Troubled waters: a social and cultural history of Ireland's sea fisheries

TROUBLED WATERS

*A social and cultural history
of Ireland's sea fisheries*

JIM MAC LAUGHLIN

FOUR COURTS PRESS

Set in 11 pt on 14 pt Garamond by
Carrigboy Typesetting Services, for
FOUR COURTS PRESS LTD
7 Malpas Street, Dublin 8, Ireland
www.fourcourtspress.ie
and in North America for
FOUR COURTS PRESS
c/o ISBS, 920 NE 58th Avenue, Suite 300, Portland, OR 97213.

© Jim Mac Laughlin and Four Courts Press 2010

ISBN 978–1–84682–258–2

Printed in England
by MPG Books, Bodmin, Cornwall.

Contents

List of illustrations   vii

Introduction   xi

1   The neglect of the maritime in Irish history   1

2   'Marauding seafarers' versus 'settled farmers': the archaeology of Irish fishing   31

3   Fishing and fish consumption in medieval Ireland   65

4   Exploitation of the marine and freshwater fisheries of pre-colonial Ireland   93

5   Imposing order on the maritime fringe   121

6   The maritime world of fishermen   156

7   Ireland's sea fisheries in the age of colonial expansion   188

8   The coastal geography of sea fishing, 1750–1880   228

9   Developmental issues in Irish sea fishing: the nineteenth-century heritage   286

10   Rural fundamentalism and the marginalisation of Ireland's sea fisheries   333

Notes   355

Bibliography   375

Index   389

Illustrations

FIGURES

Fishing boats at Moville, Co. Donegal, *c.*1900   *frontispiece*

1   John Derricke, *The MacSweeney chieftain feasting out of doors.*   8
2   Aloysius O'Kelly (1853–1941), *The return of the fisherman* (*c.*1879).   17
3   Aloysius O'Kelly, *The seaweed gatherers* (1883).   19
4   Jack B. Yeats, *The ferryman of the Dinish Islands.*   25
5   Aboriginal life in New South Wales in the 1820s.   38
6   Remains of Mesolithic fish-traps from the banks of the River Liffey.   44
7   Sketch of a medieval Irish ship from *The Book of Ballymote*
    from *c.*1400.   47
8   Map of the siege of Maguire's Castle, Enniskillen, Co. Fermanagh.   50
9   Sketch of an early Irish skin-covered currach.   52
10   Portolan map of Ireland from a sixteenth-century woodcut.   58
11   Sketch of Skellig Michael, off the coast of Co. Kerry.   70
12   Duncannon weir, Co. Wexford.   78
13   The Castle of Carrickafoyle, Co. Kerry.   85
14   The Kerry coastline as depicted in *Pacata Hibernia.*   95
15   Assaroe Falls on the River Erne, near Ballyshannon, Co. Donegal.   103
16   Sixteenth-century castle on the coast of Kerry.   106
17   Askeaton Castle and Abbey, Co. Limerick, in the seventeenth
    century.   110
18   Painting of Waterford in 1746 by C.J. Downey.   115
19   Galway fish wives on their way to market.   127
20   Fish-workers in north Donegal in the early twentieth century.   130
21   Fish-sellers from the fishing settlement of the Claddagh, Galway.   134
22   Claddagh fishermen and their wives.   144
23   Anne Bonny, a famed Irish female pirate.   147
24   The family crest of the O'Malleys of Mayo.   150
25   Detail from Boazio's *Map of Ireland.*   153
26   A *hoeker* of the type used by Dutch merchants and fishermen.   160
27   Map of the Atlantic world of Europe and North America.   164

28 'Landing the catch' at the quayside of the Claddagh in the 1830s.   169
29 Women and children in the Claddagh.   172
30 Children of Galway fishermen in the nineteenth century.   181
31 Seventeenth-century sketch of 'a portable vessel of wicker'.   191
32 Fishing boats and shipping at Carrickfergus.   194
33 *Plan de Galloway* by J.N. Bellin.   197
34 Londonderry port in the late eighteenth century.   202
35 Map of Baltimore in the 1630s.   207
36 William Petty (1623–87).   211
37 Fish press used for 'pressing' pilchards and herring.   214
38 Fishing spears from Galway, Westmeath and Roscommon.   221
39 Launching a currach on the Aran Islands, Co. Galway.   234
40 Boating and fishing activity on the Causeway Coast, Co. Antrim.   240
41 Fishing boats at Carrickfergus, Co. Antrim.   243
42 Steam trawlers at Ardglass, Co. Down, c.1900.   245
43 Fishing scene in Killary Harbour, Co. Galway.   248
44 Hunting the sunfish off the west coast of Ireland.   254
45 A wherry from Skerries, Co. Dublin.   256
46 Charles Whymper's sketch *Blessing the Waters*.   258
47 A 'pusha net' being landed in the west of Ireland.   260
48 Fish-workers processing fish at Portmagee in Co. Kerry.   262
49 Kinsale Harbour, Co. Cork, at the start of the twentieth century.   265
50 Dunmore Harbour, Co. Waterford, in the twentieth century.   271
51 The port of New Ross in the 1870s.   273
52 French mackerel boat of the late nineteenth century.   276
53 The Arklow mackerel fleet at the end of the nineteenth century.   278
54 Shipping and fishing activity at South Wall lighthouse, Dublin.   281
55 Fishing trawler with its nets down in the pre-Famine period.   282
56 Nineteenth-century schooner for deep sea fishing.   284
57 Burtonport, south Donegal, in the early twentieth century.   293
58 Methods of fishing with draft nets in major rivers and marine
    estuaries.   298
59 Hauling the catch off the east coast of Ireland.   300
60 Cape Clear Harbour, Co. Cork, in the late nineteenth century.   302
61 Two-man rowing currach from Sheepshaven Bay, Co. Donegal.   305
62 Standardised lobster traps and pots.   306
63 Sketch of the Greencastle yawl.   308
64 Baiting lines for night fishing on Rathlin Island, Co. Antrim.   310

65 Herring boats from Scotland.   312
66 Fishing boat from the Scottish coast in the late nineteenth century. 314
67 Scottish and English boats at Killybegs, Co. Donegal.   319
68 Multi-tasking fishermen in south Donegal.   322
69 Seine fishermen from Dursey Island on the Beara Peninsula,
     Co. Cork.   326
70 Tory Island in the 1940s.   329
71 Boys and young men at Baltimore Fishery School in the 1890s.   334
72 Collecting 'shore food' on the Blaskets in the 1920s.   342

MAPS

1 The location of major fish weirs in Ireland.   83
2 Hake fishing ports in Ireland, 1500–1800.   98
3 Fishing grounds and fishing ports, *c.*1900.   229

Introduction

In many ways, this book is the product of my upbringing in a seaside town on the north coast of Ireland. For the first thirty years of my life I lived within a stone's throw of the sea, and the Atlantic Ocean was well within cycling distance. Raised as a 'townie' by two parents from strong farming backgrounds who were steeped in the ways of country folk, I roamed the Inishowen coastline from an age when most young children nowadays wouldn't be allowed out of their parents' sight. From the age of four or five onwards, our mother would drag us 'down the shore' and, regardless of gender, made us pull on a unisex pair of knickers – swimming trunks being both a luxury and a rarity in our neighbourhood – and would literally drop us at the water's edge to await the incoming tide. My father, on the other hand, like many men forced to move from poor farmland to coastal towns and villages in the forties and fifties, never took to the sea. I never once remember him walking the shoreline paths outside our town. Instead, on the rare good days when he was not working, he would head inland along fuchsia-laden country lanes, as if searching for a way back home to the land.

While the parents of many of those with whom I was raised were like refugees from the countryside, their children were weaned away from rural ways in the new council houses where they settled. On moving not much more than ten miles from the farms where they were born, our parents became strange hybrid people in towns where they never really settled. They held down working-class jobs during the day, and turned tiny backyards into miniature farms where vegetables were grown, and farm animals were sometimes reared, in their spare time. However, most families had shallow roots in the housing estate where we lived. Many of those who grew up there went to sea, or moved to Scotland and England, where they often grew out of the gentle ways of the homely places where they were born. Thus our families were the first multinational institutions of de Valera's Ireland, as brothers, sisters, and not a few fathers, were scattered across Scotland and England, living in the hidden places of Glasgow, Manchester, London, Luton and Birmingham. Friedrich Engels once remarked that the English bourgeoisie knew more about foreign fields of the British Empire than they did about the back-lanes and working class districts of their own cities. The same was true of 'The Park', or 'Korea', as the housing estate in the seaside town where I was raised was known. 'Real townies' scarcely ever visited it, but stuck instead to their own streets, and to the shorefront, defending their territory in mock-battles with those of us who were from 'The Park'.

In the course of researching and writing this book, a number of close friends and academic colleagues regularly sounded me out on its subject matter. When told it was about sea fisheries, coastal communities and fishermen, fish workers, food history and cultural representation, they were surprised and somewhat perplexed. How, they asked, did this tie in with my other writings on nation building, nationalism, colonialism, racism, emigration and ethnic conflict? I have been writing on these themes for more than a quarter of a century, and I could now understand how this new interest in the amphibian world of fishermen could be taken as evidence that I had somehow or other drifted off course. A number of people asked if I had abandoned the study of class conflict and racial oppression for this more esoteric and parochial topic. Some wondered if I was now more interested in natural history than political history! However, closer examination would reveal the linkages between by my new interests and my customary social and political concerns.

The journey that brought me to this juncture began almost three decades ago. My first serious academic publication was a lengthy paper entitled 'State-centred social science and the anarchist critique', which was about political opposition to state centralisation. It was also concerned with the role of ideology in justifying the colonial and imperial ambitions of expansionist nation states in particular. This was published in the United States in 1986 in *Antipode*, which has since become a highly influential social science journal. This was followed in the late eighties and the nineties by a number of other publications examining the linkages between nation-building, industrial capitalism and the social class and racial origins of the nation-state and modern world system. Throughout this period, I had also been writing about the 'underside' of seemingly successful and affluent nations within Fortress Europe, including Celtic Tiger Ireland. Much of this work focused on the failure of nations to meet the needs of national populations, which resulted in a number of publications on emigration, racial discrimination and ethno-nationalist conflict. This research subsequently developed into a much broader study of the social and racial complexion of political hegemony in colonial and post-colonial societies.

I offer this resumé of my recent research interests in order to contextualise the present text, and to stress that it is not a product of academic whimsy or an intellectual caprice. However, I firmly believe that books also beget books, and the present study is no exception. Thus this work is not a new departure – still less is it a deviation from my traditional research interests. It has its origins in two of my earlier works, namely *Re-imagining the nation-state: the contested terrains of nation-building*, which was published in 2001, and *Donegal: the making of a northern county*, which I completed in 2007. The former was a highly theoretical assessment of competing modes of nation-building, which suggested that the nineteenth-century nation-state was constructed not only *by* but largely *for* hegemonic groups in nation-building societies. The more successful of these nations harboured the national population while also functioning as cradles for bourgeois ideas about work, respectability, morality and good citizenship. In my most recent book, *Donegal: the making of a northern county*, I was concerned with the changing social landscape and built environment of this most northern county on the outer edge of Ireland. Using extracts from a wide variety of sources, I examined social and geographical change in the county over a period of five centuries. Combining the approaches of the literary anthologist with that of the historian and social geographer, I focused especially on changes in community life and material culture in Donegal from the pre-colonial period right down to the present.

In examining the historic position of fishing and fishermen around the coastal fringe of Ireland over the *longue durée*, this study suggests that the political marginalisation of the Irish fishing industry is matched only by centuries of the neglect of sea fisheries by Irish historians and social commentators. I also argue that this tendency towards marginalisation was exacerbated by rise of rural fundamentalism in the aftermath of the Great Famine. In refusing to treat inshore and deep-sea fishing as mere footnotes in the evolution of modern Irish society, this study stresses the historical importance of the coastal economy, and the role of national and international communities in its formation. This is still very much a tentative history of maritime Ireland, and the topics examined here include the archaeology of Irish fishing; the status of fishing and fishing communities in Gaelic Ireland; the internationalisation of Irish waters in the fifteenth and sixteenth centuries; *mare clausum*, or the 'closed sea' policy and its role in the restructuring of sea fisheries and coastal communities in colonial Ireland; the organisation of fish shambles and fish markets in coastal Ireland; fish and marine produce in Irish food history; the social world and working lives of fishermen, fish workers and fish sellers; cultural representations of coastal workers in Irish art and literature; the 'crowded shoreline' of nineteenth-century Ireland, and the contribution of marine resources to the evolution of farmer-fisher communities in the post-Famine period.

Chapter one discusses the neglect of the maritime in Irish art, literature and history from the late eighteenth to the early twentieth century. It suggests that the Celtic revival of the late nineteenth century resulted in the artistic discovery of a 'hidden Ireland' along the western seaboard, a place that was a world apart from Daniel Corkery's 'hidden Ireland' of Gaelic literature and culture. However, because this coincided with the emergence of rural fundamentalism and social Darwinism that justified the territorial imperatives of the country's more powerful social groups, it failed to rescue coastal Ireland from historical oblivion. In taking a wider approach to seafaring and farming communities in prehistory, chapter two discusses the archaeology of fishing and fishing communities in Ireland, and the transformation of coastal fisheries from the ninth to the fourteenth century. This is followed by a more detailed analysis of the role of fishing and fish consumption in the Early Christian period and in medieval Ireland. It is suggested that the early Irish had a special relationship with and an acute awareness of the sea and its resources, and were, from a very early stage, acutely aware of the significance of marine resources to their cultural and political survival. Chapter four describes the exploitation of freshwater and marine fisheries in the run-up to the colonial plantations of the sixteenth and seventeenth centuries. This period witnessed growing English opposition to the presence of European fishermen in the seas around Ireland. In an effort to thwart the maritime power of pre-colonial Ireland, a *mare clausum* policy was designed to exclude foreign fishermen from Irish waters and to sever the links between Gaelic Ireland and its maritime domains. Chapters five and six have a narrower focus. They concentrate on the maritime world of fishermen, and the working conditions of fish sellers and fish workers, and describe changing attitudes towards fishermen and fish merchants in the urban centres of coastal Ireland from the fifteenth to the eighteenth century. This is followed in chapter seven by detailed discussion on the maritime impact of colonialism in Ireland and the role of 'new learning' in the privatisation and development of fisheries in the seventeenth century. Chapter eight, the lengthiest in the book, is a detailed regional geography of sea fishing and the coastal communities from the mid-eighteenth century to the aftermath of the Great Famine. Chapter nine critically assesses developmental issues confronting sea fishing around the Irish coast in the latter half of the nineteenth century. In particular, it examines the role of the Royal Dublin Society in the early development of an Irish fishing industry, and the proposals of a select number of landlords and entrepreneurs for the commercialisation of Ireland's sea fisheries in the latter half of the nineteenth century. The final chapter of the book suggests that the rise of rural fundamentalism and bourgeois nationalism prioritised the interests of landholders, industrialists and property owners, thereby contributing to the peripheralisation of coastal Ireland in the closing decades of the nineteenth century. Henceforth, fishermen and fishing communities were depicted as a people without history, a people whose history was considered to be in any progressive or evolutionary but was simply an endless and meaningless struggle with environmental forces that they could never hope to tame. To the extent that the coastal poor intruded upon the consciousness of Irish cultural nationalists, they did so as the shadowy remnants of an impoverished, pre-modern Ireland that was passing away with the hegemonic rise of substantial farmers and the urban bourgeoisie.

Finally, it should be pointed out that this study is only partly about the impact of colonialism on Irish coastal waters, and political and social exclusion of coastal communities from nation-building in Ireland. The case for a study of social and political exclusion in the process of state formation is particularly obvious in a small island nation such as Ireland. However, the arguments developed here also have more general applications. The prioritisation of landed and industrial interests in the nation-building projects of nineteenth and twentieth centuries Ireland was not a peculiarity of the Irish. Throughout this period, other maritime nations *and* post-colonial societies have similarly opted for development strategies that have studiously shunned their maritime heritage. In so doing, they have failed to effectively protect their coastal waters from international exploitation. The post-colonial world of Africa, Asia and Latin America is replete with states that have similarly turned their backs on the sea, and on their rich maritime heritages, to follow what have become highly unsustainable routes to economic modernisation and development.

Finally, this book took longer to research, and to write, than any other of my works. For this and other reasons its author was often under pressure. I would like to thank Ethel once again for her customary sound editorial comments and her usual good cheer in the long months when the book was in the making.

CHAPTER ONE

The neglect of the maritime in Irish history

EXPLAINING THE UNDER-DEVELOPMENT OF THE IRISH FISHING INDUSTRY

For almost forty years now, fishermen have criticised successive Irish governments for ignoring the fishing industry and neglecting coastal communities that have historically depended upon the country's sea fisheries. Rather than investing in coastal infrastructure and the maritime wealth of the country, the nation-state in Ireland promoted export-led industrialisation, encouraged the agri-business sector, supported regional growth and off-farm employment and, more recently, developed the country's financial sectors. At its most extreme, this line of argument has acquired the status of a political conspiracy and suggests that the internationalisation of the country's offshore waters occurred after Ireland entered the Common Market in 1973. While Irish fishermen are justified in arguing that their *national* interests have been ignored since that date, this study unearths a much deeper hidden history of fishing that emphasises the historical importance of sea fishing off the Irish coast from the fourteenth to the nineteenth century. It further suggests that the peripheral status of Ireland's fishing industry has its roots in the rural fundamentalism and petty bourgeois nationalism of the nineteenth century, when political leaders prioritised the interests of tenant-farmers and the provincial middle class and relegated coastal communities to the outer edges of the political landscape. Thus, the *territorial* imperative in Irish history and the popular association of fishing with coastal destitution meant that fishing communities have largely been ignored in most accounts of the making of modern Ireland. This neglect of the maritime was aggravated by the fact that people who looked to agriculture and the *land* as the basis for Irish prosperity tended to occupy a parallel universe to that of *coastal* dwellers that were dependent on the open sea and the shoreline for their livelihoods. One maritime archaeologist explained the resulting disjuncture separating landed societies from their coastal communities as follows:

> the two separate worlds of the seaman and the landsman must have developed very early in the course of mankind's encounter with the sea,

and they persist as separate entities to the present day. The seaman's world is alien to the landsman unless he makes a lifetime study of part or all of it; the more so since the seaman's very alienation makes him difficult to communicate with, makes his world not only the 'other', but also closed. Consequently, scholars whose lives have been involved with the history of the landsman have rightly been inclined to avoid the otherness of the world of seamen and boatmen.[1]

In most accounts of Irish history, including, not least, *economic* histories, sea fishing and the harvesting of coastal resources have received scant attention. In most cases, they have literally been relegated to the footnotes. Neglect of the maritime is all the more surprising in view of the emphasis placed by nationalists on the island status of the *political nation* in the post-Famine period, when they effectively turned their backs on Ireland's coastal geography. What has made nationalist neglect of sea fishing all the more significant was the fact that this coincided with a revival of interest in the economic potential of coastal resources among a small but relatively un-influential section of the Anglo-Irish minority. Operating outside the narrow confines of rural Catholic nationalism, these nineteenth-century defenders of the Irish fishing industry requested government support for *Irish* fishermen in order that they might compete more effectively with foreign fleets operating in waters that were then only nominally Irish. Since then, however, and with remarkably few exceptions, historians and social scientists have been studiously neglectful of coastal Ireland. 'Land matters' dominated Irish history and political discourse to such an extent that the contributions of fishing communities to the country's economic develop-ment were practically ignored.[2] However, contrary to Irish fishermen, the historical neglect of fishing pre-dates Ireland's entry into the Common Market in 1973. It has its roots instead in the political nationalism and rural fundamentalism of post-Famine decades. Throughout the colonial period, there was very strong interest in sea fisheries and coastal resources in Ireland. By examining the archaeology and ancient history of sea fishing, this study will highlight the role of fishing, and coastal foraging, in the prehistoric and medieval periods. It also shows that foreign fishing vessels were already operating off the Irish coast long before the more formal plantations of Ireland in the early modern period. The 'fabulous geographies' of Ireland drawn up by colonial authorities and travellers alike, emphasised the wealth of Ireland's coastal resources, while simultaneously stressing the country's geo-strategic significance in the sixteenth and seventeenth centuries. Similarly, statistical surveys of natural resources in the eighteenth and early nineteenth centuries repeatedly remarked upon the wealth of Ireland's sea fisheries, and showed that many landowners and merchants were well aware of the developmental potential of the country's 'fishful waters'.

Neglect of coastal communities is particularly evident in historical accounts of the Great Famine. Indeed, the failure of fishermen to 'rescue' rural Ireland from destitution in the Hungry Forties inadvertently influenced public debates on the status of sea fishing long after that crucial turning point in Irish political history. Discussing the state of Ireland's sea fisheries at the start of Great Famine, Cecil Woodham-Smith simply attributed its under-development to a number of geographical and environmental factors. Thus, she argued that

> A large part of the Irish coast … is perilous; there are cliffs, rocks, treacherous currents, sudden squalls, and, above all, the Atlantic swell, surging from America across thousands of miles of ocean. By the nineteenth century, timber was short in Ireland; in the west, practically speaking, there was none, and fishing boats were small, the largest being 12 to 15 tons … The currach was not suitable for the use of boat-nets in deep-sea fishing and, according to an expert writing at the time, the fish off the west coast of Ireland lay many miles out to sea in forty fathoms of water.[3]

She attributed the under-development of the fishing industry to the dangerous conditions of a 'tremendous coastline' measuring over 7,500km, which in places was 'lined with cliffs up to five hundred feet in height and had only one or two places where boats could shelter'.[4] Describing a period when sea fishing was arguably at its lowest ebb, Woodham-Smith conceded that the backwardness of the industry was also due to the lack of proper boats and the sheer remoteness of the country's sea fisheries from national and international markets. The pessimism in her account contrasts starkly with many nineteenth-century discussions on the economic potential of Ireland's coastal fisheries. Writing more than twenty years before the Famine, Hely Dutton in his *Statistical Survey of County Galway*, was convinced that there were 'few subjects of more importance than the fisheries, whether we consider the home consumption, the supply for which is in general below demand, or the exportation of a redundancy which could be infinitely increased'. While convinced of the economic potential of Ireland's sea fisheries, he felt that native fishing industry was 'mere peddling' and was adamant that deep-sea fishing:

might be greatly improved and extended by employing larger vessels that could meet or pursue the fish at greater distances from the shore than those usually employed, from their small size, dare attempt, for it is well known that sun fish could be caught long before April at greater distances from land, for the best fish remain in deep water; and as the small vessels must wait for good weather, the most favourable season elapses, and they dare not venture out of sight of land nor lie out at night.[5]

Among the cultural causes for the under-development of sea fishing in entire stretches of coastline were the 'overabundance of saints' days', the superstitions of the fishermen, and the lack of proper leadership from the Catholic clergy. He insisted that the fifty-two days 'held as the Sabbath' by Catholics were a cause of 'much idleness among Ireland's half-starved fishermen'. 'Where', he demanded, 'were Catholic clergy? What do they teach the ignorant? Do they think that the road to heaven is through a life of wretchedness, misery and crime? The Galway fishermen will not catch the fish themselves, nor will they allow any others to do it; no, they destroy the nets and assault the crews of the boats which come from other quarters to fish in the bay, as if they had an exclusive privilege to the produce of the ocean'.[6]

Not everyone was as pessimistic about the potential of Ireland's fisheries in the nineteenth century. In a study of the deep-sea and inshore fisheries published in the 1840s, Wallop Brabazon, describing the paltry state of native fishing in the immediate aftermath of the Famine, pointed out that there was 'no doubt of the excessive productiveness of the fishery grounds off the west coast of Ireland'. However, rather than tracing the under-development of sea fishing to geographical causes, he argued that 'want of capital' meant that native fishermen were unable to get 'more than a precarious livelihood from fishing'. While other commentators struggled to provide economic alternatives to farming along the western seaboard, Brabazon insisted that Ireland's sea fisheries were its 'greatest and only resource'. With governments reluctant to influence market forces in Victorian Ireland, he was equally adamant that the west coast needed state-sponsored 'fisheries companies' to 'provide abundant employment and income to western cottiers'. Outlining the potential benefits of fishing to coastal communities here, he argued that

From the loss of potatoes as a certain means of subsistence, the fishermen would give their undivided time to the fisheries, instead of losing the best seasons by wasting their labour on a high-rented potato garden. They would thus throw an immense quantity of cured food such as hake, cod, ling, herrings, haddock and coalfish into the interior of the country, while they could dispose of such fish as could not be cured, such as turbot, plaice, mackerel, gurnard, John Dory, ray and soles, at the markets along the coast.[7]

Writing some fifty years after the Famine, James Bowles-Daly similarly contended that Ireland's sea fisheries could reverse the social and economic decline of many disadvantaged coastal regions. Criticising the neglect of fishing by government agencies and large landowners alike, he went on to argue that

> Among the many industries of Ireland which could be rendered available towards increased comfort and the prosperity of the empire, the fisheries are entitled to the first attention. The geographical character of the island alone would be sufficient to confirm this position. Ireland is surrounded by an ocean teeming with fish of every description to gratify the most fastidious palate; her whole coast is indented with deep and spacious bays, creeks and havens, in which smaller craft can find shelter in stormy weather.[8]

Enhancing Ireland's 'national capacities' as a *maritime* nation would, he believed, halt the decline of fishing in a country where:

> Millions have been spent on Martello towers, signal posts and barracks, most of which are now mouldering away or standing idle; monuments of folly and the extravagance of war. Half the amount thus idly lavished would have made Ireland the most prosperous fishing country in the world.[9]

Stressing the role of sea fishing in defending British colonial interests in Ireland, he further added that:

> The west of Ireland might be made a great training establishment, both for sailors and fishermen, if only some of the ships, now rotting in the dockyards of England, were applied to this purpose; the cost of the experiment would be contemptible. Trained sailors and thoroughly equipped smaller craft, not unwieldy machines, will secure the empire of the sea.[10]

In *Old Ireland Improved* in the 1880s, J.P. Doyle described how vast shoals of herring regularly passed 'only seven miles out' from the Irish coast, but they were literally 'beyond the reach' of native fishermen because their 'boats were either too small', 'unsafe' and 'undecked'. Being 'too poor to improve their boats', fishermen also suffered from a 'want of proper nets for that particular kind of fishing, and the prevailing poverty of the people prevented them from reaping the harvest that Providence every year placed ready at their disposal'. Doyle felt that while 'God every year sent forth the fish of the sea for man's use', the leading men of Irish society 'would not lead', with the result that the resources of the sea lay largely untapped, at least by native fishermen, but not by foreign fleets.[11] As George O'Brien argued in his economic histories of Ireland in the seventeenth and eighteenth centuries, 'the greater part of fishing carried on in the seas adjoining Ireland was in the hands of foreigners, with whom the Irish made little attempt to compete; and from a very early time, foreign fishermen had been accustomed to fish in Irish waters'.[12] Writing in the latter half of the nineteenth century, W.E.H. Lecky suggested that the decline in deep-sea fishing off Ireland was 'due to the introduction of trailing nets around 1738 and the destruction caused among seaweed and spawn'. Added to this was the fact that 'the great shoals of herring appeared to have left Ireland at this time, and caused fishing towns like Bantry and Dungarvan to sink into decline'. Lecky was convinced that Ireland's fisheries in the eighteenth century 'seemed to have been carried on with more energy than agriculture'. He attributed this to the bounties granted by the Irish parliament, adding that the vitality of inshore fishing in particular was not unconnected with the vibrant smuggling trade then conducted around the Irish coast.[13]

Finally, in the late 1950s, in an anthropological study of Ireland's material culture, Estyn Evans found it necessary to remind the Irish people that in a country where few lived more than sixty miles from the seashore, it was hardly surprising that the country's coastal inhabitants had an intimate knowledge of the sea and the shoreline.[14] Evans was also at pains to dispel myths that implied that the coastline was Ireland's most natural habitat, the area least affected by the hand of man. He insisted that the country's Atlantic fringe, like its bogs, had been modified by human interference for centuries. Irish people gathered 'shore food' such as mussels, crabs, limpets, cockles and razor fish; dug for sea-bait; harvested sea-wrack and gathered edible seaweeds; erected elaborate fish weirs and fish-traps; made boat-slips and rudimentary piers for launching and sheltering their boats; constructed racks for drying fishing nets; and built kilns for burning lime and seashells to fertilise their potato plots. Indeed, he argued, the ancient inhabitants of the country gravitated to the coastline precisely because of 'the teeming population of shellfish' and other resources to be found there. Fishermen on the west and north-west coasts imported fishing yawls from Norway, while those on the east coast adapted the fishing 'lugger' from Cornish herring boats that traditionally fished in the Irish Sea. Evans also showed how 'hookers' transported turf along the coast of Galway in the forties and fifties, and were also used for fishing.[15] He described how Cavan fishermen used handmade lines for catching bream, which they then split, salted and stored in small ponds on the shores of lakes. In many western coastal districts, kelp was bartered for 'the two luxuries', namely spirits and tobacco, both of which were enjoyed by women and men alike. Coastal foraging for food and kelp was so prevalent around Strangford Lough in the late nineteenth century that 'every little bay where the seaweed gathered after strong tides had a little road leading down to it'.[16] The unconventional world of the small farmer-kelp-gatherer in this corner of Presbyterian Ulster was affectionately portrayed in Sam Hanna Bell's novel *The December Bride* in 1951, and in Thaddeus O'Sullivan's film of the same name in 1991.[17]

THE ABSENCE OF THE MARITIME IN IRISH CULTURE

Despite the historic importance of sea and shoreline resources to Irish coastal and riverine communities, neglect of the maritime has permeated the arts, literature and the social sciences in Ireland. With the exception Jack B. Yeats, Paul Henry and Seán Keating, comparatively few Irish artists and writers have cast a sympathetic glance at Ireland's coastal communities. Rural landscapes, landed estates, scenes from urban and rural life, ecclesiastical subjects, and the achievements of farmers and landlords have all, at one time or other, inspired artists and writers in Ireland. In the artistic traditions of pre-Famine period, the coastal poor and rugged landscapes of the west of Ireland were symbols of disorder and backwardness. Farming, including the *petite culture* of subsistence farmers in large tracts of rural Ireland, was considered morally uplifting and wholesome in nineteenth-century nationalist Ireland, whereas fishing and coastal foraging were associated with hardship and poverty. To the extent that fishermen and coastal cottiers featured in the dominant artistic traditions of colonial *and nationalist* Ireland, they did so only fleetingly. This was particularly the case in colonial representations of Irish life in the early colonial period. Take, for example, the series of wood-cuts that illustrated John Derricke's *The Image of Irelande, with a Discoverie of Woodkarne*, published in 1581.[18] The focus

1 John Derricke, *The MacSweeney chieftain feasting out of doors*, a racialised portrait of aristocratic Gaelic society from the 1580s, which suggested that Ireland's imaginary 'wood kernes', including the inhabitants of the western seaboard, were as wild as the environments that harboured them (Derricke, *The image of Irelande* (1581)).

of these illustrations, and their accompanying texts, was the MacSweeney clan from the coastal barony of Banagh in south Donegal. They particularly emphasised the 'wildness' of the Gaelic Irish, not least their uncivilised manners and disorderly ways. More than half of these twelve wood-cuts portray the well-disciplined ranks of English infantry, while reference is continually made to the ill-equipped nature of Irish forces. In one illustration, *The MacSweeney chieftain feasting out of doors*, members of the clan gorge themselves on uncooked offal, while a 'wood kern' defecates nearby. D.B. Quinn has suggested that this wood-cut 'is mainly intended as a satire on Irish residual primitiveness' that highlights the difference between the civilised English and the wild Irish. Taken as a whole, the illustrations in Derricke's work suggest that the cultivation of 'Englishness' in barbaric Ireland would involve a radical disavowal of everything linked to 'Irishness'.[19] They depict the Irish not only as the opposite, but also as inferior to the English in everything from eating habits to table manners, from toilet training to landscape management, from courtship rituals to ethical codes. Like other portrayals of the 'rude Irish' in colonial Ireland, they were never intended as accurate depictions of Irish life, and operated instead as racialised satires on what was perceived as the residual primitiveness of the Irish countryside and its Gaelic custodians. For that reason, the indigenous Irish were portrayed as a disruptive moral and political force that had to be eradicated in the peaceful Anglican commonwealth of a re-fashioned colonial Ireland. Whenever artists represented plantation landscapes and townscapes in this Ireland, they contrasted the settled nature of country's Anglicised countryside with the lawlessness and poverty of the Atlantic seaboard. Because the west coast in particular was beyond the realm of civil obedience and moral probity, it was widely perceived as a threat to English civility, a place that had to be tamed, and transformed, in order that its inhabitants could be saved from themselves.

Not until the Romantic period was the western seaboard of Ireland considered as a coastal Arcadia replete with peaceful walks through well-tended estates that swept down to a peaceful sea. Prior to that, many of Ireland's coastal districts boasted a richness of natural beauty that contrasted sharply with the well-farmed landscapes of the interior of the country. Thus, colonial art in the seventeenth and eighteenth centuries was driven by political and economic agendas that sought to attract more English, Anglo-Irish and Scottish settlers into the wilder recesses of coastal Ireland. It urged landlords, merchants and entrepreneurs to invest in the commercial development of Irish fisheries by constructing harbours and piers throughout the length and breadth of the country. Only thus, it was suggested, could 'backward' coastal Ireland be prevented from reverting to the state of lawless primitivism in which peasants, smugglers and fishermen held it.[20] Thus, colonial art and literature sought to 'tame' Ireland's rugged coastal landscapes, and seascapes, just as agents of the colonial state struggled to control the baser instincts of the 'rude Irish' who inhabited such places. It was precisely in such an intellectual environment that the painting of edified portraits of colonial settlers, and the manicured landscapes of colonial Ireland, was both a *patriotic endeavour* and a creative activity.[21] This was because writers and artists sought to dignify all that was noble about colonial society, while simultaneously denigrating all that was savage and uncouth about the native Irish and their habitations. In the late colonial era, it was sometimes suggested that fishermen, smugglers and the coastal poor existed outside of historical time, and lived their lives in an endless cycle of needless hardship and relentless poverty. Their mere presence on the fringes of gentrified *landed* Ireland was a source of astonishment and shock to social reformers and colonial settlers alike. Having constructed poor fishermen and the coastal poor as *savage subjects of colonial history*, it was only a matter of time before settled society would depict these sections of Irish society as socially expendable.[22] Like the nomadic Highlanders in Walter Scott's historical narratives, they were a-historical subjects from a lower stage of social evolution, a people who had to be consumed or otherwise 'used up' before the narrative of colonial history could proceed. This also suggested *a geography of savagery*, which implied that those located furthest from the centres of Anglo-Irish civilisation were the most savage of all Ireland's subject population. Impoverished fishermen and the coastal poor were believed to be as *unruly as the peripheral landscapes that harboured them*, not least because they lived in places where nobody went unless they literally lost their way.[23] Thus, throughout colonial history, Ireland was divided along an immutable axis of self-excluding differences that separated out 'settled Ireland' from the wilder landscapes of the west and north-west coasts. Distinctions here were centred on differences between landed Ireland and its maritime fringe, between the 'pale' and the rest of Ireland, between the settled life of farmers and the vagrant life of seafarers and the rural poor, between the civilised world of the settler and the wilder world of 'sea rogues', smugglers and fishermen. This genre of colonial art and literature was part and parcel of a much wider Enlightenment project that sought to 'tame' the rugged environments of Ireland and placate the 'rude' Irish.

Together with portraiture, history painting in Ireland in the eighteenth and nineteenth centuries also depicted colonial settlers as morally, intellectually, and even aesthetically superior to the 'rude Irish'. Unlike the densely peopled and intensely worked landscapes of seventeenth-century Dutch art, colonial art in Ireland produced landscapes that were largely devoid of working people, peasants and the coastal dwellers. In the Dutch Republic, everyday activities such as herring-fishing and cheese-making acquired such commercial significance that they imposed a strong visual presence in the country's art. Dutch pride in their successful herring fisheries in particular resonated in many pictorial renditions of herring and other fish and became popular subjects of still-life paintings. The subject of the herring banquet was a particular favourite with artists, and landscape painting fostered a deeply grounded relationship between people and their environment. Artists especially emphasised the successful struggles of ordinary people to impose order and eke a living from land and sea.[24]

If nature and its bounty were common subject matters in Dutch art, landscapes and seascapes in Irish colonial art were simply used for making obscure allegorical statements. Whereas these early Dutch painters painted men and women imposing order on both land and sea, there was little attempt in colonial Ireland to similarly honour the endeavours of the rural or coastal poor. When representing landscapes in colonial Ireland, writers and artists alike lauded the achievements of colonial outsiders who brought order to the *countryside*, not least to the wild Atlantic seaboard. In so doing, they told exemplary tales that were a source of pride for the colonial beholder, and often deeply insulting to the native Irish. Thus, for example, landscape painting, especially when it focused on urban Ireland and the 'settled' landscapes of Munster and Ulster, was part and parcel of an English nation-building project that sought to bring the coastal peripheries of Ireland under the control of the English state. Coastal regions in the west and north-west of the country were portrayed as lawless regions, as safe havens for smugglers and their unruly associates and fragile outposts of a beleaguered modernity. Thus, places here were shrouded in Celtic medievalism and pagan superstition. Colonial art on the other hand was a self-referential tradition rooted in a new geometry of power that sought to bind Ireland's out-of-the-way places to the wider British Empire. Those espousing this tradition ignored, or at least looked down upon, the very real achievements of those who managed to survive in some of Ireland's most inhospitable environments. In so doing, they failed to appreciate the autonomous qualities of Irish social life and the sustainability of rural and coastal communities. To the extent that fishermen and peasants featured in this artistic tradition, they drifted in and out of sight of the artists and travellers who visited Ireland's remote regions. Sitting hunched and alone, peasants and fishermen were depicted as social 'litter' on the genteel landscapes of colonial Ireland.[25] When visiting artists painted this Ireland, they focused upon urban and rural scenes in such a way as to unite the country in a common canvas of progress and civilisation. Máire de Paor has argued that colonial depictions of Ireland were inseparable from the military subjugation of the country and its people from the seventeenth century onwards.[26] Well into the nineteenth century, artists often portrayed rural Ireland as a land devoid of native inhabitants, a country bursting with Druidic remains, smouldering ruins and all the paraphernalia of an ancient Gaelic way of life. Not surprisingly, these representations of Ireland flattered 'settler' communities and their worlds, while simultaneously uncovering the 'wild' landscapes of rural Ireland and the 'savage' seascapes of the west coast.

Much of this elitist artistic tradition, especially outside planted Ulster, sought to define 'planted Ireland' as a haven of landed aristocratic civility set in a backward country that was steeped in plebeian Gaelic superstitions. Kevin O'Neill has suggested that many such expressions of 'settler' art were at odds with an energetic plebeian Irish culture.[27] In the seventeenth and eighteenth centuries, this latter tradition deployed a 'plastic' or 'organic' sense of community strongly in tune with the social and economic interests of Irish small farmers and coastal communities. However, the new settlers rejected the popular culture of rural and maritime Ireland, not least because it had local roots that often undermined the 'high' culture of the landed aristocracy. The very fact that Gaelic culture in the remoter corners of the country was regionally based and focused on the local rather than the national meant that the new settler elites could castigate it as un-elevating and barbaric. As O'Neill has further remarked, 'the urban elite view of popular culture, which saw "rustics" as at best rough clay, or at worst irremediable primitives, was confirmed by juxtaposing the rural culture produced by communal enterprise with its own ideologically constructed notion of the individual artist interacting with "culture{ without mediation by a collective community'.[28] Given this interpretation of indigenous culture, folk art was simply a crude act of replication, while colonial art was a product of the creative imagination. As we have already seen, settler art, architecture and estate management practices were fundamental to an enlightened *mission civilatrice* that sought to rescue Ireland from the idiocy of Gaelic life and the barbarism of an Irish nature. For that reason, representations of Ireland in the seventeenth and eighteenth centuries portrayed loyal 'civilised' subjects living in towns and well-managed estates, while remote rural areas and coastal districts were inhabited by heathenish rebels, lawless fishermen and fearless smugglers. Francis Place depicted seventeenth-century Dublin as a modernising city spreading out from its medieval core, a city whose bridges were even then linking the privileged north side with the far poorer south side of the city.[29] In treating the city as a centre of European civility, he heightened its cultural and administrative significance in an otherwise 'backward' country. Provincial Dublin was a timber-built town of less than 20,000 inhabitants in 1600, and it harboured around one per cent of the country's population. By the early eighteenth century, however, it was well on the way to becoming a citadel of urban civility and bourgeois gentility. Writing in the 1620s, Luke Gernon likened Dublin to the port city of Bristol, but he felt that it 'fell short' of its provincial English counterpart in terms of architectural grandeur, maritime traditions and business acumen. He also suggested that the 'ravaged settlements' of coastal and rural Ireland were more like 'the remnants of unfinished meals' than truly modern towns. By the start of the eighteenth century, however, the built environment of Dublin, and other coastal cities, was transformed out of all recognition. New churches were built and older ones were repaired, and recently constructed roads drew the old medieval city away from the banks of the Liffey and the shores of the Irish Sea. Henceforth, the western suburbs of Dublin looked out upon the well-tended estates of the rural interior of the country, even if the city itself still retained a strong maritime aspect and had its feet firmly planted in the Liffey and the Irish Sea. The flowering of history painting and portraiture in Britain and Ireland at this stage coincided with an even deeper marginalisation of peasants and fishermen in Anglo-Irish society. While portraiture emphasised the racial superiority of the settler over the native Gael, portrait painters and landscape artists recorded the achievements of new settlers on the land and in the business world.[30] The 'savage' Irish entered the works of these writers and artists as darker alter-egos of English and Scottish settlers. As mysterious 'anti-selves' who lived far out on the peripheries of a 'wilder' Ireland, they were located well beyond the pale of settled society and were filled with the allure of the marginal and the maritime in a predominantly rural society. Thus, suppression of the 'wild Irish' in colonial art and literature culture could occasionally give rise to a curiosity about noble Irish 'savages' who inhabited the coastline of colonial Ireland. Aside from a very occasional celebration of the Irish as 'angels' rather than 'apes', most writers looked upon the Irish, including Irish history, as both debased and debasing.[31] For many indeed, the rural Irish and coastal poor were a people without history in any meaningful or *evolutionary* sense. As a people who lived out their lives in an endless repetition of hardship and poverty, they lacked their own historical narrative and narrators. Others regarded their bawdy behaviour and lawless ways as more appropriate to the inhabitants of Britain's more far-flung colonies, than to those living at the back door to civilised Britain.

Such 'outsider' views of Irish coastal communities came to the fore in the twentieth century in Robert Flaherty's *Man of Aran* in 1934, and in David Lean's box-office success, *Ryan's Daughter*, released in 1970. The film is an epic story of a self-willed girl, played by Sarah Miles, and her unsuccessful marriage to the quiet and submissive schoolteacher, played by Robert Mitchum. It traces the marital and social consequences of a passionate affair between Miles and the shell-shocked English army officer with whom she falls in love. At another level, however, the film depicts the inhabitants of the south-west of Ireland as a bunch of rebellious simpletons, whose lives are dictated by the forces of nature, and who spend their time conspiring against the established church and state alike. In this film, the landscapes and changeable climate of the west coast are intimately linked to the volatile personalities of its coastal inhabitants.[32] The novels of Somerville and Ross perfectly portray the trials and tribulations of registered magistrates who had the 'damnable bad luck' to be posted to remote districts along the west coast of Ireland. In these novels, the weather and landscapes of the western seaboard conspire to thwart all efforts to create anything other than a fragile genteel civility in Ireland's rugged coastal environments.[33] The changeability of weather and temperament in the west of Ireland was especially pronounced in the television series, *The Irish R.M.*, an adaptation of Edith Somerville's highly successful novel, *Some Experiences of an Irish R.M.*, first serialised in the *Badminton Magazine* throughout 1898 and 1899. Her *Further Experiences of an Irish R.M.* and *In Mr Knox's Country* subsequently appeared in the illustrated *Graphic* and *Strand* magazines, as well as in the more serious *Blackwood Magazine*. The television drama opens with Major Yeates, the resident magistrate, coming to terms with his new posting in west Kerry. Leaving behind the refined and 'settled' life of Victorian London, this gentleman-officer arrives at Skebawn just as a torrential downpour is washing away the very house he has rented from Flurry Knox, his jovial Irish landlord. Nothing works in his new home, or in his rented estate, until the major puts his stamp on the landscape and the abundant retinue of incompetent servants and 'hangers-on' that accompany the property. His primary role is to impose order on a chaotic landscape and instil discipline in an anarchic population of layabouts, tricksters and likeable rogues. In one of the first scenes in the televised version of the drama, it is announced that the major is 'the sort of man who likes everything to be well planned and orderly'. Copious supplies of Dewar's whiskey, together with friendly advice from a circle of friends drawn from the local gentry and the up-and-coming Irish middle class, fortify him in this task. His great challenge is to avoid 'going native' by not sinking to the level of local custom, or accepting west of Ireland standards of 'good taste'.

The outsider's take on life on the west coast of Ireland in Somerville's novel, as in Lean's film, tends to silence Irish achievements, not least the very real achievements of small farmers and poor fishermen who struggled to make a living under extremely difficult circumstances. In both works, the ragged poverty of the native Irish is contrasted with the grandeur of the natural environment and the beauty of Arcadian Anglo-Irish landscapes that here and there hold their own in an otherwise wild Irish countryside. At one level, the novel and the film tend towards a visual realism, but ultimately they fail to convey a true image of Irish life. At another level, they simply use landscapes, and especially seascapes, as stunning backcloths against which the more enlightened and 'de-natured' members of Irish and Anglo-Irish society lived respectable bourgeois lives. Thus, in Lean's film, as in the novels of Edith

Somerville, we are presented with a range of stunning scenes of such tremendous natural beauty that they dwarf those who live and work along Ireland's rugged coastline. Rather than capturing any sense of a 'real Ireland' here, Lean's film induces a sense of escapism, encouraging the viewer to simply 'enjoy' the natural beauty of the south-west coast, without having to appreciate the struggles of those who lived there. The sheer sweep of the photography and the breathtaking nature of the scenery tend to hinder tend to development of plot and character in the film. Thus, Lean portrays nature and human emotions in coastal Kerry in a symbolic bind from which there is no escape. It has been suggested that the 'plethora of eye-catching backcloths' in the film dilutes the pastoral-tragic idiom in order to produce an escapist dream wherein poor farmers and fishermen 'dissolve in an aesthetic euphoria of scenery'.[34]

THE CELTIC REVIVAL AND THE ARTISTIC DISCOVERY OF COASTAL IRELAND

Landscape painting, environmental management and the theories of social progress have generally been responsible for cultivating a far more formal relationship with the natural environment than that which characterised the organic links between subordinate social groups and their life-worlds in colonial and nation-building Ireland. Like the literary and scientific perspective of the outsider, many filmmakers, artists and social reformers took a top-down approach to the parochial world of coastal communities and poor farmers. Prioritisation of the 'detached view', of knowledge verifiable by experiment and observation, resulted in the devaluation of the pre-scientific formulations of these communities and the spiritual dimensions of their social life. In Ireland's case, scientific treatises, travellers' accounts, the recommendations of rural reformers, and the reports of those interested in the health and social conditions of the urban and rural poor, belonged to that complex literature on human development that was concerned with the modernisation of the country's social and physical landscapes from the seventeenth onwards. By the late eighteenth and early nineteenth century, estate managers, improving landlords and all those who reclaimed land and maintained estates as places set apart from under-developed Gaelic Ireland and its natural environment, became figures of authority. Only recently have we begun to recognise the historic role of the subordinate poor in the domestication of Ireland's rural and coastal landscapes. The latter included not just those who contributed to the making of the built environments of Ireland from the sixteenth to the nineteenth century; it also included all those involved in the transformation of Ireland's coastal environment and the development of the country's inshore and deep-sea fisheries. Historically indeed, the average layperson may not have thought of the coastal landscapes of Ireland in scientific, aesthetic or even natural terms. The fields, hillsides and coastlines that excited scientists and inspired artists simply represented hard work to those who struggled to make a living from land, sea and coastline. There are at least two reasons why this may have been the case. Firstly, through no fault of their own, most inhabitants of poor marginal lands and rugged coastal regions were, until relatively recently, deprived of the more formal appreciations of landscapes and seascapes that we associate with environmental scientists, novelists, poets and artists. Equally, however, the 'educated' approach of the latter to coastal and rural environments may well have been considered as idle distractions by those condemned to work on land, sea and bog. The rural and coastal poor in particular probably regarded the natural environment as something about which they could not, and should not get excited. Like the twelfth-century Saint Anselm, many of them have considered anything other than a working relationship with land and sea as a source of distraction, as something that was essentially harmful and sometimes even sinful. Privileged individuals could take pleasure from beautiful landscapes and rugged coastlines, just as physical scientists, geologists and naturalists could take satisfaction from scientific explorations of coastal environments and natural landscapes.[35] The labouring poor on the other hand, were encouraged to believe that aesthetic appreciations of the natural environment were distractions from more pragmatic concerns, and from their devotions to God and his countless angels. Not surprisingly therefore, the majority of Ireland's coastal inhabitants looked on the natural world of sea and coastline simply as a work-a-day world. It was not so much an object of scientific interest, let alone a source of artistic inspiration, as first and foremost a world filled with hardship, risk, disappointment and disease.

First published in 1928, Peadar O'Donnell's *Islanders* clearly belongs to that tradition in Irish writing that placed great value on the expertise of poor farmers and fishermen and provides a sympathetic account of their life struggles.[36] O'Donnell began his short novella in the basement of Mountjoy Jail, where he was incarcerated during the early stages of the Irish Civil War. When asked by the present writer if his fictional writings were politically inspired, he candidly admitted that they derived instead from the stories he was told by the islanders and coastal inhabitants of his native south-west Donegal. Yet the novella offers much more than a description of coastal poverty in this

2 Aloysius O'Kelly (1853–1941), *The return of the fisherman, c.*1879. In this painting, the artist clearly idolises the austere family life and industrious self-sufficiency of subsistence fishermen on the Atlantic coast of Ireland (courtesy of the Crawford Art Gallery).

corner of maritime Ireland at the start of the twentieth century. The taut, disciplined style of *Islanders* is what sets it apart as a novel of abiding interest, and this, together with its avoidance of sentimentalism, drew praise from fellow writer and islander, Liam O'Flaherty. The book proved so popular that it ran to six American editions, five English and one German edition, and a Gaelic translation by Seosamh Mac Grianna. The title of the American edition was *The Way It Was with Them*, which suggests that the novel was 'brewed from experience'.[37] It certainly reflected a way of life still to be found in island communities and isolated coastal districts throughout coastal Ireland well into the twentieth century. So rich was O'Donnell's portrayal of Mary Doogan's struggle to keep herself and her family in some degree of decency, that we almost feel we are right there by her side as she feeds the hens or cuts a piece of soda bread for her children. Reading it today is like reading a novel from a time and place outside of the contemporary Donegal experience. Change the names of the characters and the setting, and *Islanders* could become an account of social conditions in colonial coastal Africa, or China, rather than a description of island life in Donegal in the 1920s. In an introduction to the 1979 edition, Robert Lynd wrote that *Islanders* would still be worth reading simply for its descriptions of the lives of poor people on a wild and barren coast where 'two bucketfuls of winkles may be a considerable addition to the wealth of the home'. Like O'Donnell's other novels, *Islanders* is both a rich slice of social realism and a sample of Irish heroic literature. As such, it rejoices in the heroism of a community forced to live 'in charity with one another among the uncharitable stones'.[38] That is why his characters continue to convince us of their reality. The setting for *Islanders* is a real stretch of Ireland's coastal geography at the start of the twentieth century, a local world that has all but disappeared as a result of economic change and a boom in holiday home construction since the 1980s. Yet O'Donnell received little praise from friends or acquaintances for his evocative depictions of coastal life in Donegal at the start of the century. Indeed, one could argue that *Islanders*, like Patrick MacGill's *The Rat Pit* and *Children of the Dead End*, were the *Angela's Ashes* of their day. As such, these novels often upset local and national sensibilities, and were sources of offence to those who fled coastal Ireland in search of a new life in England, Scotland and the United States in the early decades of the new state's existence. It is said that one of O'Donnell's own classmates who moved to New York stated that she would deny ever knowing the author if ever *Islanders* were mentioned in her presence! Yet the novel brought O'Donnell international fame, not least in the United States, where *The New York Times*

3 Aloysius O'Kelly, *The seaweed gatherers* (1883). In bringing a touch of colour to the coastline of Connemara in the 1880s, this naturalistic portrait is a highly romanticised, outsider's view of life and work on the west coast
(courtesy of the Gorry Gallery).

praised it for its 'quiet brilliance and power' and two Catholic book clubs selected it as their book of the month in 1935.[39]

Aside from such twentieth-century Irish artists as Jack B. Yeats and Paul Henry, a small number of nineteenth-century artists also worked on maritime themes, even if many of these confined themselves to painting 'ship portraits' and port scenes. This latter group included G.M. Wheatley Atkinson, F.W. Burton, Aloysius O'Kelly, Samuel Lover and William Magrath. From a cramped studio overlooking Cobh Harbour, Atkinson (1806–84) documented, in a typically realistic and down-to-earth manner, the wealth of Cork's merchant class in scores of 'ship portraits' painted in the decades immediately after the Great Famine. His 'maritime paintings' are filled with strongly naturalistic depictions of weather conditions, sea conditions and cloud formations, and as such are a far cry from idealised portrayal of sky and sea in the more Romantic depictions of Irish coastal scenes in the second half of the nineteenth century. As Government Inspector of Shipping and Emigrants, Atkinson also painted 'happy images of emigrants preparing for embarkation on smart and sea-worthy vessels bound for the New World in the years after the Great Famine'.[40] His contemporary, Frederick William Burton (1816–1900), was born into a landowning family in Clare and travelled with George Petrie throughout the west of Ireland in the mid-nineteenth century. Burton's *Aran Fisherman's Drowned Child*, painted prior to the Famine, is a highly theatrical and dramatic work that expresses all of the artist's sympathy for the fisher folk of the west coast of Ireland in the difficult years between 1840 and 1870. Born into a nationalist family in Dublin in 1843, and with a brother a Fenian supporter who later became MP for Roscommon, the artist Aloysius O'Kelly travelled extensively in the west of Ireland, Egypt and France. He exhibited scenes from Connemara, Brittany and Egypt at the RHA and in London, and studied at the Académie Julian in Paris from 1901 to 1903. His *Return of the Fisherman* is an idealised portrayal of family life in coastal Ireland, particularly the life of self-sufficient fishermen and their families. In contrast to the dark and sorrowful portrayals of rural poverty in post-Famine Ireland, O'Kelly's depicts a happy, smiling family group reunited when the fisherman comes home with a wicker-basket filled to the brim with fresh fish from the sea.

It other paintings by O'Kelly, the austere and frugal lifestyles of fisher folk are treated with the same sympathetic respect as that accorded by other artists and writers to struggling families in rural Ireland. Yet another painting with a coastal theme by O'Kelly was his *Seaweed Gatherers, Connemara*, painted in the early 1880s. Like other artists who came to the west of Ireland, the social aspects of kelp-burning and the seaweed harvest fascinated O'Kelly. He was especially concerned to capture, in as simple and naturalistic a style as possible, the traditional costume of the barefoot women and children who foraged for a living with patient donkeys loaded down with wicker creels.[41] His sympathetic images of the west coast set people and places here apart from the rest of Ireland. They also *ethnicised* their subject matter, and created memorable images of Irish coastal life and scenery a generation before Paul Henry and Jack B. Yeats diverted their attention to Ireland's coastal scenery and coastal communities. These paintings inadvertently contributed to a post-modern 'othering' of Irish fisher folk, by stressing their differences from other Irish people and embedding them firmly in their coastal environment. Samuel Lover (1797–1868), a Dublin-born artist with an interest in the legends and stories of the rural poor, also made several visits to the west coast between 1820 and the mid-1840s. He portrayed fishermen and kelp-gathers at work in Connemara and also painted women working on the coastline around Galway. His large canvas, *The Kelp Gatherers*, painted in 1835, is considered to be one of the earliest oil paintings of Irish coastal dwellers at work in the landscape. It is also an important social document of Connemara life in the years prior to the

Famine. However, Lover's paintings are more noted for topographical accuracy than for social realism. He was attracted to maritime scenes, not so much by the harsh life of coastal dwellers, as by 'the picturesque effects of wind-blown smoke, stormy sunsets and frothing seas that combine to form a striking coastal scene'. His womenfolk in particular are graceful and smartly dressed, with many of them clad in maroon dresses and each one wearing a different hairstyle. These are idealised and highly dramatic representations of coastal workers at one with their striking surroundings and happy in their coastal station.

If artists on the east coast painted men and women at work with horse and cart on the land or on the strand, those on the west coast were attracted to the exotica of coastal life and the cultural authenticity of fishing communities in the west of Ireland. Their paintings rarely conveyed the tedium or hardship of the work of fishermen and their families, contenting themselves instead with highly romanticised images of fish sellers. Thus they painted fish-workers with strong arms, rugged features, graceful bodies and beautiful wind-blown hair. Lover's paintings in particular convey the west of Ireland's dramatic coastline and tumbling mountain ranges with a high degree of topographic accuracy. He portrayed happy, industrious and dignified people set against dramatic landscapes of great natural beauty. William Henry Bartlett (1858–1932), the son of an art dealer from the Isle of Wight, made several visits to the west of Ireland, first visiting Galway in the late 1870s, when he based himself for some time in Connemara. He later worked on Achill and the Aran Islands, and spent some time at Burtonport in Donegal. Like Lover, he presented 'an industrious, vigorous and dignified west of Ireland life of men and women working on the rocky shore, the sea, and beneath open skies, in accordance with the seasons, the tides, their livestock and their fishing catch'.[42] His *End of the Fair, Back to the Island*, painted in 1910, is typical of such scenes and shows men and women driving their cattle on a rocky shore to their boats. This tendency to portray fishermen and coastal workers as the 'other' in rural Catholic Ireland is evident in the works of a number of other more prominent artists in the late nineteenth and early twentieth century. In his painting, *Memory Harbour*, Yeats portrays Rosses Point in such a way that the comfortable and familiar life of villagers is contrasted with the lure of the sea and the perpetual mystery of the maritime domain of the fisher folk, seamen and boat-builders of the Sligo coast.[43] In this, as in other works like *The Island Funeral, Man from Arranmore, Kelp-Burning, Gathering Seaweed for Kelp* and *The Ferryman of Dinish Island*, Yeats depicts the solitary encounters between fishermen and their maritime environment as on an altogether different plane to the experiences of rural communities making a comfortable living from the land. Certainly by the start of the twentieth century, a small number of artists and writers developed a keen interest in the seascapes and landscapes of the west of Ireland, often locating themselves and their art, in what they considered as the nation's most authentic, most neglected, and *distinctive* landscapes. This frequently resulted in a fascination with the west of Ireland, and particularly the west coast.

Jack B. Yeats, Paul Henry, George Russell, Sean Keating and Patrick Tuohy all lived in the west of Ireland for some period of their artistic lives, and all of them selected subjects from the western seaboard. Born in Belfast in 1876, Paul Henry was especially attracted to the habitats and inhabitants of the west and north-west coasts, especially, of course, Achill Island off the coast of Mayo. He once remarked that Achill 'spoke' to him, calling to him 'as no other place had ever done'. What attracted him most to these watery and cloudy places on the western seaboard was not so much the tedious work of their inhabitants as 'the wild beauty of the landscape [and] the colour and variety of [its] cloud formations'. His stated ambition was 'to study the lives of the people and their surroundings closely and single-mindedly'.[44] The result was a deeply sympathetic 'insider's' view of these 'people of the rocks' who laboured under western skies and peopled his rich portrayals of coastal Ireland. Despite their apparent simplicity, there is often much more to Henry's renditions of life on the Mayo coastline than one finds in paintings by visiting artists who always seemed to remain aloof from the lives and labours of the people whom they painted. When not producing monumental images of men and women digging turf or lifting potatoes beneath towering skies, Henry was painting dramatic images of fishermen struggling to launch currachs from storm-strewn beaches, or fishing for lobsters along the western seaboard. Hence, many of his paintings break away from the mere colourful detail and anecdotal qualities of nineteenth-century painters, and for that reason they create an altogether more realistic image of coastal life in the west of Ireland in the opening decades of the twentieth century. The sheer elemental primitivism of the figures on Henry's landscapes and seascapes, together with the vigorous style with which they are rendered, create painterly 'snapshots' of a way of life that was largely ignored in de Valera's rural Catholic Ireland.[45] At times, it seemed that the vividness of community life on the west coast defeated the ability of Irish artists to portray the struggles of poor fishermen and small farmers in this part of the country. At other times, artists captured the lives of such people perfectly, as in Henry's *Launching the Curragh*, in Keating's *Men of the West*, in J.B. Yeats' *Man of Arranmore*, in Tuohy's *Mayo Peasant Boy* and in Russell's *Potato*

Gatherers. It has been said of Henry that he understood the peasants and fishermen of Achill and Connemara in the same way that William Conor, another northern artist, understood the mill girls of Belfast. Certainly the realism and grandeur of Henry's depictions of the west coast give his canvases an abiding interest. In his *Launching the Curragh*, as in Keating's *Aran Fisherman and His Wife*, we come face-to-face with sympathetic 'insider' portrayals of life and work on the western seaboard. The works of these artists have an extreme simplicity that often consists of little more than a careful composition of sea and headland, of turf-stacks, peasants and fishermen, all set against great seascapes, towering horizons and billowing clouds. In many of Yeats' earlier paintings, lines are either absent, or they are submerged in mass and form.[46] It is as if in breaking with the convention of line, artists such as Yeats and Henry in particular wished to emphasise that there were no clear boundaries between land and sea, between earth and sky, and between that which was interior and that which was exterior in the west of Ireland.

Jack B. Yeats was perhaps the most notable exception to the sentimental artistic tradition in Anglo-Irish art. He gave clear artistic expression to the lives of ordinary people, including fishermen and their families, in the west of Ireland. Unlike so many of his literary contemporaries, including Synge, and the artist's poet brother, William Butler Yeats, Jack B. Yeats did not mythologise or romanticise the human subjects of his art. Despite the widespread tendency to do so, he rarely depicted the men and women from the islands and coastline of Ireland as handsome or beautiful. It has been said that his portrayals of islanders and coastal villagers reveal one of Ireland's most significant secrets, namely that the Irish were essentially 'a youthful people'.[47] In his west-coast paintings, we see ordinary men and women as solitary figures on the landscape determined not only to conquer nature, but also to overcome the hardships that life in the west of Ireland throws at them. When depicting the sheer uselessness of work performed on public schemes organised by the Congested Districts Board, he drew out the misery and unhappiness of people drawn away from 'ennobling' work such as fishing and kelp-making, and who were forced instead to engage in such meaningless tasks as rock-breaking and the construction of walls on barren hillsides. When painting islanders, boatmen and fishermen, Yeats portrays them as wild and colourful people. The subject of his *Ferryman of Dinish Island* was drawn from a real encounter. The ferryman had worked in Birkenhead, Manchester and Newcastle-upon-Tyne, before moving to New York, Baltimore and New Orleans. Having travelled the world, serving on land and sea, and having sailed to many of the ports and coastal towns of

Scotland and Wales, the ferryman finally returned to row his boat between two small islands and to gather kelp on the west coast of Ireland. As in countless other sketches of the west of Ireland, Yeats is less interested in presenting the Irishness of his subjects than portraying the lives of ordinary Irish men and women in natural and dignified surroundings. His artistic representations of coastal Ireland have much in common with sixteenth- and seventeenth-century Dutch artists who similarly depicted the everyday life of Dutch fishermen and peasants. Countess Markievicz once compared Yeats' art to that of the dramatist J.M. Synge. Indeed Synge was one was one of the few writers to oppose petty bourgeois rural fundamentalism and the prioritisation of property evident in so much political pamphleteering in nineteenth-century Ireland. He sympathised with fishermen, vagrants and 'tinkers' both because they represented the marginalised 'others' in an increasingly petty bourgeois Irish society, and because they rejected the mores of that society and were deeply scornful of its shallow, sanitised respectability. In plays like *The Playboy of the Western World* and *The Tinker's Wedding*, the rural and coastal poor live in a world set apart from the Ireland of substantial Catholic farmers and the town-based bourgeoisie.[48] In *The Aran Islands*, Synge's islanders are elevated to the status of a human ideal. As such, they become figures of transcendent humanism that existed 'outside of history in some vaguely timeless space'.[49] Theirs was a world that was far more spontaneous and anarchic, and consequently more authentic, than that which the latter were seeking to construct out of the chaos of post-Famine Ireland.

In his essay, *The Vagrants of County Wicklow*, Synge rescues 'tramps' and the travelling poor from cultural oblivion, giving them a place alongside islanders, fishermen and potato 'hokers'. These were the neglected and rejected in the nationalist pantheon of respectable nineteenth-century Catholic Ireland.[50] Synge idealised these sectors of a disappearing Ireland precisely because they were the social antidotes to a stultifying and puritanical Victorian world outlook that was in danger of suffocating social and cultural life in nationalist Ireland. Drawn form a beleaguered ascendancy that was finding it increasingly difficult to hold its own in Catholic nationalist Ireland, he was attracted to island communities and the coastal poor because they still held on to a way of life that was rapidly disappearing at the start of the twentieth century. Like Jack Yeats and W.B. Yeats, Synge was by no means a narrow nationalist or a romantic idealist. Rooted in an authentic Irish traditionalism, he was also steeped in a modern European artistic convention that encompassed the work of such artists as Vincent van Gogh, Paul Gauguin, Jean-François Millet and Edgar

4 Jack B. Yeats, *The ferryman of the Dinish Islands.* Yeats and Synge regarded the coastal inhabitants of the western seaboard as keepers of a secret wisdom that was in danger of extinction in modern Ireland (© Estate of Jack B. Yeats. All rights reserved, DACS 2010).

Degas. He did not occupy a neutral position between the two polarities of tradition and modernity in the emerging Ireland of his day. Instead, he preferred to defend the nomadism of 'tinkers' and 'vagrants', and the spontaneity of fishermen and poor peasants, in a country that was becoming increasing orderly, materialistic and state-centred. For Synge, spontaneity, self-sufficiency, social dignity and the autonomy of the individual were the cherished features of many of Ireland's isolated communities. As such, these were also the well-springs of their naturalism and the source of an alternative Irish authenticity. His peasants, fishermen, 'tinkers', kelp-gathers, beach workers and poor islanders were 'natural aristocrats' who upset the artificial opposition between Nature and Art in the petty bourgeois world of nationalist Ireland. Rather than portraying them as that society's poor fools, he regarded fishermen and the coastal poor as paragons of a beleaguered humanity that was increasingly relegated to the outer edges of nationalist Ireland. When these people talked, they did so in an intricate and artistic language that was in keeping with a poor but aristocratic demeanour. As the wayward 'others' in an increasingly settled society, their community life was ample compensation for the poverty of their own material circumstances. Synge did not just 'go native' by fixing a romantic gaze on poor fishermen and the travelling poor, but instead had the greatest respect for the plebeian underside of Irish society. In identifying with the fisher folk of the Aran Islands and the West of Ireland, Synge – the urbanite and sophisticated intellectual – was also placing himself in opposition to the cultural nationalist project of the Abbey Theatre of his day. His sympathetic perspectives on coastal communities were in stark contrast to the far harsher images of coastal distress found in most nationalist newspapers and journals. The following description of social conditions in and around Carraroe in Connemara in the late 1890s was fairly representative of rural nationalist views of life in Ireland's more impoverished western districts at that time. Published in the vehemently nationalist *New Ireland Review*, the author gave this account of the hopelessness of life on Gorumna, a tiny offshore island in south Connemara:

> Approaching the island from the direction of Carraroe boat slip, the visitor is struck with the appalling desolation of the scene. From the water's edge, across the whole island, the space seems to be occupied by bare rocks, those on the shore being washed white by the action of the sea … A perfect maze of granite walls, bounding the holdings of their innumerable subdivisions, hides out all view of vegetation or of land. There are no trees or shrubs on Gorumna, and were it not for the almost numberless cabins that dot the face of the island, one could hardly believe the place inhabited, it appears so utterly uninhabitable … Poverty there is on all sides, for poverty here is indigenous to the soil, or, to be more correct, the rocks, for there is no soil.[51]

Describing the 'chronic destitution' that he perceives in island life, this nationalist writer portrayed people here existing 'in a condition that appears little superior to that of the brute creation which shares their daily existence'. Houses, food, clothing 'and all the things that go to make up what we call the necessities of life are – where they exist at all – of the poorest and meanest sort'. For Synge, on the other hand, life in the Congested Districts along the western seaboard was 'strange and marvellous', and not without colour or vitality.[52] In contrast to Keogh's tough and direct account of distress, Synge is guarded and restrained in his description of island life and coastal communities. He contrasts the inhospitality of the coastal landscape with the hospitality of coastal communities. He also offers suggestions for improving living conditions in coastal districts, calling for the extension of a land-purchase scheme, and insisting on improvements to road and rail networks along the Atlantic seaboard. Instead of ignorance and idleness, Synge finds dignified labour and great vitality in these isolated communities. He understands the reluctance of many coastal dwellers to accept radical change, and is particularly sympathetic to their wariness of the expert opinions of social reformers. He praises their 'natural prudence' in the face of these experts 'who know nothing of the peculiar conditions of their native place'. He is especially attracted by the imaginative and rich cultural life of many islands and, in the letters he wrote from the west of Ireland, he stresses the distinctiveness of local places and the wealth of local customs. Unlike many of his peers, his plays were not just about the right of Irish people to decide how Ireland should be represented – they sought out a space at the centre of Irish theatre for the marginalised and dispossessed in an increasingly sanitised society.

Together with Synge, Padraic Colum, Liam O'Flaherty and Peadar O'Donnell, artists like Yeats and Henry laboured in the tradition of 'the lonely voice'. Their focus on the fleeting, the trivial and the ordinary, placed their work beyond the borders of what Declan Kiberd has called 'the national intellectual mood' of Ireland in the first half of the twentieth century.[53] They bring us face-to-face with a whole range of new characters that did not normally find a sympathetic space in more mainstream Irish art and literature. In so doing, they presented nationalist Ireland with yet another 'hidden Ireland' to that of Daniel Corkery, giving us entirely new perspectives on the coastal communities of the Atlantic seaboard in particular. Their Ireland was thus quite different from the Gaelicised Ireland of Corkery and other Irish cultural nationalists.[54] It had room within it for those who lived beyond the pale of rural Catholic respectability. These writers and artists raised the struggles of the rural and coastal poor to the level of miniature epics. They refused to consider fishermen, 'tramps' and 'tinkers' as the social jettison of a New Ireland. In so doing, they challenged imperial authority in nationalist Ireland, while simultaneously condemning the narrow nationalism and social exclusiveness of the Catholic bourgeoisie.

SOCIAL DARWINISM, IRISH NATIONALISM AND THE MARGINALISATION OF COASTAL IRELAND

Social Darwinism and Victorian moral values also had a significant impact upon social class attitudes to economic relations between rural and coastal Ireland in the latter half of the nineteenth century. From an Anglo-English perspective, post-Famine Ireland was considered more or less settled, and well on the way to becoming a vital component of a much more prosperous United Kingdom. Ireland, it was argued, had by then passed through a number of quite distinctive and separate historical epochs to become an integral part of a prosperous British nation. Real progress, it was suggested, commenced with the demise of the Gaelic lordships in the sixteenth and seventeenth centuries and continued with the ascendancy of the landed aristocracy in the eighteenth century. Colonial authorities stressed the weaknesses of Gaelic society, pointing in particular to the country's internal divisions, under-developed economy, poorly developed infrastructure, and lawless coastal regions. From this perspective, Gaelic Ireland was still locked in a 'hunting and gathering' way of life, and Ireland was a country where primitive rebels, 'wood kernes', outlaws, smugglers, pirates and the unruly poor attacked the outposts of a beleaguered colonial civilisation. For that reason, they were considered as 'disposable people', as so many obstacles to social progress and moral improvement.[55] Evolutionary theories of social progress were based on a conviction that all societies were regulated by well-defined historical social principles. It was suggested that loud echoes of Britain's historical past could still be heard in the backward regions and coastal peripheries of Ireland and Scotland. Travel to such places involved not only an expedition across space – it also entailed a journey backwards in time to an earlier, more 'barbaric' phase of social evolution. Having constructed the rural and coastal poor of these districts as the social inferiors of the civilised English, it was only a matter of time before groups such as impoverished fishermen, landless labourers and small land-holders would become social outcasts of respectable society.

Evolutionary theories of social development reached their fullest expression in the latter half of the nineteenth century in the writings of Herbert Spenser, Thomas Huxley and Friedrich Ratzel, but also influenced the social class outlook of nationalists and state-builders. Social evolutionism had profound implications for the manner in which impoverished rural and coastal communities were viewed all across nation-building Europe. Progress and development, it was suggested, were primarily the preserve of the powerful in these societies, particularly improving landowners, industrialists, entrepreneurs and the professional middle classes. Writing during a period of intense international and intra-national competition, these writers insisted that subordinate social groups could only hope to occupy a peripheral position in the state-centred projects of nation-builders.[56] Advanced societies under the hegemony of landed and urban elites had little room for those who could not compete in the struggle for national survival. Such societies were also considered worthy of emulation by those aspiring to nationhood, largely because they had managed to 'tame' the natural world and used the resources of land and sea to advance their political, economic and geo-strategic objectives. Thus, *nationalists* and social Darwinists alike insisted that the modern nation state should not only be constructed *by*, but also *for* the more advanced sectors of capitalist societies. Endorsing the commercial expansion of the nation in Europe's remaining peripheral regions, the advocates of progress called for the transformation of weaker societies into territorially cohesive and powerful states. They further suggested that the nineteenth-century colonial world should be ruled by core nations in the metropolitan world, thus rendering a handful of European nations the 'lords of humankind'.[57] Those located outside the metropolitan world, including marginalised groups within Europe and North America, were not only socially and racially inferior to the global bourgeoisie – in the words of Eric Wolf, they were also 'people without history'.[58] Because it was accepted that poor fishing and farming communities lived outside modern time and space, they too could be categorised as 'people without history'. This, in turn, hastened the demise of peasant cultivation and subsistence fishing in remote coastal areas, causing impoverished coastal communities in particular to be banished to the footnotes of mainstream history.[59] Marginalised peasants and poor fishermen found it extremely difficult to get a word in edgeways in the highly competitive environment of Europe's emerging nation-states. The histories of these marginalised communities are to be found in the slipstream of nationalist history, and well beyond the mainstream of European history.

The chapter that follows examines the archaeology of sea fishing in Ireland from the Neolithic period down to the Viking invasions of the ninth century and the Anglo-Norman incursions of the twelfth century. The contributions of the latter to the transformation of Ireland's maritime economy and coastal settlements have been widely recognised. This chapter revisits that period to assess the strength of maritime influences in the light of established and more recent assessments of the influence of early colonial settlement on the built environment of coastal Ireland. Similarly, it is argued, the degree of reliance on coastal resources and the sea was far more marked throughout the Neolithic period than has previously been assumed. In focusing on the ancient traditions of coastal and freshwater fishing over the *longue durée,* this chapter describes fishing techniques and fishing craft in the prehistoric period right up to the twelfth century. In so doing, it offers new insights into the social organisation of coastal economies in prehistoric and Early Christian Ireland, emphasising especially the reliance of early settlers and monastic settlements on the resources of marine inlets, lakes and rivers. Drawing upon a wide range of recent maritime archaeological studies of this important phase in the development of Ireland, the chapter specifically focuses on ancient methods of trapping and preserving fish, and the role of seafood in the diets of the country's original settlers.

CHAPTER TWO

'Marauding seafarers' versus 'settled farmers': the archaeology of Irish fishing

MARITIME VERSUS LANDED SOCIETIES

Describing the historical links between landed Europe and its maritime fringe, historians and archaeologists have traced conflicts of interest between seafaring and 'settled' farming communities as far back as the ninth and tenth centuries.[1] Some have located the sources of these conflicts in the great sea-raids of the Vikings who dominated the seas off north-western Europe throughout much of this period. Others have traced antagonisms between predominantly agrarian societies on the one hand, and maritime societies on the other, to the eighteenth and nineteenth centuries. It was then that the commercialisation of agriculture and the growth of industry contributed to a dramatic decline in the relative importance of subsistence farming and fishing in many European countries. Edward Fox has identified an expanding schism between landed interests and coastal settlements in continental Europe dating back to the fourteenth century. Distinguishing between seaborne commerce and localised land-based trade in the centuries before the French Revolution, he argued that

> two quite separate, and quite distinctive, societies co-existed coevally, or side by side, in Europe from the fourteenth century onwards. Landed agricultural societies are all the more familiar to us because they had a territorial basis. Their histories have been well documented by national historians. They possessed well-defined administrative apparatuses. They had clearly defined, albeit fluctuating, geographical boundaries.[2]

It was precisely the great landed and industrial societies of Europe that made history by appropriating their national *territory* (if not always their territorial *waters*), and compiling heroic histories that extolled the achievements of landed and industrial elites. It has been far more difficult to theorise Europe's seafaring communities, not least because they have been far more evasive than landed and industrial societies. Unlike the latter, they depended upon the seas off continental Europe and North America for their survival, trading across great expanses of ocean and ranging well beyond the narrow national boundaries that hemmed in urban and rural folk. Although they belonged to well-defined national territories, many coastal dwellers had little time for the type of governance and social organisation characteristic of rural and industrial societies. Nevertheless, a preoccupation with national territory and the *territorial state* has clouded our understanding of the social organisation of *international* fishing communities and seafaring nations in general. Yet these have operated in a maritime world of trade, fishing, piracy and commerce since at least the ninth century. Despite this, many find it hard to conceive of such societies successfully managing to support themselves from the resources of the sea, or through an active exchange of goods, services and information across great expanses of ocean. Nevertheless, maritime nations as far apart as Norway and Canada were for long periods of their history extremely dependent upon the resources of the sea. They also managed to retain a highly developed sense of common purpose right down to the beginning of the twenty-first century.

As Fox suggested, medieval Europe, including Ireland, was home to two quite distinctive social formations, one of which was based on seaborne trade and fishing, while the other was land-based and fundamentally rural in orientation. Each gave rise to distinctive forms of political and economic organisation, and although they were often in regular contact, they often operated independently of one another. Seafaring and maritime communities, the more extroverted of the two, contributed to the rise of quite distinctive trading towns, port cities and fishing communities.[3] Towns and cities in the interior of Europe generally functioned as market and administrative centres for the surrounding countryside. While rural and coastal areas together fostered the development of towns and cities, the critical distinctions between the two did not revolve around clear-cut divisions between town and country. They lay instead in the crucial differences between those engaged in long-distance trade and seafaring on the one hand, and those concerned with short-distance trade, commerce and industry on the other. Thus, unlike landlocked market towns and rural communities, coastal settlements, port cities, and fishing communities were in regular and close contact with each across very considerable distances. We shall see presently that this was true of the prehistoric and the medieval period. These settlements also had access to highly productive deep-sea and estuarine fisheries, and the exploitation of these resources was often more crucial to their survival than trade with their rural hinterlands. Stressing the longevity of Ireland's maritime traditions, one writer has pointed out that the inhabitants of Ireland lived on and around our coast for over 9,000 years, exploiting its resources and using the sea as a means of transport and communication. Until relatively recently, there has been great continuity of tradition along the coast with, for example, the methods of fishing changing little over the millennia. Consequently, people still live at the landfalls and harbours that would have been known to the original settlers.[4]

Moriarty has suggested that Ireland's earliest inhabitants were Mesolithic hunter-gatherers 'whose encampments revealed that they lived near rivers and the seaside around 9,000 years ago'.[5] A characteristic stone artefact of Mesolithic people in Ireland was the 'microlith', a small flint believed to be part of an early fishing spear and used to catch full grown eels as they migrated seaward in the autumn months. Moriarty also pointed to the possibility that these early settlers were capable of constructing wattle-woven barriers across lakes, rivers and coastal estuaries, in order to trap eels, trout, salmon, flounder and sea bass. Flanagan has also shown that the skills used in the construction of temporary skin-covered huts at coastal sites around Ireland were similar to those used in the manufacture of timber-framed, skin-covered boats. He has argued that it is 'virtually inconceivable' that the construction and boat-making skills of those inhabiting estuarine sites around Ireland in the Neolithic period should be quite forgotten at later stages in the evolution of farming and fishing techniques.[6]

THE ARCHAEOLOGY OF FISHING AND FISHING METHODS IN IRELAND

Fish, particularly shellfish, were very significant in the diets of coastal-dwelling peoples in Ireland in the prehistoric and medieval periods. An examination of kitchen middens near Dooey in Co. Donegal has confirmed that some forms of crude fishing and coastal foraging were important aspects of Neolithic life. Shell mounds consisting mainly of oyster remains have also been found on the shores of Cork Harbour, and the presence of large middens of seashells at many coastal districts around the west coast suggests that shellfish constituted a significant food item for many of these coastal-dwelling communities. Archaeological surveys of a number of Later Mesolithic and Neolithic coastal sites in Ireland suggest that inland areas were intensively settled by comparatively prosperous early farmers, while hunters and gatherers stuck close to the shore, where they foraged for seafood and probably also engaged in rudimentary forms of fishing. In the maritime north-west of the country, Lacey has argued that sandhill sites dating from the Mesolithic to the early medieval period reflected 'the universal economic practice of sea-food harvesting by coastal dwellers'.[7] While evidence of Mesolithic settlement is scarce in this part of the country, the modern-day county of Donegal accounts for almost one tenth of the country's Megalithic tombs, making it one of the most important sites of Neolithic and Early Bronze Age settlement in Ireland. Coastal habitation or sandhill sites are also common in Kerry, Galway, Antrim and Down, where prehistoric coastal communities subsisted on a mixed diet of meat of sheep, pig, ox, horse, red deer, shellfish and saltwater and freshwater fish. Archaeological evidence from the south-east coast suggests that saltwater and freshwater fish constituted an important element in the diet of coastal and riverside communities in the Mesolithic period. The year-round availability of fish on the coast of Wexford and Waterford meant that Mesolithic communities had ample stocks of nutritional food throughout they year. They were probably attracted to the area by large runs of spring and summer salmon that could be trapped in the estuaries of large rivers.

Kitchen middens containing an abundance of shellfish remains are a characteristic feature of Mesolithic coastal activity in the south-east of Ireland, and Stout has pointed out that one midden at Clare Island, in Bannow Bay, yielded 'a wealth of animal bone, human skulls and oysters … and contained the remains of deer, cattle and pig'.[8] The discovery of flint tools along the south-east and south coasts further suggests that this area was first settled between 5000BC and 3000BC, when coastal communities were able to exploit the food resources of shoreline and riverside. Although these communities made little impact on deciduous forests in the rural interior of the country, their impact on the coastal environment, and on the shoreline of large estuaries, was very significant indeed. Here, as elsewhere in Mesolithic coastal Ireland, there was a transitional phase during which hunting, coastal foraging and rudimentary forms of agriculture would have been practised within the same time-span. Indeed, the presence of animal bones alongside shellfish and fish remains at many sites points to the existence of a mixed farming-foraging economy in the Mesolithic period. This illustrates the importance of coastal foraging for fish, shellfish and seaweeds throughout the Late Mesolithic and well into the Neolithic period. Similarly, in the north of the country, the shoreline and sea loughs of Donegal would have been highly suitable for settlement by coastal foragers and primitive fisher folk from a very early stage. Woodman's work at Mount Sandel, the site of an important settlement overlooking the upper reaches of the Bann Estuary near Coleraine, suggests that Mesolithic coastal dwellers trapped salmon, trout, plaice and sea bass. The bones of wild pig, hares and wild birds were also found at this site, alongside 'concentrations of hazelnut shells and other seeds such as apple and water lily, from which it appears that the site had been used at various seasons of the year'.[9]

These Mesolithic coastal dwellers may have settled at sandhill sites around the north coast on a temporary basis, using great rivers such as the Bann, the Foyle and the Finn as 'water highways' for gaining access to the interior of the country. There was a coastal trade in flint on the Atlantic fringe of Inishowen during the Late Mesolithic period, and this was probably linked to rudimentary forms of fishing and coastal foraging. Dunaff Bay in the north-west of the peninsula was 'the location of a small flint industry, perhaps the part-time activity of a group of offshore Mesolithic fishermen, whose boats had the technical capacity to return home with cargoes of flint as well as fish'.[10] Lacey has argued that a group of Mesolithic hunters and gatherers may have been drawn to this area by the annual run of salmon up Lough Swilly in May or June, and by offshore seal colonies that would have provided them with a rich source of food.[11] However, in cautioning against an over-exaggerated role for fishing and coastal foraging in Mesolithic and Neolithic Ireland, Woodman has pointed out that

> The transition to agriculture remains one of the most difficult areas in European prehistory. Therefore, the role of marine resources in later prehistory is obviously viewed with certain preconceived theoretical perspectives that colour research. I would argue that agriculture only made a significant impact in Ireland when farming communities introduced a tried and tested mixed domesticated and arable farming economy. While this relied primarily on the keeping of cattle and sheep as well as growing cereals, it did not exclude the use of other resources. However, later prehistoric archaeological sites have consistently produced domesticates and little trace of the hunting of wild species … There is no doubt that marine resources continued to be used … Therefore there are some limited indicators that the sea continued to provide a component of the resources in Neolithic economies. It is probable that throughout the Neolithic, different communities used the sea in different manners but usually in a very limited fashion and probably as a supplement to a land-based economy.[12]

In the absence of bone fish-hooks, gorges and stone 'sinkers' from Mesolithic sites in Ireland as well as Scotland, therefore, it is extremely difficult to evaluate the importance of foraging and fishing in the Late Mesolithic and Early Neolithic period. Fragile artefactual and fragmentary food remains make it very difficult indeed to establish the extent of marine exploitation in Ireland at this stage. While it is probable that large quantities of shellfish were collected on numerous shoreline sites (where their remains were highly visible in the form of shellfish middens), Woodman argues that this creates an exaggerated sense of the dietary importance of 'seafood' in the Late Mesolithic period.[13] The most recent methods for analysing fragmentary food remains from Late Mesolithic sites suggest that coastal communities may well have exploited the sea and shoreline far more intensively than has hitherto been accepted.

Fishing was certainly an important source of protein in large tracts of the Irish coastline, and archaeological evidence indicates that herring and salmon were especially prized along the south and west coasts from the twelfth century onwards. Excavations at an ecclesiastical site at Drumcliffe, Co. Sligo, have identified relatively large collections of fish bones, including scad, herring and salmon.[14] The commercial exploitation of the seas played an important role in maritime economies of Ireland, Scotland, Brittany, Portugal, Cornwall and Galicia throughout the medieval period. The remains of pike and sea wrasse have been found at sites of Palaeolithic settlement in Spain and France. At the end of the Ice Age, a whole series of fishing communities extended out along the north-west coast of Europe, stretching from Brittany to the shores of the Baltic Sea. Land flora and fauna in these inhospitable environments were so poor that groups such as the Ertebølle people of Denmark, and Larnian communities in the north-east of Ireland, lived largely off fish, shellfish and game. We know that fishing was one of the major pursuits of early settlers living in close proximity to the sea in Ireland, including those who lived near major rivers and lakes.[15] Groups 'squatting' around a raised beach may have been responsible for the three Late Mesolithic middens near Rockmarshall in Co. Louth. Apart from shells, the amount of material recovered from this seasonally occupied site was quite small, and included mainly broken beach pebbles and 'roughly struck flints'.[16] While the Larnian people in the north-east of Ireland had little knowledge of farming, they managed to survive by gathering food on the shoreline of major lakes and sea estuaries. Mitchell stated that

> By the time they reached Ireland, the country had been re-smothered in
> trees, and they could not range across wide prairies in search of herds of

big game, as the Palaeolithic hunters had done. They seem to have had axe-like implements of chipped stone, but they either could not, or did not, use these for forest clearance as the Neolithic people used their hafted polished stone axes to open up cultivation patches in the woodlands. They were hunters and fishers of Mesolithic status, restricted by their inability to clear large areas to roaming along the shores of lakes and rivers and along the coast, hunting small game and catching fish, and collecting nuts and seeds, as seasonal opportunity offered.[17]

This type of coastal economy was not unique to the east and north-east of the country. Woodman's investigations in the Dingle Peninsula yielded a series of small shell middens around Ballyferriter and Ferriter's Cove.[18] Fish bones and scales, as well as wild pig and deer bones, have all been recovered from coastal sites as far apart as Kerry and north Antrim. During the Mesolithic/Neolithic 'overlap', fishing, hunting and food collection were carried on when 'settled' farming was slowly developing. Far from being rigidly separated one from the other, hunting and gathering co-existed with rudimentary forms of farming at this stage. In the Dingle Peninsula, hunting, fishing and food collection were an integral part of a slowly developing agricultural system based on pastoralism and the domestication of animals. This has caused Woodman to argue that no hard and fast line can be drawn between the end of the Mesolithic and the start of the Neolithic. Moreover, many of these prehistoric communities were more settled during the early Mesolithic than in the later Mesolithic, and may have moved from the seashore to the lakes and inland waters in a seasonal cycle of hunting, gathering and fishing. According to this interpretation, winters were devoted to hunting wild pig in forests and woodland, while the summer months saw these same nomadic peoples move to the coastline in order to collect oysters and other shellfish. Mitchell has also suggested that 'sustenance was easy on the shore-line' of Ireland around 7,000 years ago because 'both fish and shellfish were readily available'. In coastal districts where the campsites were sufficiently high to escape destruction by the sea, extensive middens containing the remains of oyster, limpet, periwinkle and other shellfish have been found. According to Mitchell

It would not have been possible to cure shellfish, crabs and lobsters, but sea fish could have been salted and dried in the way that continues in Iceland to the present day. There, great acreages of wooden fish-racks are employed in drying and smoking cod and other fish, and a substantial

5 Aboriginal life in New South Wales in the 1820s. The hunting and gathering
culture of these coastal foragers has been compared to that of Ireland's prehistoric
Larnian people from five thousand years ago (courtesy of the National Library
of Australia, Canberra).

trade is carried on in the export of such preserved fish to Nigeria and
other African countries which are short of protein. Porpoises and small
whales would occasionally be stranded [on Irish coasts], or might under
favourable circumstances be driven ashore, and after they had provided
an immediate feast, the rest of the flesh could be smoked, as mutton is
smoked in Iceland today.[19]

He also speculated that the Larnian people who settled around Lough Neagh
organised themselves into hunting parties in order to fish for salmon and eels
around the shores of lakes, rivers and sea estuaries. These hunters and gatherers
from the north-east may have penetrated as far south as Lough Derravaragh,
near Mullingar, while evidence suggests that they probably smoked salmon and
eels on the shores of Lough Beg in Co. Antrim.[20] Around 5000BC, 'Maori-style'
parties of Larnian hunters and fishermen fanned out from the north-east of
Ireland, 'setting traps for fish in the fen channels, collecting and perhaps

parching water-lily seeds, gathering hazelnuts, and giving a preliminary dressing to blocks of [flint], carrying away the semi-worked pieces to be finished elsewhere'.[21] The prevalence of small periwinkle shells of uniform size at Ferriter's Cove in Kerry suggests that young shellfish may well have been deliberately selected for their sweetness and tenderness. This has prompted one food-writer to retort that 'Irish taste buds have been millennia in the making'.[22] Some of these early coastal and estuarine settlers may have smoke-preserved salmon for winter use, and consumed large quantities of edible seaweed called 'dulse', which they collected at low tide.

Excavations at Lough Gur, in Co. Limerick, have also shown that this area was a haunt for hunters and gathers from around 3000BC. This district was criss-crossed with lakes and rivers, and interspersed with patches of limestone soils that were attractive to early farmers and fisher folk from the Late Neolithic period to the Early Bronze Age. Settlers appear to have been particularly attracted by the presence of an unfailing water supply and abundant supplies of fish and game. The area around the Knockadoon Peninsula in particular was a focus for continuous settlement from a very early age. Those who settled here were stock farmers who raised cattle, sheep and pigs, but they also trapped eels, salmon and trout in nearby rivers and lakes.[23] Fergus Kelly has argued that fish have been caught in Ireland since the Stone Age, and many techniques were employed to catch them, including spearing, stroke-hauling, tickling, netting, hooking with rod and line, and poisoning. A subsequent chapter will show that many Old Irish sources testify to the existence of fishing weirs that were erected in rivers and sea estuaries to trap saltwater and freshwater species. The Old Irish terms for weir provide clues to their method of construction, with the word *corae* referring to the commonest form of stone weir, while *aire* referred to weirs consisting of a woven wooden fence.[24] Not all weirs were used to trap fish, and early legal documents refer to weirs that were built to direct water towards a river bank in order to a drive a watermill. Weirs were especially effective in trapping migratory species such as salmon and eels, and some were constructed in such a way as to force fish into narrow channels where they could be caught with spears, forks, hooks or nets. In more complex weirs, wickerwork baskets were submerged in water in order to trap fish as they entered them.

Early Irish coastal dwellers certainly possessed a detailed knowledge of the migratory behaviour of eels and salmon, which they trapped in hand-nets set near the edges of rivers and lakes as these fish swam close to the banks.[25] Ireland's Neolithic farmers and coastal foragers suffered from severe food scarcities in the winter months, and this may have forced them to hunt for salmon and other fish entering great rivers such as the Boyne, the Liffey, the Bann, the Blackwater, the Lee and the Shannon. Neolithic farmers and the early Celts regularly fished these waters in mid-winter when salmon made their way upriver to spawning grounds. Archaeological excavations have suggested that farmer/fisher folk from Beginish, Co. Kerry, exploited this stretch of Munster coastline from the Neolithic period right down to the twelfth century.[26] Little is known about early *sea* fishing techniques, but excavations of shell mounds on the west coast of Scotland suggest that 'Neolithic man included in his fare at least eight types of fish, namely the conger eel, the Black Sea bream, the sea bream, the spotted wrasse, angel fish, tope, thorn-back ray and spiny dogfish'.[27] In addition to this, we know that coastal-dwelling Neolithic communities consumed large quantities of shellfish, crabs and edible seaweeds. Moriarty has shown that the Boyne people's diet of salmon 'was famous, even to those who lived in less favoured regions', thus implying that salmon 'was a major factor in their survival as a people'. He further suggests that it was no coincidence that the greatest centre of Neolithic civilisation in Ireland was centred at Newgrange, near the Boyne, which had abundant supplies of salmon.[28]

It has generally been assumed that the development of systematic fishing in the early medieval period capable of feeding large numbers of people had to await the development of boats capable of operating on the open sea, or at least around the estuaries of large rivers. Yet excavations of Neolithic sites in Ireland and Scotland suggest that coastal inhabitants in both these countries were skilled in the use of hooks, and may even have used primitive fish-traps. In addition to weirs, coastal dwellers also used forks and spears to trap fish, and may have been familiar with primitive, but effective, hooks known as gorges. Thorns were also used as hooks, and improved methods of working with bone and horn meant that craftsmen were able to invent a tough yet flexible hook for catching fish. The probable remains of baited fish-gorges used to 'snare' fish have been found at a Mesolithic site in Co. Antrim.[29] Fishing in later prehistoric times was probably first practised by hand in rivers and lakes, but barriers were also used to dam rivers with stones, brushwood and wattle structures. These artificial structures could be considered the forerunners of modern fish farms in that they allowed for the storage of live fish until needed for consumption.

In Ireland, as in northern Europe, prehistoric coastal dwellers also hunted whales; especially smaller whales that were simply regarded as large fish. These were sought both for food and for their oil, while whale bone was used quite extensively in the manufacture of weapons and ornaments, and was occasionally used as building material. Pieces of whale bone have been recovered from prehistoric kitchen middens as far apart as Dublin, Cork, Louth, Kerry, Donegal, Antrim, Down, Galway, Sligo and Mayo.[30] An excavation at Carrowmore, Co. Sligo, uncovered 'a dagger-like implement made of cetaceous bone' measuring approximately two feet in length. One midden at Tranarossan, Co. Donegal, revealed a fragment of rib 'drilled with a hole' from a medium-sized whale. Evidence also suggests that whales were hunted off Ireland in the early years of the first millennium, and we have references to the bones of whales, 'possibly baleen', being used in the making of hoops in the fifth century. We also know that whale bone was used in the manufacture of culinary implements at an early monastic settlement on North Inishkea off the Mayo coast. The vertebra of a large whale was even incorporated into the walls of a cottage on Achill Island. Part of a vertebra and a section of whale, possibly from a pilot whale, that were dug up in the yard of a medieval house in Cork have been dated to the mid-thirteenth century.[31]

The prehistoric inhabitants of Ireland's coastal zone must have been struck by the many opportunities on offer in the diverse mountain-lake-and-coastal environments of the south-west of the country. Coastal Munster and Ulster certainly possessed considerable resource potential for fisher folk, hunters, foragers and early farmers long before the arrival of the Vikings. These groups were particularly attracted to coastal woodlands and low-lying areas near good hunting and fishing grounds and upland farm country. Early farmers and foragers settled in coastal districts throughout Ireland around 9,000 years ago. By 4000BC, entire regions in the west and south-west were gradually transformed from open tundra to dense forest, creating an ideal environment for hunters and settlers who could survive by fishing, hunting wild pig and small game, and gathering wild plants and seafood.[32] Stone tools used by Mesolithic people have been discovered all around the coastal zone and in major river-systems.[33] There was relatively little interference with natural forests at this stage, as the banks of rivers, lakes and coastal waters satisfied the resource needs of early settlers. Throughout the Mesolithic and well into the Neolithic period, most sites of human occupation were located along the coast or close to rivers and lakes. The Bann Estuary, Killarney's lakeland district, the Blackwater Valley, the Shannon Estuary, Galway Bay and the valleys of the Barrow, Nore and the Suir all acted as important magnets for early settlement right down to 3000BC.[34] These early foragers were by no means entirely nomadic, as many of them settled in coastal locations and river estuaries on a permanent basis. The usual indication of Mesolithic coastal habitation in Ireland consists of a scattering of stone tools and extensive food middens, usually containing animal remains and fish bones, sea-shells and the leftovers of aquatic crustaceans and molluscs. Contrary to conventional images of Mesolithic folk as 'walking stomachs' or wandering hunters, many Mesolithic communities were not strictly nomadic. Prior to the onset of settled farming conditions around 4000BC, many of these people engaged in a seasonally settled way of life that was heavily dependent upon fishing, foraging and hunting.

With improvements in climate after the Ice Age, and with the onset of settled farming conditions in the fourth millennium BC, a Neolithic farming economy gradually developed, and forest clearance in coastal zones began in earnest. Far from being displaced by settled farming and animal husbandry at the onset of the Neolithic, hunting, foraging and primitive forms of fishing continued as important features of economic life well into the Neolithic period. Fish and shellfish, together with milk, appear to have been the chief sources of protein throughout much of this period. The adoption of agriculture was accompanied by land reclamation, and great effort was expended in breaking the forest canopy in coastal areas, as well as in the interior of the country. Polished stone axes were used to create these early field systems in prehistoric Ireland and they provided grazing for growing herds of cattle as farmers began the slow process of transforming hunting grounds into an organised farmscape of fields and rural settlements.[35] Most of the early field patterns that were laid down during this era of intense farming were subsequently cleared away by new farming practices in the early medieval period. The extensive landscaping of the countryside in the eighteenth century, and the peopling of marginal lands and the coastal zone in the nineteenth century, strongly affected those that survived. Nevertheless, field systems dating to the late Neolithic period have been located all across the country, most notably at Céide in north Mayo, Valentia Island in south Kerry, and in the many hills and valleys of the Dingle and Iveragh Peninsulas. In Kerry, ancient field walls and hut sites have been uncovered east of Muckross and in some mountain valleys around Killarney.[36]

As the centuries progressed, coastal communities in Ireland and Europe also traded in fish across considerable distances. Merchants from the Netherlands were travelling to Scotland to buy salted fish from as early as the ninth century. Herring fishing appears to have been the earliest established fishing industry in England and Scotland around this time, and it may be presumed that some form of rudimentary nets, possibly set along the shore, were then in use.[37] We have already seen that the most common form of fishing at this stage involved the use of man-made weirs, and these may well have been used to trap herring around the coast of Ireland, Scotland and England. Early Irish law tracts from the seventh to the ninth century regularly mention fishing coracles, fishing weirs and skin-covered boats. In *Cáin Domnaigh*, the Law of Sunday, mention is made of the fact that fishermen had to surrender their nets and coracles if caught fishing on a Sunday. The penalty for the destruction of a coracle amounted to five 'sets', payable to the owner of the vessels, while ten 'sets' were the penalty for larger boats covered with three hides as opposed to the customary one.[38] The *Uraicecht Becc* text indicates the status of the boat-builder and places him on a par with the blacksmith and the silversmith. One eighth-century law tract suggests that these early fishing communities were alert to the dangers of over-fishing particular stretches of water, with rules stating that weirs must not cover more than one third of the way across a river. Another rule laid down that a 'free gap' be left open in fish weirs in order to allow the unimpeded movement of some fish passing up or down a river. These and other medieval law tracts and annals suggest that fish weirs, known as *coar eisc*, were common throughout Ireland from the sixth to the thirteenth century. Although used in some parts of the country right down to relatively recent times, most probably began to fall into disuse chiefly from the sixteenth century onwards.[39] That said, however, it is important to note that eel weirs and fish baskets known as *giurogi* were in use in Irish tidal waters well into the nineteenth century, with examples of weirs at Bunratty in Clare, Castlebellingham in Louth and Buttermilk Castle in Waterford surviving into the twentieth century. More primitive but highly effective forms of 'fish pounds' and 'salmon walls' were found in Lough Swilly, in Co. Donegal, and at Doonbeg in Co. Clare. In coastal areas, as in the catchment areas of large rivers, land increased in value depending on its suitability for constructing weirs and fish-traps.[40] Moreover, the seventh-century law tract, *Coibnes Uisci Thairidne*, implied that privately owned weirs could be erected on a neighbour's property. Kelly has alluded to a 'grisly reference' for the year 1225 in the *Annals of Connacht*, which described how in the aftermath of a battle fought near Ballycong, drowned children were discovered in a number of local fish weirs.[41]

Remains of Late Mesolithic fish-traps around North Wall Quay and Spenser Dock in Dublin suggest that this method of catching fish may be over 3,000 years old. We know that from a very early stage, 'ebb weirs' were erected in the tidal zone of the Liffey in order to trap fish drifting downriver with the falling tide.[42] Remains discovered at North Wall Quay provide the earliest definitive evidence for the use of stationery fish-traps in Ireland, and these indicate that 'over a period of up to 200 years, the Mesolithic population of the Dublin area

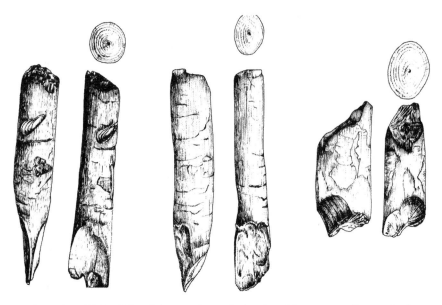

6 Remains of Mesolithic fish-traps from the banks of the River Liffey. In the late
Mesolithic period, coastal foragers around Dublin Bay were already dependent
on fish and 'shore food' (after McQuade, 'Gone fishing' (2008)).

was fishing along a 70 metre stretch of the Liffey intertidal zone (probably on
an intermittent basis)'. This fishing ground was subsequently revisited during
the Middle Neolithic, when farming was also practised and the population had
access to a wide variety of resources. Those who used these fishing grounds
invested large amounts of labour in the construction of fish-traps. Studies have
revealed that wood for their construction was carefully chosen and may
have come from managed woodland in and around the mouth of the Liffey. A
series of well-preserved wooden baskets discovered at Clowanstown, near
Dunshaughlin in Co. Meath, suggests that a mooring or fishing platform
existed here in the Late Mesolithic period. Clowanstown would have been an
ideal location for fishing and foraging, as the lake was well provided with fish
and waterfowl, while plants and animals were abundant in the surrounding
woodlands. One of the fish baskets from this site returned a radiocarbon date
of 5210–4970BC, and additional baskets of similar shape were also discovered.[43]
More recently, fragments of a fish basket from Carrigdirty Rock in the
Shannon Estuary have returned a radiocarbon date of 3875–3535BC. Like the
Meath baskets, these were also constructed of alder shoots and bear a marked
resemblance to the type of fishing baskets used by Bambi tribesmen in Mali
during sacred ritual fishing festivals.

EARLY FISHING CRAFT AND THE EXPLOITATION OF SEA FISHERIES

Some archaeologists have argued that seal-skin boats were used in Ireland in the late Mesolithic period.[44] Remains of deep-sea species of fish have also been found around Oban in the west of Scotland, along with a proliferation of skin-working tools used to trap and prepare fish in the Mesolithic and Neolithic periods. The Mesolithic Ertebølle culture of Denmark presents abundant evidence to indicate that sea fishing and the exploitation of marine molluscs were common at this stage. However, there is little evidence of an 'open sea' fishing economy in the Irish Mesolithic, and most evidence points to inshore fishing and the exploitation of the seashore, rather than the open sea. The literary evidence from the late first millennium BC onwards is more promising. Avienus' fourth-century poem, *Ora Maritima*, refers to the 'hardy and industrious peoples' of western Brittany, who used hide boats (*netisque cumbis*) to obtain tin and lead from Ireland. Extracts from a fourth-century coastal pilot's handbook mentions two-day voyages by hide boats from Ushant, off the coast of Brittany, to Ireland.[45] Pliny quoted from the third-century historian Timaeus, who referred to seafaring Britons who used sea-going boats made of osiers and covered with stitched hides.[46] A small gold model from Broighter, on the margins of Lough Foyle, probably represents one such sea-going hide boat from the first century BC. This vessel was propelled by oars and by a square sail on a mast, or by long poles used for 'punting' the vessel in shallow waters. Boats used by Celtic fishermen, lake dwellers and seafarers included log rafts, hide boats, log boats and plank boats. These could be used on inland waters for fishing, hunting and the gathering of reeds, and were also used in the transport of animals and for social intercourse.

We know that the ancient Celts had mastered the art of shipbuilding and boat design, and Julius Caesar described sea-going cargo vessels off the Irish coast that were built by coastal peoples in northern Gaul.[47] This type of craft was flat-bottomed, had heavy ribs held in place by think planks, and was usually made entirely of oak. The mast on these early ships was carried forward, and was located about one third of the way back from the prow of the boat. On larger vessels, there was room for a prow, and these were able to undertake long-distance voyages along the Atlantic coast from Ireland, Britain and northern France to Spain and Portugal. Caesar also noted that the ancient Celts made extensive use of the currach, which even in his day was used along the coast and out into the Atlantic. Such boats could measure up to twelve metres in length and while they were generally rowed, some of them also carried a sail.

The shape of the hull was perfectly adapted to Atlantic conditions, and this allowed them to bob like corks on the surface of the sea. They were ideally suited to the open ocean and were capable of regular trips between Ireland, the Faeroes and Iceland.[48] We also know that boating activity facilitated trade and social linkages between Ireland and the north-west of Europe throughout the prehistoric period. Writing around AD100, the historian Tacitus reported that Roman merchants were familiar with a number of harbours and havens around the Irish coast. More than 200 years later, another Roman historian wrote that 'the sea which separates Ireland from Britain is rough and stormy throughout the year; it is navigable for a few days only; they voyage in small boats of pliant twigs, covered with the skins of oxen'.[49] The early Irish annalists make repeated references to 'Irish fleets sailing on raiding sorties to Britain', and to numerous voyages by a number of saints to far-off places. The Annals of the Four Masters recorded that in the year AD732 'Falibhe, son of Guaire, successor of Mealrubha, was drowned, and the crew of his ship with him; they were twenty-two in number'.[50]

A limited amount of deep-sea fishing undoubtedly occurred off the coast of Ireland in the thirteenth and fourteenth centuries. Bones from a number of deep-water species have been found at excavation sites from Cape Clear to Valentia Island in south-west Munster. A twelfth-century literary text referred to deep-sea fishing at Dursey and Bere Island, and we know that dulse was widely gathered on the shoreline of Cape Clear at this time. It has also been suggested that the Irish did not engage in deep-sea fishing for cod and ling, and that Hiberno-Scandinavians were chiefly engaged in this type of fishing. The possible existence of a community of Scandinavian fishermen and farmers on Beginish Island, off the coast of Kerry, is all the more remarkable in view of the fact that Irish Scandinavian settlements were generally regarded as predominantly urban phenomena.[51] Thus, for example, bones of cod and wrasse have been found at Church Island, and at Illaunloughan, in the sea channel separating Valentia from the Kerry mainland. Remains of seal bones have been found on Church Island, thus implying that hunting of marine animals was also practised along this stretch of coast. It is not clear if seals were hunted at sea, were killed while resting on rocks, or were simply trapped in primitive nets. Certainly, marine animals were regarded as a valuable source of food in the Early Medieval period, and their remains have been found in small quantities on many archaeological sites. Written sources note the slaughter of a school of porpoises by the Vikings off the coast of Dublin in the early decades of the ninth century.[52]

7 Sketch of a medieval Irish ship from *The Book of Ballymote* from *c*.1400. A facsimile edition of this work was edited by Robert Atkinson and published in 1887.

The sizeable shoreline midden uncovered at the Early Christian site at Illuanloughan in Co. Kerry suggests that this medieval community of multi-tasking monks partially subsisted on a diet of fish and shellfish, which they supplemented with the meat of pigs, cattle, sheep and wildfowl.[53] Many of the early monastic settlements claimed fishing rights in coastal estuaries, as well as the right to trap fish and construct weirs in rivers and lakes. The monks of the Duiske Abbey, Co. Kilkenny, for example, controlled the rights to an important fishing weir on the River Barrow in the thirteenth century. *The Life of St Brigid* has references to the hunting of seals with spears and harpoons. *The Life of Colum Cille* contains a tale of a thief who lived near a seal colony and used to sail to the colony during the night in order to illegally kill and steal young seals.[54]

Boats made of some kind of skin-covered framework were common throughout Ireland from the early medieval period onwards. Skin-covered boats may have been covered with sealskin rather than deerskin, and sealskin boats were used along the coast of Donegal well into the eighteenth century. At the Ferriter's Cove excavation in Co. Kerry, some fifteen species of fish were identified, and their size suggests that these were probably a summer resource. The presence of large conger eels and tope at this site might indicate that these were caught from a boat rather than from the shore. Certainly fishing currachs figure prominently in many of the earliest accounts, but the fact that most records after the seventh century scarcely refer to them may suggest that the disappearance of the sea-going currach from the eastern seaboard in particular may well be related to the advent of a new wooden boat-building technology brought in by the Vikings. Some of the Bronze-Age rock paintings in Norway include representations of skin boats, and this has caused one authority to argue that 'the modern canvas-covered boat-types of west Britain and Ireland are the descendants and sole survivors of skin-covered boat-types formerly found along the Atlantic seaboard of north-west Europe. The sea-going currachs of today may be considered as European cultural elements 'that have found their last refuge in western Ireland, where many other elements in our cultural heritage have also survived'.[55]

Various types of boats and other craft have appeared on ancient Irish maps, and on stonework and stone insignia from the medieval period onwards. A detail from a late sixteenth-century siege map of Maguire's Castle at Enniskillen clearly shows flat-bottomed and square-ended dugouts used on Lough Erne at that time.[56] Hornell has shown that 'hide boats', sometimes known as skin boats, were used throughout Britain and Ireland from a very early stage.[57] An ancient method of fishing with nets is illustrated in a facsimile reproduced in Gilbert's *Facsimiles of National Manuscripts of Ireland.*[58] A short length of timber found at a tenth-century crannog site at Ballinderry in Co. Westmeath has been interpreted as part of a currach's framework.

EARLY FISHING COMMUNITIES

Despite its strong maritime location and the paucity of good agricultural land, considerable stretches of coastal Ireland have produced relatively little by way of fishing remains from archaeological sites. Part of the explanation for this may lie in the acidic nature of soils that inhibit the preservation of fish bones, thus rendering it very difficult indeed to establish the role of fishing in the prehistoric period. We know that merchants attached to the Hanseatic League used several sites around the southern end of Shetland as trading booths from the fourteenth century onwards. Here, coastal dwellers wind-dried and salted the catches of cod for export, mainly to Bergen and other European port settlements. This trade declined at the end of the sixteenth century, when stocks of herring moved to more distant grounds. Once the Hanseatic merchants departed, the Scots took over, and records suggest that local people then began to take an active interest in fishing and saw what great profits could be made.[59] In coastal regions in Scotland and Ireland, 'fisher-crofters' may well have been tied to merchant lairds or merchants who demanded ever-increasing rents in return for rights to use fishing vessels and fishing gear in their domain. To fulfil their obligations, fishermen-farmers often had to fish in ever-deeper waters, and it was thus that the 'haaf' fishery commenced in Scotland. We know that in historical times fishing for coalfish off the western islands of Scotland was facilitated by the Ness Yole, a six-oared boat traditionally imported from Norway in kit form, and uniquely designed to work the tidal waters around the south of the islands. The date at which the 'yole' was introduced is not documented, but it would seem reasonable to hypothesise that it was a Norse introduction that facilitated fishing for larger coalfish around the Scottish coast. Fishbone-rich middens of late Norse origins in northern Scotland, Orkney and Shetland indicate the importance of cod fishing as a resource to the Norse incomers.[60] The apparent intensification of fishing is represented by a burgeoning of fishing artefacts and increased quantities of bones at archaeological sites in large tracts of coastal Scotland. Fishing in the Viking Age, and particularly in the later Norse period, appears to have been geared towards the capture of large quantities of a single species of fish, namely cod, and possibly other species. Such evidence as we have for fishing prior to this date points to less specialised fishing strategies, with fewer fish caught from a more varied range of species.[61]

With commercial fishing as a major part of their domestic economy, coastal communities could use fish for consumption, for payment of feudal dues, and as a highly profitable and much sought after export commodity. These early

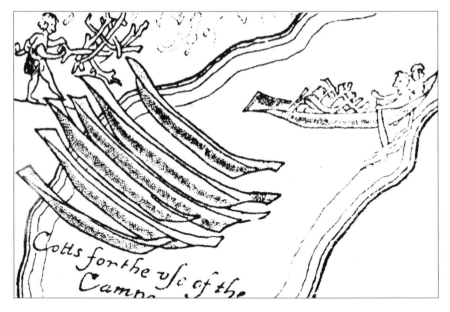

8 Map of the siege of Maguire's Castle, Enniskillen, Co. Fermanagh, from the late sixteenth century, showing dug-out canoes that were also widely used in inland waterways and coastal estuaries (courtesy of the British Museum).

commercial fishing ventures were designed to capture a single species of seasonally available fish in large quantities. By the early medieval period, specialised groups of fisher folk around the Atlantic coast were engaged in the cleaning and preservation of fish catches using locally available techniques. At that stage, the early fishing industry was characterised by a considerable degree of specialisation. This was reflected in improvements in fishing boats, design of fishing tackle, and more formalised approaches to rubbish disposal. This in turn meant that commercial fishing had a significant impact on the local economies of large tracts of maritime Europe, as large catches of fish required a significant input of manpower, at least on a seasonal basis. Fishing along the Atlantic coast of Ireland was particularly dangerous in winter months, and offshore fishing would have been confined to the spring and summer. This meant that the fishing season coincided with the busiest periods in the agricultural calendar, thereby putting heavy demands on part-time farmers and fishermen, and all those engaged in the trapping and preparation of fish. Viewed thus, commercial fishing was expensive, not only in terms of manpower, but also in terms of crops lost due to the fact that so much labour was tied up in fishing and the preparation of fish for consumption. Investment in coastal infrastructure may also have facilitated the development of small-scale, shore-based fishing enterprises, thus allowing coastal dwellers to fish from rocks, harvest seaweed and forage for driftwood and other debris on the shoreline. With a limited degree of specialisation, fishing would have provided the means to trade in either saltwater or freshwater fish, and to pay dues to a social elite who had access to the finest fish and controlled the disposal of surpluses catches.

We know that fish were an important, albeit supplementary, source of food in the medieval diet, especially in noble households and in coastal monasteries and abbeys. By the early medieval period, salmon and eels were regularly exported from Ireland to England, while eels and other species were also kept for local consumption in coastal towns and cities. The next chapter will show that eels and other migratory fish were particularly important food items in Early Christian Ireland, and were kept alive in specially constructed baskets and boxes submerged in water, thus providing important dynastic families and coastal monasteries in particular with access to fresh fish throughout they year, especially during lent and on the many 'fish days' that punctuated the Early Christian calendar. Stretches of water such as Strangford Lough and Carlingford Lough, and important rivers such as the Shannon, the Boyne, the Bann, the Corrib, the Blackwater, the Liffey and the Suir, would all have been exploited for eels, salmon, sea trout, plaice, cod, haddock, wrasse, grey mullet and skate.[62]

Bones from eels, haddock, cod and salmon have all been found in an early medieval coastal midden at Oughtymore in Co. Derry, while more recent excavations at a medieval site around Barrack Street and French's Quay in Cork city have produced the remains of significant numbers of herring, salmon, eels and flatfish.[63] The first references to the Lax Weir in Limerick occurred in twelfth-century charters, and it was later referred to in the Civil Survey of 1654 as 'a greate salmon weare'.[64] Some sixteenth-century maps of east Ulster contain the inscription *pascafdry ennomies*, which roughly translates as 'fisheries of all types'.[65] An inter-tidal survey conducted in the salt marshes and creeks in the Shannon Estuary has revealed a considerable amount of evidence of foraging and hunting activities dating back to the Neolithic period and extending well in to early medieval times. The community at the Carrigdirty site in the Shannon Estuary survived by trapping fish and collecting shellfish on the shoreline, gathering hazelnuts, berries and other plant foods further inland, and hunting for wildfowl and wild pig in nearby woodland and wetlands. A permanent village settlement situated on soils well suited to early agriculture in a site further south of here suggests that these particular hunter-gatherers did not so much precede as co-exist with early farmers. This has

9 Sketch of an early Irish skin-covered currach by W.F. Wakeman
(*Handbook of Irish antiquities: pagan and Christian* (1891)).

prompted at least one authority to suggest that some hunter-gathers at least may have made the social decision to 'stay Mesolithic' by continuing to exploit the abundant resources of their coastal wetland environment long after the end of the Mesolithic period.[66]

Some of the best preserved of these early Irish fish-traps have recently been located at Grey Abbey Bay and Chapel Island in the north-eastern corner of Strangford Lough. To date, a total of fifteen traps, dating from the eighth to the thirteenth centuries, have been located in this area. All of the Strangford traps were 'ebb weirs' designed to catch fish drifting down-river with the falling tide.[67] With wooden fences and wattle panels measuring anything between 40m and 200m, they allowed for the enclosure of considerable stretches of the foreshore. They also required a considerable amount of labour in their construction and in their repair, as thousands of hazel, ash and oak poles would have been felled, trimmed and hauled from neighbouring woodlands. In the estuaries of Sussex and Essex, as in estuaries on the south and west coasts of Ireland, medieval coastal dwellers constructed gigantic fish-traps that were among the largest timber structures known in early medieval Britain and Ireland.[68] Excavations at a number of sites around the Irish coast suggest that stone fish-traps had between one and three courses of stone laid out on loose foundations of smaller stone and rubble. They also had well-defined kerbs alongside to provide a platform for their repair, while allowing ready access to trapped fish. Aside from small traps anchored along the tidal stretches of rivers and sea estuaries, larger traps could be located on open channels and these were used on the upper foreshore and eroding drumlins as additional obstacles to free-swimming fish. Fish-traps excavated near Newtownards, in north Co. Down, had stout stone walls laid out along their base to provide protection from the sea. A particularly large V-shaped, stone-made trap that stretched out between two small islands was recently discovered in the north-west of Strangford Lough. A 'flood-fence' measuring 147m long running parallel to the shore has been revealed at Chapel Island, also in Strangford Lough. With no archaeological evidence of settlement on this site, it would appear that this fish-trap was linked to an Early Christian monastery at Nendrum, on the western side of the Lough. It would appear that the highly productive fish-traps at Grey Abbey Bay in Strangford were in use when a Cistercian monastery was established there in AD1193.[69] It is also known that Cistercian communities in Ireland were determinedly self-sufficient, thus suggesting that the exploitation of fish and shellfish may have attained new heights with the establishment of coastal monasteries and abbeys in the twelfth century.[70] A range of archaeological evidence from the mouth of the River Fergus in Co. Clare, and from the Deel Estuary in neighbouring Limerick, points to highly significant wattle-and-fence weirs dating to the mid-sixth or mid-seventh century. The weir on the Fergus is especially significant, as it is one of the earliest known examples of fish weirs in the country, and can be compared to the great Anglo-Saxon and Norman weirs found in England and Wales. The River Fergus weir was constructed with a line of pointed upright poles driven into the soil and linked together with an intricately woven wall of strong horizontal rods.[71]

EARLY COLONIAL INCURSIONS AND THE TRANSFORMATION OF FISHING IN IRELAND

Eoin Mac Neill has remarked that one of the major differences between the social structure of medieval Ireland and that of the Mediterranean was 'the presence of towns as the nucleus of community in the Mediterranean, towns that were walled for to resist attack'. In northern and middle Europe, he added, 'life was entirely rural, and the social and political nucleus was probably the assembly of freemen'.[72] The first towns in Ireland may have developed out of the fortified shipping resorts, including piratical strongholds and centres of

Viking and Norse influence in particular. Early medieval Ireland also had numerous examples of towns and villages that developed as a result of coastal trading, fishing and fish processing. In more remote coastal districts, piracy also contributed to the growth of coastal settlements, and the Aran Islands in particular contain the remains of a number of fortified enclosures that acted as safe refuges for pirates even before the fourteenth century. We also have substantial evidence of intimate relations between the maritime south-east of Ireland and the wider Scandinavian world dating back to at least the tenth and eleventh centuries. Norse traders and colonisers established a string of ports on this coast in the twelfth and thirteenth centuries, most notably at Ulfreks Fjord at Larne, at Helvick near Dungarvan, and at Smerwick in Co. Kerry. Mac Neill further maintained that 'these Norse settlements were self-governing and their customs and laws do not appear to have influenced the development of Irish law'.[73] Maritime Ireland also had close contacts with Spain and the Mediterranean world, and although geographically isolated, the country's coastal fringe was by no means economically or culturally isolated in the early medieval period.

The earliest Viking raids on the Irish coast occurred around the mid-790s. The movement inland by way of sea estuaries and river-borne raids dates from around the mid-ninth century. In 850, a Viking force had 'over-wintered' in England for the first time, signalling the beginning of a new phase of more sustained attacks by highly mobile forces. The Vikings also raided as far south as the coast of France and Spain in the 850s, and by the late 870s they were establishing settlements as far east as Russia. They also set up a number of important colonies of fishermen and farmers in Scotland, the Isle of Man, the Faeroes, Iceland and Greenland. In so doing, they united these far-flung areas into a loosely defined maritime 'proto-empire', bound together through raiding, fishing and seaborne commerce.[74] Not surprisingly, therefore, economic life in large tracts of coastal Ireland was severely disrupted and radically transformed as Viking seafaring expeditions and Norse trading ventures opened coastal districts along the east and south of Ireland to a wider maritime world of trade, fishing and coastal commerce. Whether in search of loot, trade or tribute, these early 'raids' and trading expeditions indicated the extent of Viking mastery of the seas around Ireland, Britain and north-western Europe.

Recent research suggests that these Viking incursions were not merely 'raiding' expeditions; they were also motivated by the quest for trade, tribute and colonial outposts, and the urge to find new fishing grounds in the North Atlantic.[75] Like many of their militaristic counterparts in Europe's more settled rural societies, Viking warlords ranged widely outside their domains, collecting tribute in the form of transportable wealth from subjugated communities around the Irish coast. Seaborne contact between the Scandinavian world and Ireland, Scotland, Wales and England certainly intensified from the tenth century onwards. We know that important economic change followed on from these Viking and Norse incursions. The cultivation of flax and the manufacture of sails and fishing nets spread throughout the east coast, thus contributing to a marked increase in seafaring activity and greater exploitation of coastal resources.[76] The social geography and built environment of significant stretches of coastal Ireland were also altered in the aftermath of Viking and Norse colonisation. Traditional power centres in the interior of the country, such as Cashel, Ferns and Tara, experienced gradual decline in the face of the growing economic power of the Viking and Norse settlements on the coastline. While Norse settlement in the south-east of Ireland contributed to the commercial expansion of several coastal settlements, it is important to stress that towns such as Wexford and Waterford were important trading and monastic settlements long before the arrival of the Norse.[77] However, within two centuries of their arrival, the controlling influence of the Vikings was evident in the development of maritime enclaves up and down the east and south coasts of the country in particular, and at the height of their power, Viking influence in coastal Ireland had become so strong that it had even become critical for national supremacy. This was particularly the case in areas of strong Viking influence around south Down, Dublin, Cork, Waterford, Wexford and Limerick. Unlike coastal districts in the west and north-west, which were temporarily or spasmodically inhabited by small immigrant elites, these maritime enclaves were permanently colonised from an early age. While there is little evidence that Viking and Norse colonists settled in remote headlands in the west and north-west of Ireland on a permanent basis, the early annals and poetic eulogies suggest that their bases here were occasionally occupied on something more than a temporary basis.[78] Indeed, Viking and Norse settlement in the west and north-west was comparatively weak, and one of the few place-names traceable to this period is Sheep Haven in Donegal, which probably derived from Old Norse.

Certainly by the 830s, the Vikings were also 'over-wintering' in temporary encampments around the coast of the south and east of Ireland, and in the mid-ninth century, permanent 'longphorts' and well-defended shipping ports were also established around the east and south coasts in particular. The extent of the Viking impact here can be seen from the number of Norse place-names, many of which indicate former settlements and landmarks that were widely used for navigational purposes even before the arrival of the Norsemen. Along the south and south-west coastline, the more prominent Norse place-names include Smerwick, Dursey, Fastnet, Fota, Helvick, Waterford, Saltees, Selskar and Tuskar. The name *Endilvorth*, near Kinsale, suggests the presence of a Viking seaport on this strategic stretch of coastline that already had relatively well-developed fisheries in the tenth and eleventh centuries. Norse place-names on the east coast include Wexford, Arklow, Wicklow, Howth, Ireland's Eye, Lambay, Skerries, Carlingford and Strangford, and this list is constantly growing as local studies unearth more evidence of Viking and Norse influence beyond the east and south coasts. In large tracts of coastal Ireland, a host of Norse words mainly connected with trade, seafaring and fishing were introduced into the vocabulary of the indigenous Irish from the ninth to the twelfth century. The Viking takeover of Dublin at this stage also contributed to the growth of civic and ecclesiastical institutions, and this was most evident in the growth of merchant guilds and the establishment of the office of mayor at the start of the thirteenth century. A considerable amount of infrastructural development occurred along the coastal littoral and riverbanks of many towns in Ireland throughout the twelfth century.[79] In Dublin, as in several other towns, this resulted in the construction of warehouses, piers and quayside markets, and greatly contributed to improvements in harbours and docking facilities. The new settlers in these coastal settlements not only sought to improve existing port facilities – they also set out to increase the draught of available water for larger boats and ships introduced by the Anglo-Normans and other seafaring settlers.[80] The crafts of carpentry, barrel-making, sail manufacture and net-making were all linked to the early boat-building and shipbuilding industries of medieval Dublin, Waterford, Cork and Limerick. Most of the early vessels produced in these coastal settlements then had a working life of around thirty years, and were made using supplies of native oak wood.

We know from archaeological evidence that defence was of paramount importance in deciding the location of Viking towns in Ireland. Defence was provided less by man-made fortifications than by the natural qualities of the terrain. Comparatively inaccessible lands in close proximity to water often functioned as places of refuge in unsettled times, and coastal locations that allowed access to areas such as these were especially favoured for coastal settlement.[81] Coastal and riverine sites suitable for drawing up boats were also favoured, as were coastal anchorages that had land suitable for the construction of warehouses, quays and docking facilities. It is no coincidence that Ireland's most enduring Viking towns or coastal 'longphorts' were located at the tidal head of rivers and estuaries, as such sites provided security from surprise attack and allowed coastal settlers to capitalise on trading opportunities where land and water routes converged.[82] Economic activity in maritime enclaves such as Dublin, Cork, Waterford and south Co. Down was often accompanied by the clearance of scrubland to make way for farmsteads, and trees were widely used in the construction of houses, bridges and roads.[83] Woodland clearance was so advanced in coastal districts and around the east and south coasts that several indigenous forests were already decimated by the start of the Tudor period. As we have already seen, there was also a considerable degree of town development in other parts of the south and south-west coasts of Ireland in the twelfth and thirteenth centuries. Colfer has shown that the Anglo-Norman adventurers who came to Ireland were familiar with European urban trends and, in an effort to attract new settlers and colonists to their newly acquired lands in Ireland, Anglo-Norman lords conferred borough status on a number of coastal settlements. Those who founded towns in Viking Ireland frequently also received revenues in the form of rent, market tolls and court fines, which, in the case of many coastal towns could be paid in kind with fish and shellfish, as well as with livestock and produce from the land. Towns of course also became market places and manorial centres, and Colfer has estimated that more than 300 such settlements in twelfth-century Ireland are known to have received foundation charters, while approximately fifty others attained urban status.[84]

Although generally credited with the invention of town-life in Ireland, it is more accurate to suggest that the Vikings transformed coastal districts, especially in the east and south-east of the country. Changes in the character of raids, from hit-and-run incursions to the sustained deployment of colonial settlers, meant that large tracts of coastal Ireland underwent a number of very important changes from the ninth to the twelfth century. Port facilities were improved; new quays and harbours were constructed; town government was enhanced; and a proto-merchant class came into existence as trade picked up in maritime towns and coastal enclaves. The expansion of trade and fishing at this stage may have allowed for more specialisation in fishing and fish processing, and undoubtedly prompted fishermen to find new markets for their surplus catches. Ninth-century Dublin was not so much a market centre for a large rural hinterland, but a prosperous proto-urban settlement town with links to a much wider maritime world that stretched well beyond its immediate hinterland. Thus as Simms has argued, Viking Dublin was 'an emporium, a point of interchange with a key position in a system of commercial exchange between northern Europe and the Mediterranean region'.[85] Moreover, the city's 'longphort' was largely a Scandinavian invention that served as a refuge for

10 Portolan map of Ireland from a sixteenth-century woodcut by Martin Waldseemuller, showing a remarkable concentration of seaports along the east and south coasts. It should be noted that numerous unofficial ports and landing places are not indicated on this map (courtesy of the de Courcy Ireland collection).

ships. It also functioned as a holding station for goods and provisions and was a dispatching depot for slaves. Anglo-Norman records contain copious references to salmon and herring fishing off the coast at Dublin, while Fishamble Street functioned as an important fish-market right in the heart of the city.[86] In 1261, it was resolved that 'the mayor and commonalty are to have free fishing in the water of Avenelif [River Liffey], from the bridge of Kilmaynan [Kilmainham] to the sea. The passage of salmon, gret or small, is not to be obstructed by nets, standards, weirs, other engines or implements'.[87]

The Scandinavians who founded the town were no mere plunderers and pirates. They were among the first to exploit the commercial potential of this stretch of maritime Ireland in an organised and sustained fashion. Viking proficiency in boat-building and seamanship meant that the country's indigenous coastal dwellers were also able to learn from these new intruders on the Irish maritime scene. The clinker-built boats of the Vikings were widely imitated, and Viking place-names jostled with those of local origin throughout Scandinavian Ireland. By the late thirteenth century, a port system was more or less in place along the east and south coasts. Quays and warehouses were constructed along the Irish coast to accommodate larger fishing and trading vessels. Breen has shown that artificial piers and quays were used alongside natural landing sites, and the layout of many early coastal towns suggests that they were centred on their harbours and waterfronts. This was particularly evident in the cases of Carrickfergus, Coleraine, Dundalk, Strangford, Carlingford, Ardglass, Waterford and Wexford.[88] Several of these towns witnessed development of their port facilities in the fourteenth century, as new quays and warehouses were added to enhance their trading and maritime importance. The establishment of tower houses that functioned as informal ports along the east and north-east coast demonstrated the importance of the coastal resources and fishing. Many of the tower houses built near the sea, or close to major rivers, had rudimentary port facilities. They performed military, economic and maritime functions, thus enabling them to control inshore waters and their surrounding hinterlands. The settlements that flourished in the vicinity of such tower houses also acted as communication centres and distribution outlets.[89] Although we are unclear about the types of ships using these early 'ports', we know that large 'barques' regularly anchored at a number of ports on the east coast of Ulster in the late sixteenth century. Many of the Scots settlers who came initially on naval and military expeditions were subsequently engaged in the commercial exploitation of the rich fisheries off the coast of Ulster. Ardglass was the most convenient port to a number of offshore fishing grounds from as early as the fourteenth century, while Carrickfergus retained its status as head port of Antrim and Down well into the sixteenth century. It is recorded that in 1551, one William Brabazon held the lease of all ports, creeks and islands in Strangford Lough, along with 'the customs and poundage of Strangford and Ardglass'.[90]

The local state established by the Vikings in Ireland in the ninth and tenth centuries was no mere 'raiders' headquarters'. Instead, it had its own legal and political institutions, which were quite similar to those that existed in their homeland. The early Viking parliament met on a mound outside Dublin known as the *Thingmote*, and Scandinavian Dublin was a well-organised city with extensive public works, prestigious dwelling-places, good docking and landing facilities, and a host of thriving craft industries, including shipbuilding, net-making and sail manufacture. Dublin was also a major artistic centre, whose citizens felt safe within the circuit of the city walls, the gates of which were locked and closely guarded against intruders. Although the walls of Scandinavian Dublin initially enclosed an area of some forty-four acres, by the start of the fourteenth century, the city council began to control large areas on both sides of the Liffey, including the common pastures of the citizens. On the north side of the Liffey, the city boundaries enclosed the districts of Stoneybatter, Grangegorman, Glasnevin and Ballybough. Another boundary line ran along the coast to Blackrock, turning inland by Donnybrook around Stephen's Green and back along the Coombe to Dolphin's Barn and Islandbridge. Yet Dublin's Viking 'longphort' was only one of a number of such coastal settlements established in late ninth-century Ireland. Others included Strangford in Co. Down and Annagassan in Co. Louth. Waterford, Dublin and Limerick were all expressions of Scandinavian interest in early medieval Ireland. The Irish Sea at this time was likened to a 'Viking lake' with a location at the north-south intersection between Norway and France, and the east-west intersection between Ireland and Britain. It was certainly the centre of a thriving early fishing industry. Cod and ling bones have been found in Viking Dublin, together with an abundance of cockle, mussels, oysters, periwinkles and scallops. Emphasising the early importance of fishing and coastal trade in the Lecale Peninsula of south Co. Down, Buchanan has argued that:

> Lecale's insularity, its many creeks and natural harbours, and its location on the north-western corner of the Irish Sea made the peninsula attractive as a landfall and refuge for the missionaries, scholars and craftsmen who travelled widely along the western seaways in the service of the early church. These same qualities also drew Vikings to its shores, although their legacy is now only apparent in place-names such as Strangford and Gun's Island, rather than in settlements.[91]

Moving along the east coast of Ireland at the end of the twelfth century, the Anglo-Normans left a durable legacy of fishing ports. They constructed mottes, manors and walled towns along the east coast of Ulster, and transformed the coastal economies of Antrim and Down in particular. A striking feature of this area's early social history was the high degree of dietary change that occurred alongside the development of Anglo-Norman estates increasingly dependent upon trading and fishing.[92]

It would be wrong to suggest that Viking newcomers and other colonial intruders 'invented' fishing, either in coastal or in rural Ireland. We have already seen that pre-Norse Ireland showed abundant evidence to suggest that the indigenous Irish were well-versed in techniques of weir construction and were familiar with rudimentary forms of fish-farming and inshore fishing. Early monastic settlements may well have pioneered these developments, and they certainly benefited from them. Like the more notorious Vikings, early Irish sea-raiders also possessed a detailed knowledge of the seas and estuaries around Ireland. A fifth-century manuscript of Gaelic poetry refers to the Irish as 'a seafaring people'. It has also been suggested that there was 'a continual if irregular contact by sea' between Ireland and continental Europe during the time of the Roman Empire.[93] Early law tracts suggest that land in Ireland increased in value if it was close to good freshwater or sea fisheries. The Early Christian church also controlled fishing rights on rivers and lakes and may well have managed fishing weirs in coastal estuaries and river mouths. Thus when Scandinavian settlers ranged out around the maritime fringe of the country in the course of the ninth century, they encountered evidence of a rich indigenous piscine culture. When they settled at Inis Sibhtonn, in Limerick, the Vikings selected a location that was already well known to be rich in fish and for fishing. The existence of several monasteries in the countryside around Limerick suggests that the waters of the Shannon were fished long before the arrival of the Vikings. The Viking name for Limerick was *Hlymrekr*, and we know that they introduced clinker-built wooden boats to the Shannon soon after their arrival in the closing years of the ninth century.[94]

To the monks of Gaelic Ireland and Scotland, the early Vikings were merely 'pagans from the sea'. To Gaelic chieftains, including those in Dun na nGall in the north-west of the country, they were simply *gaill*, or foreigners. Moreover, in a period when travel by sea was infinitely easier than land travel, it would be wrong to see the raiding exploits of the Vikings as exceptional. Raiding was endemic in Early Christian Ireland, as the great epic, *Táin Bó Cuailnge*, testified. In the sixth century AD, one chronicler referred to 'terrible hordes of Irish and Picts' crossing the Irish Sea 'in tiny craft' in search of slaves and other booty. Niall Naoi-Ghiallach, or Niall of the Nine Hostages, led raiding parties of Irish sea-rovers to Britain and possibly even to Gaul. The Ulster leader appears to have used Strangford Lough or Carlingford Lough as the base for these sea-going operations. Niall's fleet may have numbered one hundred currachs, manned by mariners and fighters who were said to be 'the equal of their Roman counterparts'.[95] Poised on the rugged coastline of north Antrim, and commanding strategic routes around Rathlin Island, Islay and the Mull of Kintyre, Dunseverick Castle was possibly the most strongly fortified settlement in the ancient Kingdom of Dalriada, a territory that stretched from the Cutts of Coleraine right round to Larne Harbour. It may also have been the seaport terminus of a great land-route that linked the Kingdom of Dalriada with the Hill of Tara. Similarly, Irish maritime expansion into the south-west of Scotland and south-western Wales played an important role in the evolution of Scottish and Welsh society from the fourth to the ninth century. There were an estimated thirty seaborne attacks by Irish raiders prior to the first recorded Norwegian raid on the coast of Antrim in 795. Raiding – whether across the territory of a neighbouring chieftain, or seaborne around the coast of Ireland, Scotland, Wales and England – continued to be a feature of coastal life in England, Scotland, Ireland and Wales well into the sixteenth century. Isolated coastal settlements, unprotected market towns and poorly defended monastic settlements were among the first targets of Viking raids in Ireland. Attacks were carried out by men with a deep knowledge of the maritime world of northern Europe. However, these 'raiders' were frequently also traders who relied far more upon their knowledge of sea currents, landmarks, coastal geography and the stars, than on any sophisticated navigational instruments in order to develop their command of the seas.[96] Their maritime skills and detailed knowledge of fishing in an expansive maritime world placed them at the forefront of European seafaring powers. Initially, these skills were used to enhance their power through an aggressive form of maritime imperialism.

Later, however, this in-depth knowledge of the sea was directed towards more peaceful channels, as the Vikings began to apply their seafaring skills to the development of fishing and port development in their new colonial settlements. In other words, prolonged experience of Viking trading and sea raids caused coastal communities in Ireland, Scotland and England to look seaward not just for geo-strategic reasons or out of a concern for their own defence, but also for sound economic and commercial reasons. This was especially noticeable in the growing focus on sea and coast from the ninth century onwards. Prior to the arrival of the Vikings, the coastal areas bordering the Irish Sea were scarcely mentioned in contemporary literature. As inter-action between Celtic Ireland and the incoming Scandinavians intensified, this new hybrid Hiberno-Norse society attached greater economic and strategic significance to coastal areas and engaged in a far more intensive exploitation of maritime resources. Writing at the dusk of the twelfth century, Giraldus Cambrensis found that

Sea fishes are found in considerable abundance on all the coasts. The rivers and lakes, also, are plentifully stored with the sorts of fish peculiar to those waters, and especially three species: salmon and trout, muddy eels, and oily shad. The Shannon abounds in lampreys, a dangerous delicacy indulged in by the wealthy. This country, however, does not produce some fine fishes found in other countries, and some fresh-water fishes, such as the pike, the perch, the roach, the barbell, the gardon [chub] and the gudgeon.[97]

Yet it would be wrong to exaggerate the degree of foreign domination over Ireland's fishing industry at this time. De Courcy Ireland has argued that the 'Gaelic-named Irish filtered steadily into the towns of Ireland and became merchants, shipmasters and sea fishermen alongside their fellow citizens of other origins'. Names such as Malachy Hogan, Richard Donnell, Nicholas Duff, William Kelly and John Gough litter the pages of port records from Bristol, Bordeaux and Chester, and are testimony to the indomitable determination of many of Ireland's coastal dwellers 'to face all perils of green and greedy seas'.[98] While the native Irish learned a lot about fishing and boat-building from the Norsemen, Seán McGrail has insisted that there were large fleets of ships in Ireland before the Anglo-Norman invasion in 1169–70, most notably those of the Ostmen, the Hiberno-Norse of Dublin and Wexford. He has also pointed out that there was a substantial trade in food products, including fish, between Dublin and the ports of Chester and Bristol from the first half of the twelfth century. Customs records for the period 1171–1250 specifically show a substantial amount of food exports, especially cereals and fish. Stressing the strength of this early maritime trade, McGrail has argued that early medieval Ireland was thoroughly integrated into a European trade network, with active ports at Waterford, Ross, Drogheda, Galway, Limerick, Youghal, Cork, Kinsale, Carrickfergus, Arklow and Wexford. These ports traded with Seville, Lisbon, Galicia, Bordeaux, Brittany, Normandy, Bruges, Antwerp, Hamburg, Lübeck, Gdansk, Reykjavik, Chester, Liverpool, Hamburg and Bristol. Their most prominent exports included fish, hides and leather, woollen cloth and cloaks, yarn, tallow, linen yarn, timber, grain and livestock, together with re-exported French and Iberian wine. By the early decades of the fifteenth century, flotillas of Wexford-built cotts regularly carried fish to Bridgwater and imported coal from Wales.[99]

While this chapter has touched briefly upon the role of freshwater and coastal fisheries both before and after the Viking invasions, the chapter that follows provides a much more detailed discussion of the role of fishing in the Early Christian and Gaelic Ireland. It pays particular attention to the country's indigenous piscine culture, focusing especially on native methods for catching and farming fish, and highlighting also the role of monastic settlements in the early exploitation of Ireland's coastal and freshwater resources. It shows that Christian Ireland from its beginnings attached great importance to sea and freshwater fisheries, while those living in close proximity to the coast developed a special awareness of the sea. Coastal communities not only made extensive use of the resources of the sea and shoreline – they also controlled the rights to some of the country's most important fisheries. This chapter also contains a discussion on the position of fish in the medieval diet, and the role of 'fast days' or 'fish days' in promoting the domestic consumption of fish in Ireland.

CHAPTER THREE

Fishing and fish consumption in medieval Ireland

AWARENESS OF THE SEA IN ANCIENT IRELAND

Although law-texts on sea fishing are practically non-existent in the Brehon tradition, we know that the early Irish lawyers dealt with fishing rights in rivers, lakes and estuaries in considerable detail. This material suggests that there was no such thing as a universal *public* right to fish in ancient Ireland. Instead, a king or lord employed fishermen to manage weirs and other fish-traps, and these men were numbered among the specialised servants of kings and lords. An Old Irish poem describing the household servants of King Conchobar contains references to hunters (*selcid*), fishermen (*iascaire*), fencing men (*etarpuige*) and 'various entertainers, manufacturers and attendants'. The professional fisherman in early Ireland was a person of low rank with 'an honour-price of only one yearling heifer'.[1] According to one early law-text, freemen were 'only permitted a single swift dip of a fishing-net in a stream', and entitled only to a single salmon taken from waters near their place of abode.[2] Not all fishing rights in Early Christian Ireland were so strictly circumscribed. One ancient law-text refers to the 'regulation of nets' and the management of the public fishing ground of the *tuath*, or community. Ancient legal commentaries suggest that strict fines were imposed for the theft of fish (especially salmon and eel) from nets, fish-traps and weirs. The life history of at least one ancient Irish saint referred to a miraculously heavy catch of salmon that had a fish every third mesh of the net. Nets were made from woven linen threads hand-tied into meshes, and the activities of 'nets men' were controlled by the law of *corus lin* or 'regulation of nets'.[3] The early monks who adapted the monastic landscape of rural Ireland to the country's decentralised social structure certainly took the possibilities of sustainable fishing into account when selecting sites for religious communities. The sites where they built their monasteries were often 'watery' places located close to marine estuaries or within reach of controlled salmon and eel fisheries.[4] These early monastic settlements also bred a new type of monk; one who had a special awareness of the sea, and who was also skilled in the arts of fishing and navigation. These men were capable of rowing and sailing a currach and could sustain themselves on the resources of sea, shoreline, lakes and rivers. For many of Ireland's holy men, the ocean, rather than the desert, was the great symbol of eternity. In the seventh and eighth centuries, the 'peregrination' or 'sea voyage' was the outward manifestation of a maritime wanderlust and an important aspect of Irish missionary culture. Sea voyaging in turn fostered an ascetic tradition among the early religious orders, causing monks and other holy men to cast off all ties with home and family for a proselytising life in coastal Britain and northern Europe. Some Christian hermits could even be regarded as the 'deep ecologists' of their day. These were men who had an environmentally sustainable and spiritual relationship with the remote places in which they settled. Those who opted for remote locations such as Skellig Michael off the coast of Kerry, lived at the outermost limits of human habitation and introduced the idea of 'green martyrdom' into Christian Ireland. According to one seventh-century source, they sought

> The white martyrdom of exile;
> The green martyrdom of the hermit;
> The red martyrdom of sacrifice.[5]

An ancient Irish respect for the sea was reflected in the deference shown to the three great 'voiceful waves' or *tonns* in the romantic literature of Gaelic Ireland. The latter included the *Tonn Cleena* at Glandore in Co. Cork, the *Tonn Tuaithe* across the mouth of the River Bann, and the *Tonn Rudraidhe* at Dundrum Bay in Co. Down. When stormy weather caused the wind to blow in certain directions, the sea at each of these places uttered an unusually loud and solemn roar as it tumbled over the sandbanks or ran among caves and other fissures on the coastline. Such sounds were believed to have a supernatural origin, and were interpreted as warnings of danger. They were also said to foretell the death of a king or a great chief.[6] The heroic literature that developed from Irish classical writing at this stage was steeped in maritime lore. It told of young men leaving home and going to sea, to return home again transformed by their experiences of exile. As such, these tales could almost be likened to medieval 'road movies'. They had all the hallmarks of biblical stories that dealt with rites of passage, and contained strong parallels with Christ's departure from the safety of his home, and his heroic return as a man capable of resisting the temptations of sin. Carl Sauer has suggested that this literature was not 'concerned with battle, hardship or shipwreck, but with adventure sought and enjoyed, with a sea world of marvels and incidental terrors ending in a safe return'.[7] It is now well-established that the descendants of these early mariners carried out a number of remarkable Atlantic voyages, culminating in the legendary voyages of Brendan the Navigator in the North Atlantic in the sixth century. His voyages of discovery were immortalised in the Latin prose epic *Navigatio Brendani*, a tenth-century seafaring tale that painted Brendan as a legendary voyager who travelled out into the Atlantic, and who also coasted around the shores of Scotland and Wales. Indeed, the real significance of Brendan's 'Navigation' may lie not so much in the accuracy of its geographical descriptions, as in its harking back to a time when Irish monks had been free to roam the seas unmolested by Viking warlords and other marauding seafarers. Brendan the Navigator embodied all the virtues of an Early Christian cultural hero who roved around the North Atlantic at a time when the ancient Irish were still masters of the seas around Ireland. The voyages of these early monks had their origins in a strong Irish maritime tradition, and in speculative geographies that were shrouded in mystery and legend pointing to the existence of unknown islands in the North Atlantic.

Many of these monks would go abroad in currachs, clad only in a habit of sewn skins, their feet in sandals, carrying a staff, a book of prayer and a meagre supply of food. It has been suggested that Irish monks sailing in flimsy currachs may have voyaged as far northwards as the Arctic Circle in the eighth century. Unlike the great maritime explorations of the fifteenth and sixteenth centuries, these voyages were not motivated by earthly gain or the advancement of science. They were inspired by an Early Christian missionary zeal, and by the desire to find peaceful places where monks and other holy men could engage in a closer association with God and nature. Long before they made contact with Scandinavia, early 'currach navigators' from Ireland were familiar with the maritime fringes of Scotland, England and Wales. Their 'watery world' stretched from the Shetlands and the Faeroe Islands, right round to the Inner and Outer Hebrides, and south to the coast of Devon and Cornwall. A number of Icelandic sagas refer to Irish settlements in Iceland in the seventh and eighth centuries. The interchange of family and personal names that occurred during this period also testifies to the close connections between Iceland and coastal Ireland.[8] Irish annalists made frequent references to Viking leaders by name, and one authority has listed over one hundred such individuals who were known by their personal name by those who compiled the early annals.[9] In the preface to the twelfth-century *Landnamabok*, or *Book of Settlements*, Ari Frode has argued that:

before Iceland was peopled from Norway, there were in it men whom the
Northmen called *Papar*; they were Christian men, and it is held that they
must have come over the sea from the west, for there were found left by
them Irish books, bells and crosiers, and more things besides, from which
it could be understood that they were Westmen [Irishmen].[10]

Many distinguished Icelanders traced their descent from a ninth-century king
of Ossory, whose grandson was the founder of an important Icelandic family,
and three of whose daughters had married Norsemen. The Norse called the
early Irish holy men 'papa', a word commonly found in Icelandic place-names
such as *Papos*, *Papafjordhur* and *Papavik*, and in *Papa Stour* in the Orkney, and
Papilwater in the Shetlands. It has also been suggested that the Irish may have
been in Iceland a century before the arrival of the Norsemen in the ninth
century. In his study, *Farthest North*, Fridtjof Nansen (1861–1930) maintains
that there was a substantial Irish population in Iceland prior to the arrival of
the Norsemen. It has also been estimated that one in seven of the Norse
immigrants who settled there in the early years of Norse colonisation had a
Celtic connection, and that many them brought Irish slaves and concubines.
Certainly in the tenth century, a number of famous Icelanders bore Irish names
such as *Njall* (Niall) and *Kormakr* (Cormac), and an Irish influence in Icelandic
place-names is still evident today.[11]

By the late Middle Ages, the journeys of Irish navigators and sea merchants
had taken them throughout much of Europe, and Irish ships regularly sailed to
Seville, Lisbon, Bordeaux, Brittany, Normandy, Bruges, Antwerp, Hamburg,
Lübeck, Gdansk, Reykjavik, Chester and the west coast of Scotland. At this
time also there were regular pilgrimages from coastal districts around Dublin,
Waterford, Cork, Kerry and Donegal to Santiago de Compostela in Spain, and
to Bordeaux in the south-west of France. Referring to the maritime tradition
in early medieval Ireland, the cultural geographer Carl Sauer has argued that

> Christian Ireland from its beginnings lived in a special awareness of the
> sea, not as a sea to be feared or to try the limits of man's courage, but
> which stirred the imagination and drew men to seek what lay beyond the
> far horizon. Its holy men went innocently into the unknown sea to
> experience nearness to God and learn his wonders. Being somewhat
> learned in the classics, they knew the Mediterranean Legends of the sea,
> such as of the fortunate isles which were thought to lie in the western
> ocean.[12]

The economic and cultural significance of sea and shoreline was highlighted in the richness and diversity of place-names, and this suggested that coastal dwellers had a strong working relationship with their maritime environment in the early medieval period.[13]

Closer analysis of ancient place-names along this coast would no doubt reveal a similar pattern of strong dependence on sea, shoreline and sea cliffs from a very early stage. In coastal uplands and marginal agricultural districts along the west coast, great care was taken with the naming of coastal features such as fishing rocks, seaweed beds, fishing pools, marine inlets, coastal promontories, and local sea currents. We also know that fish ranked highly among the principal exports of towns along the south and east coasts in the fourteenth century. Sailing vessels from a number of towns along the east coast were then trading around the Irish Sea, with some venturing as far afield as Bordeaux and Le Collet in France to pick up salt used in the preservation of fish and meat. Medieval Wexford was one of Ireland's leading ports and fishing towns, and English-owned and local vessels from this part of the coast transported fish to markets in the south-west of England, especially Bristol. Salmon pickled in brine were packed in casks and exported in large quantities to coastal towns on the south-west coast of England. Wexford's oyster beds were renowned on both sides of the Irish Sea. The economic significance of oysters to the town was recognised in the street name Oyster Lane, 'where taverns specialising in oysters advertised their wares by piling oyster shells outside the door'.[14] Maritime trade in ports such as Dublin, Drogheda, Wexford, Waterford and Cork in the fifteenth and sixteenth centuries often involved a system of 'combined operations' whereby boats were used both for inshore coastal and fishing.[15] We know that fish were an important element in medieval trade, a fact attested to in a number of early coats of arms and in charters of several Irish towns. Fish and trade put many medieval Irish towns on the map, and this type of trade was responsible for their commercial success from a very early age.

Given such a high degree of awareness of coastal resources, it is not surprising that fish were prominent in the diets of rich and poor alike in early medieval Ireland. Thus herring, cod, ling, haddock, place, sole and possibly also mackerel, were consumed in considerable quantities, while the consumption oysters, mussels, crab, lobster, periwinkles and edible seaweeds was already well-established by the fourteenth century. The inhabitants of Early Christian Ireland appear to have had an extremely conservative diet that was largely dependent upon cattle, sheep and pigs, the only variety being provided by the occasional consumption

11 Sketch of Skellig Michael, off the coast of Co. Kerry, by John Windele. Tradition has it that St Finian founded a monastery here in the sixth century, and monks continued to dwell in this amphibian environment until the thirteenth century, when they moved to the Kerry mainland (courtesy of the Royal Irish Academy, © RIA).

of venison, domestic chicken and sea fish.[16] By the tenth century, however, the diet of those living along the south and east coasts included a wide range of fish and other seafood. Excavations in and around Lecale in Co. Down suggest that coastal dwellers here consumed not only rabbits and other wild animals, but also a wide range of fish, including cod, salmon, monkfish, wrasse, haddock and possibly even perch. Marine molluscs such as mussels, periwinkles, limpets, oysters, whelks and razor fish have also been found at many coastal sites throughout east Co. Down. During the Anglo-Norman period, these were gradually imported into the interior of Ulster, thereby adding variety to the diet of rural, as well as coastal communities. In addition to consuming the usual fare of domesticated chicken and geese, the Anglo-Normans on this stretch of coastline also consumed considerable quantities of wildfowl, including greylag, barnacle, pink-footed and white-fronted geese.

Herring were widely fished from the late medieval period onwards as they migrated around the north and west coasts in enormous shoals. They were also highly nourishing and easy to cook. When not available, stockfish – that least-loved of Lent's slender delicacies – replaced herring during the Lenten fast. In many parts of Europe, only those who had their lord's permission had the right to sell fish, and protein-rich species such as porpoises and whales were considered the property of the king. Shellfish and other 'shore food', on the other hand, were widely consumed in coastal Ireland, with the former also being sold in large quantities in towns and cities around the coast. The urban poor in Ireland as in other European countries often found shellfish more affordable and more readily available than free-swimming freshwater and saltwater fish. Neither was it uncommon for large households to buy several hundred oysters, cockles and whelks at any one time. The urban poor could often afford 'stockfish' such as ling and cod, as well as salted herring, and herring pickled in brine. Fish such as these were probably eaten more out of necessity than for pleasure in coastal Ireland. As a preserved food, they could supplement the diet of the poor during lean seasons when food from the land was scarce. Dried fish also were the mainstay of the medieval diet, particularly in coastal towns and cities. It has been suggested that cod roe was for centuries a well-established feature of the Irish breakfast, particularly in wealthier households on the coast.[17] In continental Europe, the consumption of cod roe dates back to the late medieval period, while in northern France, fish roe formed the filling for many of the fish pies consumed in large quantities during Lent. The fillings for these early fish pies consisted of ground fish, eels or cod roe, and this was occasionally combined with wine and nuts to make them more palatable. Pies consumed on a more regular basis were simply filled with cheese and egg, to which milk or cream was added. The cooking of fish pies took considerably more time than the grilling, roasting or boiling of fish and other food. They were also a commercial success and were widely sold in streets and markets. The well-off, on the other hand, may well have bought them from commercial bakers, rather than have them cooked at home.[18] In one recipe for an old-style Irish breakfast, cod roe was sliced in half and cooked in bacon fat, or simply boiled. James Joyce was well aware of the importance of cod roe in the diet of working class Dubliners at the start of the twentieth century. In his *Ulysses*, he has Leopold Bloom sitting down to a breakfast of 'thick giblet, nutty gizzards, a stuffed roast heart, liver slices fried with crust crumbs, and fried hen-cod's roe'.[19] Writing more recently, Theodora Fitzgibbon's recipe for boiled roe involved wrapping it in a length of cheesecloth, boiling it in salt water for thirty minutes, and leaving it to cool off before eating it.[20]

Salmon was an especially valued fish in Gaelic Ireland, and its consumption was surrounded by all sorts of symbolic significance. An old Irish legal poem associating the king with salmon stipulated that he had to 'give a salmon to his judge out of every abundant catch'.[21] Judges were also entitled to the heads of all of the king's salmon. Legal ownership of fishing rights to salmon and eel fisheries can be traced back to well before the Anglo-Norman invasion. It is recorded that in 1061, one Áed Ua Conchobair destroyed a fort belonging to Brian Boruma at Kincora 'and ate the two salmon which were in the king's fishpond'.[22] Kelly has referred to a ninth-century triad referring to three deaths that were believed to be better than life. These included the death of a salmon, the death of a fat pig, and the death of a robber. The salmon in ancient Ireland was widely considered 'the crafty one of the water', and salmon fishing was the type of fishing most often mentioned in the writings of ancient Ireland.[23] Joyce found that salmon were designated by several Irish names: *bratan*; *eo*; *tonnem*; *erc*; *eicne* and *linne*. The first, under the modern form *bradan*, is now the general name. It would seem that in ancient Ireland, *bratan* meant a young salmon, and *eo* a full-grown one. The term *maigre*, a derivative from *magar*, meaning 'spawn', was used to designate an 'egg-bearing female salmon'. The word *mugna* also referred to salmon in the legal sense.[24] Lampreys, an eel-like fish with sucker mouths, were favourite fish at court festivals in the coastal areas in the north of Ireland. The finest lampreys were said to be those caught in the Severn, in England, but they were also common in River Bann in Co. Derry. Because it was believed they possessed properties of excessive coldness and dryness, lampreys were considered dangerous for human consumption, and therefore required careful treatment before consumption. While eels as a species were greatly praised by gourmets, lampreys were said to possess a phlegmatic temperament that was said to occur as soon as the fish was killed. Consequently, the usual practice in preparing lampreys for consumption was to submerge them in wine, so that their dry liquid could infiltrate into all parts of the lamprey and begin tempering it.

Although there is little information on the scale and organisation of Ireland's sea and estuarine fisheries at this stage, we know that deep-sea fishing attracted foreign fleets to Irish shores from the twelfth century onwards. It has also been established that shipbuilding was well advanced in a number of coastal districts the thirteenth century. In a history of shipbuilding in Waterford, Bill Irish has argued that

Although no medieval ships have been found in Ireland, a good number of timbers from dismantled boats and ships were excavated from the eleventh- to thirteenth-century Arundel Square site in Waterford, and almost all proved to be of Nordic origin. This strongly suggests that Viking boat-building skills were practised here. The Viking-type ship constructed by the new settlers was the template for their fleet of galleys, used to protect their stronghold but also to carry out expeditions upstream and inland. The Normans, possessing a strong maritime culture, saw the potential of the port as a centre for trade and commerce and quickly enhanced and consolidated Waterford's strategic advantages for sea trading. Strong trade links with their homelands were maintained and fostered, developing new markets and giving Waterford a significant input into European commerce.[25]

The first clear evidence of state involvement in Irish shipbuilding was contained in an edict issued in 1222, calling for the construction of galleys in Dublin, Waterford and Limerick.[26] The expansion of shipping undoubtedly fostered the development of commercial fishing, while improved methods of fish preservation permitted fishermen on the east and south coasts to take advantage of seasonal peaks in the availability of herring, salmon and eel. These developments also contributed to the enlargement of the market for fish from Ireland, as Irish fish were now sold on the west coast of Scotland and in the ports of south-west of England. Fishing boats also underwent important changes in size, shape and fittings at this stage, which meant that men were able to sail further out to sea in a variety of sea and weather conditions. We have already seen that substantial fish-traps were used in the inter-tidal estuaries of the Shannon, the Liffey and the Bann from the seventh to the twelfth century. From the twelfth century onwards, many of Ireland's larger coastal towns probably housed small fishing communities, together with their own harbours and quays, where fish were landed and prepared for market. O'Sullivan has suggested that

> detailed guidelines on the ownership and use of estuarine waters may
> have been outlined in the *Cáin Inbhir*, part of the lost law-tract
> *Muirbretha*. Early monastic foundations commonly claimed fishing rights
> on named rivers by means of both boat nets and fish weirs, and these
> must have been valuable sources of revenue. Thus, for example, the rights
> to the fish weir named as *Cordrahan* or *Chory O Dradan* on the River

Barrow were in the hands of the monks of Duiske Abbey by the late thirteenth century.[27]

Fish were caught with hooks and spears, and we have evidence that fishing nets were used well before the fourteenth century. An early form of drift-netting was probably used to catch North Sea herring in the fifteenth century, while large quantities of oysters and other shellfish were gathered by hand at low water, or were collected in crude but effective trawl nets that were dragged behind boats. Nets and wickerwork traps were commonly used to catch salmon in rivers and coastal estuaries, while trout and eels were caught as they migrated along the banks of the country's major rivers. Fish caught in these early traps were supplemented with those caught with fish spades, knives, pots, baskets, creels and barrels. Spades were used to dig both for bait and for shellfish, while lanterns attracted fish and provided light for fishermen who worked in coastal estuaries throughout the hours of darkness.[28]

Given their in-depth knowledge of lake-land and coastal waters, it is not surprising that early Irish monks and holy men were well versed in the techniques of fishing and coastal foraging. P.W. Joyce has argued that salmon and eels were commonly caught with three-pronged 'trident spears' in the Early Christian period.[29] Indeed, evidence from the Lagore crannog in Co. Meath suggests that fish spearing may have been practised by freshwater fishermen in the six and seventh centuries.[30] These early fisher folk also adopted the primitive but effective method of transfixing large fish with a single-point spear. Galway fishing spears were reputed to be the best in the country, and it was still permissible to spear fish from the bridge at Galway in the sixteenth century.[31] Eels were traditionally caught with forked-spears, and Went has suggested that fishing nets made of linen threads were used to catch salmon and herring in the Shannon Estuary in the late fifteenth century.[32] Nets were commonly used to catch migrating eels on dark nights, and when sufficient quantity of eels entered the net they were subsequently gaffed and drawn ashore. Eels trapped in freshwater or coastal weirs were usually held in a hood-shaped net called a 'cochall', a word later Anglicised to 'coghill'. The end of the 'coghill net' was then opened, and the fish were emptied into a 'throw', or side channel, which led into fish tanks that were supplied with fresh running water Those caught stealing fish from weirs or fish tanks could be severely punished.[33] In some districts, eels had a distasteful reputation, attributable to their resemblance to snakes banished from Ireland by St Patrick in Early Christian lore. Nevertheless, eels were consumed in large quantities in many parts of Ireland from the Early Christian period onwards. They were consumed for centuries in lake-land districts around Lough Neagh, Athlone and Ballyshannon. Elsewhere in the country, fishermen commonly cooked eels in their watch-houses, or ate them for supper during fishing expeditions. Once skinned and cut into lengths of about four inches, they were generally cooked in an iron pan placed over a turf fire or burning sticks. The oil from cooked eels was often bottled, as it was believed to be particularly effective against rheumatic pains.[34] A variety of methods were used to 'wind dry' or preserve fish in medieval Ireland. Cod, haddock and ling were dried outdoors in cold air, and were then traded as stockfish in coastal towns in Ireland, Scotland, England and Wales. Some modern methods for smoking eels and salmon can be traced back to the fourteenth century. Cod, whiting, herring and eels were also preserved through salting, and were then packed into crude wooden casks for home consumption, or for the seasonal export market.

Many of the religious houses near salmon fisheries took large quantities of fish from church-controlled stone and wicker fishing weirs. Given that there are relatively few references to deep-sea fishing in the Early Christian texts, it is probable that most fish were caught in weirs set in rivers and in coastal estuaries. Discussing the role of fishing in the sixth and ninth centuries, Kelly stated that

> There are few references to sea fishing from boats in Old Irish sources, [although] bones from sea fish such as cod (*Gadus morhua*) and ballan wrasse (*Labrus bergylta*) have been found in excavations at Early Christian sites. But in general, the written and archaeological evidence indicates a society which concentrated on the rich harvest of freshwater fish rather than on the fish of the sea.[35]

Depending upon the locality, weirs were made of stone or constructed from walls of woven willow rods and hazel sticks. As some were also privately owned, great care was taken to ensure that their owners did not get more than an equitable share of fish from waters that were fished by multiple owners. Landowners who held property on both sides of a river could stretch weirs out to one-third the width of the river. In cases where these limits were exceeded, the excess fish had to be donated to weir-owners upstream or downstream from the weir where they were taken, depending on which way the fish were migrating at the time of the offence.[36] Eels were commonly caught in weirs located on the shores of inland lakes. Athlone had a well-established salmon and eel fishery dating back to the thirteenth century. A mandate issued on 30 May 1216 stated that the prior of Athlone was to be paid compensation of twelve marks for the loss of 'a meadow for the site of the king's castle and fisheries'.[37] Edward I granted the weirs and fisheries of Athlone to the Abbey of St Peter in 1279, and ten years later the rent of these fisheries were estimated at £15 per annum. The great weirs and eel fisheries around Athlone grew in importance throughout the sixteenth century. In 1619, this area had no less that twenty-two weirs that were rented by thirteen different individuals, a number of whom paid rent in kind to the church.

One of the greatest salmon weirs in late medieval Ireland was located near the Falls of Assaroe on the River Erne. The nearby abbey controlled the fishing rights to a number of substantial freshwater weirs in this area in the thirteenth and fourteenth centuries. The local abbot had 'the liberty, yearly, of having two fishermen to take salmon during the season'. He was additionally entitled 'to the second draught of every one fishing there when they began to fish, and also to have a boat to take salmon and other fish from the island to the sea'.[38] An inquisition into the extent of church property in this part of south Donegal in 1588 found that the abbot and monastery at Assaroe controlled no less than ten working weirs, several of which had been in existence from a very early age. When the monasteries here were dissolved, the waters from Lower Erne to the sea, together with their impressive fish installations, passed into private hands. The author of one old Irish manuscript, *The Banquet of Dun-na-nGedh*, could scarcely contain himself when describing the 'fishful' waters on this stretch of the Erne. The Joycean quality of his adjectives was particularly pronounced in his glowing account of the famous waterfall at *Eas Ruaidh*, Assaroe. He described the latter as 'loud-roaring, head-strong, salmon-ful, sea-monster-ful, in-large-fish-abounding, rapid-flooded, furious-streamed, whirling, in-seal-abounding, royal and prosperous'.[39]

There were important eel weirs on the Corrib in the thirteenth century, and in addition to those attached to monastic settlements, a number of the dynastic families of Gaelic Ireland owned weirs on major rivers and in marine inlets. For example, the earl of Ormond controlled the fisheries on the Nore and the Suir, while the earl of Desmond continued to control an important salmon fishery at Killorglin, in Co. Kerry, right down to the sixteenth century.[40] Private ownership of fishing rights also extended to kinship groups, towns and coastal cities in the medieval period. The Lynches of Galway, who for centuries controlled the fish weirs on the Corrib, rented the best known examples of privately managed weirs. Together with the Martens of this city, they also paid an average rent of 2s. sterling per annum for the privilege of netting fish on the river Shannon in the late medieval period. Because weirs were a valuable source of income, merchants and landowners were often willing to offer higher prices for land close to rivers and coastal estuaries. Fishing rights in lake-land districts and on the country's great rivers were also subject to strict regulation in order to avoid the reckless depletion of stock, and to protect the interests of fishmongers who required a steady supply of fish for the market. The rules and regulations governing the protection of fish weirs in medieval Scotland were so strict that the law rendered a second offence of salmon poaching on a royal estate a crime punishable by death.[41] The taking of fish from rivers and lakes in medieval Ireland appears to have been less strictly regulated, at least prior to the fifteenth century, when charters were granted to private individuals who then had the sole right to fish freely on selected rivers and estuaries. This meant that the urban and rural poor were forbidden to fish these waters, and were often reduced to poaching or spearing salmon and eels in rivers and estuaries.

FISHING AND 'FAST DAYS' IN CHRISTIAN IRELAND

The strict rules governing the consumption of fish during lent meant that access to reliable sources of saltwater and freshwater fisheries was important to the proper functioning of monastic settlements. While we do not have accurate information on the number or enforcement of 'fish days' in medieval Ireland, we know that one third to one half of the calendar year in fourteenth-century France was meatless. Unlike their continental counterparts, the Irish monasteries generally did not make extensive use of fish ponds for farming freshwater fish, chiefly because most major Irish monasteries were able to draw fish from church-controlled weirs and other fish-traps. There were a number of ways in which the Irish monasteries controlled access to fisheries. A religious community sometimes owned and operated fisheries itself, or leased them to individuals outside the monasteries in return for a rent that was frequently paid in kind. Many religious houses derived a very considerable income from fish tithes and other customary payments made by fishermen. In the early sixteenth century, the abbey of St Senan on Scattery Island, off the coast at Kilrush, was still taking a tribute of '500 herrings from every herring boat once a year'. The mayor of Limerick visited the island as late as 1680 in order 'to exercise his jurisdiction among the herring boats for the city duties'. The latter amounted to '1,000 herring and 1,000 oysters out of each boat', and it has been established that these 'fish tithes' were regularly paid throughout the sixteenth and seven-

12 Duncannon weir, Co. Wexford. River and coastal weirs similar to this survived all over Ireland well into the nineteenth century and were used to trap migrating salmon, sea trout and eels in particular (from Went, 'Pilchards in the south of Ireland' (1946)).

teenth centuries.[42] By making tithes payable to the crown, colonial authorities in the seventeenth century were attacking a long-standing custom which obliged local fishermen to pay 'fish tithes' to the church rather than the state.

We have already seen that purpose-built weirs supplied early medieval monasteries with fish throughout the year. The existence of highly productive weirs on church lands made such properties all the more attractive to confiscators of Irish properties in the sixteenth and seventeenth centuries. The abbey at Mellifont, Co. Louth, managed a large fishery on the River Boyne in the thirteenth century. By the middle of the sixteenth century, this fishery was employing sixteen fishermen who used currachs covered with cowhide to supply the monks with salmon and eels. Another Irish religious house took salmon from weirs in the district around Navan, while also drawing salmon and eels from the River Boyne. The abbey of St Mary's, Dublin, held fishing rights at various locations in Co. Westmeath, and also trapped freshwater eels in nearby Lough Ennell. In addition, the abbey collected fish tithes from local net fishermen, a practice shared with a number of other religious houses prior to the dissolution of the monasteries in the sixteenth century. The friary of Lislaughtin, Co. Kerry, controlled fishing rights on the Shannon, which meant that it had access to both saltwater and freshwater fish. Similarly, the abbey of Saint Colum Cille, Co. Derry, had fishing rights to the waters around Teelin, in south Donegal, while another religious house at Newry had 'the fishing of the water of Carlingford'. The fisheries controlled by Dunbrody Abbey, Co. Wexford, were so productive that the monks were able to lease out four of their weirs to private individuals. The Franciscan friary in Cork 'had the right of fishing in a weir near the city from sunset on Saturday to sunrise on Sunday, as well as a Friday salmon from the same weir'.[43]

While religious houses undoubtedly played an important role in developing fisheries and preserving fish stocks, their fish management techniques occasionally led to conflicts of interest with secular authorities. This happened when some religious houses built weirs at particularly sensitive sites, thereby affecting the size of catches taken by other fishermen. In 1349, for instance, the abbot of Mellifont was 'indicted for erecting a weir at Oldridge', while three years later 'his successor was indicted for a similar offence'. Went uncovered evidence to suggest that some religious houses in the south-east of Ireland were responsible for 'the erection of weirs to the general detriment of the fisheries of the River Nore'.[44]

With fish ranking almost as important as bread in the households of some of medieval Ireland's wealthier families, it is not surprising that there was a market for fresh fish from a very early stage. Louis Cullen has maintained that fish were probably a much more important food source for the rural poor in the centuries prior to the Great Famine than in the medieval period, when external markets for fresh fish and shellfish were comparatively small.[45] The major towns on the east coast consumed significant quantities of herring, hake and other fish in the late medieval period. The diet of Dubliners then included oysters, cockles, razor fish and crustaceans. Oysters were part of the diet of all classes in medieval Dublin and were widely available in taverns, where they were washed down with copious amounts of ale. Court records of that time point to many cases of injuries sustained when oyster shells were carelessly thrown around in taverns thus causing injuries to customers. For example, in thirteenth-century Waterford, it was recorded that one Adam Scott, on eating oysters in a local tavern, threw a shell over his shoulder, which then rebounded off a wall and caused a customer the loss of an eye.[46] While oysters were widely consumed with beer and ale in taverns throughout coastal Ireland in the medieval period, wealthier customers consumed cutlets of salmon and large eels pickled in mixtures of vinegar, wine and beer. City folk who lived near the coast also consumed a considerable variety of saltwater and freshwater fish. The accounts of the Priory of the Holy Trinity, Dublin, give some indication of the diet of wealthier Dubliners in the fourteenth century. The priory had a number of 'granges', or farms, outside the city, and they used these to supply the priory with a wide range of food. On normal days, it was said that the inmates dined on a hefty breakfast of bread, capons, pasties, oysters and salmon, all consumed with wine or ale. Dinner consisted of lots of meat, mutton, fowl, capons, geese, pork, pigeons, goslings, rabbits, plovers and larks. Wine and beer were regularly served at main meals, while on Fridays and throughout Lent, salmon, oysters, herring and other salted fish were consumed. The ubiquitous eel was also eaten in large quantities, as well as trout, turbot, plaice and gurnard. When John de Pyllattenhale was a guest at the priory on Ash Wednesday, 1338, the cost of the dinner alone was as follows: herrings 6*d.*; salmon 18*d.*; baking the salmon 2*d.*; almonds and rice 4*d.*; ginger and mustard ½*d.* On another fast day in Lent, the cost of dinner was: oysters 2*d.*; bread 2*d.*; wine 12½*d.*; turbot 5*d.*; gurnard 1*d.*; almonds and rice 4*d.*; eels 3*d.*; salmon 5*d.* and onions 1½*d.*[47] The priory's guests were not supplied with plates, but ate their food instead from thick slices of stale bread that were afterwards given to the poor or fed to domestic dogs. We get some idea of the relative expense of such meals when we recall that farm labourers at this time earned around one penny per day, while carpenters received 2.5*d.*

In the larger towns and cities, the Lenten menu of the wealthy included salt-fish, red and white herring, and stockfish, although the latter was not much liked. Dried ling was widely consumed during fast days in medieval Ireland, while salmon pickled in brine was also popular. Herring were also popular in the thirteenth and fourteenth centuries, and there appears to have been a marked increase in their consumption by rich and poor alike by the middle of the fifteenth century. In the early years of the fourteenth century, Scottish fishermen supplied herring to the fish shambles of Dublin and Drogheda.[48] When the Liffey froze over in the particularly severe winter of 1338, the citizens of Dublin feasted on roasted eels on the frozen waters of the river.[49] The fish diets of the wealthy in medieval Ireland may not have been all that different to those of their English counterparts. When Bishop Hales of Lichfield and Coventry bid his guests to table to celebrate the Feast of the Assumption on 15 August, 1461, he offered great quantities of brown trout and salmon, and 'a choice between five other species of freshwater fish, including pike, chub, dace, grayling and eels'.[50] Similarly in Ireland, the poor tenant farmers around Ballycotton in east Cork supplied the bishop of Cloyne with cod, ling and haddock in the fourteenth century.

We know that Irish-built ships and fishing vessels were trading with Bordeaux as far back as the thirteenth century. *The Annals of Loch Cé* contain a reference to the execution in the Isle of Man in 1217 of a number of herring fishermen from the east coast who committed acts violence on the island.[51] Elaborate illustrations of fish were widely used to decorate *The Books of Kells* and *The Book of Armagh*, thus emphasising the importance of fish in the diets of Early Christian monks. A number of old Irish texts suggestd that high fish yields sometimes portended the reign of a just king, adding that it was 'through the justice of the ruler that abundance of fish swim in streams'.[52] Finally, so valuable were the herring fisheries off the south-west coast of Ireland that they may have contributed to the renewal of friaries, monasteries and Gaelic castles in the late fourteenth and early fifteenth century.[53]

The monasteries and religious houses of medieval Ireland regularly offered 'good fare' and hospitality to visiting lords and church dignitaries. From the ninth century onwards, they also acted as trading centres and were responsible for bringing considerable amounts of gold and silver into the country. This in turn enabled the inhabitants of lands adjacent to important monasteries to use coinage to increase local and long-distance trade. As they developed into more complex, and more secularised centres of population, monasteries gathered around them people from a wide variety of walks of life. Monastic sites were thus also the great market places of medieval Ireland, the sites of which were usually marked with crosses at each end of the *aonach* or market. These markets were generally held on feast days and other religious dates throughout the year. From the tenth century onwards, it was not uncommon for important Irish families to dominate the thriving markets of rural and coastal Ireland. By then, indeed, many of the great monasteries of the country, not least those located in rich coastal areas in the east and south of the country, had paved streets, industrial quarters, craft shops and rows of houses.[54] From the twelfth century onwards, some monasteries also trafficked in slaves, hides, agricultural produce and fish. Many of these early monasteries could be compared to fortified villages or farms, and consisted of a collection of small huts enclosed behind a surrounding wall, with a church, or sometimes a round tower, in which people, cattle and such other belongings could be accommodated when the community was raided by hostile neighbours.[55] Because of their connection with local dynastic families, these monastic settlements were duty-bound to provide hospitality to visiting dignitaries, and to feed and shelter pilgrims at set times throughout the year. In coastal areas, especially in areas where good agricultural land was scarce, the resources of the sea and the shoreline were exploited to feed the inhabitants of monasteries and pilgrims alike. In remote coastal areas on the west and north-west coasts, the inhabitants of ecclesiastical establishments fished and foraged for sea food, and combined farming with gardening in order to support their inhabitants. Like their English and continental counterparts, the inhabitants of some monastic settlements also engaged in rudimentary forms of fish farming. In addition to managing fishing weirs, they occasionally stocked man-made ponds, moats and other manageable stretches of water in order to satisfy the demand for fish during Lent and the numerous 'fish days' that punctuated the Christian calendar. Moats surrounding castles were sometimes stocked with fish, and these had to be kept clean of sewage and other dirt. Many abbeys and monasteries also operated fish-curing houses.

This period also witnessed the introduction of new species which, added to indigenous stocks, provided a greater variety of fish for local consumption. Among those species introduced between the ninth and the eighteenth century were pike, sea lamprey, gudgeon, bream, tench, roach, dace, perch and rudd.[56] In the last quarter of the twelfth century, Giraldus Cambrensis stated that the River Shannon already abounded in sea lampreys. In subsequent centuries, these were considered a delicacy chiefly indulged in by the wealthy. However, he added, Ireland in general did not 'produce some fine fishes found in other countries'.[57] In addition to introducing new species of fish, the Anglo-Normans also introduced rabbits, peas and beans, all of which were added to the meat- and milk-based diet of the native Irish. Mahon has suggested that the Anglo-Normans were also responsible for changing eating habits in parts of coastal Ireland at least. However, she has also shown that corn and milk provided the mainstay of most of the population in early medieval Ireland, when wheat, oats, rye and barley were widely consumed.[58] We have already seen that the great seal colonies of the north and west coasts were regularly plundered for seal oil, blubber and meat from the prehistoric period right down to the late nineteenth century.[59] In the Early Christian period, the bones of whales were occasionally used for construction purposes and in the manufacture of culinary utensils.[60] A legal tract from the fifth century referred to the bones of whales also being used in the manufacture of hoops used in the making of barrels. An early monastic settlement on the island of Inishkea, Co. Mayo, yielded a number of culinary implements made from whale bones. The latter included parts of a shoulder blade of a whale that bore the marks of numerous cuts and may have served as a chopping board. Pieces of whale bone were also uncovered at an Early Christian site near Tyrella, Co. Down. Skeletal remains

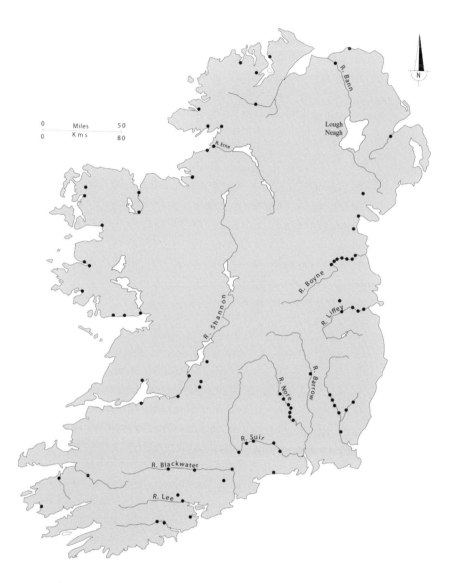

Map 1 The location of major fish weirs in Ireland (after Went, 'The pursuit of salmon in Ireland' (1964)).

of whales have been found in a medieval house in Cork city, where they lay alongside food refuse and the bones of cattle, pigs and sheep. The Arab scholar Al-'Udhri, who hailed from Moorish Spain, referred to an important whale fishery off the south coast of Ireland in the eleventh century.

Meat in most cultures has long been regarded as the basis of a substantial meal, the cornerstone of many feasts and banquets. Nevertheless, more recent research on the culinary practices in medieval societies suggests that fish occupied a central position in the diets of coastal and rural communities throughout Europe. They also played an important, albeit neglected role the history of celebrating and hospitality. Fletcher has shown that the eating of fish had symbolic significance. She further suggests that fish have appeared 'in numerous shimmering guises at feasts and festivities both in art and in life'.[61] The ancient Athenians were passionate about their fish, and a number of the Greek comedies contain innuendoes about the connection between fish and loose morals. Fish in ancient Greece were associated with luxury and decadence and, for that reason, particular species were greedily coveted. Because they were wild and 'free-swimming', refined Roman citizens were not inclined to allocate fish the same status as domesticated fowl and meat in their diets. In the Early Christian world, on the other hand, fish was the emblem of Christ, and for hundreds of years fish have formed a major part in the Christian diet because of the great many fast days during which meat consumption was forbidden. Meat, it was argued, stimulated lust and greed, while fish were believed to have soothing or 'cooling' effects on those who consumed them. It was also suggested that fish consumption put people in mind of the risen Christ. For that reason, it induced piety, controlled passions and helped man to conquer his baser appetites. Not surprisingly, therefore, large quantities of fish were required to feed people during Lent as fast days throughout medieval Europe, including Ireland. In recognition of the centrality of fish in the economies and diets of many Catholic countries, the Hanseatic League was often prepared to underwrite the debts of coastal communities when the fishing was poor.

While the diet of the poor in England, France and Ireland probably varied little during 'fish days', the wealthy could afford to relieve the monotony of a fish diet with an array of saltwater and freshwater fish. In the households of Gaelic lords, the ostentatious feasts served to discerning diners fostered the development of cooking skills and skilled cooks alike. Fish-pies in the thirteenth and fourteenth centuries were a favourite Lenten dish in many European countries, including Ireland, where they added variety to an otherwise drab diet of boiled and fried fish. Fish pies were made up from herrings, eels, salmon and sturgeon, and were sometimes flavoured with butter, spices and dried fruit. The Lenten 'ling-pie' and other salt-fish pies were reputed to be less flavoursome, and were generally enriched with egg yolks, butter, herbs and spices. By the mid-fifteenth century, well-stocked inns in and around Dublin offered a range

13 The Castle of Carrickafoyle, Co. Kerry, showing coastal waters and the surrounding countryside. Sites such as these were chosen for geo-strategic and economic reasons, and gave local chieftains control over valuable inshore fisheries (from Stafford, *Pacata Hibernia* (1633)).

of food and wines, including more than a dozen kinds of fish and half a dozen types of shellfish, along with such traditional fare as dried and smoked fish.[62] Stuffed fish were roasted on spits, and pieces of fish were commonly toasted in front of the fire. Smaller fish were boiled on a gridiron, or pan-fried in butter. The encasing of fish and meat in pies was popular throughout medieval Europe, even if many wealthier consumers did not actually eat the oil-soaked pastry. Thus 'baked in a pie' was a popular alternative to boiled or grilled fish. Many such pies took hours to cook, and at the end of the cooking process the actual pastry shell was so tough that it had to be discarded. An early recipe for baked sea lamprey explicitly states that the fish was to be lifted from the pastry, while the gravy that remained in the pie was 'mopped up with slices of bread, not pieces of the crust'.[63] In central and eastern Europe, it was customary to serve fish with gooseberries, red currants and grapes. Fish were also served with slices of orange or lemon in aristocratic households, a culinary practice that persists in Hungary, Romania and Poland to this day. The recipe book of one menagier (cook or housekeeper) in fourteenth-century Paris contained instructions for the cooking of no less than twenty-four varieties and a total of fifty-six fish dishes. This particular cook was skilled in the cooking of some sixty-eight different kinds of fish, and he could prepare a total of one hundred and thirty five fish recipes.[64] A feature of all medieval cookbooks was the sheer number of recipes devoted to fish and wildfowl and young women marrying into wealthy families were expected to be able to distinguish between wide varieties of edible fish. In some of the best cookbooks, we find recipes for pike, bass, carp, perch, bream, roach, chub, eel, trout, crayfish, salmon, gurnard, conger, whiting, dogfish, mackerel, red mullet, cod, haddock, coalfish, cuttlefish, lobsters, mussels and lamprey. Sauces were widely used in the late medieval kitchen, and these were generally sharp, spicy and brightly coloured. They also tended to be thickened with breadcrumbs rather than cream or eggs. They were particularly concocted in order to 'spice up' fish that was often fried, or roasted on a grill.[65]

Overall, it would appear, the dietary range of people in late medieval times was considerably wider than it is today. People were also extremely flexible in their eating habits, consuming seasonal food as it became available. They ate a wider range of food, including fish, than most Europeans today. Owing to the enormous demand for fish and poultry, fish farms were used to supply freshwater fish, while 'fowleries' were stocked with an abundance of wildfowl and domesticated birds. We have already seen that fish were almost as important as bread in the wealthier households of medieval Europe, including perhaps coastal Ireland. We know that Askeaton Castle on the River Deel in Co. Limerick had a great garden and at least two fishponds.[66] Cullen has suggested that because fish were so freely available in Ireland 'there may have been no need to feed fish artificially, as in the case of carp in France'. The fact that the fishpond at Eyrescourt, near the banks of the Shannon in Co. Galway, has been mentioned in historical records suggests that fishponds of this type were a rare sight in Ireland.[67] However, much more research is needed to establish the true position of fish farming and fishponds in late medieval and early modern Ireland. Bríd McMahon has argued that the Irish for centuries relied heavily on liquid, solid and semi-solid milk products, a dietary custom that had its roots in animal husbandry. Gradually, however, new dietary patterns emerged in the course of the fifteenth and sixteenth centuries, with beans, peas, bread and fish supplementing a traditional milk-based diet. Shellfish formed a major part of the diet of medieval Dublin, as is evident from the remains found in Viking excavations in the old Scandinavian quarter of the city. Cullen has also noted that the Irish diet retained many 'primitive features' that were still being consumed in considerable quantities well into in the eighteenth century. These included a very healthy per capita consumption of fish that was probably significantly higher than in England.[68]

Even when the religious reforms of the Protestant Reformation released many from the obligation to fast, some countries continued to enforce 'fish days' because a healthy fishing industry fostered the development of boat-building and provided the navy with experienced, able-bodied seamen who were skilled in the ways of the oceans. Thus, despite Henry VIII's break with Catholicism in the 1530s, 'fish days' continued to be observed throughout the fifteenth century in England, principally to encourage the nation's seamen, but also to foster the development of coastal communities. Elizabeth's Chief Secretary, William Cecil, ordained that 'fishing be maintained by the straitest observation of fish days for policy's sake; so the sea coasts should be strong with men and habitations and the fleet flourish more than ever'.[69] In addition to the traditional Friday fasts, Wednesdays and Saturdays were also set aside as 'fish days' during Elizabeth's reign, when the so-called 'political Lent' meant that people abstained from meat for approximately half the year. Thus, even after the Reformation, fasting was still encouraged for a variety of secular as well as spiritual reasons. In Elizabethan England, the dietary laws that governed the strict observance of 'fish days' were motivated by political, and not just religious considerations. Farmers held that 'fish days' helped prevent too great a drain on valuable meat supplies, while others suggested that any weakening of the rules about eating fish would result in over-indulgence of meats and fats that were believed to be the root causes of many medical problems. Lenten fasting also met with the approval of the political establishments in a number of other maritime nations, partially because sea fishing supplied men for the navy, but also because it promoted the growth of seaports and helped to revive flagging coastal towns. Viewed in this way, the sponsoring of sea fishing in England, France, Scotland and Holland at this stage may well rank as one of the earliest examples of a regional planning in modern Europe.

ROLE OF RELIGIOUS INSTITUTIONS

The promotion of fishing as a means for encouraging the supply of seamen to the navy was certainly not a feature of Gaelicised Ireland, and neither do we have much evidence of the extensive use of fishponds in the country. Aside from church authorities and monastic institutions, there was very little support for freshwater and sea fisheries in the country. In regions where fish were difficult to transport, people were limited to what was available in local rivers, lakes and sea estuaries. The mass catering arrangements of medieval Irish monasteries would appear to suggest that not only monks, but also workers on the land, travellers and those in receipt of charity also consumed fish and shellfish. Fish dishes were particularly popular at festive banquets and were regularly served up at funerals in the late medieval period. We have already seen that salmon and eels figured prominently in the diets of religious orders and were often used as tithe payments by those leasing church land. The archbishop of Armagh, for example, received annually from Kilree manor, in the bishopric of Derry, '40,000 medium eels and 60 large ones' in the fifteenth century.[70] Fish such as eels and herring were not only plentiful and cheaply available during Lent – they were also considered the 'king' of food during this season of privation. The sheer number of 'fish days' meant that the selling of fish was a lucrative business for fishermen and fish merchants alike, especially in large urban centres and in great monastic settlements. Rules dictated where fishmongers could sell their fish, the quality of fish sold, the times when they could be sold, and the personnel permitted to sell fish. By the early sixteenth century, jurors set the price of fish sold by companies of fishmongers in Dublin, Drogheda, Cork, Limerick and Galway. In parts of continental Europe, fishmongers were forbidden to offer unsalted fish for sale two days after they were caught, while mackerel, an extremely oily fish, could only be sold before and after Sunday service.

Monasteries were also the settings for some of earliest ritualised expressions of communal fasting; practices that were later transferred to lay communities outside monastic enclosures. In late medieval Ireland and Scotland, there were many more 'fast days' than 'feast days' in the church calendar, thus making fish a central item of food for many people. The forty days of Lent accounted for more than one tenth of the year, and were sometimes known as 'the tithe days of the year'.[71] Outside of this, the other fast days probably went unobserved by the majority of people, who generally got by on one or two frugal meals per day. Nevertheless, communal fasting during Lent, whether in the early religious houses, or in society at large, was an indication of the church's disciplinary control over religious communities and secular society alike. The longest and most important fasts were those observed during Advent and Lent. These ushered in Christmas and Easter, the two greatest feasts in the church calendar. Lent, the more important of the two, lasted for six week, reminding Early Christians of the forty days Christ spent in the wilderness. It was a time of year for focusing on man's failures and sins was therefore a season when all were expected to do penance. As such, it was a period of privation, prompting men, women and even children to engage in an annual 'spring-cleaning' of their souls. As creatures of water, the consumption of fish was permissible because they had escaped God's curse on earthly creatures, and because they came from an element that was 'blessed' through Christ's associations with fishermen and the sea. Prohibitions on meat consumption were also justified on the grounds that creatures that lived on the surface of the earth were flawed as a result of the fall from grace in the Garden of Eden. As 'water creatures', it was said that fish possessed the sanctifying and cleansing virtues of the element that sustained them. Lent was also the season during which entire communities were expected to offer up sacrifices to God and to compensate for their own pitiful inadequacies. By abstaining from meat and consuming only fish for considerable periods throughout the year, religious communities and those outside the religious life were united in a common endeavour. These early expressions of social solidarity in turn contributed to a strong sense of identity, fusing the inmates of religious institutions with those on the outside. In so doing, they bound lay communities to their spiritual leaders across time and space, thus creating some of the earliest 'imagined communities' in Early Christian Europe. By encouraging fish-consumption during Lent and other 'fish days', church and state in medieval Ireland were protecting the dietary codes of the landed elite and helping to stem the consumption of expensive beef. All of this suggests that the conventional image of the medieval Irish diner as a person 'draped in animal furs, tearing with his teeth at dripping joints of semi-roasted meat is an easy one to draw and a simple one to retain'.[72] However, as we have already seen, this image is by no means accurate, as fish, shellfish and a wide range of other 'shore food' were widely consumed by rich and poor alike. While meat was generally absent from the diet of the majority of people, the widespread acceptance of the teachings of the church on fasting meant that it was also absent from the diet of the wealthy for much of the year. During these periods, fish and 'sea food', and perhaps also fowl, were standard fare for many communities in coastal Ireland in particular. This was partly because religious fathers taught that fish were not imbued with earthly qualities and were therefore less likely to offend God and encourage sin.

The consumption of fish meant that status differentials in medieval Irish society were temporarily abandoned for the duration of the fasting season. Early Christian authorities went to great pains to point out that a diet of fish was good for the soul as well as the body. The eating of red meat, on the other hand, signified power and social standing. While fish was associated with coldness and the ascetic way of life, meat was a rich food that could induce a sense of euphoria and mental excitement, and give rise to a sense of 'light headedness' among those with poor constitutions.[73] Meat consumption could be confined to the wealthy on the grounds that they alone could afford it, and only they could resist its 'heady' side effects. Medieval dietary etiquette thus dictated that the aristocracy should literally feed off the fat of the land, and that red meat should be central to the dietary code of the military establishment. This suggests that regional warfare and raiding in ancient Ireland may have sustained beef consumption and contributed to the production of rich foods with a high fat content. Moreover, because meat consumption was a daily reminder of the superior status of privileged groups and the military elite, they considered it intolerable to be deprived of meat and other fat foods.

We have already seen that some fish were more prized than others, even in the medieval period. Images of ships adorn the walls of Barryscourt Castle, in south Co. Cork, and there may well have been a freshwater fishpond there in the fifteenth century. A charter granted by King John to the citizens of Dublin allowed them 'the fishery of one half of the Liffey, with the liberty to build on the banks at their will'. Another charter dating from 1215 confirmed to the citizens of the city 'in fee farm that part of the Liffey which belongs to them, together with one part of the said river, except such fishings … are held by ancient tenure'. Both of these charters point to the ancient lineage of the Liffey fishery and its importance to those living along the banks of the river. Indeed, the Liffey was a vital seaway and valuable salmon fishery in the fourteenth and fifteenth centuries. Several of these early charters emphasise the importance of local fisheries to the upkeep of religious houses in the city. It has been suggested that the Liffey's fisheries were a constant source of friction as well as fish in the late Middle Ages, and those who infringed fishing rights on the river were severely punished.[74]

Finally, we also have a number of references to the hoarding of fish as valuable property in Early Christian Ireland. There are other references to the proper management of important freshwater and saltwater fisheries. Moriarty has pointed to the paucity of references to fishing rights in the Brehon Laws; except one, which related to the right of landowners to erect a fishing weir on or adjacent to a neighbour's land.[75] While there are few references to the preservation of actual fish stocks in the Laws, many of them remark on the dangers of water pollution, especially in the Liffey, a river long renowned for its salmon. As far back as the mid-fifteenth century, authorities in Dublin passed legislation protecting salmon in the waterways in and around the city. One law ordered that 'no tanner, glover or any person use limed ware or leather work in the River Liffey on account of the destruction of salmon'.[76] The early Irish legal texts also contain references to the status of fishermen, pointing out that they were generally of low rank, and had only to offer 'an honour-pay of one heifer to their king'. Other texts state that freemen had right to a 'single-dipping of a net in a stream', and could only take one salmon caught near their place of abode.[77] These restrictions appear to have been motivated less by concerns for the preservation of stocks, than by the self-interest of those who owned valuable fisheries on lakes, rivers and coastal estuaries. Nevertheless, conservation did become an issue in the sixteenth century, when water-bailiffs patrolled some of the country's major salmon rivers in order to prevent poaching and damage to fish stocks. Early lawmakers were particularly mindful of the 'great hurt and hindrance' caused to rivers 'wherein the frye of salmon, ele and other commodious fish are bred and nourished, by townsfolk who allowed their animals to feed upon the strand, and to destroy the spawn'.[78]

Finally, the early legal texts also make a number of interesting references to the ownership of flotsam and the maintenance of ports, rivers and weirs. Joyce has argued that in Early Christian Ireland anything thrown up the seashore belonged to the owner of the shore 'as far as the value of five cows'. If worth more than that, it was divided according to the 'partition of the lawful bark'.[79] This meant that one third of all flotsam belonged to the owner of the shore, another third was divided among the heads of families of the district, and the remainder went to the king of the same territory. In places where large quantities of edible seaweed were cast up on the strand, this could be claimed entirely by the owner of the shoreline. We know from the eighth-century legal text *Crith Gablach*, that dulse was used like a seaweed salad, which, together with onions, added flavour to otherwise bland dishes. We also know that it was the duty of owners of ports and segments of the seashore to preserve from destruction any fishing vessels and other craft cast ashore in stormy weather. If, however, these proved to be utter wrecks, they were regarded as sea 'waifs', and the owner of the port could then divide them among the people of the territory in accordance with ancient law. Moreover, crewmembers rescued from sinking vessels had to be lodged and fed as long as was necessary by the people of the territory – the people from the district on whose shore the vessel was cast were 'bound to keep, protect, feed, and make provision for such parties'.[80] It was further ruled that any person who retrieved valuable flotsam floating nine or more waves out from the land, could claim ownership of it, regardless of the rights of its original owner.

The following chapter examines the history of Ireland's sea fisheries in the four centuries prior to the more formal colonisation of the country in the sixteenth and seventeenth centuries. This period, it is argued, witnessed the internationalisation of Ireland's coastal waters, as fishing fleets from Spain, Portugal, England, France, Holland and North Africa were engaged in the exploitation of Ireland's maritime resources. It is suggested that the colonisation of Ireland from the sixteenth century onwards was preceded by a prolonged *mare liberum* period, during which Irish fishermen fished alongside fleets from continental Europe in particular. Moreover, powerful Gaelic chieftains in coastal Ireland regularly collected tributary payments from foreign fishing fleets operating in the seas around Ireland throughout this period. In a number of instances, this helped prolong the ascendancy of Gaelic power in some of the country's more remote coastal areas. For that reason, it was a source of conflict between Gaelic Ireland on the one hand, and the English Crown and English fishermen and fish merchants on the other. The chapter concludes with an examination on the state of Ireland's sea fisheries at the end of the sixteenth century, with particular reference to the development of harbour facilities, fishing ports, fish processing works and the export market for saltwater and freshwater fish.

CHAPTER FOUR

Exploitation of the marine and freshwater fisheries of pre-colonial Ireland

IRELAND'S FRESHWATER AND SEA FISHERIES, *c.*1300–1600

From the historian's perspective, the period prior to the colonial plantations is arguably the blankest in the history of Irish sea fishing, and this is despite the fact that Ireland then had a thriving fish-trade and foreign fishing fleets were widely engaged in the commercial exploitation of the country's offshore fisheries. Focusing on the territorial organisation of Gaelic society and the transformations in urban and rural life in areas of strong Anglo-Norman settlement, most historians have relegated saltwater and freshwater fisheries to mere footnotes in the economic history of pre-colonial Ireland. With remarkably few exceptions, they have dealt only fleetingly with such important topics as the internationalisation of Ireland's fishing grounds, the growth of indigenous and foreign fishing communities around the Irish coast, developments in boat-building and harbour facilities, and the early emergence of rudimentary piers and harbour facilities in the fifteenth and sixteenth centuries.[1] Certainly, in the period under discussion in this chapter, Ireland was part of a European trading bloc, and fishing fleets from France, Spain, Portugal and Holland regularly fished off the country's southern and western coasts.

Recent excavations at Newhaven on the Dublin coast have unearthed the remains of one of the earliest surviving harbours in Ireland. This harbour, the jewel in the crown of late medieval Irish sea fishing, was located in a sheltered bay on the northern side of Bremore Head, where a stone pier incorporated natural outcrops of rocks along its course to define a very substantial, man-made structure. James Barnwell and his wife Margaret were granted permission to construct this 'fisher towne' in the mid-sixteenth century, and the pier was first outlined in a crude drawing of an early map of the parish of Balrothery. The harbour at Newhaven, together with similar discoveries at Inis Mór and Bunratty Castle in Co. Clare, and at Rindoon, in Co. Roscommon, has added greatly to our knowledge of medieval and post-medieval fishing harbours in Ireland.[2] An elementary fourteenth-century portolan chart also indicates a whole cluster of seaports along the east coast, extending from Strangford Lough in the north-east right round to the south coast of Munster, and with a sprinkling of other ports and coastal towns indicated on the west coast.[3] Yet another fourteenth-century map shows important fishing banks off Arklow, Dublin and Ardglass, and a sea-chart of the Irish coast at the end of the sixteenth century points to a string of ports around the south and east coasts. A number of more detailed maps give details of important sea fisheries off Arklow, Dublin and Down in the fourteenth century.[4] The concentration of wealth in maritime enclaves along the east coast had its basis in arable agriculture and in the exploitation of sea and shoreline. The waters off Ardglass, in Co. Down, were renowned for large catches of cod, herring, sole and hake, and this port had one of the most extensive complexes of tower houses and warehouses in the entire country. The latter have been described as 'a visible reminder of the extensive trade carried out by wealthy local merchants with ports in Ireland, northern England and the Isle of Man, and with continental Europe'.[5] Visiting fish merchants regularly availed of the quayside warehouses in this stretch of Ulster's coastline, and we know that fish merchants on the north-west coast were using specially constructed warehouses at the port of Assaroe in the mid-fifteenth century.[6] By the start of the sixteenth century, fishing ports around Strangford and Carlingford had acquired national significance, while many other coastal settlements around the Irish coast were also acquiring quays and improved harbour facilities.[7] A detailed map of Baltimore in the early 1630s suggests that fishermen on this stretch of the Irish coast were already using seine nets around Sherkin Island.[8] When George Carew visited west Munster at the start of the seventeenth century, he described the waters between Baltimore and Sherkin Island as an almost perfect harbour 'where infinite numbers of ships may ride, having small tides, deep water and a good place to careen ships'.[9]

Even at this early stage, Ireland had a strong trade in saltwater and freshwater fish, with salmon and herring being dispatched as far as Brabant at the beginning of the fifteenth century.[10] Basque fishermen were already exploiting an important whale fishery off the south-west coast in the thirteenth century, and put to sea in small boats to hunt the slow-moving right whales that frequented the Atlantic waters. So successful were they in harpooning and 'playing' their prey at this stage in the evolution of commercial whale fishing that they practically exterminated this species from the waters off Atlantic Europe.[11] In the early fifteenth century, merchants from Dingle had a contract with a Breton sea captain at Bordeaux to bring wine to Ireland in exchange for which they would be allowed to fish Irish waters.[12] The particularly valuable sea

14 The Kerry coastline as depicted in Thomas Stafford's military report, *Pacata Hibernia*, published in 1633. Essentially a military map to aid in the colonial subjugation of an Irish province, it also describes the rich human geography of coastal Munster in the pre-colonial period.

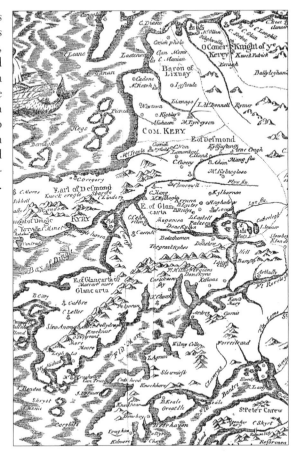

fisheries off the coasts of Arklow, Hook Head, Youghal, Galway and the northwest were already being exploited in the late fourteenth century. The coats of arms of arms of several Irish coastal towns were illustrated with ships and other craft, with that of Arklow proclaiming that the town's future rested 'on the wealth of the seas'. Fifteenth-century archival material from La Rochelle refers to merchants from Arklow exchanging herring from Ireland for salt from this section of the French coast.[13] A sixteenth-century illustrated map of Cork has fishermen fishing within the medieval walled city. This map also indicates the location of a prominent marketplace at Cross Green where the local inhabitants came to buy fish brought in from Kinsale, Youghal and Baltimore.[14] In the mid-sixteenth century, a number of English entrepreneurs petitioned Queen Elizabeth to grant them monopoly rights to the lucrative fishing industry around Baltimore. After a community of Calvinist settlers were planted there at the end of the sixteenth century, they rapidly cornered the more lucrative aspects of the fish-trade in the area, and acquired almost complete control over the local fishing industry.[15]

John Brown's late sixteenth-century map of Mayo contained comparatively accurate descriptions of Achill Island, the Mullet Peninsula and Erris Head. An inscription on one side of this map stated that 'the best havens for shippes … are the Bay of the Ownes, Brode Haven, Ennis Potyn and Enniskey', adding that the last three locations were also 'good places to take sea fishe'.[16] The islands of Inishkea are shown about four times their size on this map, indicating their possible importance to fishing fleets from Britain and the continent that fished these waters in the fifteenth century. Fourteenth-century Galway was inhabited 'by sects or colonies who got their livelyhood by cods and other sea fishes', which they dried 'by the sun'.[17] A West Country trader listed the items in Galway's export trade in the reign of Elizabeth I as follows: 'great store of salt hides, tallow, salte befe in hogsheads, Irisshe coverletts, mantels, and great store of Irish frises, both highe cottons and lowe cottons, linine yarone and heringe and salte samon when time of the year sarveth, all whiche transporte either to Rochell or Newhaven or Roane and sometimes into Flaunders'.[18] O'Sullivan has argued that the levies collected from fishermen 'contributed in no small degree to the municipal revenues of Galway City' in the sixteenth and seventeenth centuries.[19] The city had access to the important freshwater fishery of Lough Corrib, which supplied salmon, trout and eels to thrice weekly local markets. In addition to this, a plentiful supply of saltwater fish was delivered daily to the city's quays.[20] Attempts were made in the reign of Edward IV to profit from Flemish fishing fleets operating in Irish waters. Thus, a tax of 13*s.* 4*d.* was placed on every vessel of over six tons, and 2*s.* on every small boat that visited the Irish coast. Nevertheless, the 'Hollanders', as the Dutch were known, were so keen on getting into the waters off the west coast that it is said that they offered to buy the port of Galway with as many coins placed side by side that it would take to cover the city's quays.[21] After the Treaty of Antwerp in 1609, King James introduced measures to curtail competition from Dutch fishermen that prevented 'strangers' from fishing 'upon those of His Majesty's coasts and seas of Great Britain and Ireland' until they had obtained 'license for the same from the king'. Commissioners were also appointed 'at such places as the king might select, to give out licenses on such conditions as he might think fit'.[22] In the event, these restrictions did not prevent Spanish fishermen from catching large quantities of mackerel and other fish off the west of Ireland and the south-west England.[23] Nevertheless, they were targeted at all 'foreign fishermen' and suggest that the crown was very serious indeed about the management of Ireland's lucrative sea fisheries.

The Shannon Estuary was also a well-known haunt for herring, which were exported to port towns and cities on the west coast of England, especially Bristol in the late medieval period. 'Slyggaghe' in 1553 was deemed 'best town in all the country', and the fishing grounds off its shores contributed in no small measure to the early status of this coastal settlement.[24] Herring formed a vital element in the prosperity of many western coastal districts in the fifteenth century, and local wisdom had it that

> Heryng of Slegoye and salmon of Bame
> He is made in Brystowe many a ryche man.[25]

The herring fishery off the north-west coast was especially valuable to the O'Donnells of Donegal, even though it did not develop into a large-scale commercial enterprise until well into the sixteenth century.[26] O'Rorke believed that this fishery was also of 'great importance to Sligo and the whole western coast of Ireland'. Pointing to the variety of fish caught in these waters, he went on to state that

> If we add to the oysters, the salmon and the herring, the various other kinds of fish of which the Sligo waters yield, in almost equal abundance; notably the turbot, of three fine turbot banks of Milkhaven, Portavad and Eniskrone; the cod, of the whole stretch from Aughris Head to Hawlboline, as well as within the well known ledge that runs between these points; the lobsters of the rocks along the coasts of Tirenagh and Carbury, and around the island of Inishmurray; and the shoals of mackerel and whiting which visit the bay in their respective seasons; we shall the better understand how valuable the fisheries of Sligo might be made both to the town and the port.[27]

Fish also feature quite strongly in Anglo-Irish literature in the Elizabethan period. Edmund Spenser wrote of the 'fruitful fishy Bann' in *The Faerie Queene*, and in his *Epithalamion*, written around 1595, he wrote:

> The silver scaly trouts doo tend full well,
> The greedy pikes which used therein to feed,
> (Those trouts and fishes all others doo excell)
> And ye likewise which keepe the rushy lake,
> Where none doo fishes take.[28]

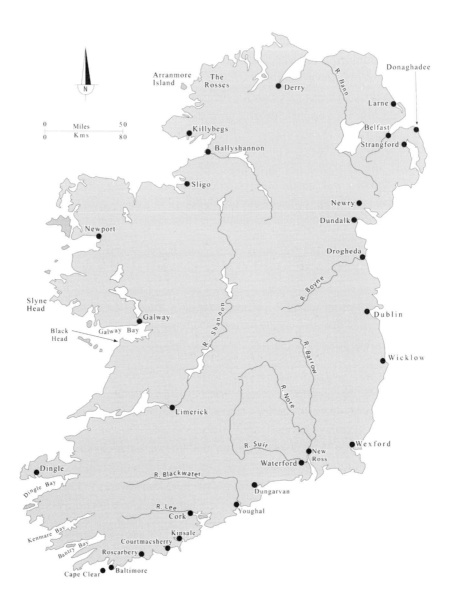

Map 2 Hake fishing ports in Ireland, 1500–1800 (after Went,
'The Irish hake fishery, 1504–1824' (1955)).

Hake, or 'haak', were exported in the thousands to Bristol throughout the late
fifteenth and early sixteenth century. In 1504, around 90,000 hake from Ireland
were landed at this port, where they fetched approximately £455 sterling. Hake

were exported both in the dried state and in the fresh state, with large hake fetching the highest prices in English and French markets. At the start of the seventeenth century, hake were estimated to be worth five to £6 per thousand fish, but when properly dried, they often fetched twice that figure. In addition to being among the most important fish exports to England, they were also exported in large quantities together with salmon, herring and cod to Spain, France and the Basque country.[29] The port of Waterford and the tiny fishing village of Duncannon did a particularly brisk trade in hake with France. The people of Dungarvan were reported to be 'very expert at salting, saving and drying this kind and most other sorts of fish'. They were able 'to cure them exceedingly well', which meant that the fish had 'a great reputation in foreign markets'. Salmon and hake were also among the most lucrative fish landed at the Earl of Cork's harbour at Youghal in the opening years of the seventeenth century.[30] In his description of the hake fishery in Waterford, Smith stated that there were

> two seasons in which the fish are taken in plenty; the first begins with the commencement of the mackerel season, that is in June, and mackerel are also the bait used at this time for the taking of them; during their first approach, they are larger than towards their second appearance, as likewise are most fish early in their season. A second shoal of this fish visits our coast towards the beginning of the herring season, viz. about September, and commonly holds till Christmas. The hake when taken is salted and dried for exportation and great quantities are consumed both fresh and salted in the country. Prior to the introduction of the pernicious system of trailing … great quantities have been yearly transported to Spain, where it is said, particularly in Bilbao, they offer a better price than cod from Newfoundland.[31]

Hake were also widely consumed in many of the fishing ports and coastal towns around the south and south-west of Ireland in the pre-colonial period. On Cape Clear, where hake were salted and dried by the wives and children of fishermen, this was the staple fish of the islanders. The Kinsale fishermen who regularly visited the island during the hake fishing season built temporary huts for curing their fish there, for which privilege they 'paid a smart rent' to the local lord.[32] Foreign and local fishermen working off the Dungarvan coastline in the 1530s were also accustomed to paying one hake for every boatload of fish landed at that town's makeshift harbour. Throughout the first half of sixteenth century, hake fishing was also well-established around the Wexford side of Waterford Harbour. Right up to its dissolution in the late sixteenth century, the Cistercian Abbey at Dunbrody was still collecting 'fish tithes' in the form of hake and other fish from local fishermen living in the village of Ballyhack. This tiny village, which probably derives its name from 'hake', was a major centre for hake fishing in the sixteenth century, and in 1541 it had nine tenements and eight cottages that were inhabited by fishermen.[33] In addition to the 'boats of strangers' who landed catches on this stretch of coast, local fishermen were also obliged pay fish tithes to those in control of coastal territories along the south-east coast.[34] In the 1580s, agents in Waterford petitioned for the imposition of duties on fishing boats engaged in hake fishing to pay for the upkeep of a 'block house' erected for the purpose of 'fysshers which yearly in fysshinge time and do resort thither'. In 1590, the lord deputy of Ireland authorised fishermen from Waterford and Duncannon 'to carry their fish called hake into France'.[35] Tolls then were generally paid in cash, rather than in kind, and were often also used to develop onshore amenities such as piers, warehouses and harbour facilities.

Although locally fixed, these tolls were generally uniform throughout the country, particularly in the coastal districts around the Irish Sea and in areas under colonial rule. In Galway, as in many municipalities throughout the east and south coasts, the tolls imposed upon fishermen also went towards the construction of town walls, fish shambles and sea barriers. In the mid-1500s, there were an estimated 600 Spanish boats in the Baltimore area, and in 1572 those in control of fortifications in an island off this coast collected customs payment from both Spanish and Biscayan fishermen. Further along the coast from Baltimore, the Spaniards paid £300 per annum to the local chief MacFineenduff for the right to fish in and around Kenmare Bay.[36] Spanish, and to a lesser extent Dutch, French and Portuguese fishing craft, were also active off the south coast of Ireland throughout the sixteenth century. In 1569, one John Corbine, who had a pass for safe conduct that permitted him to travel through the territory of the Mac Carthys of Glencarr, stated that 'every year 200 sail fysheth' in the seas off this part of Munster.[37] Charles Smith referred to an incident involving an English ship that captured a Spanish fishing vessel near Dursey, in 1531. On receiving notice of what he considered the 'high-handed' action on the part of the English captain, Dermot O'Sullivan, the 'prince' of Bear Island and Bantry Bay, 'manned a small squadron of ships and brought in both the Englishman and the Spanish vessel to Bearhaven'. The English captain was subsequently hanged, while the Spanish fishermen were set free to fish the waters around Dursey under the protection of the Gaelic chieftain.[38] The Spanish presence around Dingle in the sixteenth century was so strong that houses here were 'built in the Spanish fashion, with ranges of stone balcony windows'. The seas off this part of Munster were also 'much frequented by ships of that nation [Spain], who traded with the inhabitants, and came to fish on this coast'.[39]

One of the earliest references to valuable sea fisheries around Ireland points to the presence of Spanish fishing vessels off the west in the fifteenth century. The practice of Spanish vessels putting ashore on the west and south coasts was thus already well-established by time of Elizabeth I. In the Elizabethan period, it was reported that the seas around Baltimore and the Blasket Island were said to be the favoured centres for Spanish fishing vessels in Ireland.[40] The strong Spanish presence in Irish waters was also reflected in the number of place-names with the prefixes 'Spain' and 'Spanish' around the west and south-west coasts in particular. Many of these fishermen may actually have resided, albeit on a temporary basis, around Baltimore and on Cape Clear Island, and had well-established linkages with Galway dating back at least to the fifteenth century. In the mid-nineteenth century, Francis B. Head stated that

> The connection which formerly existed between Galway and Spain is not only recorded in history – is not only to be traced in the architecture of Lynch's Castle, also in the wide entries, arched gateways, stone-mullioned windows, and outside stars of several ancient mansions in the town, but the traveller … can most legibly read it in the dark eyes, noble features and high-bred demeanour, that in Galway in particular, and throughout Connemara in general, I repeatedly met men and women whose countenance, to say nothing of their garb, would have induced me to address them in Spanish rather than in English.[41]

There appears to have been a particularly strong Spanish and Breton presence all along the Atlantic coast of Ireland from the mid-sixteenth century onwards. In 1543, Sir Anthony St Leger reported that 'from Limerick to Cork, the Spanish and Bretons have the trade as well as the fishing there … and furnish Irishmen upon the south coast of Munster with salt'.[42] In a dispatch to Henry VIII in 1543, we learn that 'the Spanyardes and Brittons had the trade from all the marine havens in O'Donnell's country' in the north, right down to 'the haven of Limerick' in the south, and 'fewe or none Englishemen come there'.

In the sixteenth century, boats from Tenby, Milford and Carmarthen exchanged salmon, hake, salted fish and hides from Ireland for salt, wine, cloth and iron from England and Wales. Pike, an introduced freshwater species largely unknown in contemporary Gaelic literature, were dispatched from Cork, Youghal, Dungarvan and Kinsale to Padstow and Penzance on the Cornish coast.

Coastal districts in late medieval northern Europe had access to two major herring grounds in the North Atlantic and the Baltic Sea. The first of these was centred on the western Baltic and was largely controlled by ports belonging to the Hanseatic League. The other was located off the east coast of England, and ranged right round the coast of Ireland. By the mid-fifteenth century, herring migrating from the Baltic Sea poured into the North Sea, the Irish Sea and down along the western and southern shores of Ireland. From the fifteenth century onwards, this great migration ushered in a new era of prosperity for English, Scottish and, to a much lesser extent, Irish fishermen.[43] This was helped by the fact that the Dutch successfully managed to salt herring, thereby laying the foundations for a commercially viable, international herring trade in the fourteenth century. The main centre of herring fishing in Britain then was the great port of Yarmouth, but a whole string of lesser ports around the English, Scottish and Irish coastline were also engaged in this fishery. There were two divisions in the late medieval Irish herring fishery at this stage. One of these was centred in the Irish Sea and had the port of Dublin as its principal base, while the other was off the south-west and west coasts of Ireland and was widely exploited by foreign fleets. Scottish vessels from small ports in the Clyde Estuary fished for herring off the east coast of Ulster throughout the fifteenth century. Large quantities of herring were also shipped from Drogheda to Dublin, with consignments also going to the port of Chester, in Cheshire.[44] The chief herring ports in the Irish Sea at this time were Dublin, Rush, Howth, Malahide and Drogheda, and we know that herring remained plentiful in the Irish Sea throughout the sixteenth century, with an estimated 600 English boats operating in Carlingford Lough in 1535.[45] The Atlantic herring fishery was almost the equal to that of the Irish Sea, and foreign vessels operating off the west coast regularly went ashore to process and pack fish caught by local fishermen.[46] Large-scale commercial fishing for herring was especially important for small fishing ports along the Dublin coast and, to a lesser extent, to coastal towns and villages between Waterford and Kinsale. Fishermen from Rush and Bullock Harbour had ready access to the Dublin market, and ranged as far north as the Shetlands in their quest for fish.

15 Assaroe Falls on the River Erne, near Ballyshannon, Co. Donegal. Famed for their salmon from a very early stage, the waters off the coast of Tír Chonaill attracted fish merchants from Bristol in the sixteenth century. The chief of the O'Donnells was then known as 'king of the fish' (courtesy of Seán Beattie).

The rich salmon and eel fisheries of the medieval lordship of Tír Conaill had long attracted the attention of English fish merchants. Foreign fishing fleets in the latter half of the sixteenth century also exploited the sheltered bays and inshore waters around this stretch of the Irish coast. As we have already seen, this region had well-established links with Bristol, Glasgow, Ayr, Wigtown and the north-west of France. Bristol fish merchants, some of whom may have had a working knowledge of Gaelic, visited this outpost of Gaelic Ireland on an annual basis in the 1400s, staying up to two months at time at O'Donnells port at Assaroe.[47] Approximately thirty licences were granted to the Bristol men between 1400 and 1416, as part of a strategy for opening open trade links between the north-west of Ireland and the south-west of England. The region also attracted fish merchants from Galway, Drogheda and other ports on the Irish Sea. Bristol fish merchants maintained resident agents in this stronghold of Gaelic Ireland, and one merchant, John Fagan, became secretary to both Aodh Dubh and Manus O'Donnell. A number of Breton fish merchants also resided in Tír Conaill prior to the plantations, and emissaries from the O'Donnells looked after the family's interests on the continent. Hundreds of foreign fishing vessels exploited the rich herring grounds off the north-west coast in the fifteenth century, when Spanish fishermen paid one tenth to one sixth of their catch to local overlords for protection and the right to fish in these waters. These fleets also paid for the use of onshore curing and packing facilities. The lord of Tír Conaill was famed as a prominent promoter of the fish-trade in the sixteenth century, and one contemporary described him as 'the best lord of fish in Ireland ... [who] exchanged fish always with foreign merchants for wine, by which he is called in other countries, the king of the fish'.[48]

The O'Donnells of Tír Conaill were not the only Irish lords to collect tributary payments from foreign fleets fishing around the Irish coast. O'Sullivan Beare received tribute for the 'protection' offered to Spanish fishermen operating off Dursey Island and in Bantry Bay. Breen has argued that 'the extent to which the O'Sullivans went to protect their interest in the fisheries is unsurprising, given the limited terrestrial resources of the Bantry region'. In the late 1580s, the rent due from this territory was a mere £40, as the country over which this coastal lord held dominion possessed

> no good farm land, but all valleys, cragged rocks and hill, can yield no great commodity thereof, as his fishing, his wrecks, and such like. And for the fishing it is a thing uncertain, for some years if fishing do fall upon the coast, then Dunboy is worth much; if fishing fail, it cannot yield profit. For the ships and boats, the rent of them is but as the lord and they can agree, according as the fishing do continue all the season of the year, or fail, as sometimes it doth fail within one month &c.[49]

Given their secure base in and around Baltimore, the O'Driscolls of west Cork were also able to collect tribute from foreign fishing fleets in the pre-colonial period.[50] Similarly, dynastic families such as the O'Malleys of Mayo and the O'Flahertys of Galway were also indirectly dependent upon the fisheries off the west coast and regularly collected tributary payment from foreign fishing fleets. Likewise in the reign of James I, merchants and fishermen in Limerick were 'compelled to give tribute of wine and merchandise from their ships, not only to the Okehanes of Kilrush and the O'Connors of Foynes, but to each possessor of a castle between the city and the sea'.[51] So valuable were the sea fisheries off the south-west coast of Ireland, that one Spanish sea captain cautioned his fellow countrymen to tread lightly when dealing with the Irish lest they might prejudice the interests of Spanish fishermen who were heavily dependent on the trade in fish from Ireland and England at this time.

Thus, from the late Middle Ages onwards, fishing fleets transported large quantities of hake, herring and salmon to England and Scotland, chiefly in boats from these countries that were then operating around the Irish coast. These fish were usually salted or dried, and were less commonly sold in a fresh state. Herring were divided into three categories, namely fresh white and slightly salted fish known as *allecia alba*; red smoked herring known as *allecia rubra*; and 'full herring' charged with roe, which were known as *plenum*. Full white herring were the most valuable, with those from Youghal fetching very high prices in Cornwall in the early years of the sixteenth century.[52] The great fish exporting towns on the south coast at this time were New Ross, Cork, Youghal, Dingle and Kinsale, with the last named being especially famed for its pilchards, herring and hake. Waterford and Wexford also exported very considerable quantities of saltwater fish. Drawing attention to the early links between Waterford and Bristol, one historian has pointed out that twelve of the thirty-five Irish ships engaged in the import trade between Ireland and Britain in the early 1500s were from Waterford.[53] Meanwhile, fishing fleets working out of Dublin, Drogheda and other east-coast fishing ports largely controlled the sea fisheries of the Irish Sea. The sea fisheries off the south coast, on the other hand, tended to draw in fleets from Spain, France, England and Holland. Fishermen from Bristol, Poole and Bridgewater regularly visited Waterford, Wexford and Dungarvan, and their boats frequently landed fish catches at these and other ports on the south coast. Portuguese fishermen also fished the waters off the south coast of Ireland in large numbers right up to the seventeenth century, when foreign craft probably outnumbered native fishermen in Irish waters.

While it is impossible to gauge how much of the decline in foreign fishing fleets in these waters was due to restrictions imposed by English authorities, it is probable that Spanish and French fleets found it less and less profitable to visit the Irish coast after the opening of the Newfoundland fisheries. The gradual weakening of maritime links with these countries meant that many small fishing ports along the south and west coasts failed to prosper in the seventeenth century, while northern and eastern towns, which were almost entirely dependent on trade with England, grew in importance. The reduced prosperity of southern ports was most obviously reflected in a decline in their capacity, most notably at Youghal, Kinsale and Dungarvan. Despite their locational advantages, these coastal towns never really developed into major ports capable of capitalising on the opportunities presented by the opening of the Greenland and Newfoundland fisheries. Goods dispatched from the south of Ireland were sent abroad on foreign vessels, rather than in Irish ships.

16 Sixteenth-century castle on the coast of Kerry that was once a Fitzmaurice stronghold. Many Gaelic chieftains in pre-colonial coastal Ireland collected 'fish tithes' from foreign fishing fleets operating in Irish waters (from Coyne and Willis, *Scenery and antiquities of Ireland* (1841)).

Waterford, Wexford and New Ross were the only sizeable ports to maintain successful fishing fleets at the start of the colonial period. For that reason, they were capable of exploiting opportunities made available by the development of slave-holding economies in the Caribbean and the expansion of the Newfoundland fisheries. In 1598, it was estimated that Waterford and Wexford alone had more ships than the whole of Ireland, and at a time when there was even a lack of locally owned ships in Dublin.[54]

THE COMMERCIALISATION OF FISHING AND IRELAND'S MARITIME FRINGE

Pre-colonial coastal Ireland was a complex matrix of Gaelic over-lordships and maritime regions that benefited considerably from the presence of foreign fishing fleets off the Irish coast. Prior to the regulation of trade in the fifteenth and sixteenth centuries, goods traded out of Ireland included horse hides, stag skins, goats, rabbits, squirrels, martens and foxes, and a wide variety of saltwater and freshwater fish and shellfish. We have already seen that herring ranked highly in Ireland's coastal trade in the fifteenth and sixteenth centuries, as did shellfish, which were consumed in large quantities in the maritime towns and cities of Ireland and the south-west of England. We know that herring remained plentiful in the Irish Sea throughout the sixteenth century and the fishery off the coast of Down provided the earl of Kildare with a considerable income in the form of tithes and other payments. An estimated 600 English boats were operating in Carlingford Lough at the beginning of the sixteenth century, while the Atlantic herring fishery off the north-west coast was favourably compared to that in the Irish Sea. As we have also seen, foreign vessels fishing off the south and east coasts in particular regularly went ashore to land fish, or to buy catches from local fishermen. The tributary payments made to the dynastic families who controlled territories adjacent to these coastal fisheries were an increasing source of discontent to English authorities and fishing fleets alike. Thus, steps were taken from the early fifteenth century 'to prevent foreign vessels from fishing among the king's enemies'.[55] By the close of the sixteenth century, complaints were regularly made about the treatment of English fishermen by a number of powerful Irish Gaelic chieftains in coastal areas around the west and south-west coasts. Fulk Greville, in a letter to his cousin on 2 July 1558, bitterly referred to O'Sullivan Beare's 'extortionate dealings' with English fishermen off the Munster coast.[56] Evidence suggests that English authorities may even have considered enticing Dutch pirates to abandon piracy to take up the role of an elite coastguard to guard fishing fleets in some of Ireland's more intractable coastal stretches.[57] Authorities clearly regarded the tributary payments made by foreign fishermen to these leaders as unacceptable, not least because they helped support Gaelic chiefs in some of the country's most unruly regions. In the mid-fifteenth century, the English parliament sought to prevent commercial fishing off Baltimore because of the profit it brought to Fineen O'Driscoll on this stretch of Munster coastline. Around this time also, it was estimated that 'the Spaniards paid £300 per annum to Mac Fineen Duff of Arden, a local chief, for the right to fish in Kenmare Bay'.[58] Writing in the mid-eighteenth century, Smith noted that the Kinsale fishermen who regularly visited Cape Clear during the fishing season, built huts for curing fish on the island, for which privilege they were obliged to pay 'a smart rent'.[59] By the close of the sixteenth century, there were large numbers of Spanish vessels fishing off Cape Clear, and a number of these were also obliged to pay a rental to the O'Driscolls for the use of rocks in the area between Baltimore and the Fastnet.[60] Likewise, O'Rorke has remarked that Spanish fishermen who frequented the north-west coast had to pay 'fish tithes' to local overlords.[61] Such payments continued to be paid to landlords and religious authorities in parts of coastal Donegal right down to the start of the eighteenth century. When a Presbyterian community was established around Dunfanaghy in the late seventeenth century, the local inhabitants had to 'to raise £25 a year for a minister, and furnish his house with fish all the days of the year'.[62]

Perhaps the most notable feature of coastal Ireland in the late sixteenth century was the high level of international exploitation of the country's offshore waters. As we have already seen, Spanish, French, Portuguese, Dutch, English and Scottish fishermen operated in considerable numbers off the Irish coast. Some of these fleets fished in Irish water from as early as the thirteenth century. In July 1306, a Scottish fishing vessel seized near the coast of Ireland was subsequently released when it was established that the crew were not a raiding party, but were simply fishermen who made a living fishing the waters off the Irish coast.[63] In the reign of Charles I, the Dutch government paid £3,000 for a licence to fish in Irish waters, while in the late 1300s, Irish fish merchants were using techniques pioneered by the Dutch to preserve herring for the export market.[64] When caught, herring were immediately gutted, salted and packed in barrels with a layer of salt in between to preserve them. Swedish fishermen also obtained a licence to fish off the Irish coast in 1650. By the start of the seventeenth century, the French were among the main exploiters of Ireland's sea fisheries. They were especially well-established off the north coast in the waters between Portrush and the north-west of Donegal.[65] Herring were said to be so abundant off Wexford at the end of the sixteenth century that fishermen from Cornwall and Devon were attracted to this stretch of the Irish coast in very large numbers. The quantities of fish taken off Baltimore were said to be so great that after the neighbouring district was amply supplied, and considerable quantities of fish were dried or salted for export, the rest were simply used as manure. Fishing vessels from Yarmouth also came to Ireland on a regular basis in search of cod, ling and herring, and the families of fishermen in towns from Wexford to Kinsale barrelled large quantities of fish for the English and the continental market.

Among the new installations established around the south-west coast at this stage in the evolution of Ireland's sea fisheries were the fish palaces, ice houses, salt houses and quayside warehouses. Fish palaces, which probably pre-dated the colonial period, were particularly suited to the processing of pilchards, but fish exports at this time also included herring, cod, hake, salmon, eel, turbot and whiting. While a number of fish palaces were already operating in the creeks and inlets of the south-west coast at turn of the century, others were established in the course of the seventeenth century by new settlers from coastal areas of England, and especially from the West Country. While references to fish palaces in pre-colonial Ireland are scarce, there was a pilchard fishery off the south-west coast in the early 1590s, and it is probable that these fish were processed in local fish palaces.[66] Most fish palaces were located in sheltered bays and estuaries around the south-west coast, where fishing communities sprang up in order to service the capital-intensive pilchard industry, and to cater to the expanding herring fishing industry. As often as not, however, prosperity favoured these communities only intermittently, and the volatility of herring migrations around the Irish coast meant that this type of fishing was extremely unreliable. It has been suggested that the decline of isolated settlements around the coasts of Cork and Kerry in the latter half of the seventeenth century was not so much due to civil unrest as to the disappearance herring and pilchard from offshore waters.[67] 'Colonial' involvement in more substantial fishing ports such as Kinsale, Youghal and Waterford was already evident in the 1580s, when these towns already had sizeable fishing communities. Foreign fishermen who 'off-loaded' large quantities of fish to be processed by local families regularly visited these towns at the end of the sixteenth century, when Youghal and Kinsale had populations of around 3,000 inhabitants. The 'intrusive settlement' of tenants and fishermen around the coast of Munster, south Leinster and the eastern fringes of Ulster at this stage certainly contributed to the commercialisation of sea fishing off large stretches of coastline. This was particularly noticeable in the south of Ireland in coastal towns such as Waterford, Kenmare, Youghal and Kinsale, where Cromwellian families were to play a significant role in the development of enclave economies heavily dependent on trade and fishing. Elsewhere in coastal Ireland, the local sea fishing industry was much more rudimentary. This was particularly the case in remote districts around the north-west coast, where, for centuries, local fishermen simply beached their boats on sandy shores, or used the mouths of larger rivers as harbours.

Fish palaces were the very nerve-centres of many small fishing ports in the south-west of Ireland in the early colonial period. Here, herring, pilchards, sprats and sometimes even cod, were layered with salt in four-foot piles, prior to being stuffed into huge wooden casks and exported to England, France, Italy and the Americas.[68] At particularly busy times in the fishing season, women

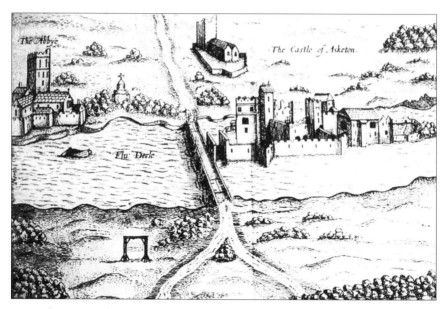

17 Askeaton Castle and Abbey, Co. Limerick, in the seventeenth century. Situated on the banks of the River Deel, this seat of Desmond power had access to the resources of land, rivers, lakes and coast (from Stafford, *Pacata Hibernia* (1633)).

and children were also engaged in the task of salting and crating fish. Contemporary sources state that fishing settlements around the south and east coasts provided employment to considerable numbers of female 'fish gutters', in addition to bakers, brewers, coopers, ship carpenters, smiths, net-makers, rope-makers, pulley-makers and many others.[69] The larger of these coastal towns often had the right to make by-laws, try minor offences and otherwise enforce law and order. As often as not, they had to augment the harvest from the sea by growing potatoes, cabbage and turnips, and keeping a small number of livestock and poultry around their settlements. Larger coastal towns also functioned as market centres, serving their surrounding hinterlands, while also operating as nucleated settlements in a seaborne world of commerce, fishing, smuggling and piracy. A subsequent chapter will show that in many areas around the Irish coast, the spoils of smuggling and piracy were sold off to merchants, especially innkeepers, a practice that continued right down to the middle of the seventeenth century. Pirates and smugglers brought in fine wines, brandies, tobacco, salt, spices and weaponry, which they exchanged for wool, linen, leather goods and animal pelts.[70] Their links with other towns and cities around the maritime fringes of Ireland, Britain and indeed continental Europe were crucial to the survival of these coastal towns. Larger towns and cities such as Dublin, Drogheda, Waterford, Wexford, Limerick and Galway acted as points of interchange between Britain and northern Europe on the one hand, and continental Europe on the other. In this manner, whole tracts of rural Ireland were integrated into an extensive arena of primitive accumulation that was firmly anchored in port cities and fishing towns strung out around the Irish coast.

The consolidation of the mercantilist state system in the fifteenth and sixteenth centuries meant that coastal enclaves along the south and east coasts were drawn into a much more commercialised world of sea-going trade, fishing and resource exploitation. The protracted process of colonisation penetrated the social fabric of this part of the country, giving its coastal towns and fishing communities a solid social structure from as early as the fifteenth century.[71] Discussing the status of sea fishing in Gaelic Ireland at this stage, Nicholls has stated that

> The fisheries carried on off the southern and western coasts of Ireland were of great economic importance during the late medieval period, and brought in large revenue to the lords of adjacent coasts in the form of fishing dues, charges for the use of harbours and of drying grounds for nets and for fish itself, etc. The fishery itself, however, was always carried on by foreign vessels, although Irish merchants might on occasion take a stake in it ... The fisheries off Hook Head in the south-east, those centred on Baltimore in the south-west, and the herring fishery off Aran Island in Co. Donegal are noted as being especially valuable.[72]

Nicholls and others have suggested that the abundance of rich fertile grassland then militated against any significant exploitation of Ireland's sea fisheries, at least by the indigenous Irish. In arguing thus, he underestimates the direct and indirect importance role of fishing to Gaelic Ireland, and treats colonial conquest as a purely *territorial phenomenon*. Most writers have failed to note that the informal colonisation of *Irish waters* by foreign fishing fleets long pre-dated the more formal plantation of the *Irish countryside* in the sixteenth and seventeenth centuries. The maritime expansion of Britain, Spain, Holland and France into the waters around Ireland deeply affected all those who made their living from these seas in the run-up to the plantations. Gaelic overlords especially felt the effects of these maritime intrusions. So too did coastal communities that were even then directly or indirectly dependent upon fishing, or were otherwise engaged in the exploitation of the shoreline resources. As power and influence passed to colonial authorities in the late fifteenth and early sixteenth centuries, Gaelic overlords and dynastic families in many of the country's coastal regions were forced to relinquish their rights to offshore fishing, including their rights to trade in fish and collect tribute from foreign fleets. As a result, an increasingly powerful class of merchants, colonial settlers and venture capitalists acquired control over significant segments of Ireland's maritime economy. These groups used their power and influence in order to establish corporate control over port cities and fishing centres, especially along the east and south coasts. In so doing, they consolidated their grip on a vibrant trade in such items as animal skins, hides, timber, salmon, eels, herrings, pike, turbot and hake. Thus, while large tracts of late medieval rural Ireland exhibited high degrees of regional autonomy and self-sufficiency, the east and south coasts were already locked into an extensive maritime world of trade and resource exploitation. By the start of the seventeenth century, merchants and colonial *parvenus* also began to occupy new positions of power in these regions. Inshore and deep-sea fishing, together with the trade in fish and other natural resources, were the basis of their newly acquired wealth. In the course of the seventeenth century, this disparate group of merchants, town burgesses and venture capitalists also monopolised the collection of tolls and 'murage' payments (that is, payment imposed at point of entry into harbours). Fishermen around the east and south coasts in particular were long accustomed to paying 'murage' taxes on entering Irish ports and coastal towns and cities. In fifteenth-century Galway and Waterford, for example, boats were subject to murage taxes on passing the walls of their respective cities. Such high levies did not deter foreigners from entering Irish waters, and murage payments and other tolls may have been used to improve harbours, build quays and ware-houses, fortify coastal towns and villages and provide the basic infrastructure for the development of fishing. Ports such as Dublin, Drogheda, Waterford and Galway, and even smaller towns such as Carrickfergus, Dungarvan, Youghal, Kinsale and Wexford, were all permitted to raise taxes and impose customs payments on fishermen in order to improve their fortifications and enhance harbour facilities. For these and other reasons, a number of coastal districts in the east and south of the country experienced a veritable urban revolution in the fifteenth and sixteenth centuries. This manifested itself in the expansion of existing port facilities and the establishment of new fishing communities in more isolated tracts of coastline. Later in the colonial period, landlords and local merchants were instrumental in the establishment of rudimentary whaling stations, pilchard fisheries and herring fishing stations. This resulted in the development of important sea fisheries at Arranmore, Inver and Inch Island in Co. Donegal; Inishkea, Achill Island, Blacksod Bay and Belmullet in Co. Mayo; Cape Clear, Baltimore, Dursey and Roaringwater Bay in Co. Cork; and Kenmare and Ballinskelligs in Co. Kerry. In post-plantation Ulster also, a string of new ports emerged alongside improvements in existing ports at Carlingford, Ardglass, Carrickfergus and Coleraine, all of which were engaged in sea fishing prior to the introduction of new settlers in the seventeenth century. In the aftermath of the plantation, small ports such as Newcastle, Dundrum, Donaghadee, Bangor and Hollywood also rose to prominence, while further down the coast, towns such as Drogheda, Malahide, Skerries, Rush, Dalkey, Arklow and Wicklow matured into fishing ports of some considerable significance.[73] Many of the older Viking and Anglo-Norman settlements on the south-east coast experienced renewed growth at this stage, both as a result of the commercialisation of offshore fisheries, and because the influx of new settlers added new vigour to sea fishing along this coast. Larger ports such as Waterford, Arklow, Drogheda and Dundrum exported large quantities of fish to Britain, and to the American colonies. Fishing ports to the west of Kinsale tended to be much smaller and had poorer harbour facilities, and many grew up around fish palaces and rudimentary harbours in the late sixteenth and early seventeenth centuries. Tiny coastal settlements such as Baltimore, Bantry, Castlehaven, Crookhaven, Courtmacsherry and Leamcon in West Cork thus owed their origins to a combination of strategic and economic factors, and benefited considerably from the commercialisation of sea fishing in the colonial period.[74] Here, as on the west coast, coastal towns were probably far less orderly than landlord villages and planned towns in the interior of the country. Since many of them were also dependent upon the volatile shoals of herring and mackerel that migrated around the south-west coast, they regularly underwent periods of expansion and contraction.[75]

By the close of the sixteenth century, the export market for Irish fish was in serious decline. Customs house accounts for a number of Cornish and West Country towns show that large quantities of fish were now coming in from Newfoundland, rather than Ireland. Indeed, when cod fishing took off on the Newfoundland coast in the sixteenth century, it was conducted with all the enthusiasm of a gold rush.[76] Of all fish in the very large order of *gadiforms*, including pollock, haddock, whiting and hake, the Atlantic cod was the largest and had the whitest meat. For that reason, it was the choice fish for curing. By the mid-sixteenth century, cod accounted for 60 per cent of all fish eaten in

Europe, and this figure would remain stable for the next 200 years.[77] The expansion of the Newfoundland fisheries at the end of the sixteenth century led to a radical remapping of fishing ports all along the Atlantic fringe of Western Europe. However, most of Ireland's fishing ports were too under-developed, or too far off the beaten track, to really benefit from this new phase in the commercialisation of the North Atlantic fisheries. In the days of slow sailing, a western location was considered a tremendous advantage to towns on the Atlantic fringe of Europe, and Ireland's maritime geography seemed to suggest that the country was ideally situated to take advantage of the opportunities thrown open by these highly lucrative fisheries. However, these geographical advantages were offset by the lack of political will and investment, and most Irish ports did not have distant water fleets capable of fishing off the Newfoundland coast. That said, however, Irish fishermen and rural emigrants from the south-east of the country did participate in these great cod fisheries. Many of these were poorly paid deckhands who experienced the most appalling conditions both on board fishing vessels, and at onshore fishing stations along the Newfoundland coast. Mannion has pointed out that Newfoundland-bound fishing vessels from Devonshire in the seventeenth century regularly

> called at Waterford in late spring, and provided passage for several thousand young men engaged in the cod-fishing season off the Newfoundland banks. This spawned the first organised mass movement of labour to far-away shores, the migrant worker, 'spailpin' or 'navvy', leaving Waterford in spring and returning in November. The 3,000–5,000 young men were amply rewarded for the season – but the fact that so many would undertake a hazardous voyage in conditions of severe hardship that would last a month or more merely for seasonal work gives a fair indication of how harsh and intolerable the conditions at home were.[78]

In his detailed study of the role of Irish emigrants in the Newfoundland cod industry, he has shown that the Nova Scotia ports where they settled were spawned by the transient fishery and resident operations of Irish-based fishing fleets operating out of the south-east of Ireland from the sixteenth to the eighteenth century. Thus, according to Mannion, Irish migration to Newfoundland at this time

> was intimately related to the exploitation of the Newfoundland fishery. This was organised by merchants and their agents, many of whom

18 Painting of Waterford in 1746 by C.J. Downey. A renowned nursery
for fishermen and seamen, Waterford in the eighteenth century was one of
the few Irish cities to benefit from close contact with the Newfoundland cod
industry (from Downey, *The story of Waterford* (1914)).

originated in the south-east of Ireland. Indeed, Catholic merchants,
barred from a wide array of private enterprises as a result of the enact-
ment of penal legislation, may have found lucrative outlets for investment
in the national and international fishing industry in the seventeenth and
eighteenth centuries. A number of these Irish merchant families accumulated great wealth as a result of their fishing enterprises, and dominated
the political landscape of Newfoundland for generations.[79]

Right from the start, these early Irish migrations to coastal Newfoundland were
well-organised and comparatively successful fishing projects that were highly
dependent upon this trans-Atlantic fishery. The early fishing expeditions
matured into much more sophisticated operations in the late seventeenth and
early eighteenth centuries, when fishing boats from Devonshire called at
Waterford and other south-eastern ports to collect provisions and manpower
for the Newfoundland summer cod-fishing season. By the end of the eighteenth
century, a handful of merchant families from around Wexford 'owned more
than a dozen deep-sea fishing vessels that linked together Spain, Ireland and
Newfoundland in a triangular network of a trade based primarily on cod, that
lasted down to the early nineteenth century'. At the height of the Newfoundland
fishery, two Irish-owned firms, namely the Sweetmans and the Saunders,

dominated the Irish cod industry in Nova Scotia, where they employed around 500 fishermen in 140 fishing vessels, in addition to some 250 workers engaged in a wide variety of fish-related onshore operations.[80] By then, English authorities in Newfoundland were increasingly worried about the growing influence of Irish fish merchants and fishermen in the region's rich cod industry. They specifically complained about the number of unlicensed Irish fishing vessels operating from French-occupied harbours in and around Placentia Bay, while one official in particular complained that fishing boats from Ireland were bringing with them 'a number of Irish servants, some of whom they leave in the winter and by that means stake out the very best of the ancient fishing rooms'.[81]

ENGLISH OPPOSITION TO CONTINENTAL FISHERMEN

The foreign exploitation of Ireland's fisheries was a constant source of irritation to English fish merchants and fishermen in the pre-colonial period. Government officials also looked on offshore fishing by native and continental fishermen as a convenient cover for seditious intercourse that could lead to the importation of arms into some of the country's more intractable coastal regions. Certainly by the seventeenth century, it was widely believed that the continental fish-trade linking Ireland to mainland Europe was in breach of colonial policy in Ireland, and many felt that it also posed a threat to local fishermen and fish merchants in the south and west of England.[82] Ireland's sea fisheries, it was argued, were major commercial enterprises whose profits should accrue to English authorities, rather than enriching Gaelic lords and continental fishermen. The evasion of customs duties, and tributary payments made to Gaelic lords, also rankled with tax officials of the crown. In addition to this, the significant gains lost to English fish merchants from trade with Holland, Spain, France and Portugal were an even greater source of irritation. Thus, an Act of 1465 sought to 'close' the seas around Ireland to all but British fishermen, but this appears to have had little effect, as continental fishermen continued to operate in Irish waters without much molestation until well into the age of formal colonisation. In an effort to impose a stricter policy of *mare clausum*, another Act of 1535 sought to have all 'foreign' fishing craft banned from Irish waters until such time as they 'had been duly entered in the customs books'.[83] The trade in fish between the south of Ireland and the south-west of England in particular drew complaints from English fishermen from the mid-sixteenth century onwards. For example, in 1543, a number of fish merchants in the

Bristol area sought protection from cheap fish imports sold by the 'men of Erlond' in 'the countrys of Gloucester, Somerset, Monmouthe, Dorset, Haffordwest, Worssiter, Waryke, Shropoesher and Wiltes'.[84] Complaints were regularly made throughout the century regarding 'the injury' done by herring fishermen from Ireland to towns along the south coast of England. In some cases, the chief complaint about Spanish fishermen in Irish waters was that they paid 'no dues to the Queen's Majestie'.

At other times, French and Spanish fishermen were accused of over-fishing, thereby leaving no fish for the English, Scottish and Welsh fishermen who fished these same waters. In 1515, it was argued that Breton fishermen were conveying so many 'salmonds, herrings, dry lengs, haaks and other fishe' out of Ireland that 'they leve none within the land to vitall the king's subjects here'.[85] English authorities particularly complained about the number of Spanish fishing craft operating off the south and west coasts. It was estimated that Spain kept some '600 sail of ships, and barques for fishing only' off the south of Ireland in 1570s, when Sir Humphrey Gilbard called for Spanish fleets to be cleared from their stronghold in and around Baltimore Harbour. Emphasising the lawless state of coastal Ireland, he pointed out that the 'wild Irish and savage people' on this stretch of coastline regularly cut the cables of foreign fishing vessels, thus causing boats filled with fish to run ashore where they could be plundered. He further insisted that the English crown should police Irish waters with a view to outlawing such acts of piracy, and demanded that the Spaniards and 'Biscayans' who fished off the Blasket Islands should set aside one sixth of their catches as taxes to the crown.[86] In 1580, Lord Justice Pelham was still demanding that Munster's 'creeks and havens' should be fortified 'to prevent the commodities which the Irish make by entertaining pirates, and also Portingalls and Spaniards that yearly come to fish in these harbours, bringing with them powder, muskets, targets, swords and other munition'.[87] Giving evidence at Kinsale in 1611, one Robert Cogan stated that this Munster town had one of the best harbours in the kingdom, and pointed out that catches of herrings, hake and pilchards were enriching many continental fishermen. By the 1690s, one commentator stated that the cargoes of salmon, herrings and pilchards that were transported from Ireland to the ports of Spain and Venice were 'so great … that they would startle the common people'.[88] Earlier in the same century, in a letter to the English privy council, the lord justice complained that Dutch and French fishermen alone were earning between £15,000 and £20,000 from pilchard fishing off the south coast.[89] Another commentator, writing in the 1620s, argued that 'as fishing in general in Ireland runs for the most parts into the hands of strangers', no foreigners should be permitted to fish in Irish waters, or to land their catches at Irish ports, without first being licensed to crown authorities. The fact that continental fishermen were still paying no customs duties to the crown on the large catches that they took out of Irish waters was clearly a source of annoyance to early colonial authorities. In 1623, one observer stated that 'most of the income from fishing along the Irish coast is now enjoyed by foreigners, who fish upon these coasts and carry all away and pay no custom to the king for the same'. He added that 'between 500 and 600' continental fishing vessels, all 'deep-laden with fish' caught in Irish waters, regularly descended on the British coast, and took away huge quantities fish 'without yielding any custom, impost or any other advantage to the king'. Insisting that the sea fisheries of Ireland and England 'belong as property to these islands as the river fishes do', he demanded that those who exploited them should pay 'regal duties' and taxes to the English crown.[90] Still, however, continental fishermen continued to be a source of irritation to English fishing fleets well into the seventeenth century. In 1671, Robert Southwell, whose family had a stake in the lucrative pilchard fishery, complained of the 'injurious effects' of French fishermen on the valuable herring, pilchard and mackerel fisheries off the south-west of Ireland. According to Southwell

> About thirty to forty French fishing boats are come to this coast, each of 30–40 tons burden, having very long strings and rafts of nets, which they call 'mackerel nets'. They have both herring and mackerel nets; the mackerel they place uppermost next the ropes and the herring under the same raft and joined together, each boat having 100 nets and about 30–40 men carries out in length about 2 miles. By these long and unlawful nets, they break and destroy all the great shoals of fish on this coast, to the great destruction of the fishing trade here and particularly of the pilchard fishing in the West of Ireland, set forth at very great charges of the undertakers and of the hookers and fishermen of this town, consisting of 60–80 boats, and also those of Youghal and Dungarvan, to their great disheartening and impoverishment.[91]

The exertions of Irish fishermen at this stage were hampered by colonial restrictions, and by the commercial jealousy of English fishermen and fish merchants. In an effort to eliminate competition from French fishermen, and to defend against the threat posed by pirates in large stretches of the Irish coast, a petition of 1670 called for 'two frigates of the king' to be stationed off the coast of Munster. By then, however, the continental fishing vessels that fished these waters were less and less answerable to Gaelic overlords in coastal Ireland, and were increasingly subject to the regulatory authority of the crown. Colonial control of tithe collections and other customary payments contributed to the demise of Gaelic lordships in coastal Ireland and ultimately resulted in the exclusion of continental fishing fleets from Irish waters. The extension of the crown's authority to coastal Ireland contributed to the Anglicisation of Ireland's sea fisheries, protected English and Scottish fishing fleets from continental rivals, fostered the growth of an intrusive merchant class in coastal Ireland, and made it increasingly difficult for poorly equipped Irish boats to compete with Scottish and English fishing fleets in waters that were now only nominally Irish. In so doing, it allowed colonial settlers, fishermen and merchants to acquire a greater degree of control over the *maritime* resources of Gaelic Ireland. Thus, prior to the formal colonisation of the country in the seventeenth century, fish tithes and other customary payments were important sources of income for many towns and cities in coastal Ireland. Here, as in other arenas of 'primitive accumulation' around the coast of Great Britain, local authorities regulated trade, outlawed piracy and smuggling, protected commercial fishermen in the country's inshore waters, and encouraged the export of a wide range of agricultural and maritime resources.[92] This resulted in the growing dominance of port towns and coastal cities, and contributed to the marginalisation of indigenous traders and local fishermen who found it increasingly difficult to compete with 'outsiders' in the new environment fostered by the development of capitalist relations of production and exchange. There were two main ways in which these new rising social classes consolidated their position in Gaelic coastal Ireland. Firstly, they exploited the wealth and confiscated the property of traditional power-holders without offering anything in return. This occurred when traditional owners of property, including those with monopolistic rights to exploit natural resources such as timber, game and fish, were either pushed aside by colonial intruders, or opted to exchange power for money in the new social order. Secondly, the consolidation of colonial authority followed on from the confiscation of the resources of churches, monasteries and dynastic Gaelic families in the sixteenth and seventeenth centuries. Among the more valuable resources to pass into colonial ownership at this stage were the fishing rights to many rivers, lakes and sea estuaries. In addition to this, colonial authorities and individual landlords acquired control over fishing weirs and fish-traps, coastal harbours, fish palaces, processing facilities, quayside warehouses and a whole range of other marine resources.

The chapter that follows examines the broad issues of fish marketing and the role of fish merchants in the early modern period. It begins with a discussion on the development and management of fish 'shambles', or fish markets, in the sixteenth and seventeenth centuries, focusing specifically on the gentrification of urban space and the marginalisation of fishermen and fish sellers in Irish towns and cities. This is followed by a more general discussion on the policing of coastal waters and state-sponsored strategies for controlling piracy and smuggling in the seas around Ireland.

CHAPTER FIVE

Imposing order on the maritime fringe

FISH SHAMBLES AND THE GENTRIFICATION OF URBAN SPACE

Public hygiene was first taken seriously in European cities in the fifteenth and sixteenth centuries. The public thoroughfares of well-managed towns and cities were then regularly cleaned, pigs and other farm animals were prohibited from roaming the streets, and home-owners were prevented from housing these animals in their gardens. Authorities in many European cities, especially busy ports and thriving fishing towns, kept a watchful eye on all those who traded in meat, fish, dairy produce and cereals. This was to ensure that the produce of land and sea would be sold in good condition, and at prices fixed by city fathers, rather than by farmers, fishermen and small merchants. In fifteenth-century Venice, for example, only fishermen over fifty were permitted to sell fish, and anyone caught selling fish considered unfit for human consumption could be publicly flogged. On payment of a hefty fine, the culprit could be imprisoned for a month and was forbidden to trade in fish for four years. Venetian authorities were especially concerned with public hygiene and the prevention of plagues that ravaged the city on average every eight to ten years. While the source of these plagues was unknown, they were generally thought to be associated with refuse and filth that accumulated on the city's streets, not least in canals where the urban poor were forced to scavenge for food. A whole range of measures was therefore adopted to prevent street sellers, shopkeepers and fishmongers from throwing rubbish onto the streets, and otherwise disposing of waste in the city's waterways. Particularly harsh measures were implemented to ensure that fish markets and meat stalls were kept in a clean and healthy condition.[1]

Purpose-built fish markets or 'shambles' were built in Irish towns and cities at various times from the sixteenth to the nineteenth century. While fish shambles controlled the sale of fish in coastal towns and cities, holding weirs and salmon traps were widely used to supply fish in the Irish countryside. There was also a whole variety of often highly informal arrangements for meeting the demand for fresh fish from the sea and rivers. Many coastal dwellers simply fished off rocks, or from cotts and other small boats, while poaching in rivers and weirs was such a problem that laws were enacted against it as far back as the ninth century. Wealthier landowners and other dignitaries in the Irish countryside could procure freshwater fish from their own weirs and fish-traps. Those who lived in or near busy fishing ports could avail of the open selling of fish on the shorefront and riverbank, and could also buy fish on selected days at country markets. Street vendors often met boats as they arrived in harbour, bought up their catches and sold fish openly in the streets. Thus, for example, eels trapped in weirs in the Lough Gur area 'were sent direct to Limerick market or taken by Meggy-the-eels, an itinerant vendor who came from Bruff to buy 'the take', which she peddled from house to house'.[2] In the of the seventeenth century, many local authorities took measures to prevent the indiscriminate 'hawking' of fish on city streets, and confined street vendors to designated fish shambles. Hereafter, the association of 'hawking' with vagrancy meant that the practice was forbidden, at least in more respectable neighbour-hoods, and new legislation confined fish vendors to specific streets and public places. This made it easier for city fathers to tax fish merchants and control the quality of their produce. The fact that fish and meat shambles had to be constructed in the first place was an indication of the sheer volume of fish, shellfish, meat and poultry being sold in Irish towns in the centuries before the Great Famine. Moreover, fish and shellfish probably held more prominent positions in the diets of people in Ireland in the centuries before the Famine than they did in the late nineteenth and early twentieth century.

Rules and regulations governing the sale of fish and other meats were intimately connected with the civilising mission of the bourgeoisie in many European towns and cities. Elias has suggested that the entire notion of 'civilisation' in seventeenth-century Europe confidently expressed the self-consciousness of an emerging bourgeoisie in relation to other sectors of society, not least the urban and rural poor.[3] The category 'civilisation' encapsulated the specific character of bourgeois society, including everything that set it apart from primitive societies abroad, and the 'great unwashed' at home. As such, it referred not only to artistic accomplishments and scientific achievements, but also to social attitudes towards public hygiene and health, dress codes, manners of speech, private and public morality, and all the social arrangements for the preparation, sale and consumption of foods. Crucially for Elias, the 'civilising process' entailed the gradual elimination of external constraints on human behaviour and their replacement by internal systems of moral restraint for regulating the baser instincts and cleaning up society. Changes to the material and moral structures of everyday life over what Braudel termed the *longue durée*, could be observed through changing attitudes to private and communal property, not least in attitudes towards work, leisure, dress, idleness, cleanliness, good manners, health and disease. They could equally be observed in changing attitudes towards vagrancy, 'foul language', aggression, filth, cruelty and suffering.[4] On account of their association with 'ribaldry', lawlessness, filth, sweat and 'unpleasant odours', groups such as fishmongers, street vendors, vagrants, butchers, cattle drovers, horse dealers and all those who 'fouled up' city streets, were especially prone to the lowering of thresholds of tolerance that separated these from refined sectors society. As the sensibilities of the latter became more 'sophisticated', their tolerance of unsanitary conditions, sweaty bodies, filthy wastrels and putrefaction was similarly lowered. Many of those who serviced the early modern city, including sewermen, fish gutters, street sweepers, rag gatherers, drain cleaners, 'dredging gangs' and all those who worked with slime, rubbish, excrement and offal, were lumped together and treated almost as untouchables. As 'comrades in stench', they were the subjects of city reformers, social engineers and urban planners. Obsessive images of 'nauseous bilge' and 'foul-smelling bodies' also informed urban authorities' perceptions of the 'putridity' surrounding the 'lower orders'.[5] The novelist Patrick Suskind evoked the 'barely inconceivable stench' over eighteenth-century Paris in the following terms:

> The streets stank of manure, the courtyards of urine, the stairways stank of mouldering wood and rat droppings, the kitchens of spoiled cabbage and mutton fat, the unaired parlours stank of stale dust, the bedrooms of greasy sheets, damp featherbeds, and the pungently sweet aroma of chamber-pots. The stench of sulphur rose from the chimneys, the stench of caustic lyes from the tanneries, and from the slaughterhouses came the stench of congealed blood. People stank of sweat and unwashed clothes; from their mouths came the stench of rotting teeth, from their bellies that of onions, and from their bodies, if they were no longer very young, came the stench of rancid cheese and sour milk and tumorous disease. The rivers stank, the marketplaces stank, the churches stank, it stank beneath the bridges and in the palaces. The peasant stank, as did the priest, the apprentice, as did his master's wife; the whole of the aristocracy stank.[6]

Maria Kelly described living conditions in Dublin at the time of the Black Death as follows:

The conditions in which people lived in towns provided the perfect incubator for nurturing fleas and rats and facilitated the transmission of epidemics. Towns, and especially coastal trading towns, are the natural breeding habitats for the black rat, whose preferred habitation is a warm place with a temperature of 38.09 degrees centigrade. Fleas lodged in the merchandise of ships and warehouses. Dublin port provided these conditions, as did the town itself, which was similar to many European cities at this time. Streets were made of packed earth or mud, full of ruts and holes, though some streets had been paved by 1348 … Drains ran in the middle of roads. Butchers killed animals on the streets and deposited their remains on the city's streets or in the river. Complaints were constant about the dumping of waste in public places and in rivers, as well as about contaminated water supplies and noxious smells. Pigs roamed freely, mainly because almost every household kept them, and foraged among the waste dumped outside houses. The city's authorities made repeated efforts to forbid them within the city's walls, to require licences for ownership and to fine unlicensed owners, but the repetition of the ordinances suggests limited success.[7]

The stench of the poor and the disease-carrying capacity of the 'filthy wastrel' clearly acquired strong symbolic significance in the early modern city. Fear of the obtrusive presence of 'dangerous elements' and the 'foul-smelling' bodies replaced an earlier obsession with carrion and ooze as the chief threats to public hygiene. Repugnance to smell also affected attitudes towards the urban poor, and many of those who served the city with food, drink and sex. It focused particularly on street urchins, vagrants, prostitutes, the hovels of the poor, 'the filthy rags' of street vendors, and on the 'greasy and fetid sweat' that impregnated the very skin of fishermen, fishmongers and all those who worked with animals. The gathering places and homes of fishermen, fish-gutters and fish vendors were avoided because the 'emanations' from rivers, estuaries, harbours and fishing boats were considered sources of contamination. The cramped living quarters of fishermen and fish workers in particular made for unclean and unhealthy living conditions. Fourteenth-century Dublin and other coastal towns were pervaded with 'excessive and noxious stenches' emanating especially from quarters where fish were landed and gutted. City fathers in the fifteenth century complained that 'dung heaps, swine, hog sties and other nuisances in the streets, lanes and suburbs of Dublin infect the air and produce mortality, fevers and pestilences throughout that city'.[8]

Contaminated air and 'noxious stenches' were increasingly mentioned in the public records in the early modern period, and these were generally traced to manure heaps, animal corpses, decaying fish and fish offal, slaughter-houses and tanning works located within the walls of coastal towns and busy ports. If access to freshwater and sea fisheries helped reduce chronic shortages of food in Dublin, Cork, Limerick and Waterford, it also added to problems of waste disposal and contributed to the unsanitary conditions found in many urban areas. Exposed drains flowed above ground and along the sides of work-places, slaughter-houses and fish shambles, carrying their contaminated water and sewage to nearby rivers and open cesspits. Detaching the 'filthy' quarters of the urban poor from those of 'respectable' citizens was a major concern of public health inspectors. This frequently involved the 'uncrowding' of congested districts and their separation out from the rest of the city.[9] The institution-alisation of new divisions of space was central to this process of urban segregation. It also prevented the 'filthy poor', including poor fishermen and 'fish gutters', from unduly encroaching on richer neighbourhoods. While social segregation influenced poor people's use of urban space, it inevitably resulted in the damming up of 'putridity' and 'social emanations' in specific sections of the early modern city.[10]

In the case of Ireland, the 'civilising process' clearly affected attitudes towards the management of food stalls and fish markets from the fifteenth to the nineteenth century. With the establishment of designated fish and meat shambles in the country's larger towns and cities, selected streets and districts were set aside for the preparation and sale of food. In time, these were gradually protected from the elements by the construction of markets and the erection of overhanging canopies that often carried the names of the fishmongers and butchers who managed them. The streets where fish and meat were 'vented' for sale were gradually also paved, or otherwise kept clean from everything offensive to sight or smell. In the larger coastal towns and port cities of the country, the streets and lanes where fish were prepared for sale were often subdivided into stalls and allocated to individual fishmongers. The word 'shamble' initially referred to the bench or block used by butchers and fish-sellers, but was subsequently applied both to a butcher's slaughterhouse, and to any open-air market where meat, fish and agricultural produce was sold *en pleine aire*. The new purpose-built meat and fish markets allowed for the preparation and sale of fish and meat on the same site. For that reason, at least from the point of view of city officials, they were a considerable improvement on the looser arrangements of earlier centuries, when meat, fish and poultry, as

well as a whole range of other farm produce, was openly sold on the streets and
in open-air markets. These loosely organised meat and fish markets existed in
Irish cities well before the sixteenth century. A recent study of the urban street
markets of Cork has suggested that Anglo-Norman influence in this part of
Munster contributed to the economic development of fisheries and the
expansion of maritime trade all along the south and south-west coasts of
Ireland in the thirteenth and fourteenth centuries.[11] At this early stage in the
evolution of the maritime economy of the south of Ireland, small ports on the
coast of Cork were exporting a wide variety of goods, including oats, wheat,
fish, beef, pork, malt and hides, and importing wine, cloth and manufactured
utensils. Records of toll payments on a range of commodities dispatched from
Cork suggest that the city did not participate to any great extent in the overseas
trade of saltwater fish to England in the fifteenth and sixteenth centuries. Most
of this trade, together with a surreptitious trade in beef, tallow and hides, was
instead conducted between the native Irish one the one hand, and Spanish and
French merchants on the other. In the early sixteenth century, exports from the
small but industrious coastal towns of Kinsale, Youghal and Dungarvan
included animal hides, linen, wood, wooden board, oars, salmon, pike and
herrings. This 'disordered trade of aliens' was commonly conducted in 'creeks
and unhaunted ports' along the Munster coastline, and for that reason was
frowned upon by English traders who were strongly opposed to it.[12] In the
fourteenth and fifteenth centuries, fish, hides and timber were dispatched in
particularly large quantities from coastal towns in Munster and Leinster to port
cities in England and continental Europe. Salmon from Cork and other fishing
ports along the coast of Munster were exported in quantities considerable
enough to merit mention in official pronouncements in the sixteenth century.

   Given the level of trade in the port cities of the east and south coasts in
particular, it is not surprising that changes occurred in their infrastructural
arrangements for the processing and sale of animal products, fish, poultry and
agricultural produce. Fishamble Street in Dublin, the location of one of the
country's oldest fish markets, may even date to the tenth century. Known
officially as *Vicus Piscarorium* (Fishmongers' Quarters), it became Fish Street
around 1470, and Fisher Street in 1570. It was so called because it was the place
where fish were 'exposed' or 'vented' for sale to the citizens of the city.
Anciently known also as *Le Fyschamlys*, the street appears on Speed's map of
Dublin in 1610. The name Fishamble probably dates back to the start of the
fifteenth century, and excavations at Fishamble Street have provided evidence
of trade between Dublin and France that may have pre-dated the Anglo-

19 Galway fish wives on their way to market. The wives of fishermen in large seaports often had a considerable degree of financial autonomy and were responsible for the sale of fish (from O'Dowd, *Down by the Claddagh* (1993)).

Norman invasion.[13] In 1365, we find the government 'prohibiting, under penalty of imprisonment, the sale of fish anywhere in the city except in the shambles, and at a proper hour of the day'. Fishmongers sometimes engaged in the 'forestalling' or 'stockpiling' of fish, and when this happened, citizens were obliged to pay exorbitantly for it on fast days. Dublin's 'forestallers' (that is, those who held back fish when prices were low and who sold them on when prices were high) were known as *privati mercatores, broggatores, braggars* and *loders*. To remedy the problem of forestalling, four commissioners were appointed to supervise the harbours in and around Dublin, while special care was taken to ensure that all fish forwarded for sale in the city went directly to the fish shambles. The new commissioners were 'empowered to enter the houses of suspected persons, and to imprison such as were found guilty of forestalling fish'. The western side of Fishamble Street in the medieval heart of Dublin also had 'garths' (that is, gardens or tenements), some of which may have dated to the tenth century, when Dublin became, in Edmund Curtis' words, 'a real town instead of a mere fortress'.[14] Medieval Dubliners subsisted on what they produced on their own plots of land or 'garths' inside the city, supplementing the produce of the land with a whole range of saltwater and freshwater fish and shellfish from the surrounding hinterland. In 1630, the proceedings of the privy council stated that 'antientlie there was a fish market in Fishamble Street', and the shambles occupied by the fish vendors were described not as houses, but as 'voyde buildings or booths'. In the seventeenth century, butchers and possibly also fish-traders erected stalls against the church in St John's Lane in the centre of medieval Dublin. However, in 1682, several of these buildings were pulled down, having been declared a nuisance by the Court of King's Bench. After this date, the city fathers ordered that neither stalls nor shops should be erected against the church. In the late 1580s, the fish-traders of Dublin were at liberty to sell fish, but only if they 'were not injuring the mayor's market'. Other 'fishers' who sold fish in the streets of the city were obliged to set up in the newly appointed fish shambles, while 'unfree fishers' were compelled to sell their fish at prices below the free men in the market'.[15]

Smith referred to 'an excellent flesh market' in the centre of Cork that was built by the corporation for less than £50 at the end of the seventeenth century. At the start of the following century, another market was erected on the south side of the city for the selling of meal and milk.[16] A Fishamble Lane, near to present day Liberty Street, was indicated in a mid-eighteenth-century map of Cork. The riverside location of Cork's fish shambles meant that they were easy to clean and cheap to maintain. Smith described them as 'very convenient, being erected on a branch of the river, which runs through arches under the middle of the town, by which means they are kept clean, cool and sweet'.[17] These shambles were 'well supplied with fish, chiefly from Kinsale', which were sold on Wednesdays and Saturdays of every week. There was also 'a flesh market' on the north side of Cork city, and 'a market place for purchasing live cattle, particularly bullocks and cows, great numbers of which are slaughtered here during the winter season'. Smith also remarked that public walks in the city were 'very few, and not over commodious, in comparison to the number of inhabitants'. The Mall, situated in the south of the city at a short distance from the meat and fish markets, was 'most frequently used, but had little to recommend it, except for its being planted with trees'. Because this street was close to a tidal stretch of the River Lee, it was reputed to be a 'pleasant' place when the water was high, but 'equally offensive' in summer when the tide was out and the surrounding streets reeked of fish, offal and other matter. Although the Mall, Cork's most prestigious street, was still not paved in Smith's day, it was 'filled with the *beau monde* of the city, and, during assizes, with considerable numbers from the country'. Moving out from the Mall to the less salubrious Mallow Lane in the north side of Cork, Smith found this part of the city to be 'much frequented by country people, both for buying and selling their commodities'. In Blarney Street, he encountered 'an infinite number of slaughter houses' that made the city's north side 'very disagreeable'. Even then, the southern suburbs of the city had 'not as much trade' as the north side. 'The poorer sort of inhabitants' were to be found in the north side of the city where, 'notwithstanding their hard fare, coarse diet and the labour of their parents', their offspring were 'more strong, lusty and healthy, than children more tenderly reared'.[18]

Meat shambles and fish markets also featured on the urban landscapes of other Irish towns and cities from around the late seventeenth century onwards. Limerick had a 'Fish Street' in the early sixteenth century, when townspeople were also accustomed to buying fish near the Island, in the centre of the medieval city. The city's 'Fish House' was built around 1585, while its milk and meat markets were of medieval origin and were even then protected by ancient laws. There were fish stalls in Wexford as far back as the eleventh century, and the streets and lanes of this thriving coastal city 'rang with the sound of the names of foreign ports'. Companies of fishmongers were formed in a number of Irish towns and cities in the late 1500s, when more care was taken to ensure the quality of fish proffered for public sale. Unsalted fish had to be sold two days after they were landed, while in some cities, mackerel, a very oily fish, could only be sold on Sundays. Salmon from Ireland, which were greatly prized by wealthy customers at Irish fish markets, were also pickled in brine for the highly lucrative markets in London. Lampreys were a favourite fish at court festivals in medieval England.

A decree issued by Waterford town council in 1740 ordered that all fish 'intended for public sale' should be brought to the new fish market on the quay. Hucksters and other street sellers who previously sold fish openly on the streets and at the quayside were henceforth 'suffered to expose fish for sale to the public upon pain of forfeiture'. In this city, as in other coastal towns and cities, a bell ringer was employed to announce the arrival of 'parcels' of fish at quayside markets. Thus in Waterford, one John Thomas, porter at the Fish House, was instructed 'to be in constant attendance and to ring the bell upon fish coming in at any time'. He had to keep the market clean, and 'to have some staff or signal in his hand by means of which he might be known in his office'. For his 'constant and faithful attendance' at the fish-market over the years, Thomas was 'paid three shillings and three pence a week out of the city's revenue when he retired'.[19] The establishment of a new improved fish market in Waterford in 1715 had been part of a general process of gentrification that

20 Fish-workers in north Donegal in the early twentieth century. Unmarried 'herring gutters' and female fish-workers in particular were among the poorest sectors of society. They have largely remained hidden from history to this day (courtesy of Seán Beattie).

coincided with the introduction of public lighting 'for the conveniency' of the inhabitants of the city. Prior to this, the citizens of Waterford had complained 'that fish caught in the river were sold in other places besides on the Quay'.[20] In the early eighteenth century, local merchants had sent a petition to the city fathers 'pointing out that for many years, large quantities of herrings had been caught in the harbour, and that ships had been induced to come to Waterford and take away other merchandise for the sake of getting herring cheaply'. To facilitate merchants in the city, the old Custom House on the quay was pulled down and a new exchange was built on the site. The city's new 'fishboard' or fish market was established on the site of a much older fish shambles that dated to the fifteenth century. Writing in the nineteenth century, Downey described this as 'a neat, plain building, supported by arches of hewn stone'. Here also, a bell hung above the market and was 'tolled to give the inhabitants of the city notice of the arrival of fish'. Downey noted that Waterford for centuries had a 'considerable number' of coopers making barrels for packing fish, and large numbers of workers were employed curing herrings for the export market. The latter occupation provided casual employment for the 'poorer sorts' of people who would otherwise have begged or starved on the streets of the city. Another reason for the construction of the fish market was that local merchants wished to control the sale of fish in the city, and were unhappy with fishermen 'exposing' or selling fish at Duncannon, Passage West, Ballyhack and 'other places in the harbour'. The town council also offered 'a licence to fish in the harbour to foreigners, or others who would enter into a bond to take all fish they caught up to the city quay and expose it there for sale, and if any foreigners should attempt to fish without a licence, that the mayor would order a sufficient number of persons to destroy, cut or take away the nets of each boat transgressing'.[21] This deterred neither foreigners nor poachers, and a fresh remonstrance had to be issued by the city merchants in 1736, insisting that 'a boat or sloop should be fitted out to preserve the royalties and privileges of the mayor and citizens'. It was also resolved that, 'for the better encouragement of all fishermen', they should 'bring their wares to the quay where they were to be exempted from the quayage dues normally paid to the Water Bailiff'. One historian of old Waterford remarked that 'while the municipality displayed commendable anxiety for the welfare of the visitors who brought supplies of fish to the city', they were 'not unmindful' of the necessity 'to keep the fish market clean'. In 1721, it was declared that there was 'a great nuisance of fish and dirt enough to breed infection leading from St John Street to James Bayon's back gate, and that the same ought to be cleansed and the pavement mended at the expense of the inhabitants on both sides of the way and a gate to be fixed at the charge of the city'.[22] Many of the roads linking the city to the ferry at Grenagh were also repaired, thereby contributing to the gentrification of the urban environment of Waterford. Another reason for the construction of the 'fishboard' or fish shambles was that 'it was greatly to the disadvantage of fisher folk coming from Dungarvan and elsewhere by land that there was no fit place to rest themselves or their loading, or to shelter them from the injuries of the weather'.[23]

In late medieval Ireland, as in other European countries, it was an accepted axiom that fish, fowl, meat and the other necessities of life sold in marketplaces should be of reasonable quality and within reach of all sections of the population. In confining marketing to particular streets and specified market days, civil authorities, including the church, sought to monitor the quality of produce and impose their authority on traders and food producers. They particularly tried to regulate the behaviour of fish-traders and to improve standards of hygiene at open-air fish markets. In 1588, for instance, the corporation of Dublin arranged a place on Cork Hill, above Dublin Castle, where the 'free fishers' of the city were compelled to sell or 'utter' their fish. In order to participate in the new market, traders were obliged to pay the corporation the very substantial sum of £4 10*s*. for 'boards and other necessary furnishings'.[24] This also marked the beginnings of a gradual secularisation of the regulatory bodies set up to control the maritime economy, as henceforth merchants and city officials, rather than religious leaders, were increasingly responsible for the development and regulation of fisheries.[25] The city fathers in sixteenth-century Galway 'hedged in' fish sellers and street traders with an elaborate system of rules and regulations to control the market for fish and farm produce and to improve their quality.

As in towns throughout Ireland, city officials in Galway also stipulated the price of fish, bread, meat, ale, butter and practically every item of the city's food supply.[26] While these rules and regulations were supposed to benefit the entire community, including fishermen and fish merchants, they tended to favour larger merchants, and the removal of fish sellers from their traditional market places limited their ability to operate freely in the urban environment. Because they infringed on the customary rights of small traders, the new regulations were strongly opposed by poorer fishermen, farmers, street vendors and all those who purveyed food in the city. The frequency with which penalties were imposed on those who circumvented local trading laws suggests that fishermen continually tried to evade them whenever and wherever they could. One authority on trading practices in Galway at this stage argued that the net effect of the new trade laws was to give rich wholesale merchants an additional advantage over the poor traders and street sellers. The latter were often in no position to pay fines imposed by the city fathers, while the more powerful merchants regarded such fines as mere trifling sums.[27] In the event, the wealth accumulated by Galway's merchant class enhanced their social status in the city, or was used to financing public projects there. The murage payments and other tolls paid by fishermen as they passed through the city gates helped to finance harbour improvements and other quayside installations.

O'Sullivan's account of economic life in Galway in the fifteenth and sixteenth centuries shows that fish had an important role in the diet of people in this city for centuries. Half of all faunal bones found by archaeologists in medieval layers in the city were of fish, with large cod, ling, pollock and haddock being especially prominent. The majority of bones found during an excavation at Athenry Castle were of ling, cod, whiting and haddock, and it has been suggested that these may have come from a nearby port, probably from Galway. O'Sullivan has suggested that there were no less than seven market places in the late medieval city, including those that dealt in freshwater fish, sea fish, meat, cattle and horses. Galway's Little Market and Corn Market dealt in a wide variety of goods, while on certain days, local traders and fish sellers streamed into town, exchanging the produce of land and sea for commodities made the city's craft workers. The inhabitants of the surrounding countryside entered Galway through the east and west gates, bringing with them cattle, turf, wood, butter, grain, honey and poultry.

The corporation even prescribed the time of fishing in and around Galway Bay in the sixteenth century. In 1557, one Richard FitzGeffre demanded that the postern gate at the side entrance to Galway be opened night and day to allow fishing boasts and other vessels to pass in and out of the city. However, the mayor and council emphatically refused his request, deeming it 'very discomodyus and perells [perilous] to this town to have such a gape or dore so oppenid in such dangerus tymes'. They ordered that 'such fishers as be appoynctid to fish shall go befor the said gattes be closed or shute for their ffishinge and so to remayn withoute all night untill the mornings that the said gates be openid'. The corporation always kept a watchful eye on all sea-going traffic entering the town 'with a view to the convenience of the inhabitants and the due preservation of public order'. Market officials acting in the name of the town's mayor were particularly anxious to prevent 'forestalling' or stockpiling of goods, and kept a close watch on weights and measures. They appraised the quality of meat, fish and fowl at local markets, superintended their disposal and regulated prices of products sold in the city. When a ship arrived at the port, the mayor, acting with the bailiffs or two or three of the most 'discreet men' of the town, called before him the merchant to whom the cargo was consigned, as well as the sailors of the ship, and obtained from them on oath the exact prices of the goods on board and the costs of transportation. Only then did he fix a price for fish, and other such goods and wares that were destined for the town's markets. Anyone departing from these regulations was severely punished. The penalties imposed included fines and 'sometimes even forfeiture of goods was visited upon all persons who, by trying to circumvent the law, put their private gain before the good of the community'.[28] Galway's old fish market had fallen into such a disreputable state by the close of the eighteenth century that it 'proved no inconsiderable annoyance to the public'. Laneways in its vicinity were 'frequently impeded, and the smell of fish and filth [was] often insupportable'. At the start of the nineteenth century, General Meyrick, who was in command of the market district, 'induced some of the principal inhabitants to enter into a subscription for the purpose of providing another fish market, and a convenient site on one of the quays, near the river, was

21 Fish-sellers from the fishing settlement of the Claddagh, Galway,
on their way to market in the early nineteenth century
(from Halls, *Ireland: its scenery, character etc.* (1841–3)).

chosen, where it was soon after erected'. The new market contained 'several
sheds, a pump and porter's lodge', and, according to Hardiman, 'no other
similar market in the kingdom was better supplied with fish of every
description'. An inscription over the entrance of the market read: 'This fish
market was built by subscription, under the patronage of general Meyrick,
who, during his residence here, acquired the praise of a grateful people, for his
admiration of justice and benevolence'. Nevertheless, Hardiman noted that 'the
old Poissardes loudly vociferated against this innovation, and refused to bring
their fish to the new market until coercion was resorted to … [and they]
obstinately continued to expose their fish for sale in the street outside the
marketgate, to the great annoyance of the passengers'.[29]

Improvements to fish markets and fish ports were not confined to larger
towns and cities. The process of gentrification also extended to riverside towns
and coastal areas under the control of enlightened landowners. Thus prior to
its improvement by the Duke of Devonshire at the start of the nineteenth
century, the small port of Dungarvan was considered a 'crowded place with
miserable houses, irregular in appearance, without any or at all events an
efficient police'. For that reason, it was felt that the town 'deserved the

reproachful epithets which travellers universally bestowed upon it'. There were no regular market places or public water-works in the town, and no bridge to link the riverside town to its hinterland. The lack of a bridge meant that there was 'no way of passing from the town to the Waterford side of the river, except by a ferry boat or, as was generally the case with the lower classes, by fording the river at low water'. It was pointed out that this latter custom, 'particularly as practised by females, gave rise to ridiculous and indelicate jests, which served to impress upon travellers an unfavourable opinion of the inhabitants of the town'. The rich sea fisheries off Dungarvan were scarcely exploited when the duke of Devonshire directed his attention to the improvement of the town and its outlying district. His first 'great work' involved the building of 'a new bridge across the river, at a little distance above the town, where it should not interfere with the approach of the shipping'. A neat square and handsome street were then built to connect the town with the bridge, and this 'served to make an opening to the penetralia of the place'. Reservoirs of clean water were also established and, what were hitherto unknown in Dungarvan, marketplaces for the sale of fish and meat were also added to the town. As a result of these and other improvements, the sea fisheries off the southern coast of Ireland became 'a nursery for seamen' and afforded employment 'to a superabundant population'. At the same time, they yielded 'an ample supply of nutritious food' and 'presented to the enlightened statesman a wide field for the exercise of political sagacity'.[30]

POPULAR PERCEPTIONS OF FISHERMEN AND FISHING PORTS

From the seventeenth century onwards, fishermen, fish sellers, 'fish-gutters' and many of those associated with the fish-trade were considered a social category set apart from bourgeois society. This was especially the case in port towns and cities where these groups were associated with uncouthness, ribaldry and lack of respect for many of the mores governing respectable settled society. One writer traced the roots of growing social distance between fisher folk and the rest of society to 'their narrow sordid shelters, the unseemliness that surrounds and penetrates them, their life in contact with filth which they have neither the time nor the means to get rid of, and which even their education has not taught them to fear'.[31] Another authority on late medieval Dublin noted how the thatch and wattle houses of Fishamble Street, some of which dated back to the twelfth century, were positioned with their long axis at right angles to the roadway, thus giving access to the rear of these dwellings through the actual house, rather than by a pathway running alongside.[32] The thatched windowless structures that housed Dublin's early fishing communities had post-and-wattle walls, with smoke from their central hearths escaping through the roof. Like the abodes of poor craft-workers, they occupied long narrow plots and presented their gable-ends to the street-front. The back gardens of these houses were used for a variety of purposes – as latrines and rubbish dumps, for storage and the keeping of animals, and for the growing of fruit, herbs and vegetables.[33] To this list we could certainly add the storage of fish and fishing gear, as well as boat-building and repair, net-making and the preparation of long lines for fishing.

Given prevailing prejudices against street vendors and those connected with the sale of fish, meat and fowl, it is easy to imagine how fisher folk in Ireland's major cities could be discouraged from bringing their 'debauched customs' and 'bodily odours' into the more respectable quarters of their respective cities. In medieval Wexford, the marketplace for fish and other produce was 'situated just outside the town wall within convenient distance of the monastic enclosure and settlement'.[34] The marketplace and the monastic settlement were situated within 200m of the shoreline of the medieval town, along a road that followed the route of present-day Abbey Street. Similarly, an early plantation map for the city of Londonderry shows the fish shambles just inside the walls, but in a separate street near the back of the walled city close to present-day Bishop Street.

For occupational reasons, but also on account of strong prevailing social attitudes that led to fisher folk being perceived as unruly and uncouth, fishermen and fish workers in general were often confined to the littoral margins of coastal towns and cities. In many instances, they would remain in these occupational enclaves right down to the beginning of the twentieth century. As far back as 1371, authorities in Dublin attempted to deny freedom of movement to fishermen and fish sellers because of their 'continuous befoulment' of that city. As Lydon has pointed out, 'the over-crowded conditions, the large numbers of animals which wandered the streets, the killing and cleaning of animals, fish and poultry in the open air, the lack of latrines or lavatory facilities in most houses meant that the streets and public highways of medieval Dublin 'quickly became filthy, smelly and sometimes impassable'.[35] In an effort to regulate standards of hygiene on the city's streets, the municipality made a series of provisions for fairs and fish markets to be located well away from respectable businesses and residential areas. Special bye-laws were passed to make life tolerable for those living in the city, and a whole range of sanitation laws was gradually introduced throughout the fourteenth and fifteenth centuries to protect the health of those living in well-off areas. 'Articles of grievance' brought before the courts regularly demanded that streets should be cleaned at least twice a week. The frequency of these bye-laws, as well as the complaints that prompted them, suggest that the problems of urban sanitation, including those associated with the gutting and sale of fish and the slaughtering of farm animals, were not easily remedied. One regulation stipulated that each house-holder in Dublin 'must cleanse the portion of the street before his own door, under penalty of twelve pence'. Similarly, in other Irish towns and port cities, bye-laws were introduced to eradicate filth from the streets and improve the sanitary condition of the built environment. Every house-holder in Kilkenny was obliged 'to cleanse the pavement against his house and this twice a week; that is, on Wednesday and Saturday'. The keeping of pigs in towns and cities was a perennial source of annoyance. In 1489, a letter complaining of unsanitary conditions in Dublin stated that

> The king has been informed that dung heaps, swine, pigsties and other nuisances in the streets, lanes and suburbs of Dublin infect the air and produce mortality, fevers and pestilence throughout the city. Many citizens and sojourners have thus died in Dublin. The fear of pestilence prevents from the coming thither of lords, ecclesiastics and lawyers. Great detriments thence arise to his majesty, as well as dangers to his subjects and impediments to his business. The king commands the mayor and bailiffs to cause forthwith the removal of all swine, and to have the streets and lanes free from ordure, so as to prevent loss of life from pestilineal inhalations.[36]

In considering the overall condition of hygiene in medieval Dublin, Lydon concluded that the city 'was dirty, overcrowded, unhealthy, and a dangerous place to live'.[37] Nevertheless, people did manage to live and work in and around the city. Houses were small, dark and damp, with few if any windows. For that reason, they were also full of smoke from fires that in most cases burned in the middle of the floor. Dirt was everywhere, especially underfoot, and rats and mice abounded. Rushes and straw made poor floor covering, especially when it became dirty or wet. Most people slept on beds of bracken, devoured by fleas and bedbugs. The conviction that disease in general was caused by filth and decaying flesh, including rotting fish and other offal, and then spread through the air, made city authorities particularly vigilant about the slaughtering of animals and gutting of fish in city's laneways and side streets. In 1459, Dublin's municipality issued an ordinance that 'every fisher that hath a board in the fish shambles, and casteth cuts under their boards after they have done their market, shall pay a groat (4*d.*) as often times as they be found guilty thereof'. In Kilkenny, a decree of 1337 proclaimed that 'if anyone be found washing clothing or the intestines of animals or anything else in the fountains of the said town they shall be forfeited, and if anyone be found committing any other enormity in the said fountain they shall be put under the tumbrel'. Beggars, who could easily also include itinerant fishmongers, came in for particularly harsh treatment because they were perceived as carriers of pestilence. In the early thirteenth century, the provosts of Dublin had to take an oath promising to 'banish all beggars in time of sickness and plague'. In 1455, an assembly of city fathers decreed that 'no manner of beggar dwelling within the said city, no scholar [shall] walk by night at all abegging, upon the pain of forfeiting what may be found with them'.[38] Beggars and strange street sellers were feared as 'outsiders' who operated as spies in times of war by entering the city under the guise of honest poor men and women deserving of charity. In 1489, the mayor of Dublin was ordered to expel all beggars and mendicants from the city. Clark has traced the growing power of corporate or civic government in Dublin from the early modern period to the start of the seventeenth century, the period during which so many controls were imposed upon the baser elements of society. Certainly by the latter date, the city's lord mayor and council had considerable control over the social fabric of the city. The council was responsible for a whole range of urban functions, from the maintenance of the city's defences and the upkeep of the Liffey bridges, to the implementation of rules and regulations to improve hygiene and safety standards in the city. Thus, for example, fines of 20*s.* were imposed for an outbreak of fire inside a house, and this rose to 40*s.* if an entire street were burnt down. Throughout the sixteenth century, Dublin's city council met quarterly at the city hall, or tholsel, situated at the junction of High Street and Skinners' Row. Here, they discussed breaches to rules regulating trade and the organisation of guilds, public hygiene, maintenance of the built environment and the defence of the city. The aldermen and merchants who dominated the council were particularly concerned about water pollution and the proliferation of dung and offal on Dublin's streets, lanes and pavements. In 1546, city officials approved legislation for the provision of facilities, including an extra cart for the 'clenyng of the cittie'. By then, groups of citizens were mobilised to clean animal dung and other offal from the streets and, in 1560, a company of 'good and able workmen' were sought out 'to remove donge from Hangman

Lane and make it cleane'. Ten years later, the council passed legislation penalising those found dumping animal dung and other waste material on the city's streets. It was further mandated that 'no person or persons shall caste any donge in the streets or lanes within the franchises of this cittie, but to carrie the same donge to Oxmanton grene, the Hogen grene, Corker's Barris and the Coombe upon payne of forfacitur of three shillings and three pence for every tyme the shalbe founde giltie thone halfe to the spier and finder and thother halfe to the treasorie'.[39]

McNally has suggested that the designation of official dumping grounds outside the city walls was a strategy for preventing the 'noxious odours' from animal offal and fish from contaminating the more salubrious districts of Dublin city. As a result, areas such as the Coombe and Oxmantown were places where dirty work and 'dirty business' were conducted.[40] By the 1560s, it was the responsibility of residents to keep their own street clean and safe for the general public. Stray livestock, a perennial source of complaint, were a menace to the public, and to themselves. In 1570, the council hired wardens to control wandering animals, and one Henry Ellis was appointed overseer of swine in the city. Whatever the immediate effect the council's efforts, the condition of Dublin's streets and laneways continued to decay. By the mid-seventeenth century, conditions were little better, as complaints continued to flood into the mayor's office about 'the foulness of the streets, the swine which fed and roamed without restriction, and the number of beggars with infectious diseases'.[41] 'Fear of pestilence' resulted in incessant demands that town councillors and mayors remove pigs, cattle and other wandering farm animals from city streets, and have the streets and lanes 'freed from ordure in order to prevent loss of life from pestilineal exhalations'.[42]

We have already seen that the proper management of fish, meat and other markets was crucial to any attempt to improve sanitary conditions in Irish towns and cities. This, in turn, was an elaborate affair, requiring spacious pens for cattle and sheep, and properly maintained fish shambles for the sale of the extensive array of fish and shellfish that were consumed in such large quantities in the early modern city. Badly managed markets, especially those located on unsuitable sites in densely inhabited inner city areas, were considered threats to public hygiene. Fisher folk living in urban areas were also closely monitored to assess the impact of their activities on the rivers, estuaries and coastal districts where they lived. The text of an Act of 1569 suggests that the Irish parliament was not unmindful of the care of Irish rivers, including the Liffey, the Lee and the Shannon, and other waterways that traversed the country's major towns and cities. Those responsible for drawing up this particular Act referred in particular to the 'great hurt and hindrance' caused near the estuaries of rivers 'wherein the frye of salmon, ele and other commodious fishes are bred and nourished' by those who 'allowed their herds to feed upon the strand and so to destroy the spawn'.[43] It was precisely because salmon fry and elvers were commonly fed to pigs in coastal towns, than an Act of Queen Elizabeth's reign prevented swine from feeding on the shores of tidal rivers. Foraging pigs and other farm animals also contributed to the destruction of 'a great quantity of salmon and eel fry'.[44] New legislation was thus enacted which meant that 'no swine, hogge or pigge' was allowed access to rivers and estuaries containing valuable fisheries. The penalty for breaking this law was 'forfeiture of the animals concerned'. While it is difficult to establish whether or not legislation had much effect in protecting fish stocks in rivers and estuaries, we know that farm animals continued to forage many stretches of the coastline right down to the late nineteenth century in parts of coastal Ireland. Writing in 1683, William Montgomery recorded that the new Scottish planters of Co. Down found that their sheep 'kept fat and wholesome all spring by feeding on the oare'.[45] Here, as elsewhere in coastal Ireland, cattle and sheep regularly grazed on seaweed and rough grassland, particularly during hard winter months. This was especially common on islands and on the coast of many western counties where animal fodder was hard to come by and grazing land was in short supply.

It is possible to argue that fishermen and fish workers in general occupied two quite contradictory positions within the social structure of the early modern city. Because of their association with 'putridity' and 'nauseous bilge', they were often considered unclean and a threat to public hygiene. On the other hand, as suppliers of cheap and nutritious fish, and other costly luxuries from sea, shoreline, lake and river, they held a special position in port towns and coastal cities. As a privileged group who supplied cities with food, fishermen were occasionally forbidden to engage in farming if it interfered with their fishing. However, their association with rough and dirty working conditions rendered fishermen and fish gutters 'uncouth' in the eyes of many. The port towns of medieval England, Scotland and Ireland were reputed to be 'swamped' in the 'putrefying blood and ordure' of slaughtered animals, decaying fish and domestic fowl. Rivers running through such settlements were little more than open sewers that discharged their fetid contents into the sea, or onto streets, during periods of flooding. The 'vapours' associated with fish guts, and the stench of slaughtered animals, were said to be so foul that they were capable of 'corrupting' the 'strongest blasts' of sea air. From the fifteenth to the late nineteenth century, images of 'nauseous bilge' clung to fishing communities, and even to the bodies of fishermen and sailors.[46] The stench of fishing ports and the heavy smells around working fishing boats and other vessels were attributed to the 'fetidity engendered by so many men collected together in a small place'. Deep-sea fishing boats in particular were likened to 'floating swamps'. Here, 'seawater seeped through the seams in the bulwarks; fresh water stagnated in puddles after rainfall, washing, soaking the rigging, eroding the timbers, and combining with the ballast to form a blackish and murderous ooze'. Their 'fetid odours' and 'exhalations' meant that mooring places, harbours and warehouses came to be identified with marshes and swampland as places where disease was rife. 'Fish palaces', where fish were gutted, salted and packed in containers, were 'noisy crucibles of bustle and industry' that gave off such an overwhelming stench that sedate visitors found such places 'intolerable'.[47] Not surprisingly, areas such as the Marsh in Cork, the Liberties in Dublin and the Claddagh in Galway were long considered breeding grounds for disease, pestilence and social disorder.

The containment of 'putridity' and the eradication of filth from city streets were fraught with difficulties from the start. It was stated that in the reign of Elizabeth I, one Wiley Barnaby Rathe of Dublin, 'preferred a life of relative ease in the house of St John in Fishamble Street, to the impossible and unsavoury task of killing pigs and ridding the city of its pestilineal beggars'. As late as 1659, 'idle boys and women were imprisoned in a large cage in Dublin's Cornmarket, prior to examination and punishment by the justices of the city'.[48] In fifteenth-century Galway, butchers were prevented from 'exposing for sale' any kind of meat before 'it be preysed by the officers in the shambles'. It was an offence punishable by fines to store cowhides, whether salted, fresh or dried, in anyone's house for more than two nights before being 'exposed' for sale.[49] Similar strict restrictions undoubtedly applied to the sale and storage of fish in the port towns and coastal cities. It was said that the country's busy fishing ports always had 'the smell of a warm vapour and an unpleasant odour that could make a delicate person faint'. Harbours were choice areas for fermentation, and here fishermen and their sizeable families usually lived in simple one-roomed or two-roomed cottages. The fresh, salty air of fishing ports and villages along the south and east coasts in particular was often polluted with the tang of rotting seaweed and the fishy stenches given off by fish palaces. This was mingled with the rich organic smells of cows, sheep and goats, and the stench of human excrement and urine. Richard Carew's description of a fish palace in Cornwall at the close of the sixteenth century could equally apply to the fish palaces of Munster. In preparing fish for sale, Carew wrote that

> Some are polled (that is, beheaded), gutted, split, powdered [salted] and dried in the sun, as the lesser sort of hake. Some headed, gutted, jagged and dried, as rays and thornbacks. Some gutted, powdered and dried, as buckthorn made whitings, the smaller sort of conger and hake. Some gutted, split and kept in pickle, as whiting, mackerel, mullet, bass, peal, trout, salmon and conger. Some gutted and kept in pickle, as the lesser whitings, pollocks, eels and squary scads [Spanish mackerel]. Some cut in pieces and powdered as seal and porpoise and lastly some boiled and preserved fresh in vinegar, as tunny and turbot.[50]

Aside from the hustle and bustle of life around fish palaces and in busy ports, coastal towns were ribald places frequented by all sorts of characters and given over to an assortment of diversions not usually accessible to those living in the comparative seclusion of rural Ireland. In eighteenth-century Cork, for example, local butchers celebrated the end of Lent by holding a mock funeral for a herring, the fish that most symbolised poverty and abstinence in the city. Each Easter Sunday, a single herring was carried aloft by the city's butchers on a nine-foot pole 'and was subjected to insult and ridicule as it passed through the streets of Cork'. During the parade, the herring was beaten with rods until all that remained were the remnants that were then flung into the Lee.[51] Conjuring up the social atmosphere of Wexford in the early 1600s, one historian has stated that

> There were taverns and merchant houses, shops, fights, murderous skippers and 'hard chaws' and, in a maritime economy, sailors' wives on the lookout for the house money. There were drinking bouts and rows between deep water and shallow water sailors; there was rivalry between the sailors' enclaves around the Faythe and Maudlintown and the land employed families of the John Street area. The overwhelming bulk of the population refused to conform to Protestantism and remained loyal to the old religion. This factor, along with the international political significance which that choice signalled to London, added a major dimension to the character of the town.[52]

Late Medieval Dublin was also the scene of raucous public pageants that attracted pilgrims from all parts of its coastal hinterland. 'Pilgrims' were

particularly attracted by the street theatre and great processions held on Corpus
Christi, St Patrick's Day, St George's Day, and during the week running up to
Christmas. The many trade and craft guilds of the city, including the
fishermen's guild and organised groups of 'salmon-takers', adopted Corpus
Christi in particular as their principal festival and performed elaborate pageants
throughout the medieval heart of the city on that feast day. In the early
sixteenth century, Christmas plays were performed on Hoggen Green in the
centre of the city, and here different trade guilds performed roles appropriate
to their trade. Vintners related tales about Bacchus, blacksmiths identified with
the god Vulcan, mariners, ship-carpenters and 'salmon-takers' paraded in
made-up versions of Noah's ark, while carpenters acted out biblical tales about
Joseph and Mary. In other medieval plays set in the city, suitably 'bloodied'
butchers acted the role of 'tormentors', fishermen paraded as Christ's apostles,
while skinners provided a model of a camel for public entertainment.[53] Public
plays and pageants were strictly regulated, as fear of the 'pestilineal exhalations'
attributed to hordes of poor pilgrims was common in Dublin, and in other
towns and cities throughout the late Middle Ages, where they were associated
with fever and death. Lydon has pointed out that the taverns and ale-houses of
medieval Dublin were generally packed with customers. In ale-houses along the
quays in particular, cheap oysters and other shellfish were consumed in large
quantities. At a time when the smallest coin available was well in excess of a
normal portion of beer, tokens were used instead of coinage. Excavations in the
vicinity of the city's Winetavern Street produced a hoard of no fewer than
2,061 tokens, some dating from before 1282 and decorated appropriately with
figures of pilgrims and animals slaking their thirst.[54] Not surprisingly, excessive
drinking was especially serious in Dublin's poorer districts, especially in the
quarters frequented by sailors and fishermen. In an age when alcohol-induced
violence was endemic, and when many customers carried weapons of sorts as a
matter of course, quarrels resulting from drink could all too easily lead to
bloodshed. No strictures by priests or churchmen could curb the fisherman's
drinking. Drink indeed was considered one of the few escapes of poor fish
workers from the drab and gruelling work that was their daily lot. Not
surprisingly, therefore, fishing ports and towns that traded in the export of fish
were widely considered as immoral places. Here, danger hung in the air, and
'noxious vapours were exhaled from supplies, from rigging, from strongly
smelling or fermented liquids or victuals, from decomposing rats and insects,
from the rubbish that had piled up in dark corners to generate a melange of
odours that threatened fishermen and passers-by alike'.[55] The 'olfactory

22 Sketch from *The Illustrated London News* (1880), showing Claddagh fishermen and their wives settling the price of fish before going to market.

emanations' arising from such places were so strong that passers-by practically suffocated when they walked through them.

Seamen and fishermen ran the greatest risk of falling victim to 'vile-smelling effluvia'. It was said that fishermen smelled 'unpleasant and were disgusting'; their customs were 'debauched', their lives 'immoral' and, like sailors, they found their greatest enjoyment in the 'supreme happiness of drunkenness'. The 'stench' associated with fishermen and seamen alike was reputed to be 'wedded to the vapours of wine, alcohol and other coarse foods that they like to eat'. It was said that the 'perfume' of their clothing was impregnated with sweat, filth and tar, thus making it repulsive for many to be near them. This, it was argued, was notoriously the case with those engaged in hunting whales. The stench of sailors and fishermen was also considered 'robust and libidinous'. For that reason, it was said to be sexually arousing and added 'a strong spermatic secretion to the effluvia' with which these men of the sea were associated. It was suggested that those who worked with fish could easily be recognised by their odour, even on the street, because the smell of fish impregnated their bodies and stuck to their skin. Bourgeois sensibilities and popular literature would later convey this perception of fisher folk as 'stinking', 'repulsive' and 'slovenly'.[56] In the 1830s, one commentator described 'lower town' in Arklow, where the families of local fishermen lived, as 'a wretched segregation of huts, a huddled assemblage of squalid hovels, a magnified copy of a Hottentot or Caffre kraal, with the putrid excrement of the accumulated offal of a slovenly fishery'.[57] When James Tuke visited Galway in 1848, he complained of piles of unwanted fish and 'the most disgusting effluvia' that lay everywhere around the vicinity of the market when catches were high and fishermen could not dispose of fish.[58] Writing some twenty years before the Famine, James Hardiman described the Claddagh district in Galway's as 'a very ancient village whose streets and exteriors were as remarkable for want of cleanliness as the interior of most houses was for neatness and regularity'.[59] On a visit to Galway in the early 1850s, Francis B. Head wrote that

> After admiring for some time the dock, which appears to me the most admirably constructed, I observed close to it, quite apart from the town of Galway, a little city of cabins, entirely inhabited by fishermen and their families. It is called 'the Claddagh'; and as I had heard so much of their strange habits, customs, prejudices, superstitions, and of their being governed almost exclusively by their own laws, with considerable curiosity I slowly dived into it. I must own, however, I was woefully disappointed; for although it certainly was strange to wander by oneself through the winding streets of huts, containing a population of nearly 1,300 people, yet with this eccentricity was mixed up so much filth and misery that the amalgam altogether was anything but attractive. As might naturally be expected, the first thing I ran against in the city of the Claddagh was a tall dirty woman, with a long fish dangling, as if it had grown there, from her right hand. On each side of every street, the doors of the cabins were wide open. On entering one of them I found, kneeling on the ground in the middle of her chamber, an old woman, with one tooth, preparing in a wooden bowl, for two little pigs a quantity of potato-parings, which they were eyeing and she chopping very attentively. Around her were walking, now and then interjectionally hopping, three hens … In another cabin, I found four women rapidly making nets, and a very old man, in rags, slowly combing his hair. After passing through several streets of cabins, in which I usually saw, mixed up in different proportions, half-naked children, pigs, fowls, women and nets.[60]

Given these prejudicial perceptions of fishermen and their habitations, it is not surprising that many of those who traded in fish were condemned not only to live, but also to marry and 'breed' among their own kind. This enhanced the endogamous nature of many fishing communities, safely anchoring fisher folk within their own marriage fields and extending their social distance from so-called respectable society. This further contributed to social closure in many fishing communities by cutting fisher folk and their families off from the rest of society.

PIRATES, SMUGGLERS AND SEA FISHERIES

The continental fishing fleets that paid a medieval version of 'protection money' to local chiefs in the fourteenth and fifteenth centuries may well have facilitated the development of maritime trade in Ireland by keeping Irish waters relatively free of pirates and privateers. In 1277, for example, the merchants of Galway were paying Dermod More O'Brien, lord of the Aran Islands, a tribute of '12 tuns of wine per annum 'in consideration of his protecting the harbour and trade from all pirates and privateers, by maintaining a suitable maritime force for the purpose'.[61] Merchants in sixteenth-century Limerick were similarly compelled to give a share of wine, and other merchandise from their ships, to the powerful Gaelic families along the Shannon Estuary. This rule equally applied to all owners of stone castles between Limerick city and the sea.[62] Foreign fishermen and coastal traders prior to the plantation of Ulster were also required to pay for protection on sea-routes around the wilder west and north-west coasts. Payment of 'protection money', of course, did not always ensure the safety of merchant shipping and other vessels. In 1256, a merchant ship carrying a cargo of wine, cloth, copper and iron was attacked and plundered off the Connemara coast by a fleet of Scottish pirates operating out of the Hebrides. The medieval lordship of Tír Conaill had well-established trading connections with Scotland, the south of England and France, all of which were prone to attack by pirates and organised gangs of smugglers. So great was the fear of pirates in parts of the west and south of Ireland in the late sixteenth century, that the lord justice called for the use of force to clear them out of the creeks and havens on this coast. Thus, the development of Ireland's sea fisheries and maritime trade was predicated upon the elimination of piracy. It was equally central to a much wider *mission civilatrice* that sought to 'improve' the wild and lawless towns and villages around the south and west coasts of Ireland in much the same way that landlords improved rural settlements.

The Munster coastline and the waters around the north-west of the country were renowned strongholds for smugglers, pirates and all those who depended

23 Anne Bonny, a famed Irish female pirate, from the Dutch version of Charles Johnson's *General history of the pyrates* (1724). Reputedly from Co. Cork, Bonny was accorded a prominent place in a chapter dealing with her 'remarkable actions and adventures'.

on them, throughout the fifteenth and sixteenth centuries. Piracy, like smuggling, paid off in these remote areas, and many coastal communities made their living from the illegal trade generated by these activities. 'Portingalls' and Spaniards were regularly involved in a late medieval version of arms-dealing, bringing muskets, gunpowder, swords and other munitions into secluded coastal districts in the west and north of the country. The piratical raids that occurred along this coastline could be compared to the great 'land raids' that were such a feature of Celtic Ireland. They certainly enabled Gaelic chieftains to exert control over considerable stretches of coastline. Similarly, the localised plunder of Gaelic overlords in the sixteenth century was frequently overlaid by organised, long-distance piracy and smuggling. Scottish and English pirates raided the ports and sea-lanes of Tír Conaill throughout the sixteenth century, causing the O'Donnells in particular to protect offshore fisheries and sea-lanes with a fleet of ten or twelve wooden boats that were much sturdier and larger than the local currachs. McGettigan has shown that they occasionally raided the island haunts of pirates around the coast of the north-west of Ireland with these craft.[63] In the sixteenth and seventeenth centuries, English merchants repeatedly complained that 'pedlars' and other illegal traders were taking advantage of creeks along the east coast of Ulster and the west coast of Munster, to engage in smuggling and piracy and to transport goods abroad. It was reported that 'pedlars out of Scotland' were taking advantage of 'unguarded creeks' along the Antrim coast and that they swarmed 'about the country in great numbers [in order to] sell all manner of wares, which they may afford at easier rates than poor shopkeepers that live in corporations'. Merchants at Coleraine similarly complained of Scottish pedlars who were 'desiring to load and discharge at petty creeks where they may have advantage to steal'.[64] One of the geo-strategic objectives of the plantations was to eliminate or at least curtail such illegal 'peddling' and trading and the centralising tendencies of colonial policy caused many of the country's smaller outlying ports to fade into insignificance.

The spectacular actions of pirates and smugglers had an impact upon some of the fundamental issues in the social and economic life of Atlantic Europe in the early modern period. Poor fishermen and others who entered the nomadic world of piracy and smuggling dramatised concerns about nationality and proper social behaviour. In so doing, they represented threats to private property at sea, and challenged the hegemony of the state in inshore and deep-sea waters alike. When aristocratic women took to the sea, whether to fish or to become pirates and smugglers, they profoundly challenged prevailing conventions surrounding gender and social class. In sixteenth-century Ireland, Grace O'Malley clearly belonged to that most subversive of all social groups, namely those women from well-off backgrounds who commanded respect at sea as well as on land. Such women engaged in piracy for political as well as economic reasons. To English authorities O'Malley was 'a woman that hath impudently passed the part of womanhood and been a great spoiler and chief commander and director of thieves and murderers'. Known variously as Gráinne Ní Mháille or Grainne Mhaol, to English authorities she was the 'nurse to all rebellions'.[65] Born in the vicinity of Clew Bay in or around 1530, she spent a good part of her youth at the family residence on Clare Island. As a member of the regionally powerful Uí Mháille family, she belonged to 'a hardy seafaring people on the west coast of Ireland'. Married twice, her first husband was Donal O'Flaherty, from an important seafaring family on the west coast of Connaught. After the death of her second husband in 1583, she continued to command a fleet of ships that were manned by fighting men and fishermen from coastal districts along the west coast. The O'Malleys were typical of a number of dynastic families in the west of Ireland in the pre-colonial period in that they derived their living mainly from the sea, and fishing was one of their principal sources of revenue. Their motto, *terra marique potens*, suggested that they were powerful on land as well as on the seas around west Connaught, where herring, cod, ling, turbot and salmon was a good source of income. Piracy and smuggling supplemented the incomes of these and other seafaring clans off the coast of Connaught and Munster at this time. The career of Grace O'Malley pre-dated by almost 150 years the careers of such widely known women pirates as Ann Bonny (1702–82), and Mary Read (d. 1721). The former was probably born in the vicinity of Kinsale, but she grew up in South Carolina. She took to piracy in the waters off Jamaica and her story was told by Daniel Defoe in his *History of the Pyrates*, which was published in 1724.[66]

Powerful Gaelic leaders such as the O'Malleys in Mayo, the O'Flahertys in Galway, the O'Donnells in Tír Conaill, and the O'Driscolls and O'Sullivan Beare in west Munster all owned large fishing fleets and exported great quantities of fish in the sixteenth century. The ancient annals regularly referred to the piratical incursions of the O'Malleys all along the west coast, from Kerry in the south, to Donegal in the north. In 1513, it was stated that Eoghan O'Mhaille 'went with the crews of three ships against *Na Cealla Beaga* (Killybegs) in the night … [to] raid and burn the town and take many prisoners'.[67] The secluded Clew Bay area, where the O'Malleys held sway, was ideally suited for smuggling and other illicit activities. Its tides, channels, dangerous reefs and sandbanks, as well as its remoteness, rendered it difficult for state authorities to exert control over this coast. Grace O'Malley would have accompanied her father on numerous fishing and trading voyages all along the Connaught coast. Indeed, in the sixteenth century, this part of the west coast of Ireland was sufficiently removed from English control to merit comparison with other havens of piracy in the West Indies. Merchants in Galway regularly complained to Dublin of their inability to suppress 'piratical raids'. One local official stated that 'the O'Malleys and O'Flahertys, with their galleys along our

24 The family crest of the O'Malleys of Mayo, affirming that they were powerful both on land and at sea (from Chambers, *Granuaile: Ireland's Pirate Queen* (2003)).

coasts, have been taking sundry ships and barks bound for this port town'. He went on to describe one incident in which they overpowered the owners and merchants on board one vessel and 'most wickedly murdered divers of the young men'.[68]

In the fifteenth and sixteenth centuries, the merchants of Galway had succeeded in building up a considerable foreign trade in fish, hides, tallow, wool and other commodities, the bulk of which went to the continent. In addition to the threats posed by pirates and smugglers, and the treacherous weather conditions, the merchants of Galway were exposed to the 'rough handling' of vessels voyaging between Ireland and Spain throughout the greater part of the sixteenth and seventeenth centuries.[69] The south-west of Ireland also drew in 'huge numbers of English pirates who had been pushed out of their homeland' when James I announced a crackdown on privateering. The waters off Baltimore were so 'infested' with pirates in the early sixteenth century, that English money was rarely seen in the region, the most acceptable currency being the Barbary ducat.[70] There was also an easy familiarity between local fishermen, pirates and smugglers along this coast, and this would have led to a high degree of collusion between coastal towns and fishing villages on the one hand, and their illegal 'benefactors' on the other. In an episode that occurred in 1608, an English naval captain who tried to take a pirate vessel off Baltimore was overwhelmed when his crew, among whom were local men, 'made merry with the pirates' who showered them with 'gifts [of] ... twenty chests of sugar and four chests of coral'.[71] The most notorious act of piracy along the Irish coast occurred just before daybreak on 20 June 1631, when 'a joint force consisting of 230 elite troops of the Turkish Ottoman Empire and pirates from the Barbary coast, stormed ashore at the little port of Baltimore and spirited almost all of the villagers away to a life of slavery in Algiers'.[72] The victims, most of them English settlers not long resident in this remote district, included 'fifty youngsters ... even those in the cradle', together with thirty-four women and some two dozen men. Des Ekin has described this coastline in the early seventeenth century as 'a centre of local freebooting under the locally powerful O'Driscolls'.[73] This mixed company of Algerian and Turkish pirates also swooped on a number of vessels on their way to Baltimore, including two small fishing craft from the Waterford area that they captured off the Old Head of Kinsale. It is said that John Hackett, skipper of one of these vessels, acted as a pilot for the pirates, and may have had a number of motives for doing so. In the first place, having been captured by the pirates, a danger faced by many fishermen in Irish waters at this time, he had little choice but to do their bidding. Secondly, a native of Dungarvan, Hackett had little sympathy for those living in the west Cork port of Baltimore, as this port was regularly used by the O'Driscolls to plunder trading ships and fishing vessels passing from Waterford to the west coast of Munster. Finally, there may have been an ethnic dimension to the Waterford fisherman's motives, as the inhabitants of Baltimore were English Protestants, while Hackett was a Roman Catholic.

Ohlmeyer has shown that Wexford was also a renowned haven for smugglers and privateers in the sixteenth and seventeenth centuries. During the rebellion of 1641, one government official described it as 'a place plentiful in ships and seamen, where the rebels have set up Spanish colours on their walls in defiance of the king and kingdom of England, and have gotten in from foreign parts great store of arms and ammunition'.[74] By the mid-1640s, Wexford was temporary home to a cosmopolitan community of privateers drawn from France, England and Flanders. Their ranks were greatly augmented towards the end of 1646, when an incursion of privateers who had been expelled from Dunkirk arrived in the town and threatened to make Wexford 'the Dunkirk of Ireland'. Flemish privateers apparently dominated this band of pirates, but they 'were numerically matched by Irish commanders who, though less experienced in the ways of professional privateering, were also fine sailors, thoroughly familiar with the treacherous seas along the south-east coast of Ireland, and therefore valuable as pilots and navigators'.[75] The privateers were clearly familiar with the sea-routes used by Scottish, English and Dutch fishermen who regularly fished the waters off the south-east of Ireland at this time. They also knew the itineraries of ships trading grain and fishing vessels operating between the Baltic and the Iberian Peninsula at this stage. Evidence suggests that they may have attacked Scottish and Dutch herring fleets off the western isles of Scotland throughout the sixteenth century. Further south along the coast of Ireland, privateers operating out of Wexford harassed fishing fleets off the coast of Devon and Cornwall, and regularly captured vessels working out of the busy fishing ports of Bristol, Weymouth, Torbay and Plymouth. The booty picked up on these privateering expeditions was rich and varied, with the most valuable items being captured ships ranging in size from small fishing boats and merchant vessels to heavily-armed frigates and men-of-war. One contemporary pamphlet produced around the time of the 1641 rebellion reported that the inhabitants of Wexford regularly enriched themselves 'by robbing and pillaging at sea all English merchants they could light on since the war began, and making a trade of that piracy'. The anonymous author listed 'household furniture, trading commodities and merchandise' among the pillaged booty taken in by Wexford merchants.[76] Because of the extent of their catchment area, pirates operating off the south-east coast were able to harass merchant ships and fishing fleets from England, Holland and France. The cargoes stolen from these vessels were disposed of in Wexford and other towns along the east coast, and consisted of herring, cod, beef, pork, butter, malt and wine. Much of this booty went directly to merchants in Wexford, including prominent aldermen who benefited from a 'constant stream of basic foodstuffs and luxury items'. Thus, Ohlmeyer has argued that

> The local community not only purchased the privateers' booty and the
> vessels, thus turning cargoes of wine, corn or herrings into hard cash, but

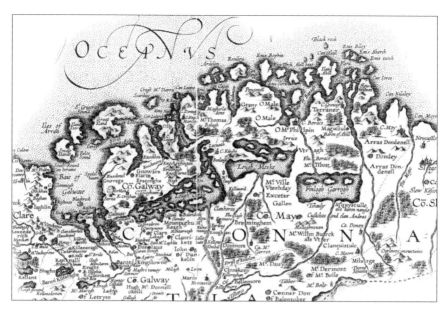

25 Detail from Boazio's *Map of Ireland, with the principal lordships and chieftains*, published in 1609. The map shows the amphibian territory of the O'Malleys, who controlled the coastal waters of west Connaught right up to the start of the seventeenth century (from Chambers, *Granuaile: Ireland's Pirate Queen* (2003)).

they also became involved in the business of privateering itself. Some offered specialised services to the sea rovers. In Wexford, for example, Patrick O'Quonny, a local carpenter, later reminisced how he had often been employed to repair privateers' frigates. Others provided entertainment for the sailors. No doubt the tavern enjoyed a flourishing trade, as did the brothels or 'whattling shops' (as they were known). Certainly during the early seventeenth century, prostitutes were extremely numerous in the piratical havens along the Munster coastline: there is no evidence to suggest that forty years later Wexford was any different.[77]

The social and economic significance of piracy in Irish waters began to decline around the 1620s, although piracy continued to pose a problem in the wider Atlantic long after that date, particularly in the Caribbean. In the 'Golden Age of Piracy' following the War of Spanish Succession (1702–13), Irish seamen and fishermen accounted for a significant proportion of pirates operating in Atlantic and Caribbean waters. The 'boom' conditions of these years saw huge quantities of wealth, including fish and fishing craft, moving between ports on both sides of the Atlantic Ocean, as men, and sometimes also women, took to piracy as an alternative to a life of poverty and oppression ashore.[78] It has been estimated that around one half of pirates in the early part of the eighteenth century were of English origin, while one tenth were 'in some manner Irish', and one in fourteen were Scottish. Not surprisingly, most of these men hailed from major ports such as London, Liverpool, Bristol and Plymouth, while Irish and Scottish pirates hailed from Dublin, Cork, Waterford, Wexford, Glasgow and Aberdeen. Rediker has labelled these 'the outcasts of all nations'. They included refugees from poverty and the dispossessed, as well as ex-fishermen, convicts, prostitutes, political prisoners, debtors, vagabonds, indentured servants and religious radicals, all of whom had migrated beyond the line of respectable society. While those belonging to this world of piracy were generally poor, they often expressed high ideals. 'We should remember them', Rediker suggests, 'so long as there are powerful people and oppressive circumstances to be resisted'.[79]

The decline of piracy did not mean that Irish seamen were free from press-gangs that later operated around the Irish coast in the eighteenth and nineteenth centuries. In a rare account of press-gangs off the coast of Cork, O'Mahony has shown that many men, including part-time fishermen, were captured off the coast of Cork and Kinsale in the late eighteenth and early nineteenth century. In February 1804, it was reported that

> In no part of the United Kingdom has the Impress service been carried on with more benefit to the service, and less inconvenience to the public, than in Cork and its out ports. Upwards of 1,500 seamen have been put into service since Captain Chilcott's command of this duty took place; and what is singular of this number, zeal and activity of Lieutenant Townshend, collected about 400 at Cove during the short space of three months – a number which has been often not exceeded in the course of a war.[80]

In May of the following year, press-gangs were once again active off the coast of Cork and Cobh. One of the most daring episodes of press-ganging occurred off Kinsale in the autumn of 1812. Despite an admiralty order exempting fishermen from naval service, *The Cork Mercantile Chronicle* of 8 September in that year reported that a strange ship sailed into Cork Harbour and immediately set about press-ganging the crews of a number of small fishing craft and a pilot boat. When the pilot boat came alongside one boat, its four occupants were immediately seized, while three other longboats, each containing an armed gang, set off after the fishing boats. Realising what was happening, some of the fishermen tried to swim ashore, 'while others who attempted to climb nearby cliffs were dragged back with boat hooks, and numerous shots were fired by the press-gang'. This operation resulted in the capture of thirty to forty men, including three men from Oysterhaven and seven farm labourers from Robert's Cove who had come to Kinsale for a day's fishing.[81]

This chapter has suggested that the imposition of order on Ireland's maritime fringe and the attempted gentrification of coastal ports, town and cities were already well advanced by the time of the Ulster and Munster plantations. These attempts at 'ordering' and 'improving' the coastal landscape of Ireland led to a closer monitoring of fish markets and fishing activities, and a rudimentary gentrification of urban space. As such, they were central to a much wider *mission civilatrice* that sought to transform the country's maritime economy, regulate the fish-trade, eliminate piracy and smuggling, and prepare the way for a much more orderly exploitation of the country's sea fisheries. This was a long drawn out process that was resisted by some, but welcomed by others. The extension of control mechanisms to marketplaces and coastal waters affected the status of a number of Gaelic families who benefited from the presence of foreign fishing fleets, and smugglers, off large tracts of coastal Ireland. By the close of the sixteenth century, their ability to control stretches of the western and northern coast in particular was seriously undermined. The imposition of order on marketing arrangements for fish and other food products fostered the development of the merchant class and contributed to the commercialisation of fishing. Henceforth, small fishermen, fish workers and petty fishmongers were often unable to compete with foreign fishing fleets and their activities were subjected to a comparatively high degree of control. Certainly, the elimination of piracy and the control of smuggling, motivated as it was by a mixture of geo-strategic and socio-economic considerations, paved the way for a much more orderly exploitation of Ireland's coastal fisheries.

The following chapter discusses the position of fishermen and seafarers in early Irish history, with special reference to the experiences of those employed in the deep-sea fisheries off the Irish coast from around the fifteenth to the eighteenth century. It also examines the early history of port and harbour development, focusing especially on the modernisation of the country's coastal infrastructure in this important period in the history of Ireland's sea fisheries. Finally, it examines the quite unique world of seamen and fishermen, including their distinctive work practices and social behaviour that set them apart from rural and urban Ireland from a very early stage.

CHAPTER SIX

The maritime world of fishermen

SEAFARERS AND FISHERMEN IN THE EARLY IRISH HISTORY

The phoenicians of northern spain may well have been the first to engage in large-scale deep-sea fishing in North Atlantic waters. Given the geographical extent of their maritime world, it is by no means inconceivable that their fishing range extended to the waters off the south and west coasts of Ireland. Homeric sources suggest that hunting and trading for fish were important aspects of colonial Greece in the sixth century BC, when the security of the Greek Empire rested as much on its oarsmen as on its armies and cavalry forces. Its great shipping fleets consisting of hundreds of ships were extremely important to this 'island empire' as it struggled to maintain hold of lands that stretched from the Black Sea to the Mediterranean, and from the Aegean to the Nile delta. Although many of the men who manned the ships that held the empire together were 'hired foreigners', most were lower-class Athenians who had amassed experience through years of sailing and fishing in its offshore waters.[1] The spread of Roman power in the second century BC contributed to the early growth of intensive sea fishing, both in the Mediterranean and in Atlantic waters. In Caesar's Italy, thousands of slaves trained as fishermen were engaged in catching and preserving fish for mass consumption.[2] De Courcy Ireland has argued that Irish seamen 'helped finish off the dying Roman Empire'.[3] From the eighth century onwards, Irish seafarers and fishermen carried out many remarkable sea voyages, the first echoes of which have come down to us in the great maritime legends of Brendan the Navigator. Thus, from the earliest of times, the Irish had a strong connection with the sea and close contact with the cosmopolitan fleets of fishermen who exploited the deep-sea fishing grounds of the North Atlantic.

The American cultural geographer, Carl Sauer, was among the first to recognise the special relationship of the ancient Irish with the maritime world of northern Europe. As the inhabitants of a strategically located island set under the 'northern mists' of the North Atlantic, the Celts, like the Basques and the Scandinavians, regarded the sea as a 'frontier of opportunity to provide food, to build and man vessels in which to go out and to move to new homes'.[4] Situated midway down the European frontage of this North Atlantic world,

Ireland belonged to a maritime world of great biological diversity. Prior to serious over-fishing in the nineteenth and twentieth centuries, the shallow seas around its coast were an immensely rich feeding ground for vast quantities of fish, and other forms of marine life. Knowledge of the hazardous geography and shifting moods of this sea world, including an ability to read the signs of sky, tides and bird flight to detect the whereabouts of shoals of fish, were essential skills for all who made their living from fishing and farming in this extensive maritime world. Ireland's Early Christians did not fear the sea, nor did they permit it to set limits to their courage or explorations. Many ancient Celtic traditions betray a profound reverence for 'the waters and the wild', and Irish holy men went bravely, and often innocently, into unknown seas to be close to God and his wonders.[5] Brought up in the tradition of Greek and Roman classics, many early Irish scholars were familiar with Mediterranean sea-legends, not least those relating to 'the Fortunate Isles' that were believed to lie far out in the western ocean. Fragments of that lore were subsequently woven into ancient Irish sea-tales, some of which are older than Irish Christianity itself. The literary genre of the *immram* deals with the high-spirited ventures of these early Irish travellers and missionaries in the North Atlantic. Unlike the Vikings, their sea-tales are less concerned with battles lost and won, or hardships endured, than with 'adventure sought and enjoyed, with a sea world of marvels and incidental terrors, ending in a safe return home'.[6] Not surprisingly, these tall seafaring tales often placed great emphasis on courage in the face of adversity, and could be regarded as the maritime equivalent of the frontier literature of seventeenth-century North America. These were also *disjunctive* narratives that described departures from the safety of the home community and all the dangers that attended those who journeyed into unknown worlds.

While fishing and shoreline foraging declined in Ireland with later developments in agriculture and rural industry, a mixture of fishing and farming has persisted in many coastal communities down to recent times. Given the longevity of native and foreign fishing traditions in maritime Ireland, it is not surprising that specialised sub-groups within coastal communities put to sea from a very early age to catch a considerable variety of fish. Because of the under-development of the native sea fisheries, many of these men fished alongside the much more advanced fleets from Britain and continental Europe. Ireland was not unique in this respect and, from the start, deep-sea fishing was a cosmopolitan affair involving fishermen from many countries. The organised exploitation of sea and freshwater fisheries developed along the Atlantic coast of Western Europe, and in the major rivers and lakes of Central and Eastern Europe, from the seventh century onwards. Fishermen from Holland and the Hanseatic ports of northern Europe dominated the herring industry of northern Europe in the late medieval and early modern period. Their fishing grounds encircled a maritime trading empire extending from Russia in the east to Scotland, Ireland and England in the west, running southwards to the waters off the south-west of Spain and Portugal. By the middle of sixteenth century, the merchants and mariners of Holland and Zealand also commanded the preponderant share of the carrying trade between the Baltic and Western Europe.[7] The growth of Dutch power at this stage was partially attributable to the geographical position of the Low Countries at the edge of the North Sea, which gave them access to the markets of Germany, France and England. The chapter that follows will show that many of these 'Hollanders' were long familiar with Ireland's sea fisheries, and fished the waters off the south and west of the country throughout the sixteenth and seventeenth centuries. Even in the confined waters of the Irish Sea, fishing in the relatively shallow waters off the south-east coast was not without its difficulties in the twelfth century, and sea travel from England to Ireland was fraught with dangers for fishermen, as well as for pilgrims and other travellers who wished to make the journey by sea to England and Wales. Fishermen and other sea voyagers may have had more to fear from privateers and smugglers than from the natural elements. Giraldus Cambrensis described the Irish Sea as 'surging with currents that rush together … [which] rendered it nearly always tempestuous, so that even in summer it scarcely shows itself calm, even for a few days'. Travelling from Clonmel to Jerusalem during Easter of 1323, Symon Semeonis was frightened by 'the very stormy and dangerous Irish Sea'.[8] While prevailing winds made the sea-trip from Ireland to England comparatively easy, crossings from the other direction were often dangerous in the extreme. Depending on weather conditions, sea-going vessels could do one hundred miles per day on the Irish Sea, while a trip from Dublin to Avignon could take more than a fortnight.

The North Atlantic was a 'great aquarium' that was 'extraordinarily rich in life, both in quantity and diversity'. These waters were supplied with mineral and organic nutrients from a large part of north-west Europe, and were constantly 'kept stirred, mixed and aerated by current, wind and tide, within temperatures, salinities and insulation favourable to organic reproduction'.[9] Microscopic plants and animal plankton formed the great 'sea pastures' off the coast of Ireland, Britain and continental Europe. The relatively shallow waters of the North Sea were one of the best fishing areas of Western Europe in the fourteenth and fifteenth centuries, rivalled only by the narrow straits linking the North Sea with the Baltic off the coasts of Denmark and Sweden. Huge shoals of herring spawned just off the Scania Peninsula of southern Scandinavia and made their way southwards towards Ireland and Scotland in the autumn months. From August to October, these waters were so crowded with herring that one 'fishy tale' decreed that 'you could cut them with a sword'. One fourteenth-century observer declared that there were no less than 45,000 boats at work in this narrow sea, employing a labour force estimated at around 300,000.[10] Some of the catch went as far south as Spain and Italy, its transportation requiring large and well-protected fleets to ward off attacks from 'sea beggars' and privateers, many of whom operated out of comparatively safe havens around the Irish coast.

The more profitable aspects of sea fishing at this stage lay in distribution rather than in the actual catching of fish. The success of the Dutch fishing industry was partly attributable to the fact that the Dutch possessed large boats, or 'busses' of twenty to thirty tons, capable of carrying ten to fifteen men. These boats fished with huge lengths of netting and could cure fish on board rather than having to put ashore to salt and preserve them. The great herring, haddock, cod and ling fisheries of the Baltic and the North Sea were 'the chiefest trade and principal gold mine' of the United Provinces between 1580 and 1640. By the closing years of the seventeenth century, these fisheries employed more than 1,000 'busses' of 48–60 ton burden. Together with ancillary onshore trades such as boat-building, net-making, fish-salting and barrel-making, the entire industry employed an estimated 450,000 persons. Compared to the 200,000 employed in agriculture, and approximately 650,000 in other industries, this was a sizeable figure indeed.[11]

Unlike the predominantly rural interior of late medieval Europe with its nucleated villages and peasant communities, fishing ports and coastal villages were often the basic units of social organisation in large tracts of the North Atlantic coastline. Here, many communities – not least those located on the coasts of Ireland, Norway, Scotland, France, Spain and Portugal – owed their very existence to a combination of sea-going trade, fishing, smuggling, piracy and coastal foraging. The sheer intractability of many upland and rural areas in the interior of these countries resulted in a strong reliance upon inshore fishing and shoreline foraging right down to the nineteenth century. This was particularly the case in coastal Norway and Newfoundland. However, even in countries such as Ireland, Scotland, Spain and Portugal, coastal towns and villages often supplied inland areas with the produce of sea and shoreline.

26 A *hoeker* of the type used by Dutch merchants and fishermen in the seventeenth and eighteenth centuries, and claimed by some as the forerunner of the Galway hooker (courtesy of Timothy Collins).

Fishing communities in the south-east of Ireland also supplied saltwater and freshwater fish, and shellfish, to towns and cities in England and continental Europe from at least the fourteenth century. Braudel has documented 'a continual coming and going' between towns and cities in the hilly interior of the Mediterranean world and its coastal villages and fishing ports. While fishing communities were often the basic units of social organisation along the Mediterranean coast, they rarely matured into regional capitals, a function that was largely confined to coastal cities and other centres of population.[12] Moreover, while the Mediterranean was long regarded as an immense 'nursery' for fishermen and sailors, it trailed behind the Atlantic economies of northern Europe in terms of numbers employed in fishing and related industries.

At this stage also, maritime Ireland was home to small groups of fishermen, and foreign fishermen and fish merchants regularly visited the country's coastal towns and villages. Fishing and trading centres along the east coast in particular had links with La Rochelle, Bordeaux, Rouen, Dieppe, Flanders, Glasgow, Chester, Liverpool and above all Bristol. Seafaring communities here were long accustomed to the comings and goings of sailors, traders, merchants, international travellers and deep-sea fishermen. Furlong has suggested that seventeenth-century Wexford was 'daily accustomed to sailors, foreign vessels, passengers, cargoes, the gossip and lore of cities and civilisations from Pembroke, Bristol, Rotterdam, Bordeaux, Cadiz and points west across the Mediterranean as far as Constantinople and up through the Black Sea to Galatz on the Danube'.[13] Dublin, Waterford, Wexford, New Ross and Drogheda were all filled with vagrants, beggars, street sellers, wandering fishmongers and dealers in every imaginable form of farm produce. Trade between these and other coastal towns was generally conducted along well-established sea lanes, while long-distance land-routes also linked Dublin with Cork, Waterford, Galway, Limerick and Derry. The coastline of Ireland was dotted with an estimated eighty-eight ports of varying size and capacity at the end of the sixteenth century. Irish-built ships operating out of these ports were engaged in an extensive trade with France, Spain and England in the fourteenth and fifteenth centuries. Merchant vessels from Ireland visited ports as far apart as Seville and Gdansk in the sixteenth century. Irish fishing boats and small trading vessels regularly harboured at Chester on the west coast of England, while herring boats from Wexford and Waterford also docked at the Welsh ports of Milford and Carmarthen. De Courcy Ireland has suggested that there 'was a lot more seafaring and fishing off the west and south coasts of Ireland in the sixteenth century than later on'.[14] The country's major ports included Ardglass, Drogheda, Dublin, Malahide, Wicklow, Arklow, Wexford, Waterford, Dungarvan, Youghal, Kinsale, Baltimore, Dingle, the Aran Islands, Galway, Killybegs, Arranmore and the Bann Estuary. Fishing vessels and larger boats working out of Dalkey and the coastal settlements of Strangford Lough in the medieval period rode at anchor offshore while their cargoes were unloaded into smaller boats or carted by pack animals that met boats in shallow waters. In fishing ports all around the coast, unloaded cargo was stored in fortified tower houses prior to its removal to towns and cities along the coast and in the interior. The revitalisation of regional economies on the east coast in the fifteenth and sixteenth centuries led to the construction of well-built stone warehouses in many quayside locations. The new-found importance of Ardglass in south Co. Down at this stage was reflected in well-built stone warehouses used for the storage of fish and agricultural produce.[15] These structures, the maritime equivalent of rural tower houses, were similar to those found at Bristol, Weymouth and King's Lynn on the English coast. They functioned as retail and storage establishments, frequently enclosed an inner harbour, fronted onto one or more quays, and often formed the nucleus of expanding coastal settlements. In areas lacking proper harbour facilities, fishing boats were simply dragged ashore, by both men and farm animals, and beached at landfall clearances. This was the case around the intensively fished Strangford Lough as far back as the thirteenth century, and was probably common practice along other stretches of coast well into the early modern period.[16]

In many coastal districts in the south and east, merchants and other property owners were also instrumental in the development of rudimentary piers and harbours. They regularly complained of the lack of onshore facilities capable of accommodating larger vessels, and suitable for harbouring offshore fishing fleets. In a petition to the king in 1358, Dublin merchants stated that 'for want of deep water in the harbour, there has never been an anchorage for large ships from abroad laden with wine, iron and other commodities. All such anchor at Dalkey within six leagues of Dublin, a town of the archbishop of Dublin. No other place is suitable for laden great ships'.[17] With the improvement of harbour facilities to accommodate these 'great ships', fishermen and small coastal traders were in a position to better exploit the coastal resources of the Irish Sea. Breen has described the 'tiered system' of ports that emerged in Ireland in the sixteenth and seventeenth centuries. These ranged from small marine inlets and river mouths, right up to well-developed ports and harbours.[18] Legislation enacted at the start of the seventeenth century put many Irish ports and harbours on a sounder basis. Customs collectors were appointed in more settled districts on the east coast. Ports here were more closely monitored, and more loyal to the state, than those on the more remote west and south-west coast. In all probability, these ports were also subjected to more state surveillance. Certainly, the appointment of port officials and early 'fisheries inspectors' meant that the state had more control over fishermen, and coastline, than in more remote stretches along the west and north-west coasts. The barrage of legislation enacted from the sixteenth century onwards sought to protect port towns along the east and south coasts on whose loyalty the early colonial state depended. Murage payments on goods entering coastal towns financed the development of piers and harbours. They were levied on a very wide range of goods, including butter, cheese, oats, wheat, herrings, salmon, lampreys, eels, badgers, martens, cattle, horses, deer, goats, rabbits, wolves and foxes. When the local archbishop got permission to establish a market at Dalkey in the early fifteenth century, he imposed levies on a range of goods, including fish, in order to finance improvements to the town's fortifications. A water-bailiff was appointed in the town in 1419, when considerable quantities of fish caught off the Leinster coast were either sold locally, or exported to Bristol and Chester.[19] Even small towns such as Carrickfergus, founded by John de Courcy in 1177, prospered during this period. Protected by its castle from the close of the twelfth century, this town acquired all the trappings of a small medieval city in the fifteenth and sixteenth centuries. A mid-sixteenth-century map of Carrickfergus shows boats, sailing ships and a well-maintained harbour. At the close of the century, the town was transformed into a flourishing port and regional trading centre.[20] Further down the Irish Sea coast, the Anglo-Norman settlement of Drogheda saw substantial urban development on both sides of the River Boyne, as it also became an important centre for shipping and fishing in the fifteenth and sixteenth centuries. This town's street pattern of narrow lanes with steeply rising steps emerged in the medieval period. With just over one hundred acres of urban land enclosed within its fortified walls, Drogheda was one of the largest and most important walled towns in the country. The old Viking settlement of Waterford, captured by the Anglo-Normans in the late twelfth century and developed over the next four centuries, was another prosperous coastal city. Its half-mile long medieval quays were able to accommodate sixty ships. An important shipping, trading and fishing centre, Waterford exported hides, fish and wool to Flanders and the imported wine and other luxury goods from the south-west of France.[21] As a result of rapid expansion in the late medieval period, it became a major port city with a well-established fishing community. Limerick, a Norse settlement from the close of the tenth century, received its charter from Prince John at the end of the twelfth century and underwent significant port development in the late medieval period. When the city was incorporated in the thirteenth century, its fisheries were already a major source of revenue and profit. The fishermen of Limerick 'enjoyed no small share of opulence' in the fourteenth and fifteenth centuries, and this was evident in the quality of their houses and the extent of their properties.[22] The fisheries on the Shannon constantly drew public attention, and inquisitions were frequently required to settle rival claims to tithes and other tolls collected from weirs and other fish-traps in the river and its estuary. The city's prosperous salmon and eel fisheries were a particular source of grievance, and after many disputes, one of the most important weirs

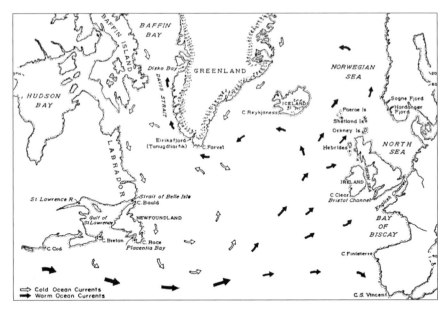

27 Map of the Atlantic world of Europe and North America, by the American cultural geographer, Carl Sauer. Sauer claimed that the Irish 'from a very early stage' had a deep knowledge of the sea and marine resources (adapted from Sauer, *Northern mists* (1968)).

was made over to the corporation, which leased it for just over £28 in 1679.[23] A very extensive network of weirs and fish-traps was used to exploit the highly productive eel and salmon fisheries of Athlone in the thirteenth and fourteenth centuries. The Anglo-Norman settlement of Kinsale received its royal charter in the early fourteenth century. Other privileges conferred on the town in the fifteenth century helped to encourage the exploitation of the offshore fisheries. With the construction of James' Fort between 1601 and 1603 and the establishment of Charles' Fort in the 1670s, Kinsale possessed a well-fortified harbour and subsequently became an important naval and fishing centre.

Many of the coastal towns and fishing centres in late medieval and early modern Ireland belonged to a maritime world that transcended the political boundaries of the country, a world united by the seafaring activities of native and foreign fishermen, pirates, traders, navigators and seamen. The expanding trade in fish prior to the opening of the Newfoundland fisheries had a threefold effect on the development of fishing around the Irish coast. Firstly, it encouraged the growth of specialised fishing communities and contributed to the separation of fishing from farming in many coastal districts. In most parts of the country, however, this simply fostered the growth of farmer-fisher communities, and in these districts fishing supplemented, but rarely replaced farming as the primary economic activity. Secondly, the trade in fish contributed to the development of 'backward linkages' with other labour-intensive crafts such as boat-building, net-making, sail-making, salt-refining, sawing, milling, barrel-making, and a whole range of activities associated with fishing and fish processing. Finally, this in turn fostered the growth of specialisation within a number of the more important fishing communities, thus augmenting the social distance between fishing ports on the one hand, and predominantly rural or urban settlements on the other. Thus, while the link between farming and fishing remained close in Ireland, as in many other European countries, a number of fishing ports were home to seafaring communities that were almost totally dependent upon fishing. In Ireland's case, this was especially the case in fishing villages on the Dublin coast, and in important fishing centres such as Waterford, Wexford, Drogheda, Arklow, Kinsale and Galway. In smaller ports around Strangford Lough and Carlingford Lough, and on the north-west coast of the country, fishing supplemented rather than replaced farming. Nevertheless, by the sixteenth and seventeenth centuries, fishermen were becoming much more experienced in the practice of their craft, moving from inshore to deep-sea waters, and fishing for particular species as the season demanded. Moreover, the shift from one type of fishing to another was frequently costly, as the skills, tackle and boats required in fishing for herring, salmon or pilchard could not easily be adapted to deep-sea cod and hake fisheries. Similarly, fishing techniques used in one branch of fishing often differed from those used in another. Thus, for example herring and mackerel fishermen used nets and comparatively small boats (including currachs and coracles), while those who hunted cod, ling, hake and conger fished with several fathoms of long lines baited with hundreds of hooks.

THE SEPARATE WORLD OF FISHERMEN AND FISHER FOLK

With no universal right to right to fish in medieval Ireland, fishermen were often prohibited from exploiting the rich resources of freshwater lakes and rivers. Those who fished in the inshore waters appear to have been less restricted. Legislation in the sixteenth century suggests that professional fishermen and their families occupied a privileged position in the social order of a number of Irish ports and cities. In 1585, for example, it was ordained that no seaman or fisherman in Galway should 'take in hand either the plowghe, spade or teithe, that would barr them from fyshinge'. It was further decreed that fishermen and their families should be served before all others, excepting the mayor and his peers, in the city's food markets.[24] This suggests that coastal fishermen in this stretch of maritime Ireland at least, belonged to the labour aristocracy rather than the *lumpenproletariat*. Together with fish processors and fishmongers, they usually lived separately from the rest of the community in port towns and fishing centres around the Irish coast. An inability to compete with foreign fishing fleets meant that many of them lived impoverished lives, and the districts that housed fishermen and their families generally had their own special ambience and social identity. The Claddagh fishing community of Galway, for example, developed separately from the rest of the city from a very early stage. Prior to the eighteenth century, this was one of the most impoverished quarters of the city. Situated a quarter of a mile west of Galway in the mid-nineteenth century, the Claddagh was described 'a very ancient village' which retained its own customs and social mores right down to the start of the twentieth century. In the late eighteenth century, the inhabitants of the district were persuaded to 'appropriate a small proportion of their weekly pay for the purpose of cleansing about their houses'. They were also encouraged 'get rid of many of those contagious disorders which generally prevail in large villages'. In the mid-nineteenth century, Hardiman stated that the Claddagh fishermen and their families 'lived in thatched houses of great thickness, or black beehive huts whose architectural style goes back to Christian times'.[25] On visiting this area in the 1830s, Henry Inglis commented that

> The fishermen of Galway form a large portion of the population, but are, in fact, a distinct people. They inhabit that part of the shore which lies on the right of the harbour, apart from the town, and which is called the Claddagh, and were formerly rued by a mayor and by laws exclusively their own. This usage, however, has been some time discontinued; though they are still governed in all matters regarding fishing, by their own laws, and are still an interesting and peculiar people.[26]

In the early 1840s, the Halls described Claddagh as

> a singular community that was still governed by a king, elected annually. At one time this king was absolute – as powerful as a veritable despot; but his power yielded like all despotic powers, to the times, and now he is, as one of his subjects informed us, 'nothing more than the lord mayor of Dublin or any other city'.[27]

A decade earlier, Hardiman also found that

> This colony from time immemorial has been ruled by one of their own
> body, periodically elected, who somewhat resembles the *Brughaid* or head
> villager of ancient times, when every class resided in its hereditary canton.
> This individual, who is dignified with the title mayor, in imitation of the
> head municipal officer of the town, regulates the community according to
> their own peculiar laws and customs, and settles all their fishery disputes.[28]

Discussing the peculiarities of the Claddagh fishermen in the post-Famine
decades, a contributor to the *Illustrated London News* wrote:

> It is said that they have, like the gypsies till of late, a code of law and
> form of government administered by an elective monarch who is called
> in Galway 'the King of Claddagh' and who is yearly chosen by 'the
> Claddagh Boys' on the eve of St John. A procession of men and women,
> bearing long faces of dock-stems, escort him through the quarter, and
> when the proclamation has been duly made, bonfires are lighted in
> honour of his reign for ensuring the twelve months. His ensign is a white
> flag, and he is empowered to decide all quarrels and punish all minor
> offences among the Claddagh population, without troubling the police
> and legal magistracy at all.[29]

Black's *Guide to Galway, Clare and the West of Ireland*, published in 1888, stated
that

> The Claddagh is the name given to that part of Galway adjoining the
> harbour, and inhabited chiefly by fishermen, the total population num-
> bering about 4,000. They may undoubtedly be regarded as representing
> the original Celtic inhabitants of the town, as they have never married
> with the 'transplanters', that is, with the Saxon and Norman colonists
> introduced at different periods. Formerly, they were recognised as a
> distinct community, governed by their own magistrate or mayor, called
> the 'king of the Claddagh', and although now under municipal rule, they
> still acknowledge the authority of their own 'king' as supreme in regard
> to many of their affairs.[30]

The population of the Claddagh increased steadily in the seventeenth and
eighteenth centuries, rising from an estimated 528 inhabitants in 1695, to over

2,300 in the opening years of the nineteenth century. The village was estimated to have 468 thatched cottages in 1812, housing approximately 500 families. In the early 1820s, the population reached over 3,000, and a large proportion of the 2,500 fishermen in Galway Bay hailed from the Claddagh.[31] The streets and footpaths of the district were greatly improved in the opening decades of the nineteenth century. Gentrification of this nature was usually carried out in rural towns in Ireland under the supervision of state agencies in the late nineteenth century. In the Claddagh, however, it occurred as early as the 1820s under the supervision of an officer in the Royal Navy who 'prevailed upon fishermen to use a portion of their earnings to pave their village with cobbled stones and install much needed drainage channels'.[32]

Writing about the Claddagh district in the opening years of the twentieth century, the nationalist writer Stephen Gwynn stated that he had 'never found any other community in Ireland so alien, so shy, and so hard to know'. A rough equality of the sexes was a marked feature of this and many other fishing communities throughout Ireland in the pre-Famine period. O'Dowd, the district's historian, has stated that

> Whereas the men went to sea and caught the fish, the women of the village took over the unloading and sale of the catch. In fact, when one looks a little closer at the social scheme of things in the nineteenth century, one is struck by the powerful influence exercised by the women in matters of selling the fish and dispensing with the proceeds. It was they who controlled the finances of the home, including what their menfolk spent on such luxuries as whiskey and tobacco.[33]

Hardiman commented on the position of women in the Claddagh as follows:

> The women possess unlimited control over their husbands, the produce of whose labours they exclusively manage, allowing the men little more money than suffice to keep their boats in repair, but they have the policy, at the same time, to keep them plentifully supplied with their usual luxuries, whiskey, brandy and tobacco, of which they themselves also liberally partake. They are equally illiterate with their husbands, and very seldom speak English, but are more shrewd and intelligent in their dealings. In their domestic concerns, the general appearance of cleanliness is deserving of particular praise; the wooden ware with which every little dwelling is stored rivals in colour the whitest delft.[34]

28 'Landing the catch'. Fishermen and their wives unload their catch at the quayside of The Claddagh in the 1830s (courtesy of Paul Francis Duffy).

Another visitor to the district in the early 1880s concurred, stating that

> The women [in the Claddagh] in the matter of the rule, were always the equal of men. The boats were unladen by them, the fish carried by them to the market, the husband not interfering. The women paid for everything, maintaining the complete control of the purse.[35]

Finally, when S. Reynold-Hole visited the Galway coast in the aftermath of the Famine, he also found that here, as in other Irish fishing communities

> The men give up their cargos to the women on landing, only stipulating that from the proceeds they may be supplied with a good store of drink and tobacco, and so get due compensation on the shore for their unvarying sobriety at sea.[36]

Fishermen in ports and towns on the east coast were also segregated from urban and rural communities in the eighteenth and nineteenth centuries. This was particularly noticeable in fishing ports around Strangford and Carlingford, but was also a feature of larger fishing towns such as Drogheda, Arklow,

Waterford, Youghal and Kinsale. An anonymous Frenchman who visited Connemara in 1797 stated that

> It is a singular thing that I have often had occasion to note that the uglier the country the prettier are the women – they are charming here. Connemara is said to be the most abominably ugly place in nature, and therefore ought to be inhabited by angels. I had thought of visiting it, and this sweet reflection confirmed me in my resolution. It is most extraordinary that this country, forming part of the county of Galway, and not more than fifteen miles from the city of that name, should be less well known than the islands of the Pacific Ocean. Of the persons from whom I asked information, some replied vaguely, others begged me not to visit such a barbarous country, where I should not find a dry stone to sit down on, and where the few inhabitants were as barbarous as the Iroquois. The Galway men in former times held it in such dread that, over the city gate leading to it, they engraved the word 'Lord deliver us from the ferocious O'Flahertys', and they made a law that any man of the name of O'Flaherty who should spend a night in their town should be put to death.[37]

Writing at the start of the nineteenth century, H.L. Bayly stated that

> The fishermen of Arklow, it must be observed, are a race distinct from the other inhabitants; occupying a separate part of the town, and being solely devoted to their own particular pursuits. Neither will they, even when reduced to absolute distress, employ themselves in any occupations not connected with their favourite element. Their lives afford an incessant variety, which seem the zest of their existences. Sometimes they are enduring all the hardships of the sea-faring life; at others they are sitting at home in perfect indolence for days together. Sometimes they have money in abundance; at others, they are suffering under the bitterest effects of poverty and improvidence. But, probably, in these particulars, they differ little from the same class of men in all parts of the world; and both their defects and good qualities, it is likely, may be traded in all cases to the same cause – a life of chance and adventure.[38]

Women and young girls who worked as fish-gutters and packers were always among the poorest members of these fishing communities. Married fishermen who had families to support, but who were forced to spend a good part of the year away from home were also prominent among the maritime poor. These men, and their womenfolk, often endured working conditions that made the life of an agricultural labourer appear comfortable by comparison.

That said, however, the fisherman's life had its compensations. At a time when most people in rural Ireland lived out their lives under the narrow horizons of the townland and country parish, fishermen inhabited a much wider world that sometimes stretched as far as the fishing grounds off the Irish and Scottish coasts. Fishermen from coastal towns around Dublin and the Irish Sea regularly fished off the north-west of Ireland, where local fishermen occasionally attacked their better-equipped boats. Likewise, those on the south coast fished up along the west coast, some going as far as the coast of Galway and Mayo. Fishermen from the north coast fished along the west coast of Scotland, and around the Western Isles. In the mid-nineteenth century, young men from all around the coast of Ireland occasionally found work on English and Scottish fishing boats. For these raw recruits to fishing, work on a boat was but a step away from emigration, as many of them moved to England and Scotland with the fleet at the end of the herring and mackerel seasons. Deep-sea fishermen in particular toiled alongside a diverse and globally experienced body of fishermen from Scotland and England. Some even found employment in fishing fleets from Holland, Spain, France and Portugal. Fishermen from these countries linked together the countries of coastal Europe. In the eighteenth and nineteenth centuries, large numbers of fishermen from coastal and rural districts in Waterford and Wexford worked alongside fishing fleets from all over Europe in the cod-rich waters off Newfoundland.[39] Before these men could become fully socialised into the world of sea fishing and seafaring, they had to undergo the equivalent of a maritime rite of passage. This meant that they had to be stripped of parochial attachments to land and locality, and were often obliged to drop all the home comforts and social supports to be found in close-knit rural communities. They also had to learn a new language of the sea, a language that would forge seamen and fishermen into a quite distinctive speech community. Full-time fishermen especially had their own language, which often included a generous portion of swearing and cursing. Deep-sea fishermen who kept themselves apart from other sections of urban society were notoriously renowned for 'rough talk'. It was said that they had 'tongues that swore and did not easily give way to prayer'.[40] The foreign fishermen who visited Ireland's larger ports along the south and east coasts were not only reputed to be 'foul-mouthed' – they were also lacking in deference

29 A satirical caricature of women and children in The Claddagh awaiting the return of their fishermen husbands. This sketch was taken from *A little tour in Ireland* by 'An Oxonian' and published in 1859.

to those set above them, whether on land or at sea. As 'plain speakers', they were suitably suspicious of the dealings with merchants and were among the hardest candidates for conversion that priests and other proselytisers were likely to encounter. It was said of these men that they liked short voyages in the same way that they liked short prayers. It was precisely because they were often 'men of short prayers' that proselytisers sought them out in order to tame their ribald ways.[41] Yet many of these men placed more faith in folk customs and religious superstitions than in the teachings of church and state. The deep-sea fisherman's religion was a rich mixture of superstition, doubt, disbelief and fantasy. Some held religious beliefs that helped them through seasons of hardship and very real danger. Others had a deeply sceptical attitude towards the religions of the pulpit. As one historian of Europe's maritime culture so aptly put it, the worldview of seamen and professional fishermen was 'an amalgam of religion and irreligion, magic and materialism, superstition and self-help'.[42] It often surprised many of those on shore that such men were rarely in awe of the beauties of nature and the sea. Yet fishermen were much more likely to be respectful of the sea and its unpredictable ways.

Fishermen also had an unmistakable way of talking. Their language included a rich array of 'slang' words and technical terms, unusual syntax and distinctive pronunciation. Raw recruits to deep-sea fishing especially had to learn names of boat parts and equipment, as well as picking up an entirely new vocabulary about sea and weather conditions that was indispensable to their survival at sea. When ashore in Ireland, they were numbered neither with the 'saints' nor with the 'scholars'. They belonged to a liminal world that was perched between the comparative security of a sedentary onshore life, and the complete insecurity of life at sea. The work-places of those engaged in gutting and packing fish, whether on the shore, on the quayside or on the street, were places where hard, often dangerous work was the norm. Here, physical prowess and self-help necessarily took precedence over all forms of mediation. When at sea, many fishermen lived under the sail or under the stars. The following account describes life under the 'towel', or sail, in small lobster-fishing boats off the south-west coast in the late nineteenth century:

> The only shelter available to the lobstermen in the entire six or seven-week fishing trip was a tent of sorts, temporarily erected in the bow when the boat was at anchor. The tent was originally referred to in the local Irish dialect by the term *teabhal*. Cooking was done at the mouth of the towel, on an open fire contained in a bastible pot, just forward of the mast and the main thauft. The pot, referred to as the 'fire-pot', was set on a mound of white clay under which was a large flat stone or a sod of earth. The bottom of the pot was also lined on the inside with a further layer of white clay or gravel. In some boats at least, the fire was set alight with the aid of hand-bellows, and a piece of corrugated iron, standing abaft the fire-pot protected the thauft and the mast. Bread, baked in a second bastible set on the fire-pot, was the mainstay of the lobstermen's diet. Two cakes were baked for each of the three daily meals, spread with butter and eaten hot. So-called 'griddle cakes' were baked in a frying pan … The salted mackerel used for baiting the pots was sometimes eaten, preferably after it had been in the pots overnight so that much of the salt had dissolved … Meat was rarely eaten. In the days before it became fashionable to have a floor in the holt, the pot of boiled potatoes was tipped on to the ballast, and the crew ate directly from the mound of steaming potatoes without the use of plates … Cans and enamel mugs were used for drinking, and the tea was brewed in a kettle. Milk was contained in a four-gallon earthenware whiskey jar, which was sometimes

fitted with a protective sheath woven from straw … When cooking was in progress, the bag of flour was put under the main thauft near the fire. When the crew was sleeping, it was covered over and used as a pillow.[43]

Foreign fishermen, who for centuries fished off the Irish coast, had an even tougher life than many of these inshore fishermen. They could be absent from home for weeks, and when their stint at sea was over, many were simply paid in kind, rather than cash. Inshore fishermen had comparatively easy lives compared to those attached to deep-sea fleets. Like the lobstermen from west Cork, they also had a wide and quite distinctive vocabulary, and often spoke a technical language that would have been all but incomprehensible to towns-people and rural folk. Hardiman described fishermen of Galway Bay as 'an unlettered race' who rarely spoke English, and whose Irish was 'harsh and discordant and scarcely intelligible to the townspeople'. Their separateness from other inhabitants of Galway was reflected in the fact that they rarely married outside their own community. They also married on set days, such as Saint Patrick's Day, midsummer's eve, and on selected fair days in May and September. Marriage was often preceded by elopement, and women were 'generally prolific' in giving birth to 'fine healthy children' rarely to be seen outside 'more opulent communities'. Strangers, known as 'transplanters', were 'not welcomed' in the Claddagh district, whose inhabitants were described as 'fiercely independent' people who 'stubbornly obeyed their own rules, and observed a whole array of superstitions relating to the sea'.[44]

Separated from loved ones, fishermen who fished off the Irish coast for days, sometimes weeks on end, also developed a distinctive male work culture. This had its own rituals, songs, language and sense of comradeship. The core-values of this culture were collectivism, anti-authoritarianism and equalitarianism. The seas where they fished, while more productive than the land and inconceivably richer than they are today, were steeped in superstition and danger. A vast body of prophetic sayings and incredulous beliefs was embedded in the sea lore of these men. It was difficult to know where superstition ended and where religion began in the belief systems of native and foreign fishermen. Catalan fishermen, for example, would confess to the sea by casting a pebble into it for each of their sins. If the water remained calm, it was a sign of God's forgiveness, but if the weather turned to storms, it was a sign of God's anger. Others would throw a dozen gourds – which were used as buoys – into the water, and read the future in the patterns made by their movement. Spanish fishermen in the seventeenth and eighteenth centuries bought special bells and other ornaments for their churches. They also whitewashed their topmost spires and bell towers in order to see them from afar. While at sea, many fishermen had special ways of blessing, and thus controlling, the sea. Some of the continental fishermen who fished the waters around Ireland in the sixteenth and seventeenth centuries believed that the souls of those lost at sea could be glimpsed at dusk. The sea was a widow-maker, a stingy task-master, and a 'dominating mistress in her own right'.[45] It was also the cruellest of elements, not least because it kept men from wives and sweethearts, often for weeks on end. The fishermen's loved ones were condemned to live 'a life of fearful uncertainty'.[46] The sea of course could also be 'bad tempered', and even jealous at times. It was home to an entire array of spirits, ranging from those that at could raise a storm in calm waters, to others that had the ability to sing a wind into existence. The worst storms of the year in Irish waters were those that raged between November and March, and these were often considered the work of demons. Naturally, for many deep-sea fishermen, superstition often shaded into religion. Just as Saint Peter was regarded as the saint who looked after the fisherman's catch, Saint Elmo was in charge of the boat's gear and the crew's fortunes.

The attitude of most fishermen towards the sea was usually a combination of affection and gratitude. They were grateful for the bounty of the ocean, even though they lived in constant fear of its strength and unpredictable nature. Most would not have thought of seascapes and coastal landscapes in spiritual or even aesthetic terms. For them, the seas, coastlines and skylines that excited moralists and inspired artists were simply associated with strenuous and often unrewarding work. Privileged individuals could enjoy stunning seascapes and coastal landscapes and take great satisfaction from scientific explorations of the physical environment. In so doing, they 'civilised' nature and portrayed themselves as defenders of the civil from the natural order. The labouring poor who harvested the seas and the shoreline of Ireland may well have considered such aesthetic and moralistic appreciations as so many distractions from their more pragmatic concerns with making a living. For some, indeed, time spent admiring nature was a distraction because it diverted them from a proper religious devotion to God and his angels. Although they lived lives close to nature at its most spectacular, fishermen therefore were also believed to have no real appreciation of the wonders of the natural world around them. In a rare description of the fishermen in Irish literature, novelist Joseph Tomelty gives a more sympathetic insight into their views on spiritual matters. In *Red is the Harbour Light*, one character who compares the religious attitudes of Ulster fishermen at sea with those of his urban and rural counterparts on the land, quietly states that

> at sea people don't feel the same about religion as they do on land. On the land, they never seem to find God, so they must fight about Him all the time. But at sea you can see Him everywhere, in the water, in the moon, in the stars, and you can hear Him in the wind. He's always there, like a strong but silent friend.[47]

Yet, historical accounts from the seventeenth to the nineteenth century have portrayed fishermen and other coastal dwellers as 'uncouth' and 'unmanageable'. As such, they were a breed apart from the manageable tillers of soil and the respectable society of country towns. Recognised as both keen-eyed and alert to the wily ways of the sea, fishermen were believed, by some, to lack feeling and to suffer from 'sensory inferiority'. Their 'sensory apparatus', it was suggested, was 'paralysed by lack of exercise of the intellectual faculties' and worn out through hard work.[48]

We have suggested that many of the British and continental fishermen who for centuries fished off the coast of Ireland had their own distinctive speech communities. This may have been the basis of their strong sense of social solidarity and collectivism. The speech of these men did not constitute a total language, or a language in its own right, but was primarily a language of work that did not encompass all aspects of these men's social existence. The language of fishermen and others who worked with fish was frequently grafted onto other aspects of plebeian culture. This made it all the more difficult for those outside their immediate circle to understand them. Fishermen and sailors in the larger Irish ports and harbours also had their own lifestyles. Ashore in Ireland, they would have congregated among their own kind, especially in their own drinking dens. They were constantly exposed to the temptations of 'grog shops', and churchmen frequently harangued them for their overindulgence in hard liquor. Referring to the evils of the floating 'grog shops' that sold hard liquor, tobacco and other contraband to fishermen off the coast Munster in the 1880s, the Reverend Green warned that

> It behoves everyone interested in the welfare of our countrymen and in that of fishermen who visit our shores, to use all the influence they can to prevent the fishermen from having any dealings whatever with these boats. The great saving of a deep-sea fisherman's life is that no matter

how he may be tempted on shore, he was free from temptation while at sea. If these copers continue to visit our shores this is all at an end.[49]

The culture of sea-going men had traits that were borrowed from other coastal communities. It shared many of the rebellious characteristics of plebeian culture at its most plebeian. For that reason, it was not so much a culture in its own right, but a 'proletarian particle within the larger plebeian culture'.[50] There were always definite commonalties between fishermen and other coastal workers in the terms of language, social beliefs, attitudes to authority, and attitudes to life. As in the case of all manual workers, fishermen were by no means stereotypical labouring automata who drowned their sorrows and boosted their joys in hard liquor and boisterous boasting. As the writings of Tomás Ó Criomthain and other island fishermen testify, they were cultured people who could debate politics and hold their own in discussions on religion, history and social affairs with anyone. They knew the words of hundreds of songs, and many probably knew just as many poems. They could play musical instruments and conduct conversations in English as well as Gaelic. Historically, when ashore in foreign countries, they would crowd into rowdy punch-houses, brothels and the haunts of 'lewd dissolute fellows'.[51] These places were remarkable for 'the swearing, obscene, masculine talk and behaviour of their women'. Coastal towns and cities in England, Scotland, North America and Western Europe also provided Irish sailors and fishermen with all sorts of entertainments not readily available in rural Ireland. This was especially true of those who put ashore at Bristol, Liverpool, Glasgow and Greenock, and others who sailed to the ports of France, Spain and Portugal. These are the forgotten passage migrants and unsung 'wild geese' of Irish maritime history.

Localised seasonal famines in Ireland over the centuries may well have augmented the number of men and youths who took to fishing at home in Ireland, or abroad in Canada, Scotland and England. These men experienced migration in a dual sense, leaving the land for a harsh life at sea, and abandoning rural work practices for the very different work experiences of fishermen and seafarers. While integration into this wider maritime culture certainly created new social bonds that often replaced the old, it stretched the social distance separating those who made their living from full-time fishing from those who worked the land. In the case of part-time fishermen (who made up the bulk of fishermen in large tracts of coastal Ireland), fishing fused with farming to produce a hybrid culture that linked fishermen and small farmers in a common struggle for survival on land and sea. Right down to the end of the nineteenth century, these part-time fishermen and farmers were occasionally abducted off the Irish coast, while others were press-ganged into the navy.

Fishermen and seamen have historically been associated with hard work, danger and the adventure of the open seas. Jack B. Yeats recurrently portrayed fishermen, kelp-gatherers, boatmen and ferrymen as active and purposeful individuals, as people who were constantly engaged in an arduous and not always bountiful partnership with sea and shoreline. He also 'pictured' them enjoying work and achieving something substantial in their humble but meaningful lives. For Yeats, it was their dignity and purposefulness that set fishermen and coastal foragers apart from dispirited peasants who worked the land, and from recipients of charity in town and country alike. He depicted the female kelp-workers and fish-workers on the western shoreline as dignified and upright individuals who held their backs straight when not toiling over fish and seaweed, and carried heavy baskets more than half their size. Their fishermen husbands were similarly portrayed in a sympathetic fashion, dragging currachs ashore after a day's fishing, or carting panniers of fish and shellfish ashore under a western Atlantic sky. Such images not only revealed the pride of fishermen and kelp-gatherers in their own work – they were also statements of the artist's conviction that fishing and kelp-gathering were worthy of recognition in modern Irish society.[52] In his portraits of people who made their living from sea and shoreline, none seemed to have beautiful faces, yet all radiated with life and character. The artist focused on the liveliness of personality in his maritime subjects and, in so doing, avoided the more conventional images of beauty in the work of others who portrayed life on the west coast of Ireland as a romantic engagement with sea and weather.[53] Yeats' fishermen were quayside philosophers as well as good sailors. They were 'swaggering men' who made their living in some of the harshest of environments, men who used their earnings to hold families together when emigration was emptying out coastal communities and scattering their Gaelic-speaking youth to the outer edges of the English-speaking world.

Many of the deep-sea fishermen who fished off the coast of Ireland belonged more to the broad macho world of male 'bravado' than to the narrow local world inhabited by the rural poor. Historians of maritime Europe have long recognised the central role played by seamen and fishermen in the formation of the Atlantic economies from the sixteenth century onwards. Certainly the English, Scottish and continental fishermen who for centuries exploited the great fishing grounds off the Irish coast, played a crucial role in the formation of a North Atlantic economy. Writing in the seventeenth century, William Petty described fishermen and sailors as 'the very pillars of the nation and empire'.[54] Historically, however, fishermen could often be as parochial and provincial as any farmer on the land. Although they travelled great distances in search of fish, when ashore, their wanderings were of a narrower sort. If, for example, he was from a village near Barcelona, the Spanish fisherman might never have visited that city, or if from Baltimore, he might never have visited Cork city. Such men regarded physical strength and a strong sense of male superiority as natural virtues, the essential attributes of those forced into a social partnership with sea and weather. Not surprisingly, the macho culture of the deep-sea fisherman placed numerous prohibitions on female contact with the male domain of boats and fishing gear. It was considered bad luck to even allow a woman step on board a fishing boat. However, crews made up exclusively of women occasionally also fished the waters of the Irish Sea in the nineteenth century. The bravado of fishermen who gambled their lives on life-threatening seas and in dangerous weather conditions was an important component of the self-image of these 'swaggering men'. They were arguably the most macho of Irish males, men who cast their very bodies and souls against the sea in order simply to make a living. Their admissions of failure, like their expressions of humility, emerged only intermittently, and chiefly only in a private setting shared solely with other fishermen.[55] It was most noticeable when they emerged safe and sound from their duels with waves and foul weather.

Fishermen of course not only worked in a very different environment to that of the farm labourer or tenant farmer – the tools of their trade were fundamentally different to those of other working people. The very nature of their work occasionally rendered their boats more important, and valuable, than land and other property. This was especially the case with islanders, but it was equally true of fishermen in remote coastal areas who made their living from the sea and by foraging on the shoreline. Such men were responsible for the upkeep of their boats and the maintenance of netting and other tackle. Despite the intense competition at the height of the fishing season, their boats brought fishermen together, both at launching time and when boats had to be beached at the end of the season. These were tasks that were beyond the ability of individual fishermen. As highly laborious tasks, they required young and old members of the community to 'pull together' as they dragged their boats ashore or struggled to hold them steady when they were being launched from the land. The communal launching of larger fishing vessels involved the joint efforts of as many as thirty men and boys. Fishing boats and currachs were the life and soul of Irish fishing communities, especially in the high seasons of herring, mackerel and salmon fishing, when the skill of their crews meant everything. Such men often had far stronger emotional ties to their boats and fishing gear than to their tiny plots of often unproductive land. Although always perceived as vital for survival, land rarely possessed the same emotional qualities for fishermen as their boats clearly did. As they themselves were wont to put it, 'no one ever died digging potatoes'. They expressed a similar sentiment when they claimed that 'there was no danger in planting barley'.[56]

Although they could be as emotional about land as other rural dwellers, fishermen rarely looked on it in the same way they did the sea and the boats that sailed on it. Boats could take on the qualities of 'magical bridges', linking the fishing community together, and linking the community both to rich fishing grounds and to the world at large. For that reason, they were much more than simply a means of transport. In the proper hands, and under the careful management of a skilled skipper, currachs and other fishing craft took on properties and values that were over and above their mundane uses. These craft also held meanings for their crews that were frequently expressed in song and poetry when men were under the influence of strong drink, and especially after a fishing disaster when a boat and its crew 'went down'. On larger boats, as also on the longer currachs used on the west coast, fishing crews often consisted of several family members, supplemented with friends, cousins and in-laws from the extended family. When fishing boats were lost at sea, or when the fishing season proved disastrous, this meant that the male side of entire families could be wiped out. At such times, grief was less a personal or even a family affair, but was something experienced at first hand by the entire community.

The boats that made up the foreign fleets off the coast of Ireland in the fifteenth and sixteenth centuries were highly complex affairs. With their pulleys, ropes, nets, endless lines of baited hooks, buoys and other gear, they were among were the most complicated 'machines' of their day. As such, they required constant maintenance and respect. Compared even to small farmers who gradually adapted to changes in farming practices, fishermen were often profoundly conservative. There was comparatively little in the repertoire of many nineteenth-century fishermen that would not have been recognisable to their seventeenth-century counterparts. Many of these men would have considered it sacrilegious to use the timber from old or decaying boats for any non-marine purpose. In some cases, they preferred to burn their boats, rather

30 Well-dressed children of Galway fishermen in the latter half of the nineteenth
century, with one child dressed in a petticoat to protect him from the 'faeries'
(from the *Illustrated London News* (31 Jan. 1880)).

than permit carpenters to dismember them.[57] Unlike landowners, merchants
and property owners, fishermen were not represented on any of the institutions
of the medieval or early modern state. They were 'fixed' on the sea rather than
on the land, and at sea each boat was a mini-state where the skipper's authority
was absolute. Their life at sea has been described as 'a rigorously fixed
combination of absolutism and communism, sanctified by tradition and
impervious to change': absolutism, because the skipper's word was law; and
communism, because the catch was divided more or less equally.[58] Historically
speaking, the strict equality governing relationships between fishermen on
board was particularly evident in eating and sleeping arrangements. The fierce
loyal bonding that was such a characteristic of such fishing crews was a form of
primitive communism. In his account of Catalan fishermen in the sixteenth
century, for example, Hughes pointed out that fishermen rarely owned their
own plates, although each had his own spoon, with which he ate from a
communal pot. Generally speaking, the crew kept the best fish for themselves,
and sent the rest to market, which was considered a modest compensation for
the low pay and the hard work and danger that they endured during long
fishing trips that took them many miles from home.

In Ireland as elsewhere in Europe, fishermen had their own peculiar way of dressing that marked them out from their urban and rural brethren. Such differences in dress code were especially pronounced in fishing communities on the Aran Islands, Cape Clear, the western coast of Donegal, south Co. Down, and many districts in the south-east of the country. Levis has given the following description of the apparel of lobster fishermen in west Cork at the end of the nineteenth century:

> Many of the lobstermen were fitted out with oilskin aprons or long smocks made from calico and, in later years, from flour bags. They were waterproofed by applying several coats of a mixture of linseed oil and egg yolk. Between coats, they were rolled up and put aside to allow the oil to soak into them before being put out to dry. It was the egg yolk that gave them their traditional yellowish orange colour, still a feature of modern-day 'oilskins'. Prolonged exposure to sunlight had a detrimental effect on them, gradually eroding their water-resistant qualities. Beeswax was also sometimes used for waterproofing. Some lobstermen also wore the leather, knee-length boots more commonly worn by the mackerel fisher-men. They had a strap at the side, near the top, for pulling them on, and they were made specifically for the fishermen by local shoemakers. They were regularly treated with oil or goose grease.[59]

Dressing differently, fishermen wore baggy breeches made of heavy material that was tarred against the cold, numbing wetness that they encountered at sea. Being adept at net-making, many fishermen probably mended their own clothes, and had them made by their wives and families. For that reason, each region often had its own distinctive style of clothing, and this was most remarked in the case of woollen jumpers worn by fishermen on the Aran Islands and around the north-west coast. Hardiman gave the following description of the dress of fishermen in the Claddagh in the mid-nineteenth century:

> Three flannel vests, under a fourth of white cotton or dimity (stout cotton fabric woven with raised stripes used for bedroom hangings), trimmed with tape of the same colour, over these a fine blue rug jacket with a standing colour and horn buttons, blue plush breeches never tied or buttoned at the knees, blue worsted stockings, a pair of new brogues, a broad brimmed hat neither cocked or slouched, and a red handkerchief

about the neck completes the holiday dress of Claddagh fishermen: at all other times they wear the common jacket and trousers usual with persons of their trade. The women still retain their ancient Irish habit: consisting of a blue mantle, a red body-gown, a petticoat of the same colour, and a blue or red handkerchief bound round the head after the old fashion. On Sundays and festivals, however, they make a more modern appearance; a matron's dress being generally composed of a blue cloak trimmed with fine ribbon, a rich calico or stuff gown, with a red flannel bodygown, occasionally worn over it, and a silk handkerchief on the head. They are seldom known to wear ribbons – women who cannot speak English are not allowed to wear ribbons in their caps.[60]

Because they were unable to choose when to fish, the act of fishing for these men was by its very nature compelling. In the centuries before the development of sophisticated aids that enabled fishermen to locate and catch fish, fishing times were determined by the condition of the sea and the state of the weather. All members of the community respected older fishermen and seamen for their experience and knowledge of the sea. Younger men respected their elders for their ability to 'read' the sea and the weather. The routines of fishing were strict, and were strictly observed. The daily lives of fishermen required a structure that, if they were to be successful, could not vary. Discussing the 'compelling' nature of fishing for coastal communities in Ireland, Hugh Brody has shown how work on the sea dominated the lives of such communities. He argued that fishing, by its very nature, created dependence upon a form of life which 'compelled' the very details of how a day be spent, how much cash income was earned, and how much each of the other elements in the lives of coastal communities had to be ordered around the sea. Discussing the Gola islanders off the coast of Donegal, he further added that:

> Work on the land is not as compelling as work on the sea. Its separation from money rewards renders it subsidiary in the islanders' concerns ... The islanders' attitudes towards farming constantly reflect the secondary significance of the land. There is not the same enthusiasm for growing things as there is for fishing. There is not the discussion of how a crop is progressing, nor particular interest in the fertility of the land. And farming's secondary place is evidenced in the rhythms of the day as it is in the rhythms of the year: a man can choose his time for work in the day without strict reference to the demands of soil and plant. A crop must be

picked when it is ripe, but ripeness spreads through time; the ground must be tilled on a fine day, but fine days are not specific days. If one chance is missed of working on the land, another will probably come. So if it is the moment to go fish, the men go fishing. The work on the land must wait. The very qualities of land work, be it farming or turf stacking, assist the islander in giving priority to work on the sea. The land is less compelling, and its moments less exact.[61]

This description of the primacy of fishing in the island of Gola in the 1960s could equally be applied to many coastal communities living between the land and the sea in the poorer agricultural districts of Ireland from the fifteenth to the nineteenth century. It could certainly be applied to historic fishing communities such as Killybegs, Kinsale, Arranmore, Claddagh, the Aran Islands, Cape Clear, Baltimore, Youghal, Dingle, Dungarvan, Skerries and Dunmore East. Describing the primacy of commercial fishing over subsistence farming in a fictional Scottish village in the nineteenth century, Neil Gunn wrote that many of the young men

had a hunger for a bit of land, but seeing it could not be got, they gave more and more of their whole attention to the sea. A row of potatoes here and there on a croft each would have, and he gave harvest labour for it, but he now bought his oatmeal. With fresh fish, salt fish, a barrel of cured herring, meal, potatoes and – for the greater part of the year – milk, butter and cheese, life was given a solid back that neither chance nor mischance could affect greatly. A side of pig, a barrel of porter, meat on more than one day a week, syrup, eatables bought out of a shop, would be encountered in many a place, and when there was no milk for porridge, children grew excited over the change to treacle, nursing a dark spoonful in the centre of the place. The rise of the fishing had pushed poverty from the door and beyond the little fields, and though its spectre might haunt the mind now and then, there was a good way of dealing with it, especially when a stranger came … It was the hand into the store of hidden shillings then for swift feet for 'something special' to the shop. For the women were jealous of hospitality's good name and, to come near the truth, they would indulge in hospitality as men on a market or settling-day would indulge in drink. They loved it, its carefree giving, its talk, its laughter, its swept house, its clean table, its bright face, its delicate pride.[62]

Unlike rural communities, with their acutely perceived gradations of power and influence, fishing communities such as these were often characterised by a high degree of 'equalitarianism'. In a study of 'belongingness' in the Shetland community of Whalsay, Anthony Cohen showed how equalitarianism led to the intentional masking or muting of social differentiation. Rather than being a moral principle, this was a pragmatic imperative that facilitated intensive long-term social interaction within small, peripheral communities. In such communities, the achievement of consensus was frequently more important than leadership, and it was the community as a whole, and not any elected representatives of it, which made important day-to-day decisions in their confrontations with the sea and the outside world. In Ireland, Peadar O'Donnell described close-knit island communities on Arranmore, Tory Island, Cape Clear and the Blaskets as 'a special kind of townland'.[63] Danger at sea 'made one heart of all their people' on stormy nights when the boats were out. It was said that people in such places were not so much 'fed' as 'bred' to take the strain of sea fishing, and a good herring catch could cause the entire community to 'leap from naked poverty to comparative wealth'.[64] Fishing communities such as these have historically also tended to treat all members alike, insisting, for example, that they 'were all the same', despite differences in material circumstances and social status. This in turn kept the community ensconced within a local world that had well-defined social borders. Not surprisingly, such communities also tended to be hostile to 'transplanters', or strangers, just as they were superstitious, secretive, self-satisfied, self-sufficient, introspective and impenetrable. Again, this was most marked in island communities in the past, but for centuries may have been a marked feature of fishing communities all around the coast of Ireland.

Fishermen were also one of the largest and most important groups in the 'labouring classes' in the international economy of northern Europe in the seventeenth and eighteenth centuries. As such, they were the pioneers in the construction of a transnational and international labour market. Their numbers included all those who laboured on board fishing vessels, in addition to the thousands employed as fish-curers, packers, gutters and a host of other jobs associated with the processing and marketing of fish. This was also the case in coastal Ireland, where large numbers were employed in offshore British and continental fishing fleets. While ashore, many more were employed in the processing and packing of fish for home consumption and the export markets. In the comparatively small port of Bantry, for example, up to one thousand workers were employed in local fish palaces in the opening years of the seventeenth century.[65] The men who fished the waters around the Irish coast in the late medieval and early modern period were also forced to endure a quite different regime of discipline and punishment than that experienced by their rural Irish counterparts. Harsh discipline was considered a necessary accompaniment to the increasing productivity of seafaring labour at this stage in the evolution of the fishing industry. On larger continental fishing vessels, men experienced social class discipline at its harshest, while on smaller Irish fishing smacks they were expected to eat, sleep and work in the most primitive of conditions. Whether on board boats or ashore, fishermen were expected to perform a whole range of tough and dangerous tasks. This included 'shadow work' such as repairing and oiling the gear, overhauling the rigging, coiling and making ropes, mending sailing canvas, swabbing the decks of larger vessels and guarding the cargo of their boats. As such, fishermen were the great 'multi-taskers' of their day. Because the work of fishermen was highly visible, they were also under constant surveillance. Whether within the close confines of boats or on the open pier, they were constantly under the eyes of their strict task-masters. Fishermen were also expected to exchange the open space of life on shore for the confined world of the boat. Those working on board the larger foreign fishing vessels that fished off the Irish coast were regularly submitted to the despotic rule of skippers whose control of the crew was absolute. For many of these men, indeed, life at sea was a life of incarceration. One commentator has suggested that life on board fishing vessels in the seventeenth and eighteenth centuries was comparable to 'a binding chain of linked limits: limited space, limited freedom, limited movement, limited sensory stimulation and limited choices of leisure activities, social interaction, food and play'.[66] Many fishermen lived out much of their lives in 'wooden worlds' of limited space aboard their boats. They were poor, underprivileged and overworked, but they were also considered 'irresponsible', 'uncouth' and 'careless'. Their attitude to life was summed up in the saying 'let us live while we can'. Their sayings glorified the life of the present, as they demanded the right to 'a merry life and a short life'.

The following chapter focuses on the social and economic consequences of colonial policy on Ireland's sea fisheries from the sixteenth to the eighteenth century. It particularly examines the role of colonial settlers and venture capitalists in the commercial exploitation of the country's sea and freshwater fisheries from the sixteenth to the eighteenth century. It traces the development of the *mare clausum* or 'closed sea' policy that sought to exclude continental fishermen from Irish waters in the run up to the more formal plantations of

Ireland in the sixteenth and seventeenth centuries. Finally, it traces the impact of colonial governance on the maritime economy of Ireland, and the effects of settler colonialism on the country's dietary patterns and fish-trade from the time of the plantations to the pre-Famine period.

CHAPTER SEVEN

Ireland's sea fisheries in the age of colonial expansion

PLANTATIONS AND COASTAL IRELAND

Nowhere has the neglect of the maritime been more noticeable than in historical accounts of social change in Ireland in the aftermath of the plantations. Ignoring the effects of colonial governance on Ireland's sea and freshwater *fisheries*, most historians have reduced the plantations to mere transfers of forfeited *territory* from Gaelic overlords to individual grantees and companies of venture capitalists. The neglect was partially due to the fact that new power holders in colonial Ireland were grouped together in *land* precincts corresponding in most cases to the territorial baronies into which the counties had been divided. Not surprisingly, in most accounts, the plantations have been synonymous with the transfer of *land* to English and Scottish settlers in the sixteenth and seventeenth centuries. In the case of the Munster plantation, the lands confiscated by the crown in the wake of Desmond rebellion were divided into *seigniories* or lots, varying in size from 4,000 to 12,000 acres. These were then granted to 'undertakers' who pledged to plant them with English-born families. Under this scheme, Sir Walter Raleigh alone acquired approximately 40,000 acres of prime agricultural land, including whole stretches of the Munster coastline. He was certainly aware of the development potential of the province's freshwater and saltwater fisheries. He noted for, example, that England's great sea rivals, the Dutch, then had more than 3,000 vessels that employed some 50,000 men on the waters off Great Britain and Ireland. This resulted in an estimated 30,000 tons of salted fish exports valued at £2.5 million and represented a considerable drain on the national wealth. While the plantation in Munster was far less effective in execution than originally envisaged, nevertheless the movement of population was impressive, even by Elizabethan standards. An estimated 12,000 settlers moved into the province, many of whom settled in the coastal districts in the south and south-east of the country.[1] The plan of plantation in what came to be known as the 'escheated counties' of Ulster was devised between 1608 and 1610. By the mid-seventeenth century, the population of that province was around 260,000, including an estimated 80,000 immigrants from Scotland, many of whom originated in coastal areas that already had a flourishing fishing industry.[2] Plantation 'lots' in Ulster were significantly smaller than in Munster, the largest being around 2,000 acres. In coastal areas in the east of the province, a significant number of small farmers, fishermen and craft workers were established alongside already established farming and fishing communities.[3] In the north and west of the province, as in large tracts of Munster, the longer-term effects of plantation meant that whole sections of the indigenous population had to eke out a living on some of the most infertile land in the country. In a significant number of cases this resulted in communities being pushed up into marginal uplands, or further out onto the maritime fringes of the country where they were forced to subsist on the resources of inshore waters and the shoreline. The amount of land held by 'New English' and Scottish settlers practically doubled between 1640 and 1688. The seven million acres transferred to 'undertakers' and merchant adventurers represented accounted for approximately 80 per cent of all Irish land by the end of the seventeenth century. By this time, new settlers and colonial authorities accounted for an even higher proportion of prime agricultural land, while Catholic landowners retained only 22 per cent of the land, much of it in poorer districts along the west and south-west coast. This figure dropped to around 5 per cent a century later, when the 'plantations' had effectively contributed to the relegation of Gaelic society to some of the most remote districts of Ireland.[4]

The introduction of merchant companies and investment agencies had a profound effect on the utilisation of coastal resources in colonial Ireland. Despite early efforts to establish small-scale settler farming in parts of Ulster and Munster, most land was consolidated into large estates under the control of powerful families who also claimed fishing rights to the lakes, rivers and estuaries of the country. As far as sea fisheries were concerned, the plantations simply contributed to the Anglicisation of waters that had already been 'colonised' by foreign fishing fleets well before the seventeenth century. In the course of the eighteenth century, significant regional imbalances began to emerge in colonial Ireland, as commercialised systems of farming and fishing spread across the south-east and east coasts, while subsistence farming and fishing continued to characterise marginal lands and coastal tracts in the west of Ireland. The population of the country as a whole expanded rapidly between 1750 and 1830, especially in the west, where potato cultivation supplemented rough grazing, turf cutting and the gathering of 'shore food', or *cnuasach tra.*[5] Throughout this period, therefore, poor families in many coastal districts along the west and north-west coast readily availed themselves of the natural resources of seashore and inshore waters in order to obtain cheap food, fuel and housing. For many, the coastal west of Ireland constituted 'the poor man's paradise'. Driftwood from the sea and bog oak from the hillside were available for putting roofs on houses built with locally available stone, while rushes, reeds, bent grass and heather 'scraws' were widely used as thatching material. In many remote coastal districts, the traditional barriers to early marriage were largely absent, and landlords and the institutional church had comparatively little influence over the social norms of coastal communities. It has been shown that settlement limits in large tracts of rural Ireland were set at roughly 500 feet above sea level in the mid-eighteenth century, and climbed to roughly 800 feet in the early 1840s. The alarmingly high population densities experienced in this period led to the construction of new human landscapes on barren hillsides and remote coastal uplands of the west of Ireland in particular. Moreover, while such communities may have appeared primordial or pre-colonial, they were in fact the product of comparatively recent adaptations to rural and coastal landscapes in some of the country's harshest environments.[6] Potato cultivation, a limited amount of rough grazing, and the assiduous use of shoreline and inshore waters, crucially underpinned the success of many coastal communities in the eighteenth and nineteenth centuries. When the fishing failed, or when poor weather conditions made it hazardous to harvest sea wrack or collect shellfish, many coastal communities faced temporary *coastal* famines. Thus, well before the Great Famine, those living on an ecological knife-edge between marginal uplands and a rocky coastline were frequently pushed to the limits of survival. Although they availed themselves of a wide variety of produce from sea as well as the land, life for such communities was lived at the margins. The census of 1841 revealed that almost half the rural population of Ireland were living in one-roomed mud cabins. In coastal districts in Kerry, the figure was as high as 66 per cent, while in the Beara Peninsula in Co. Cork it reached 80 per cent.[7] In the late 1830s, in a letter to the lord lieutenant of Ireland, a teacher from a coastal parish in west Donegal stated that there was 'not more than ten square feet of glass in windows in the whole [parish of some 1,500 houses], with the exception of the chapel, the school house, the priest's house, Mr Dombrain's house and the constabulary barracks'.[8]

Military conquest and plantation also brought about a radical break with traditional methods of resource utilisation in colonial Ireland, thereby altering social and environmental relationships in many coastal districts. This was particularly noticeable in coastal Ireland, where the mixture of farming with

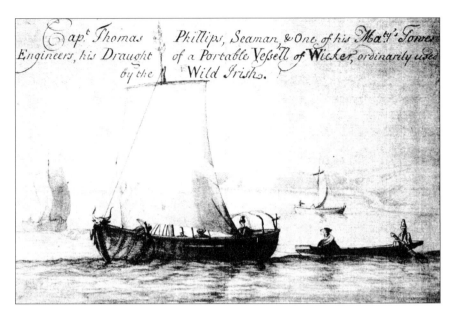

Cap.t Thomas Phillips, Seaman, & One of his Ma.ty. Tower Engineers, his Draught of a Portable Vessell of Wicker, ordinarily used by the Wild Irish.

31 Captain Thomas Phillips' late seventeenth-century sketch of 'a portable vessel of wicker ordinarily used by the wild Irish' in the pre-colonial period (courtesy of the de Courcy Ireland collection).

fishing meant that communities were never simply dependent upon the land, or narrowly confined to rural parishes. They lived instead in an open world of sea and coastline, organising themselves around quite rudimentary fishing ports adapted in the course of the eighteenth and nineteenth centuries to the needs of a much more commercialised fishing industry. The extrovert character of large tracts of coastal Ireland was evident in many aspects of social and economic life, and in the material culture of coastal communities. Thus, for example, the 'drontheim' – a fishing yawl widely used in remote districts along the north coast – was an eighteenth-century adaptation of a Norwegian fishing boat.[9] The 'hookers' used for fishing and transporting goods along the Galway coast may well have developed from the 'hoekers' used by Dutch merchants and fishermen in the seventeenth and eighteenth centuries.[10] Given the rounded nature and geographical spread of the colonial population, it is hardly surprising that the new settlers contributed to the demographic re-mapping of large expanses of coastal Ireland.[11] The inhabitants of coastal Leinster, east Ulster and colonial Munster in particular witnessed dramatic changes in the structures of their everyday lives, as areas that had formerly been beyond the reach of state control were now much more firmly under the centralising influence of state institutions.[12] Maritime Ireland, with its long history of commercial and cultural contact with the Mediterranean, Scandinavia and Atlantic Europe, also became locked into a much tighter core-periphery relationship with Britain. These trading associations entailed new power relationships, as settler society gained increasing control over land, coastal resources, freshwater lakes and well-stocked rivers. The twin acts of 'civilising' coastal Ireland and 'planting' the peripheries of the country with colonial settlers radically reduced the area under Gaelic control. Prior to the plantations, and for a considerable period afterwards, commercial relations of production had barely existed in many remote communities along the Atlantic seaboard. Here, inshore fishing was a survival strategy that permitted farmer-fisher communities to supplement their meagre agricultural surpluses with the produce of the sea and the shoreline.[13] In the colonial period, farmer-fisher communities were forced into a much more intensive relationship with coastal environments. The modernisation of agriculture in coastal Leinster and east Ulster caused improving farmers to exploit the resources of sea and shoreline in a much more thorough fashion. Small tenant farmers gathered seaweed, burned seashells to produce lime for fertiliser and generally supplemented the meagre produce of their infertile fields with saltwater fish and a wide variety of molluscs and crustaceans harvested from the shoreline. This was particularly evident in the Lecale district of south Co. Down, where farming techniques introduced by the settlers fostered a 'new husbandry' based on novel systems of crop rotation and large inputs of seaweed and limestone. In time, these were heavily dependent upon regular applications of lime-rich sand, seaweed and even sometimes fish, to enrich soils and maintain productivity.[14]

Viewed thus, colonial intrusions had a number of important consequences for Ireland's sea and freshwater fisheries, and for its maritime economy. Firstly, from as early as the fifteenth century, there were repeated attempts to 'close' the seas around Ireland to continental fishing fleets, and to bring the country's sea fisheries more firmly under English control. This culminated in a loose version of *mare clausum* when the commercial concerns of English and Scottish fishermen coincided with the geo-strategic interests of the colonial state and sought to exclude foreign shipping, including fishing vessels, from what were now only nominally Irish waters. Secondly, the much more formal Ulster and Munster plantations contributed to the demise of Gaelic Ireland's control over freshwater and marine fisheries, as fishing rights now passed into private ownership and colonial control. Thirdly, and more positively, colonial settlement was accompanied by comparatively high levels of investment in fishing fleets, and in the development of freshwater and inshore fisheries. This occurred alongside the upgrading of transportation networks, harbours, docking facilities, quayside warehouses, 'salt houses', 'ice houses' and other rudimentary structures for the processing and packaging of fish for export.

This was especially noticeable in coastal Munster and the east coast of Ulster, where individual landlords and venture capitalists invested significant amounts of money in upgrading facilities for processing and marketing fish. William Petty's thriving but short-lived pilchard fishery in Kenmare Bay bears testimony to the innovative role of an individual planter in the development of Ireland's fisheries in the seventeenth century. William Nesbitt's bold attempt to develop a whaling industry off the coast of Donegal in the latter half of the eighteenth century was another example of this type of initiative.[15] Finally, the plantations resulted in a reconfiguration of the urban landscape of colonial Ireland as coastal ports became the new channels through which the surpluses of the rural and maritime economy were dispatched, and even small ports facing the Atlantic had a precocious trade with the new world.[16] As Robinson has argued in relation to early colonial Ulster, coastal ports now served

> as entry points for colonists, and so the communications network also functioned as a framework for their dispersal. The ports attracted town-dwelling merchants and traders, while the conditions of the plantation provided a unique attraction for British farmers to settle and exploit the hinterland. For seven years from 1610, the produce of the undertakers' estates could be exported free from tariffs, while for five years, household goods and a limited quantity of livestock could be similarly imported. This provided a massive incentive for the export trade in grain, butter, cattle and hides from Ulster, particularly to Scotland.[17]

In the minds of colonial rulers and settler communities alike, the military conquest and subsequent 'peopling' of Ireland with 'improving' planters also found their shaping metaphors in the prior subordination of nature as feminine and woman as a category of nature. Yet to describe the conquest of coastal Ireland as 'rape' is to liken it to a 'once-off' act of aggression inflicted on a vulnerable victim by a powerful male 'other'. The Ulster and Munster plantations were not like that. They were certainly not spontaneous events. Neither were they passively accepted historical happenings that scarcely impinged on the lives of 'feminised' or 'taciturn' natives. They were meticulously planned, long drawn out, and strongly resisted affairs that were more akin to forced

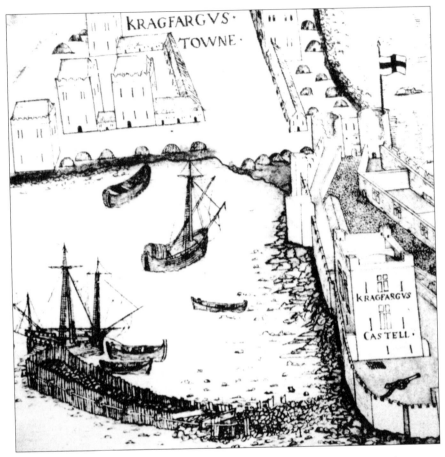

32 Fishing boats and shipping at Carrickfergus on the Antrim coast in the mid-sixteenth century (courtesy of the British Museum).

marriages than spontaneous acts of rape. Certainly, in the aftermath of the plantations, whole sections of the indigenous population were considered as a 'debased people' who lacked the skills to manage the land of Ireland and to properly exploit its fisheries. New settlers, it was argued, would husband the resources of land and water more effectively than the native Irish ever could.[18] Colonial settlers were brought to Ireland in very large numbers, with William Petty's calculations suggesting that one third of the population in the latter half of the seventeenth century were either immigrants or of immigrant stock. These 'in-migrants' spearheaded the social and economic transformation of colonial Ireland, refashioning parts of the country into a fair imitation of the places they left behind. They cleared woodland, reclaimed land, planned new settlements, introduced improved methods of boat-building and net-making, and transformed the indigenous fishing industry.

At yet another level, the plantations contributed to a Manichean construction of Ireland as a country inhabited by 'civilised settlers' and 'avenging natives'.[19] While the former were largely confined to the agricultural heartlands, the latter, including poor peasants, landless labourers, smugglers, fishermen and pirates, were believed to inhabit the coastal wastelands and bogs of the west and north-west coast. Thus, while settler communities were considered a civilising force in a 'barbaric land', the coastal poor belonged to the realms of lawlessness and disorder. The inhabitants of this 'disordered' Ireland were believed to be engaged in a whole range of illegal activities, including piracy, smuggling, harassment of sea-going traders and fishing vessels and the extraction of tribute payments from foreign fishing vessels in the waters off the coast of Ireland. This meant that the coastal poor and impoverished fishing communities were at the centre of settler objections to Gaelic cultural practices in early colonial Ireland. The mere presence of impoverished natives in these 'backward places' was a cause for concern for the country's colonial modernisers. It was also suggested that sea fishing and smuggling had fostered distinctive 'human types' in coastal Ireland, especially island communities, people whose moral and physical characteristics set them apart from Irish and colonial society. It was suggested, for example, that the twin forces of coastal geography and a life spent harvesting the ocean were responsible for the development of a hardy and independent race of men eminent for their height, strength, stealth and cunning.[20] The inhabitants of Cape Clear were regarded as a seafaring race set apart from Irish society by their 'reputation of being simple, honest and worthy people'. Their simplicity resided in an aversion to luxuries, their chief indulgence being a fondness for strong drink and the comforts of community life. Isolated island communities such as these 'delighted in listening to old tales when the winter's fire afforded a delightful contrast to the storms of the Atlantic'. Cape Clear islanders in particular were 'so attached to their sterile home that they never quit it, even for a short time, without evident reluctance; and they view an expulsion from the island as the greatest of all possible calamities'.[21] The Claddagh fishermen of Galway were considered to be 'an isolated fragment of the past, carried to the present on the current of time'. Their fishing craft was said to be 'inferior to the "currach" used 2,000 years ago', while the 'language and manners of this singular colony had undergone no change since the days of St Endius'.[22] Because remote islands and coastal communities produced such 'natural seafarers', they attracted the attentions of naval officers and captains of foreign fishing vessels from a very early age. For centuries, therefore, the latter were drawn to the coasts of Cork, Galway and Mayo 'because of their supply of skilled seamen and fishermen'. During the Elizabethan period, ships trading with Galway regularly recruited crews from surrounding districts, 'with fishermen from Claddagh being highly valued for their expertise'.[23]

IRELAND'S FISHERIES IN AN AGE OF TRANSITION

Ireland's foreign fishing trade declined rapidly in the seventeenth and eighteenth centuries with the opening of the far more profitable Newfoundland fisheries, and continental fishing fleets found it increasingly less profitable to visit the Irish coast. Nevertheless, new investors in colonial Ireland were well aware of the economic potential of the country's freshwater and sea fisheries. Many English settlers were attracted to the country by the 'great and plentiful fisheries of salmon, herrings and pilchards, which salted and barrelled are every year exported for foreign ports and yield a considerable return to merchants'.[24] From the start, colonial authorities were convinced that, under judicious management, the seas off the north and south-west coast would afford an inexhaustible supply of wealth. One commentator asserted that

> No country in Europe, or probably in the universe, is so admirably situated for an extensive trade in fish as Ireland. From Cape Clear in the south, to Malin Head in the north-west, the coast is studded with numerous banks, such as those off Brandon Head, at the entrance of the Shannon; Moyman, near Westport; the great banks extending into the deep sea from Slyne Head, Achill Head and Inishboffin Island on the Connemara coast, probably a continuation of the great Newfoundland Banks, and, like them, abounding in fish of the most valuable description, such as ling, cod, equal to those on the North Sea, haddock weighing from 15 to 30 pounds. The sea along this coast is often speckled with marine animals of a larger size, such as the Greenland and Spermaceti whale, the sun fish etc, producing oil of the most valuable description. Here, then, is a field open for the employment of 100,000 fishermen, whose operations would give sustenance to millions of people.[25]

From the opening decade of the fourteenth century, boats from Rutherglen in the Firth of Clyde had been fishing for herring off the north-east coast and in the Irish Sea. The thriving Atlantic herring fishery off Ireland's west coast was

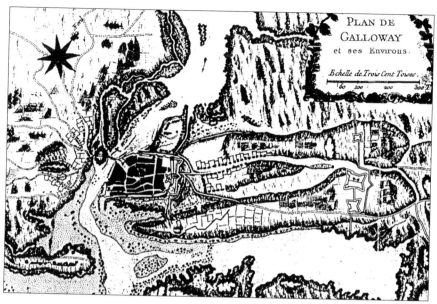

33 *Plan de Galloway* by J.N. Bellin, published in Paris in 1764. Historically, Galway's fishermen were prohibited from farming lest this would distract them from fishing and reduce fish supplies in the city (from O'Dowd, *Down by the Claddagh* (1993)).

on a par with the highly productive east coast fisheries. Certainly by then, the sea-routes between Ireland and Britain experienced an increasing amount of sea-going traffic, much of it linking the north-east of Ireland with the western islands and the west coast of Scotland. Much of the traffic on the Irish Sea at this stage was directly concerned with military campaigns in Scotland. The latter, in turn, were 'made possible only by constant supplies of men and provisions carried by ships from Dublin and Drogheda to the port of Carlisle, or to Ayr'.[26] Ireland was not only 'one of the king's great grain stores'; at a time when armies on the march consumed immense quantities of salted fish, the country supplied British ports with abundant catches of hake, herring, cod, ling and salmon. Indeed, long before the formal planting of Ireland with settler communities, English and Scottish fishermen were regular visitors to coastal towns and fishing villages around the east and south coasts of the country in particular. The rich cod banks and herring fisheries off the country's Atlantic coast were as much sought after by European fishermen in the fifteenth and sixteenth centuries as those off Newfoundland and Greenland in subsequent times. In the mid-sixteenth century, Anthony St Leger wrote to his monarch urging him to take over the rich sea fisheries off Ireland's south coast. Earlier in the fifteenth century, a number of English investors sought licences to exploit fisheries off this productive coast. In the opening decades of the sixteenth century, English and Scottish fishermen had penetrated as far south as the waters off Munster. In 1535, Oliver Cromwell received intelligence from the treasurer of war in Ireland stating 'that an English fleet of some 600 sail were at the herring in the vicinity of Carlingford Lough and Greencastle'. This informant added that rents in this part of Ulster would increase significantly 'if the fishing there continued as it has done'.[27] Here, as in other stretches of coastal Ireland, a thriving fishing industry meant that rents were well paid and regularly paid.

The right to import wine through Irish ports, known as *prisage*, was frequently used to control fishing rights in the pre-colonial period. *Prisage* rights benefitted powerful Gaelic families in coastal areas, enabling them to export fish, hides and agricultural produce, in return for wines, weapons, manuscripts and luxury garments from continental Europe. This allowed them to control considerable stretches of the Irish coast, with some local chieftains taking between one sixth and one tenth of fish caught by foreign fishing vessels in Irish waters. Tolls were also levied on foreign vessels using anchorages and harbour facilities. At this stage, a local chieftain, one MacFineenduff, earned £300 per annum from Spanish fishing fleets in Kenmare Bay.[28] Tribute collection on this scale was gradually brought to an end during the reign of Queen Elizabeth. English merchants, not least powerful fish merchants, sought to keep the profits of all possible branches of Irish commerce in English hands, at a time when colonial authorities frowned upon any intercourse between Gaelic Ireland and continental Europe. Still, however, the waters off the south-west coast of Ireland, the jewel in the crown of Ireland's sea fisheries, continued to be 'much frequented by French, Spaniards as well as English and Irish'. In the mid-sixteenth century, Philip II of Spain paid the Irish exchequer one thousand pods per annum for a license allowing Spanish fishermen to fish off the north coast of Ireland for a term of twenty-one years. In his *Discourse of Ireland*, Humphrey Gilbard reported that there was 'a great traffic' of Spanish vessels in the south of Ireland, with 'at least with 600 sail of ships and barks for fishing only'. He accordingly petitioned the queen:

> To have a grant of the isle of Balletymore with a friary standing therein;
> To have an island in the harbour of Balletymore, in which the Spaniards lie aground during the time of the fishing and wherein a fort must be made [and reliable subjects settled there];

To have customs from the Spaniards and Biscayans, who use year to fish from the foreland of Blaskey;

To have the sixth or tenth fish from all such fish as they take there.[29]

By the end of the sixteenth century, however, the continental fleets that customarily fished the intractable waters off this coast faced increased competition from English vessels working out of Bristol and the west coast of Scotland. Sir William Temple, writing in the early 1670s, believed that Ireland's sea fisheries 'might prove a mine under water, as rich as any under ground'. The coasts of Ireland, he added, were 'the resort of vast shoals of herring, cod, ling, hake, mackerel, turbot, sole, haddock, plaice, sprats and numerous less useful fish'.[30] The country's rivers and lakes, on the other hand, were 'abounding in salmon, trout, pike, eels, perch, tench and fish of other delicate kinds'. Pike were brought into the smaller English ports, particularly from Youghal, Cork, Dungarvan and Kinsale, in the early part of the sixteenth century. Cod, ling and hake, all of which were associated with 'the white fishery', were plentiful on the Irish coast, particularly in the vicinity of the Nymph Bank off the south-east of the country. Those concerned with the development of this fishery insisted that, 'if cultivated with skill and activity', it would one day equal that of Newfoundland. The western coast was believed to be 'particularly well adapted to an extensive fishery'.

With fish ranking as one of the most important exports of sixteenth-century Ireland, visiting merchants and colonial speculators frequently remarked that the produce of sea, rivers and lakes were among the country's most important products. Even before the plantations, English fish merchants kept 'factors' or 'buyers' at the more important Irish ports. One sixteenth-century account suggests that West Country fish merchants sent boats to fish Lough Swilly and the west coast of Scotland as a matter of course. Boats destined for Irish fishing grounds were generally made ready at Michaelmas, the best time for fishing cod and ling. In addition to fishing gear, they carried goods for trading, including 'all sortes of corrupt wines' to the north of Ireland, where the 'salmon fishing is'.[31] Almost 1,200 barrels of herring were shipped from Ireland to Gloucester in one week alone in 1592. A *Port Book* from 1607 reported that fishing boats from Poole, in Dorset, voyaged from 'Killeborge' [Killybegs] with over 200 barrels of 'white herring'. Accounts show that fish other than salmon and herring came chiefly from the southern towns of Dungarvan, New Ross, Cork, Youghal, Dingle and Kinsale. Waterford and Wexford supplied large quantities of herring to Bristol, Bridgewater and smaller ports along the west coast of England.[32] The main centres for salmon, herring and ling fishing around the Donegal coast were Killybegs, Assaroe, Culmore, Culdaff, Buncrana, Trabreige, Lough Swilly, Greencastle, Leanan, Rathmullan, Ballyshannon, Inver and Arran.[33] A tract published around the end of the sixteenth century proposed settling a colony of Dutch Protestants around Lough Foyle and Lough Erne in order to exploit the fisheries there. Although this proposal fell through, it indicated the importance of saltwater and freshwater fisheries in this part of Gaelic Ulster. Killybegs and Assaroe had access to offshore sea fisheries, and this played no small part in cementing trading, and even diplomatic relations between Gaelic Ulster and Catholic Spain. An emissary from Spain landed here in 1596, and in April of the following year a Spanish vessel put ashore on the Donegal coast laden with supplies for the O'Neills and the O'Donnells. Far from being an undeveloped backwater, pre-colonial Donegal had highly productive saltwater and freshwater fisheries, a thriving agricultural economy and close trade links with continental Europe. The O'Donnells, famed for their wealth in Spain, France and Belgium, exerted control over a coastal stretch extending from Dunluce on the north coast of Antrim, to Erris Head in on the coast of Mayo. As Mac Eiteagain has pointed out, 'they took particular care to control the Moy Estuary, the cockets of Sligo, and the valuable fishery in the River Bann'.[34] So great were the revenues derived from these and other fisheries that the north-west of Ireland attracted 'sea robbers' and pirates from Iar Connacht and the Hebrides. This region also had strong trading links with Bristol in the south of England, with Wigtown, Glasgow and Ayrshire in Scotland, and with St Malo and Morlaix in Brittany.[35] Its extensive salmon and herring fisheries were reputed to be among the largest of their kind in Europe.

Following the plantation of Ulster, the lucrative salmon fisheries of the Bann, Lough Neagh and Lough Foyle were granted to the corporation of London, while many lesser 'fishing-places' in Ulster and Munster were assigned to new owners who were immediately impressed with the wealth of Ulster's fisheries. One seventeenth-century account deemed the coast around Tír Conaill to be 'the very best fishing-grounds in Europe'. 'Who', its author asked, 'has not heard of the magnificent fishings of cod, turbot and plaice off the coast of Tír Conaill ... who has not heard of the productiveness of the Hempton and Otterainoile banks?'[36] Early into the plantation project, agents representing a company of London merchants in the lordship of the O'Cahans, were instructed to 'furnish a true account of its natural resources – whether it might be expected to yield great numbers of red deer, foxes, sheep, lambs, rabbits, martens and squirrels, which would be valuable mainly for their fells or skins'. O'Cahan country was described by one visitor to the province as 'fruitful and pleasant'. Off the coast, and in the waters adjacent to the islands of Scotland, the sea was well stocked with fish, 'which attracted Scottish, Breton and Flemish fishermen every year in considerable numbers'.[37] Writing in 1611, Sir Thomas Phillips also referred to the presence of considerable numbers of Breton fishermen off the coast of O'Cahan country, adding that:

> There was long since at Port Rush a fishing used by the Burtons [Bretons] in France who came every season thither for dogfish and rays, which being well handled are a great commodity in Spain.[38]

Colonial agents in seventeenth-century Ulster were required to report on 'the extent of the several fisheries in the sea and the rivers; together with an account of what sea fowl could be had on the coast; and whether, as reported, pearls were to be found in the River Foyle'. Their employers were particularly interested in establishing whether or not ports on this stretch of the coast of Ulster could be used in the exploitation of the recently opened Newfoundland fisheries. Their agents in Ulster were directed to ascertain 'whether the coast was adapted to purposes of traffic with England and Scotland ... or most fitted, by being comparatively the nearest point, for the voyage to Newfoundland'. In their final report, the agents stated that:

> The harbour of Derry is a most commodious harbour, and convenient for all sorts of shipping. Portrush is distance from thence 12 miles, and Lough Swilly, 30 miles ... It is likely upon the said coast, store of cod, ling, skate and other fish might easily be taken, if they were as diligently sought for as elsewhere ... it is certain that infinite store of cod and herring are there, and upon the near and adjacent islands of Scotland, yearly taken by Scots, Flemings and French, whereof they learn there are 200 sail many times together ... In the rivers of Lough Foyle and Bann, besides salmon and eels, there is a great plenty of trout, flounders and other small fish, and the said rivers by computation yield 120 tons of salmon yearly, and sometimes more ... The coast is apt and safe, taking a first wind to go to all parts, and as such convenient for trade, both to the north and the south.[39]

With the plantation of Ulster, a small salmon fishery in the Roe, together with another at Faughan, both of which flowed into Lough Foyle, fell to the

34 Port life in colonial Londonderry in the late eighteenth century.
With the plantation of Ulster, fishing rights once held by the Catholic
church and Gaelic families passed to private landowners and colonial
entrepreneurs (from *The Copper Plate Magazine*, 1 (1793)).

possession of the crown. Following the Flight of the Earls in 1607, and with 'much manoeuvring and no small outlay', Sir Arthur Chichester and Sir James Hamilton managed to 'clear the River Bann from Lough Neagh to the sea of all other minor plotters against its salmon and eels'.[40] Records from the seventeenth century show that two fisheries in the peninsula of Inishowen, namely Culdaff River and Culdaff Bay, were in the 'king's possession, while the fishery at Trabreige was also Chichester who subsequently leased it to one of the O'Dohertys. Around this time also, Sir William Godolphin from Cornwall acquired 'the whole water or river of the Banne with the fishing and taking of salmon and all other kinds of fish, for twenty-one years at a rent of 10 pounds'. Shortly after acquiring the right to exploit fisheries in mid-Ulster, Chichester subsequently surrendered part of his newly acquired possessions, including 'very valuable fishings and 300 acres' in order to attract more London investors to the region. As Hill has argued, in order to 'encourage the Londoners' it was Chichester's 'patriotic duty' to make these valuable fisheries available to new investors.[41]

From the 1680s onwards, a number of attempts were also made to set up companies to promote fishing off the west coast of the country. Sir George Rawdon provided boats and nets to Irish fishermen in order to curtail the export of Irish fish by Scottish fishermen from this section of the Irish coast. Even then, however, the success of the fishing industry was still hampered by competition from French fishermen who came here in great numbers and resisted all efforts to expel them. It was also pointed out that, prior to the arrival of French commercial fishermen on the south coast, it 'was very usual for the hookers and fishermen of Kinsale, with about three men and a boy in each boat, to take 3,000 or 4,000 mackerel a day; but now they take few or none, and also other fish grow very scarce'.[42] In an effort to extend colonial control over the southern and western fisheries, 'forty gentlemen' from England applied for a patent to set 20,000 fishermen to work 'at overthrowing the Hollanders' and other fishing fleets who had traditionally fished in Irish waters.[43] At this time also, efforts were made to exploit the rich fishing grounds off the Mayo coastline, while the earl of Cork sought to improve Munster's offshore fisheries by building boats and establishing salting and 'fish palaces' on the coast from Youghal to Bantry. With the clearing of pirates from the creeks and estuaries along the Munster coastline in the late 1630s, it was reported that the 'take' of pilchards on this coast was 'the largest on record'. Some twenty years later, the indigenous fishing industry of Munster and south Leinster suffered a severe blow when the only fishing vessels operating in Irish waters that were allowed to enter English ports were those registered in England.[44]

This growing commercialisation of fisheries in the seventeenth and eighteenth centuries led to investments in onshore facilities for preserving and packaging fish for export. Colonial settlers along the south in particular introduced 'salt houses' and 'ice houses'. Occasionally known as 'snow wells', the latter began to appear in Ulster in the second half of the eighteenth century. Rudimentary though they were, these facilities were crucial to the expansion of Ireland's saltwater and freshwater fisheries. Ice houses in the north-east of Ireland were generally built near a lake or a pond so that winter ice could be packed into them.[45] Cruder versions had been established in England and the south-west of Ireland in the sixteenth and seventeenth centuries. Many early ice-houses were little more than open pits in the ground, filled with ice and then thatched over with a roof of straw. Elizabeth David has shown that the use of ice to preserve fish was largely confined to the luxury trade in salmon at this stage.[46] By the seventeenth century, however, fish merchants in remote fishing ports in colonial Ulster and Munster were using ice to preserve herring and pilchards. The rapid increase in the use of snow and ice in the preservation of fish contributed to the development of more sophisticated storage facilities along important salmon rivers and fishing ports in Scotland, Ireland and England. The supply of ice to large fish markets was big business by the eighteenth century, and often drew in Norwegian dealers who could supply it in bulk to ports and fish markets throughout Great Britain and Ireland.[47] Tons of ice were packed into specially constructed ice-houses in ports all around the Irish coast at this stage. Remote coastal districts were at a disadvantage if they lacked ice-houses or salting facilities. This was particularly so in summer months, when lobster and other shellfish and large seasonal catches of oily herring, pilchards and mackerel could rot away on lonely landing stations due to the lack of proper facilities. Writing in the 1750s, Pococke referred to 'fish palaces' where fish were preserved at a number of sites around the coast of Munster, including the islands of Sherkin, Cape Clear, Dursey and Whiddy, and the ports of Bantry, Baltimore, Crookhaven and Mizen Head.[48] In the eighteenth century, it was customary for small farmers and fishermen along the east coast of Ulster to flood fields in upland areas in order to create sheet-ice for supplying ice to local fishing stations. Elsewhere in the country, ice was harvested from lakes and ponds when it attained a thickness of two or three inches, and in the early nineteenth century, small farmers could earn up to 3*s*. per day filling ice-houses. In the 1830s salmon exported from Derry to Liverpool were packed in boxes filled with ice that was usually obtained in neighbouring districts. However, in the unusually mild winters of 1832, 1833 and 1834, it was necessary to import ice from Norway, and the cost of ice used in the Foyle fisheries alone was put at £600 per season.[49]

ENGLISH JURISDICTION AND IRISH FISHERIES

John Appleby has shown that the English high court had comprehensive jurisdiction over much of Ireland's loosely defined territorial waters in the sixteenth century.[50] New legislation was then enacted to consolidate English control over Irish waters, and to put an end to 'criminal actions' and 'illegal activities' on the seas and shoreline around Ireland. The criminalisation of pre-colonial customary practices was a marked feature of capitalist development in the maritime fringe of Ireland from the sixteenth to the eighteenth century. These included the collection of tithes from foreign fishermen by Irish chieftains; customary fishing rights of the Irish in the country's inshore waters, lakes and rivers; the pollution of rivers and bays by foraging animals; the spearing of salmon and other freshwater fish with hooks and forks; the non-payment of murage taxes and tolls by fishermen entering Irish ports; the collection of seaweed on the shorelines of private estates; and the grazing of farm animals near the spawning grounds of freshwater fish. Estate owners and colonial authorities in the eighteenth century banned the use of spears to catch salmon and other freshwater fish in Ireland. A penalty of 20s. was imposed on those using spears in the country's major salmon rivers and it was an offence 'to make, have or keep, any *leister* or spear for killing salmon, or make use of any light upon any freshwater river'.[51] Persons without a warrant were allowed to seize salmon spears and bring the offenders to a justice of the peace who then paid the informer the 20s. fine. Despite these restrictions, salmon spearing continued in many Irish rivers and estuaries until well into the nineteenth century, and lightweight casting spears were used to catch fish in the shallow waters of bays and estuaries around Wexford well into the twentieth century.

While there was little mention of legislation to protect the spawning grounds of salmon and trout in the early literature, we know that authorities in Dublin for example were concerned about water pollution in the Liffey from the fifteenth century onwards. In 1446, the corporation, by then a major controller of fishing rights in and around the city, ordered that 'no tanner, glover nor any person' who used lime in the preparation of leather goods should be permitted to 'work in the River Liffey on account of the destruction of salmon'. The penalty for each offence was three farthings, half of which was to be paid to the detector of the offence, and the other half to the court. Most of the tithes collected from Liffey fishermen at this stage appear to have belonged to the prior and convent of Holy Trinity. In 1577, the dean and chapter of Holy Trinity presented a bill to the lord chancellor for the recovery of tithes payable on herring. Among the protesting fishermen involved in this non-payment of fish tithes were Tomas Heiwarde of Malahide, Thomas Carre of Howth and Patrick Managhan from Clontarf. In defending their right to fish, the men insisted that 'the custom of Ireland was to give one half of such tithes to the parish church where the fish were landed, and half where the fishers dwelt'.[52] This was one of the earliest of many recorded examples of a clash between native custom and 'foreign practice' in matters relating to fishing and fishermen in Ireland. Protection of local oyster beds was probably the reason for an ordinance of 1461 that prevented fishermen in Dublin from flooding the market with oysters bought at ports outside the city. Water-bailiffs were appointed to supervise the harvesting of oysters in and around Dublin in the fifteenth century. These were paid in kind with one hundred free oysters from every boatload arriving in the city from beyond the Liffey Bar. Oysters were also taken inside the bar of the Liffey, and in 1578 Richard Browne complained to the corporation that one Richard Rouncell, a fishmonger, 'did molest him and would not permit him to dredge oysters within the bar, as it was lawful for him to do as a free citizen of Dublin'. In response, the city fathers passed an ordinance stating that 'no freeman be forbidden to dredge oysters within the bar', provided that no one should take any other fish while ostensibly fishing for oysters.[53]

A deposition of 1567 called for an admiral to be appointed to regulate fishing seasons in Ireland and to impose levies and fines on those who infringed fishing regulations. These new regulations were not only designed to keep Irish fishermen in check – they equally applied to Spanish, Dutch, French and Portuguese fishermen who sailed in large numbers around the Irish coast. Well-equipped Scottish, English and continental fishing fleets often fished alongside smaller vessels working out of Dublin, Drogheda and other ports in the Irish Sea in the sixteenth century. These were also subject to state regulation. The monitoring of saltwater and freshwater fisheries, by no means unknown in the pre-colonial period, was increasingly the function of the colonial state and its local representatives. We have already noted that powerful dynastic families along the west and north-west coasts benefited significantly from the presence of foreign fishermen in Irish waters. The herring fishery off the north-west coast was a particularly lucrative source of wealth for the O'Donnells in the sixteenth century. There was also a flourishing salmon export trade in this part of the country as far back as the fifteenth century, the bulk of it going through the English port of Bristol. The lordship of Tír Conaill also had a valuable seal fishery in the late medieval period, and in addition to the tribute payments from foreign fishermen, and from vassal territories within their domain, the leader of the O'Donnells could claim toll payments from the port of Sligo.[54]

Control of fishing rights on such important rivers as the Liffey, the Shannon, the Lee, the Blackwater, the Bann, the Foyle and the Roe was a topic of growing concern in the sixteenth and seventeenth centuries. Judging from the frequency of cases taken to court, the poaching of salmon and other fish was common in rivers and lakes throughout Ireland. Yet, despite the vigilance of the owners of fishing rights on the Liffey, medieval Dubliners were able to indulge in what for many was not just a form of recreation, but a necessary means for supplementing an inadequate urban diet. Judging from court records from that time, medieval Dublin had many such poachers. Those engaged in what was increasingly regarded as *illegal* fishing, especially those caught taking freshwater fish from water flowing through private estates and church land, or from the urban stretches of the Liffey, the Lee and the Shannon, were severely

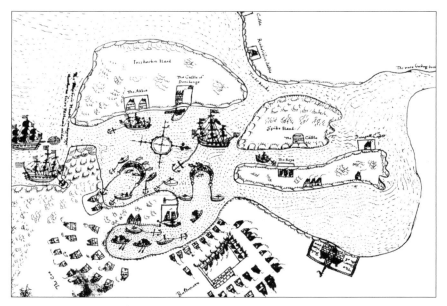

35 Map of Baltimore in the 1630s, showing the modest homes of fishermen and seine netting for fish in The Cove. Prior to its sacking by Algerian pirates in 1631, this small town was a model fishing village, complete with fish palaces and fish presses (courtesy of Sheffield Library).

punished. Salmon-poachers in particular were sternly treated. In 1425, one John Dyrre from the north side of Dublin helped himself to two salmon on a section of the Liffey controlled by the church. For so doing, he received a punishment beating from the curate of St Michan's and was ordered to wear a loincloth for six days. Similarly, fishermen who put their nets into the Liffey between vespers on Saturday and tierce on Monday were liable to a fine of one ounce of silver. As punishment, they could also have their nets, coracles and clothing burned. The existence of such rules and regulations not only testifies to the harshness of the legislative code, it also suggests that fishermen worked in unison and that they were well practiced in the art of net-fishing. They used wickerwork boats covered with one or more animal hides.

We know that the pilchard industry in Ireland was also subject to protective legislation from the earliest of times. In 1625, it was ordered that fishing rights on the south Irish coast were to extend ten leagues out into the sea. Within these limits, it was ordained that 'no nation whatsoever shall fish without licence of the inhabitants'. By the early 1620s, the earl of Cork held the tithes from pilchard fishing around Crookhaven. Some forty years later, continental fishing fleets were forbidden to fish for pilchards off the south-west coast.

Those engaged in this fishery were also banned from fishing from June to the end of October, and the penalty for breaking the ban was forfeiture of nets and boats.

New settlers also sought patents granting them exclusive rights to entire sections of the Irish coast. Sir Warhame Sentleger, for instance, wished to have a patent for the fishing rights to the entire coast of Munster. At the end of the sixteenth century, John Appleyard obtained the right 'to plant and inhabit Baltimore with colonists who would fish its waters'. By 1630, the lower part of the town, known as the Cove, contained some twenty-six single or two-roomed thatched cottages arranged in three concentric rings around the curve of the shoreline. The inhabitants were mostly fishermen and their families who worked at the village fish palace, the vital nerve centre of the town. Baltimore by then had adopted preservation techniques that had been tried and tested at fish-processing works in Cornwall and Devon. Pilchards were 'layered with salt in four-foot piles before being stuffed tightly into huge casks … before being shipped off as far as France, Italy and the New World'.[55] Baltimore was not the only fishing village to attract the attention of colonial entrepreneurs. On 20 July 1630, Sir Thomas Buttons requested that the fort at Kinsale be repaired 'because it stands where the greatest fishing of pilchard, herring, haak and salmon are to be had, and where the greatest provision is made of fishing for all the western parts of any port in the west of Ireland'. Further along the coast at Bantry, a 'handsome abbey' was demolished in 1734, 'for the conveniency of the pilcher palaces'.[56] In 1672, Sir Robert Southwell addressed a letter to one Mr Reeve in Rotterdam with a view to inducing a number of Dutch fishermen to settle in Kinsale and to form a fishing company. Southwell's father had established a pilchard fishery there in 1665, when it was alleged that some fishermen 'took £1,300 worth of fish in one pull of the net'. In the event, his request fell on deaf ears and the Dutch did not accept his offer. In a tract published in 1576, John Dee condemned the practice of allowing Spaniards and Frenchmen to fish 'without molestation' around Cork, Kinsale, Youghal and Baltimore, 'as if they were within their own king's peculiar limits'. He went on to add that the fishing port of Blackrock, in Cork Harbour, was frequented by 'three or four hundred sail' of foreign fishermen who were attracted there by the rich cod banks that lay offshore. In 1623, the lord deputy, writing to one Sir Oliver G. Calvert, stated that 'Last year the Hollanders came to the herring fishing on this coast and are making preparations for taking liberty again this year without leave or license, according to the encroachment they have made of late years at Shetland in Scotland'.[57] Spanish fishermen were particularly aware of the rich pickings to be had off the south and west coasts of Ireland. In a message sent to Captain Juan Pita de Beiga, the Alcalde of Ferrol, in March 1580, Captain Sidee counselled the Spanish official 'not to do anything that might prejudice the interests of the subjects of Spain who use the trade and fishing of England and Ireland'. In June 1606, James I granted the earl of Ormond:

> the haven of Skerries, which is now in a ruinous state, by reason whereof there are now only in Skerries 2 boats, out of which the lord or tenant of Holmpatrick had the best fish, whenever they took fish for a custom; but when the said fort was built, many ships and boats from England, France, Spain and Scotland came thereto annually, as well for security as to fish, and there paid customs.[58]

A memorandum written by Lord Justice Pelham and dated 28 July 1580, recommended that the government should build forts 'to prevent the Irish from entertaining pirates and Portingalls and Spaniards that yearly come to fish in those harbours'.

'NEW LEARNING' AND THE SEA FISHERIES OF COLONIAL IRELAND

From the sixteenth and seventeenth centuries onwards, the fishing potential of the west and south-west of Ireland was regularly assessed by colonial authorities and new settlers alike. Drawing attention to the number of fishing vessels operating around Gregory's Sound, off the Aran Islands, Sir Oliver John pointed out that any 'enemy possessing this sound may be master of all the isles of Aran (which are well inhabited) and command all the bay of Galway'. He called for the 'building of a fort in the Great Island, which would be of great use and importance' due to the fact that this coast had 'a good fishing for cod, ling and other fish [which hitherto was] conducted by the English, the Bretons, the Portugalls'.[59] By the mid-seventeenth century, the waters off the south of Ireland were said to have the best pilchards in Europe, while Irish cod and ling were much esteemed in England, France and Spain. Some investors pointed out that cod and ling, 'with the train of oil that comes from them', were also 'vented in large quantities through the fishing ports of the west coast of England'. Others sought to develop the fishing potential of the Galway and Mayo coastline, where the chief obstacles to the commercialisation of the local sea fisheries included lack of salting facilities, poor harbours, inadequate fishing boats, the distance from markets and the fact that pirates and smugglers plagued this coastline well into the seventeenth century.[60]

The development of the pilchard industry in the 1620s and 1630s had a significant impact on the coastal economy of Munster. Pilchard fishermen alone accounted for 40 per cent of customs receipts from the coastal region between Kinsale and Baltimore at this stage. The use of seine nets to catch pilchard was well developed in Cornwall in the sixteenth century and spread along the coast from Kinsale to Kenmare in the opening decades of the seventeenth century. At this stage also, new methods for salting, pressing and barrelling fish were introduced, and a string of 'pilcher palaces' for 'pressing' pilchards was built along the south-west coast. Dickson has remarked that:

> the momentous growth of the pilchard fishery was funded by New English venture capital, some coming from past earnings in piracy (as in the case of Thomas Cooke and William Hull), some from new landowners, including Thomas Roper, Vincent Gookin and Richard Boyle, and some from speculative traders attracted over from London and the English West Country.[61]

We have already seen that Richard Boyle was especially instrumental in developing the fisheries of coastal Cork, where, 'under his fostering care, comfortable farm houses sprang up in deserted villages, and lonely sea bays changed into harbours crowded with fishing smacks'.[62] The pilchard fishery in this part of Munster was 'cantoned in about a dozen settlements, of which Clonakilty, Crookhaven and Baltimore were perhaps the largest'. At its peak, it provided seasonal employment to over 2,000 people. New English settlers accounted for the bulk of the skilled personnel in the industry, and there is 'almost no record of the direct involvement of indigenous merchants or of Irish labour in the fishery'.[63]

The career of William Petty was to have a very important effect on the development of fishing in colonial Ireland. A member of the Royal Society, Petty had studied medicine at the liberal Dutch University of Leyden, and as such would have been familiar with developments in the Dutch fishing industry. He belonged to that group of colonial investigators and amateur scientists who regularly communicated the results of their scientific investigations to the Royal Society. Aside from his scientific work, Petty also lived the life of an enlightened estate owner and entrepreneur. A stout supporter of the natural sciences, and defender of what came to be known as the 'new learning', he pioneered the development of statistical science, political arithmetic, map-making and colonial geography.[64] Born in 1623, he spent time as a cabin boy

36 William Petty (1623–87). Political economist, statistician and landowner, Petty developed the pilchard fishery of Kenmare Bay in south Kerry in the latter half of the seventeenth century (courtesy of the National Portrait Gallery, London).

on an English merchant ship when he was only fourteen years of age. He held the post of Deputy Assistant to the Professor of Anatomy at Oxford in 1684, and was appointed Professor of Anatomy two years later. In 1652, he was appointed physician to the Cromwellian army in Ireland and acted as clerk to the Irish Council. As Surveyor General of Ireland he produced the Down Survey in 1655–6 with the aid of that other defender of 'new learning', James Ussher. Petty's work on the Cromwellian Land Settlement, more commonly known as the Down Survey, was the starting point of a grand seventeenth-century design to 'improve' Ireland's remoter regions by exploiting their natural resources, including not least the resources of the sea and the coastline of the west and south of the country.[65] His survey of colonial Ireland has been described as one of the most remarkable scientific works carried out in Ireland in the seventeenth century. It was also one of the first modern surveys of the country. Demography as 'political arithmetic' had much of its origins in the seventeenth-century tradition of writing about Ireland that Petty represented. According to this school of thought, improvements in the public 'weal', and in the very constitution of society, could only occur when those guided by clear, rational and scientific principles were entrusted with public office. This was considered essential in under-developed societies such as seventeenth-century Gaelic Ireland and in the wider colonial world of the Americas, Australia and India in the eighteenth and nineteenth centuries.

This line of thinking reached its fullest developments in Petty's *Political Arithmetic* and *The Political Anatomy of Ireland* and in Hobbes' *Leviathan*. Students of demography in Ireland after Petty did not just collect information about the country's population; they also warned of the putative consequences of untrammelled population growth, and were alert to what they perceived as any deteriorations in the social fabric of society. They particularly focused on the social class and ethnic 'mix' of Ireland's population, both at the level of the nation as a whole, and at the regional level. In so doing, they transformed the category 'population' from the 'natural' entity that it was in pre-plantation times, into a pseudo-scientific and ideological construct. Viewed thus, the population of Ireland, not least the communities that made up the 'barbarous' west of the country, rapidly took on the features of a threatening spectre hovering over an Enlightenment nation-building project. From the start, therefore, the populations of 'backward' coastal districts were widely perceived as threats to the success of colonial civilisation. The term 'population' lost all links with actual people, and was used instead to refer to the reproductive capacities of the 'lower orders' living in 'backward places' and remote coastal districts. New settlers and colonial authorities in Ireland were especially concerned about the 'native' preference for a life of 'filth' and 'idleness', which they contrasted with the settled life of industry and reason represented by new settlers and colonial entrepreneurs. Throughout the seventeenth and eighteenth centuries, English observers in Ireland's 'wilder' regions condemned traditional methods of farming and fishing, and by the mid-seventeenth century we find English visitors to the west of Ireland deploring the Irish aversion to 'honest industry'.[66] Prior to the plantations, Ireland was perceived as a country that had more in common with the 'backward' interior of medieval Europe than with the dynamic societies on the maritime fringes of Atlantic Europe. Despite its small size, however, some argued that it straddled both these worlds, and that its social structure was a mixture of the mercantile world of Atlantic Europe and the far more secluded and medieval world of pre-modern Europe.

Plantation, new methods of farming and fishing, and the commercialisation of the coastal economy were all viewed as strategies for drawing Ireland's 'backward' regions away from the 'idiocy' of native customs and into an evolving world system of maritime trade, industry and mercantile capitalism. Petty and his followers firmly believed that the natural sciences could make a significant contribution to the development of industry, farming and fishing in seventeenth-century colonial Ireland. In typical colonial fashion, he insisted that innovative experiments in resource utilisation and regional development were 'better tried out upon poor Ireland than upon proud England', since royal authority was 'somewhat more absolute in Ireland than in England'. In the preface to his influential *Political Anatomy of Ireland*, written in Kerry in the late 1660s but not published until 1691, he held that just 'as students in medicine practise their inquiries upon cheap and common animals, I have chosen Ireland as such a Political Animal'.[67] The economic orientation of his thought revealed a distinct interest in the development of the extractive industries, fishing and shipping. The latter, he argued, could raise living standards and increase productivity in under-developed regions undergoing rapid population growth.

In regarding the population of colonial Ireland as the embodiment of its wealth, he held that the latter in turn was 'the result of man's social actions on the resources of nature'. Having been impressed by the fishing industry of contemporary Holland, he was anxious to promote the exploitation of Ireland's coastal zone, especially the estuaries around the west coast of Kerry and south Munster. In his *Political Anatomy of Ireland*, he remarked that the Irish were masters of 'the art of Fishing and ... everywhere gather cockles, oysters, muscles [sic], crabs etc. with boats and nets'.[68] Petty also suggested that the under-development of the Irish fishing proceeded

> from want of imployment and encouragement, than from the natural abundance of flegm in the bowels and blood; for what need they to work, who can content themselves with potatoes, whereof the labour of one man can feed forty; and with milk, whereof one cow will, in summer time, give meat and drink enough for three men, when they can everywhere gather cockles, oysters, muscles, crabs etc., with boats, nets, angles, or the art of fishing; can build an house in three days?[69]

He further stated that there 'were only 1,000 people in Ireland engaged in fishing in 1672', adding that '[t]here are in the west of Ireland about 20

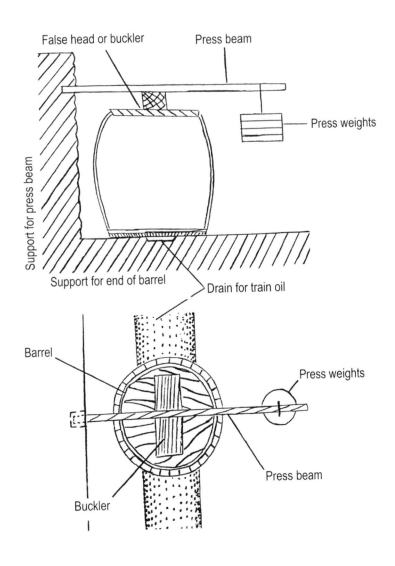

37 A fish press used for 'pressing' pilchards and herring prior to packing them in barrels for the export market (from Went, 'Pilchards in the south of Ireland' (1946)).

gentlemen who have engaged in the pilchard fishing, and have among them about 160 saynes wherewith they take about 4,000 hogsheads of pilchards worth about 10,000 pounds'. On acquiring 'a huge and wild estate' in Kerry in the 1660s, he immediately set about exploiting the region's natural woodlands and inshore waters. Much of this estate was acquired in the aftermath of the Cromwellian invasion, when many of those granted land in Ireland did all in their power to avoid settling in remote places along the west coast 'because of the apparently rough and unprofitable character of the soil and the wildness of the inhabitants'.[70] However, Petty was alert to 'the facilities which the geographical situation, the land-locked harbours, the extensive forests, the valuable quarries and other natural resources of the county might give in the development of *other than* agricultural wealth'.[71]

Having established a colony of Protestant settlers in the baronies of Iveragh and Dunkerron, he set about organising the sale of timber from the native woodlands around Killarney, set up a pilchard fishery in Kenmare Bay, and introduced iron works, lead mines and marble quarries to this remote corner of colonial Munster. He also built 'fish palaces' and ice houses for the preservation of pilchards and herring at a number of locations around Kenmare and Ballinskelligs. Seine nets, especially useful for catching pilchards, herring and mackerel in remote areas where larger fishing craft were considered too expensive or unmanageable, were also introduced into this region at this stage. Like several other new settlers in colonial Munster, Petty was well aware of the substantial profits to be made from the herring, cod and pilchard fisheries on this stretch of coast. At the start of the seventeenth century, it was estimated that the tiny port of Baltimore could produce up to 30,000 tons of dried fish per annum, and earn around £20 per ton of fish exports. To further develop the fishing, 'pilchard palaces' for packing pilchards and the extracting their oil were established around the south-west coast in the opening decades of the seventeenth century. Being delicate and subject to deterioration when exposed to the sun, pilchards had to be processed prior to being exported. Smith has provided the following detailed account of the preservation techniques used in the processing of pilchards and other 'oily' fish in the seventeenth and eighteenth centuries:

> They first cover the pavement with salt, which is made so as to have a fall to let the pickle run-off. Then they lay the fish with the heads all outward on the ground, and strewing salt between every layer they raise the bulk between 2 and 3 feet high, or higher, if pinched for room. Thus they remain for 21 days if the summer, and 15–16 if in the winter; then they take them and shake off the salt, and wash them at least twice if possible in freshwater, until they are perfectly clean; after this they are brought to the yard where the presses are, and having filled them in casks in which

they are closely packed, having holes in them to let out the water, blood and oil, they are thus pressed; those casks are all placed in a row against the press wall, being supported on wooden stands which prevent the bottoms from being pressed out, on the top of each cask is placed a round piece of timber or plank an inch thick, somewhat less than the head of the casks which they call bucklers; these bucklers are squeezed in by placing one end of a pole or lever in a hole made in the wall for that purpose, and by applying weights at the outward end, these bucklers are forced into the casks. As the pilchards are squeezed down, the barrels are again filled up, and so again until they can hold no more; under the casks are convenient receptacles for holding the oil, blood and water; the oil is got by scumming off the top. The fish being thus pressed, the barrels are headed and sent to market.[72]

Carew's account of the pilchard fishery at the start of the seventeenth century is one of the earliest descriptions of fishing methods in Ireland. He described how fishermen with their boats and nets

hovered upon the coast … directed in their worke by a Balker, or Huer, who standeth on the Cliffside, and from thence, best discerneth the quantitie and course of the pilchard; according whereunto, he cundeth (as they call it) the master of each boate (who hath his eye fixed upon him), by crying with a lowd voice, whistling through his fingers, and wheezing certain diversified and significant signs, with a bush, which he holdeth in his hand. At his appointment they cast out their net, draw it to either hand, as the choel lyeth, or fareth, beate with their oares to keep the fish in, and at last either close or tucke it up in the sea, or draw the same on lande, with more certain profit if the ground be not rough of rockes. After one companie have thus shot their net another beginneth behind.[73]

Charles Smith stated that pilchards in the seas off Co. Cork were

taken either by day or night, but mostly in the day, by means of hewers placed on the adjacent high grounds above the bays. The nets are from 100 to 140 fathoms long, and from 6–9 fathoms deep; the net being shot or dropt into the sea, they surround the fish, having two boats to attend them, one of which is called the seine boate and the other the follower. The pilchards being thus enclosed between the two boats, by drawing both ends of the net or poles together, they begin to haul the net up, and bring the bottom and top of it together, this is called tucking the net; then by means of oval baskets which they call maons they empty the net of fish into their boats. The fish are brought out of the large baskets and are laid in the fish-house, which they call a palace.[74]

While Petty and his associates contributed to the commercialisation of the sea fisheries off the Munster coast, Roderic O'Flaherty commenced the systematic study of marine life in the west of Ireland with his *Chorographical Description of West or h-Iar Connacht*. Written in 1684, but not published until 1846, this work provided a detailed account of the bio-geography and natural history of Connaught. Unlike the accounts of Giraldus Cambrensis in the twelfth and thirteenth centuries, O'Flaherty's work reflects the extent of local knowledge of fishing, and marine lore, in this part of Ireland at the end of the seventeenth century. He listed some fifteen marine 'finfish' and nine freshwater species, which together with shrimp, lobster, crab, freshwater pearl mussel and five marine mussels, emphasised the wealth of marine life to be found around an otherwise desolate west coast. O'Flaherty's very considerable knowledge of the names and habits of fish, and other forms of marine life, suggests that he had a deep understanding of the coastal geography of this part of colonial Ireland. Moreover, many of the fish he described were habitually caught by fishermen off rocks, or in small boats, in the inshore waters off the coast of Connaught.[75] This suggests that O'Flaherty may not have been the sole possessor of the marine lore of coastal of Connaught. His systematic study of marine and freshwater fish was built on local lore, and on a deep working knowledge of the west coast of Ireland gathered from indigenous, and possibly also foreign fishermen. Certainly, his account of fish life in the rivers, lakes, bays and estuaries of west Connaught contains some of the most authoritative treatises on coastal geography, marine biology and animal behaviour to be recorded in Ireland since the publication of Giraldus Cambrensis' *Topographia Hiberniae* at the start of the thirteenth century.

Finally, the maritime geography of Ireland at this stage was also charted by Gerard Boate. A native of the Low Countries, Boate devoted almost one third of his study of *Ireland's Natural History* to the country's coastal waters and shoreline.[76] Published in the early 1650s, this work broke with a Gaelic tradition that generally ignored Ireland's maritime geography. Boate had a fascination with the lakes and rivers of Ireland, which he classified according to their size and depth. He also compiled a whole series of micro-geographies of the country's inland waters, complete with detailed descriptions of the location and natural history of the islands located on them. Boate also collected scientific data on the ebb and flow of tides, the salinity of water, the direction of sea currents, and the nature of the submarine physical geography of Ireland. His *Natural History* does not so much 'marvel' at the wonders of nature. Instead, it described natural phenomena and classified plants, animals and fishes according to scientific principles. Boate was particularly impressed with the number of 'fishing cots', which he found were 'very common throughout Ireland, even upon the great rivers and loughs'. He described how labour-intensive fish weirs were constructed 'of big stones set close together from one side of the river to the other', adding that a basket was laid in front of these 'wherein local fishermen took a great quantity of fish'.[77] He was clearly writing at a time when Irish maritime affairs were attracting very considerable attention, not just from statesmen and the naval establishment, but also from fish merchants, the merchant class and urban entrepreneurs.

COLONIAL INTRUSIONS AND DIETARY CHANGE

One of the most notable long-term effects of the plantations was the severing of the centuries-old linkages of powerful Gaelic families and monastic settlements with the country's highly productive sea and freshwater fisheries. This was to have significant effects on Irish diets, and on food consumption patterns in general in the centuries after the plantations. From the sixteenth century onwards, new forms of 'husbandry' were introduced, just as new methods of estate-management and novel techniques of resource exploitation were imposed upon the land, seas, rivers and lakes of Ireland. Irish diets changed significantly in the transition from a complex native society, with its own traditions of feasting and hospitality, to one wherein an amalgam of new dietary practices existed alongside novel forms of feasting and aristocratic dining.[78] Hospitality in particular, which was such a marked feature of Gaelic society, was subject to profound change. Castigating native dietary habits on the eve of the Ulster Plantation, one traveller decided that the 'wilde Irish' here were 'not much unlike to wild beasts … [as] they eat no flesh but that which dies of disease or otherwise of itself'. Adding that they lived 'mainly on whitemeats and esteem for a great dainty sour curds', this commentator stated that the native Irish had 'no tables, but set their meat upon a bundle of grass and use the same grass for napkins to wipe their hands'.[79] At its most extreme, this genre of anti-Irish racism suggested that the native Irish showed a total disregard for good manners and simple hygiene, were without the 'steadying' instinct of animals, and entirely devoid of the 'ennobling intellect' of civilised settlers.[80] For these very reasons, the defenders of settler society called for a rigid policing of the boundaries separating 'civilised colonial society' from its social inferiors in Gaelic society. This in turn was to lead to a strict separation of the 'civilised spaces' of settler society from the 'natural' landscapes and 'wild coastline' of a decaying Gaelic Ireland.

Dietary change was not unique to the plantation period. New culinary practices had also been introduced into the strongholds of Anglo-Norman society in an earlier phase of colonisation. In the thirteenth and fourteenth centuries, the most obvious contrast in food consumption was between regions heavily dependent on oats, butter, milk, cheese, fish and potatoes on the one hand, and the coastal colonial core of the south-east on the other. Here, people relied on a range of foodstuffs, including grains, beans, fowl and a large variety of meat, fish and shellfish.[81] Gradually, in the course of the thirteenth century, the dietary tradition of Gaelic and Anglo-Norman Ireland coalesced, as beans, peas, bread and fish began to supplement the diet of the indigenous Irish. Supported primarily by beef, milk and other dairy produce in summer, and by fish, shellfish, bread and beans in winter, the Irish now had a year-round food supply. From the early medieval period onwards, the Irish population already had a long tradition of fish consumption. This was partly explainable in terms of church teachings on the needs to avoid meat during 'fish days' in the medieval calendar, but it was also linked to a long-standing historic reliance on primary animal protein staples such as meat, fish, milk and butter.[82] With the arrival of the Anglo-Normans, the diet of the people in coastal areas throughout the country became much more varied. Henceforth, a wide range of fish, many of them introduced species, as well as shellfish, wildfowl and wild and domesticated animals, were added to the diets of people living near the coast.

Compared to many other European countries, Irish food traditions were comparatively unstable from the early 1600s to the late 1800s. Whereas grain provided the basis for diet in most European countries, in Ireland this tended to be replaced by the potato, which was often accompanied by herring and other fish in coastal districts in the course of the eighteenth and nineteenth centuries. Moreover, as Cullen has argued, it is the range and richness of Irish food that most strikes the food historian in Ireland from the fifteenth to the nineteenth century. Prior to the nineteenth century, Irish people were highly flexible in their eating habits. They ate a wide variety of seasonally available food and probably consumed a wider range of fresh food, including far more varieties of fish and shellfish, than they did at the end of the nineteenth century. Joyce has suggested that 'all the fish used for food at the present day were eaten in Ireland in old times'. He added that

> The people fished with net and with hook and line, both in the sea and in lakes and rivers. The *slatt*, or fishing rod, was 10 or 12 feet long: the line was called *ruaim* and the hook *buban* ... The net was sometimes the common property of the family group of relations, each individual family having a right to use it in turn, or a claim to a share of the fish caught. Both salmon and eels were often caught with trident spears, or with spears of more than three prongs: and sometimes people followed the primitive plan of transfixing large fish with a single-point spear. Eels are still caught with forked-spears: and until lately salmon were taken in a similar way, the trident spears having handles about five feet long and a cord attach at the end. The spear was flung from the bank with aim that seldom missed.[83]

Went has suggested that fish spears, many of which were unaltered from prehistoric times, were one of the most popular implements for catching saltwater and freshwater fish, both before and after the plantations. In superseding the use of hands and hand-lines, they may well have increased the range of species captured by fishermen from the fifteenth to the nineteenth century. Eel spears 'prodded blindly through the weeds at the river sides from a boat' were for centuries widely used along the lower reaches of the River Bann, and were still being used in many coastal estuaries and rivers in the pre-Famine period.[84] A 'vicious looking' eel-rake, 'similar to the type of eel rake used in China to fish for herring ... [and] first described by Captain Cook in 1778', was traditionally used on the banks of the Bann 'to jab among the weed'. In the nineteenth century, the silver eel fisheries of the Bann were considered the largest of their kind in Western Europe.[85] In Westmeath, fish spears, some-times known as 'rock spears' or 'sun-spears', were 'used on rocky bottoms in hard sunny weather when eels could be readily seen and stalked'. Not everyone agreed with this method of landing freshwater salmon and eels. A popular angling book published in 1845 condemned the 'piking' of eels with 'long spears' in Co. Clare. This cruel practice involved eels being dragged through the teeth of the spear, after which they were strung up 'on a large cord half alive'. The author insisted that if this 'custom was to be permitted at all, [it] should only be tolerated in bog holes, but not in any lake or river, as it scares

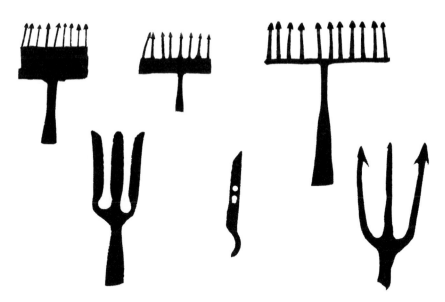

38 Fishing spears from Galway, Westmeath and Roscommon. Spears were one of the earliest implements used to catch salmon and eels in rivers, lakes and estuaries (after Went, 'Irish fishing spears' (1952)).

away the fish, and often destroys them.[86] Evans has pointed out that in Wexford Harbour, eels and flatfish were for centuries speared with two-pronged spears of Scandinavian origin. When the tide here covered the mudflats, fishermen would lie in wait in punts with spears in each hand in order to catch eels and flat fish. At low tide, the men wore wooden mud shoes known as 'scooches' to prevent them from sinking in the soft mud. Salmon were commonly speared with 'leisters', or three pronged spears, and were attracted at night by 'burning the river with split bog-fir or lumps of turf soaked in oil'.[87]

Dietary patterns probably exhibited marked regional variations in the early colonial period. A letter from a visiting churchman in the 1640s stated that fish were 'plentiful', oysters 'cost little' and there was 'an abundance of milk, butter and cheese'. He added that 'the fish of both river and sea are so exquisite and so abundant that the common people have pike, hake, salmon, trout, indeed all sorts of fish and these are to be had for astonishing value'.[88] Oyster consumption was prevalent in many coastal districts at the end of the sixteenth century, and we know that men engaged in recovering ordinance from sunken Armada ships off the Galway coast in the 1580s requested beer, bread and oysters from some local victuallers.[89] Writing in the 1660s, Petty singled out

Cork, Kinsale and Bantry as 'the best places for the eating of fresh fish, though Dublin is not or need not be ill supplied with the same'. In the closing years of the sixteenth century, people gathered regularly at the mouth of the Garavogue River in Sligo 'to gather great store of oysters, cockles and mussels, all of which [were] a great help with her Majesty's stores'. When Pococke toured Ireland in 1752, he noted that the inhabitants around Blacksod Bay sold pickled oysters to Dublin merchants for 'a penny a hundred', and added that 'on the bank they will load a horse for four pence'.[90] Pilchards and herrings were eaten in large quantities in the seventeenth and eighteenth centuries. In 1764, the *Dublin Magazine* claimed that Wexford was 'as celebrated for its fine women as for its beer and oysters'.[91] 'September herring', known as 'harvest herring', were widely consumed in the months leading up to Christmas, while salted herring or 'winter kitchen' were widely consumed around the coast and at some distance inland. Potatoes in many rural areas were supplemented with readily available staples such as whiting, hake, dried ling and cod, and with herring and mackerel in spring and autumn. In the southern half of Ireland particularly, the rural poor consumed lake pike and saltwater mullet. Crabs and shellfish, including barnacles and razor fish, were also a feature of the diets of the coastal poor until comparatively recently. In the 1780s, Joseph Cooper Walker commented that the usual summer diet of the people of the Rosses in Donegal 'consisted of milk, curd and butter with most excellent fish of several kinds'. Here, he added, 'rabbits, lobsters, crabs, scallops and oysters in abundance made every meal a feast'. In wintertime, the people of this district 'feasted on potatoes, fish, rabbits and butter', while the inhabitants of small offshore islands also consumed the flesh of salted seals.[92] When Arthur Young visited Killala in Co. Mayo in the summer of 1776, he noted that fish were cheap and 'plentiful' and added that the food of the people consisted of 'potatoes, cockles, herrings, and a little meal'. At one memorable meal, he 'partook of three gurnet, two mackerel and one whiting, at the bishop's table, which his steward bought for sixpence halfpenny, enough to dine six people'. At Galway, he noted that 'a middling night's take' of salmon was 5,000 fish, the bulk of which local fishermen 'sold into the country'.[93] In some coastal districts, particularly in the midlands and in the east of the country, lobster, oysters, hake, halibut, salmon, sole and turbot could have prestige conferred upon them through their association with upper-class palates. Amhlaoibh O'Suilleabhain, a Kilkenny diarist writing in the 1820s, 'considered himself something of a gourmet' and confessed to eating 'only fresh fish'. He added that these were regularly brought up from Waterford and Dungarvan, and were often considered 'too dear' by most people. Yet, even in the heart of rural Ireland, wealthy families always managed to have access to fresh fish from the sea, especially in the interior of Munster and Leinster.

After a particularly poor year in the early 1780s, a local landlord in Sligo learned 'with great satisfaction, that last August my worthy countrymen … were able to purchase a horse load of herrings for 3 pence – many a nak'd back was comforted by a full belly – and the parson will make his fortune next year by christenings'.[94] By the start of the nineteenth century, oyster beds were 'seeded' by the local gentry to provide employment for their tenants, and to increase the supply of shellfish available in urban areas. Dublin's Sandymount Strand was a favourite cockle strand for Dubliners until its waters became severely polluted in the nineteenth century. Local lore in many coastal areas suggested that cockles should not be eaten until they had three drinks of 'April water'. Ling, cod, hake and other white fish were salted and hung in the rafters until needed, and were then taken down and cooked. Oysters were sent from the Burren to Dublin throughout the nineteenth century and, at the end of the century, oyster boats from Carlingford were 'almost as familiar as the potato boats along Dublin quays'.[95] By then, salmon and oysters were pickled to improve their flavour and to facilitate their transportation. Writing at the start of the nineteenth century, Maxwell 'saw more crabs and shellfish than would load a donkey, collected during one tide by the children of a single cabin'. He remarked that cockles, scallops, clams, mussels and razor-fish were widely consumed throughout Connaught at this stage. The widespread consumption of shellfish was considered a welcome development in this part of the country because it provided 'change in an otherwise unvarying potato diet'. Dublin was long renowned for its 'capital oysters', the quality of which was provocatively celebrated in raunchy street ballads sung by poor female oyster sellers.

Freshwater and marine fish, and 'sea food' from the shoreline may well have been more widely consumed in coastal Ireland than in industrial Britain in the eighteenth and nineteenth centuries. However, consumption patterns changed quite drastically in the course of the nineteenth century. Consumption of pike, mullet, pollock, wrasse, haddock and eels dropped off dramatically in the aftermath of the Famine, when poor fishermen were either wiped out, or were unable to reinvest in boats, netting and other equipment. Nevertheless, fish appear to have been much more widely consumed prior to the Famine than after it. For centuries, rich and poor alike in many districts consumed salmon, and we meet with constant references to its superiority over all other fish. Salmon taken from the 'salmon-full Boyne', and from Lough Neagh and the

River Barrow, were particularly prized. Throughout the seventeenth and eighteenth centuries, the country's principal rivers were the haunts of 'vast quantities' of salmon that were 'sold at a moderate price throughout nearly the whole of the island'. Cullen has noted that in the seventeenth and eighteenth centuries, 'salmon were caught in enormous quantities, especially in the estuaries where they often numbered hundreds in a single draft'.[96] The Irish salmon was 'universally allowed to be of a very superior quality'. Variously known in colonial Ireland as 'the sea-smelling salmon' and the 'king-fish of the river', it was a favourite food of prominent Anglo-Irish families and was much sought after by English fish merchants. It was also considered the most highly prized of all fish exported from Ireland. In the mid-nineteenth century, Ireland had 'upwards of one hundred rivers that were frequented by salmon in great abundance, and in the primest condition'.[97] Given their locations at the estuaries of two of the country's greatest rivers, Galway and Coleraine were able to exploit huge numbers of salmon migrating upriver through these towns to spawning beds further inland. Throughout the eighteenth and nineteenth centuries, salmon were also widely trapped in freshwater and saltwater fishing weirs, and in great 'fishing machines' that were located all around the Irish coast.[98] Salted salmon from many of the country's larger rivers were sent to coastal towns and cities throughout the country in the eighteenth century. Fresh salmon, on the other hand, were often, but by no mean exclusively, reserved for more refined tastes. Writing in the mid-eighteenth century, Smith found that Lough Allua, near the source of the River Lee, 'abounded' in salmon, while trout there were 'almost as large as salmon'. The saltwater lake at Lough Hyne near Skibbereen, then the property of Sir John Freke, was particularly noted for prime salmon and good white trout, in addition to 'excellent oysters, crabs, escalops and small deep oysters'.[99]

The Irish diet retained many 'primitive features' well into in the eighteenth century, including a very healthy per capita consumption of fish, meat and potatoes that was probably higher than in industrial England at this time.[100] When demand for fish could not be met from local supplies in some parts of the country, the well off regularly imported fish from England and Scotland. In the great houses of the Anglo-Irish ascendancy, where breakfast was often a feast in itself, fish was served alongside ham, eggs, venison and porridge. Letters written by the secretary to archbishop of Rinuccini while in Ireland during the 1640s, provide a vivid picture of the diet of wealthy ecclesiastics in seventeenth-century Ireland. Massari found that 'fish was plentiful', oysters 'cost little', and there was an abundance of milk, butter and cheese. His letters also reveal that fish and meat were comparatively cheap in Ireland. After commenting on the size, flavour and abundance of Irish oysters, he added that

> the fish of both river and sea are so exquisite and so abundant that the common people have pike, hake, salmon, trout, indeed all sorts of fish and these are to be had for astonishing value. We bought pilchard and oysters very cheaply indeed.[101]

Pilchards were also eaten in large quantities in Ireland in the sixteenth and seventeenth centuries. Shellfish, crabs and lobsters were everywhere prized by country people, and by town-dwellers living near the coast. Herring was eaten in both urban and rural settings, and Jonathan Swift evoked the street cries of Dublin's fish sellers in the late seventeenth century in the following verse:

> Be not sparing,
> Leave off swearing,
> Buy my herrings
> Fresh from Malahide,
> Better was never tried.
> Come eat them with pure fresh butter and mustard,
> Their bellies are soft, and as white as custard.
> Come, sixpence a dozen to get me some bread,
> Or like my own herrings, I too shall be dead.[102]

The playhouses of eighteenth-century Dublin, especially those around Smock Alley and Aungier Street, echoed to the sounds of street sellers purveying their wares in the very pits of the city's theatres and concert halls.[103] The cries of fishmongers were for centuries a prominent feature of street life in Norse Dublin. Fresh hake, sole, turbot and salmon were all to be had on the tables of the prosperous merchants and landowners in the sixteenth and seventeenth centuries.[104] Hake was a staple food for the islanders of Cape Clear and the inhabitants of coastal towns from Waterford to Galway from the sixteenth to the eighteenth century. However, many households, particularly in inland areas, seldom if ever ate fresh saltwater fish, even though they may have had access to freshwater salmon, trout, pike and eels. Dried whiting, ling and rock cod were often hung from the rafters of small cabins or prosperous farm-houses, and together with salted fish, could be bought in small country shops. Further inland, dried fish occasionally replaced bacon as the only accompaniment to the potato when times were bad. Moreover, while the Great Famine appears as a major divide in the history of Irish food, the commercialisation of food production in its aftermath also contributed to the standardisation and impoverishment of diets in many parts of the country. Cullen has cautioned that

> It is misleading to see the evolution of Irish diet as divided into two periods separated by the Famine. In fact, Irish diet had been in a continuing evolution during the two preceding centuries. The diet was characterised both by change, in the form of increased emphasis on grain and the potato, and continuity in the persistent consumption of meat and butter in quantities.[105]

Much of the misunderstanding about Irish diet, not least the exaggerated emphasis on its poverty and over-dependence upon the potato, stems from the misguided assumption that the population was socially *and regionally* undifferentiated. The marked regional variations in standards of living, and the complex structure of urban and rural communities, have all but been ignored in most accounts that treat the Irish as uniformly poor, malnourished victims of coastal and rural poverty. Fish and shellfish, particularly herring, pollock, mackerel, crabs, oysters and molluscs, were important items of food in poorer coastal districts long before and for a considerable period after the Great Famine. In richer regions on the other hand, and especially in the homes of the well-off in Dublin, Cork, Limerick, Galway and Belfast, fish came to be associated with poverty, and for that reason were often shunned. Nevertheless, improvements in transportation meant that the new middle classes could now consume fresh fish and shellfish that heretofore would only have been available to those living within easy reach of the coast. Prior to the eighteenth and nineteenth centuries, rich and poor alike consumed fresh oysters and other locally available shellfish in considerable abundance. However, some food traditions that had been quite strong in the pre-colonial period, gradually wilted by the late nineteenth and early twentieth century. Fish and cheese consumption decreased significantly in his period, as did the consumption of ale and cider. Herring and mackerel, on the other hand, long considered 'poor food', were so strongly associated with poverty and famine that better-off sections of society shunned them. Fresh hake, sole, turbot, halibut and, of course, salmon, were all to be had at the tables of prosperous merchants and landowners throughout the nineteenth century. An article in the *Folklore*

Journal of 1888 pointed out that no sooner had Dublin fishmongers advertised the sale of halibut, than members of the Jewish community in the city 'rushed to buy pieces of it, and all try to get the head if possible'.[106] This suggests that Dublin's wealthier Jews dined on fish and were especially fond of good quality fish. A unique feature of the Irish diet in the early nineteenth century was the manner in which the potato practically dominated the diets of almost two thirds of the population.[107] However, as we have also seen, the diet of those living on the south coast and on the Atlantic fringe of the country consisted of the produce of the sea as well as the land. For the coastal poor, the most readily accessible items of 'shore food' were limpets, cockles, mussels, periwinkles, dulse and carrageen moss. Traditionally, edible seaweeds were cooked, though dulse was simply dried in the sun and then eaten raw. When food was scarce, however, beaches and rocky shorelines in impoverished coastal districts throughout the west were frequently stripped bare of their tidal crop.

Chapter eight contains a detailed discussion on the geography of sea fishing in Ireland from the mid-eighteenth century to the late nineteenth century. It focuses especially on the regional organisation of Ireland's sea fisheries, and the economic status of fishing in the country's coastal economy.

The coastal geography of sea fishing, 1750–1880

THE NORTHERN COAST

The early nineteenth-century statistical surveys of Irish counties provide rare insights into the state of Ireland's sea and freshwater fisheries at a crucial stage in the evolution of the modern Irish economy. An Irish Fisheries Report of 1823 estimated that there were a total of 44,892 fishermen engaged in fishing around the Irish coast, and the entire fishing fleet consisted of 306 full-decked boats, 286 half-decked boats, 2,516 open sail boats and just over 6,000 rowing boats.[1] A census of fishing boats in 1829 estimated the total number of fishermen in Ireland at 63,421. In that year, there were an estimated 3,634 men employed in the country's 1,360 curing houses, 2,094 men and women engaged in packing and gutting fish, and an additional 4,770 net-makers and 300 coopers. In all, it was estimated, there were almost 74,500 fishermen and tradesmen employed in the Irish fisheries.[2] The ports with the largest number of 'decked vessels' in 1829 were Balbriggan (85), Dungarvan (81), Dublin (59) and Ardglass (39), which together accounted for more than 70 per cent of this category of boat in the entire country. The largest concentrations of smaller 'open sail' boats were recorded for Galway (484), Wexford (396), Belfast (327), Dublin (245) and Dingle (203), and these accounted for 70 per cent of the country's 'open sail' boats. The greatest concentrations of half-decked boats were recorded for Kilrush (163), Kinsale (160), Ardglass (93) and Wexford (76). Despite their apparent accuracy, these figures fail to explain the uneven development of inshore and deep-sea fisheries and the volatile nature of sea fishing in particular in the late eighteenth and early nineteenth centuries. For many coastal dwellers, particularly those along the west coast, fishing was a highly precarious activity. Herring shoals came and went, and a good harvest on land meant that small farmers devoted considerably less time to the sea, and the shoreline, in their struggle for survival. Currachs and other small craft were relatively easy to build, and since crews were easily assembled, the numbers employed in fishing could vary considerably from one season to the next.

In a survey of the sea fisheries off the north-west of Ireland in 1801, James Mac Parlan reckoned that the herring fishery off the west coast of Donegal had 'dwindled within the last ten or twelve years to a 100th part' of what it was in

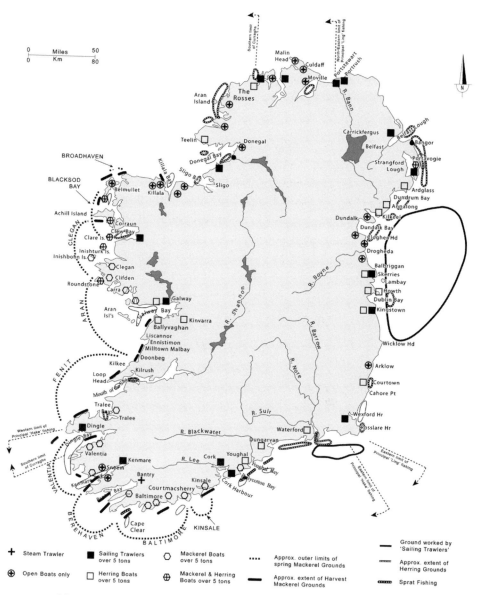

Map 3 Fishing grounds and fishing ports, *c.*1900 (adapted from Green, 'The sea fisheries' (1902)).

the 1780s.[3] Nevertheless, at the time of Mac Parlan's survey, the coast between St John's Point and Donegal town was still yielding 'an abundance of fish' in the summer months, while the winter fishing for herring, and other fish, had 'almost failed entirely'. In the mid-1780s, on the other hand, the herring fisheries had 'produced to the inhabitants of the Rosses a sum of £40,000', and in some years they 'loaded with herrings upwards of 300 ships'. This induced the Marquis of Conyngham to spend £50,000 in building a model fishing village, complete with houses and stores, on tiny Rutland Island. In 1784, there were 1,200 men employed in the herring fishing there, but then in 1793, when only one street of the village had been completed, the herring abandoned this coast, leaving huge numbers of local fishermen without a livelihood.[4] Arthur Young's animated account of the great herring fishery off the west coast of the county in the 1770s stressed the commercial potential of herring fishing and its importance to local farmers and part-time fishermen. He described the scenery around Inch, at the southern end of Lough Swilly, as 'amazingly fine, the lands everywhere high and bold, with one of the noblest outlines any where to be seen'. Inch itself was 'a prodigiously fine extensive island, high lands, with cultivation spreading over it, little clusters of cabbins, with groups of wood: the water of a great depth, and a safe harbour for any number of ships'.[5] Here, he reported, was 'the great resort of vessels for the herring fishery', which began in around mid-October and ended at Christmas. When Young visited, the island's herring industry 'had been five years rising', and no less than 500 boats were employed in this tiny corner of maritime Ireland. Small farmers and local fishermen built their own boats and sent 'them out either to fish on their own account, or let them to others'. There were usually five men per boat, with each man taking half a share, each net half a share, leaving one complete share for the owner of the boat. Boats cost around £10 on average, and each one of these had six 'stands' or 'lengths' of net costing £2 per stand. In a reasonably good year, he reported, some boats could take up to 6,000 herrings per night, and fished six times per week during the season. Averaging only around 'four shillings per thousand fish', however, prices were higher on the east coast. Home consumption accounted for a considerable quantity of the herring caught by the Inch fishermen. However, the islanders also availed of the services of offshore fishing boats, and coastal trading vessels, to dispatch 'a great bulk' of herring to England and Scotland, with some of the catch going as far the Caribbean, where salted herring were the staple diet of slave communities on a number of sugar plantations. The tonnage of the larger British vessels operating around the north-west coast at this stage ranged from twenty to one hundred tons, and these boats received a premium payment of 20s. per ton of fish landed at Scottish and English ports. Young noted that 'the merchants who owned these ships both buy fish themselves; cured fish for export and made their own barrels of American staves'. A local businessman called Alexander, 'one of the principal merchants of Derry', had developed a commercial herring fishery in this part of Donegal in the early 1770s, employing 'two sloops and a brig of 100 tons, the latter of which he sent to Antigua with 650 barrels of fish'. Local boats supplied Alexander with fish, which were then sent 'coastwise' to other parts of the country. In addition to this local trade, Mr Alexander 'regularly sent herring to the West Indies'. 'Carrying vessels' and fishing craft engaged in the herring trade were not immune from robbery if they chose to put ashore in isolated districts along the north-west coast. In 1775, Alexander employed 'a brig and three sloops' on this coast trade, and when one of these put ashore at Blacksod Bay 'the country people came down, obliged the crew to go on shore, and then not only robbed the vessels of her cargo, but of every portable material'. On a more favourable note, Young reported that one of Alexander's boats successfully dispatched a colossal 1,750 barrels of herring to the West Indies, while an additional 1,008 barrels were exported in other vessels. With such strong catches, Young concluded that there were 'fish enough in the Lough Swilly for all the boats of Europe', as they 'swarmed' around the lough in such dense shoals that it was 'difficult to row through them'.[6]

Travelling along the west of the county, Young came to at Mountcharles on the shores of Donegal Bay, where he found Lord Conyngham's agent 'deeply engaged in the fisheries on this coast'. His lordship's agent, Alexander Montgomery, took him on a tour to the marine inlets around Killybegs and Inver, where 'the fisheries were most carried on'. Afterwards, he gave the following estimates of the number of boats engaged in fishing around the coast of south Donegal in 1775 and 1776.[7] The summer season for herring off the coast at Inver generally started around the end of July, and ran on to late December or early January, depending on weather conditions. Young estimated that the construction cost of fishing boats varied between £18 and £20, while nets made of hemp were 8*d*. per pound. Young noted that most fishing boats around Killybegs and Inver had crews of six hands, comprising a skipper and five crewmembers. He estimated that 'ordinary fishermen' could earn around 10*s*. per week during a good herring season. At the time of his visit, boats were landing an average of approximately 100,000 herrings per week, the bulk of which were cured, packed into the holds of fishing vessels, and sold all around the adjacent coastline. He further calculated that more than seven tons of salt were needed to cure 80,000–100,000 herrings, and this came at a cost of just over £24 per ton. Larger, well-equipped vessels were able to carry 500,000–600,000 herrings, which represented the catch of five smaller boats in a good season. The trade in smoked herring to England was 'considerable' at the time of Young's visit and he felt that it could be 'carried on to much greater advantage if there was wood enough to do it with'.[8] Remarking that the smoke houses of the Isle of Man were well supplied with wood from Wales, he reprimanded Donegal landlords for neglecting to 'plant some of the monstrous wastes in this country with quick growing copes wood, which would, in five or six years, enable them to begin the trade in smoked herring'.[9]

Table 1: Fishing boats at selected harbours in Donegal, 1775–6

Fishing Port	Number of fishing boats	
Year	1775	1776
Inver	52	72
Killybegs	50	60
Teelin	47	47
Bruckless	20	25
Boylagh and Rosses	50	50
Cloghanealy	18	18
Dunfanaghy	20	25
Sheephaven	30	30
Totals	*287*	*327*

The highly commercialised herring fishery off the west coast of the county in 1770s and 1780s co-existed alongside the far less commercialised ventures of subsistence farmers and local fishermen. Cullen has remarked that the abundance of herring in this stretch of the Donegal coastline also helped to relieve near-famine conditions in the neighbouring Sligo in 1784, when 'horse-loads of herring' were sold for 3*d.* per load.[10] The herring fishery off the Rosses was still prospering at the beginning of the nineteenth century. Between 1822 and 1831, the fishery off Killybegs attracted as many as 700 boats, many of them from the east coast of the country. In a good season, they caught over 200,000 herring, which were cured sold for as little as 10*s.* per thousand. Writing in the 1880s, George Hill described 'the natural harbour' of Killybegs as

the safest on the whole coasts of Donegal, and hundreds of vessels large and small have been frequently crowded into it at the same time, and in perfect safety, during the herring-curing season. It affords the very best rendezvous for the fishing vessels, although they could not sail from it in a strong west or south-west gale.[11]

In the late 1890s, attempts were made to open a spring herring fishery off Donegal, and the revival of herring fishing off the Rosses saw Scottish firms transporting large quantities of cured fish to the markets of Glasgow. Brabazon found that cod, ling, hake, haddock, dogfish and conger eels were also caught with baited long lines, known as 'spillards' or 'spillets', along the west and north-west coast of Ireland. Similar to herring fishing, this fishery for 'round fish' was open to small fishermen and generally confined to stony or rocky fishing grounds where waters were too deep for the use of either trawl or drift nets. This did not affect the quality of fish landed, and Brabazon insisted that the finest of haddock were caught off Clew Bay and weighed between 15lbs and 30lbs.[12] However, by the time these fish were offloaded at Newport or Westport, the lack of ice and salting facilities meant that they were 'so far gone that no one, unless the natives of the place, would eat them'. The long lines used in this fishery measured more than 200 fathoms, with each line holding around 200 hooks and each rowing boat having five long lines. In 1847, three long-line fishing boats from Rush, Co. Dublin, fished off the Donegal coast, and 'returned with a cargo of 36 hundred of ling, which they sold for 8*d.* each'. In addition to this, they caught cod, hake and conger eels.[13]

For much of the nineteenth century, spring salmon ran along the north-west coast of Donegal in very large numbers, with a denser run of smaller fish beginning around June and continuing until the end of July. These fish traditionally marked the beginning of the salmon season for part-time fishermen around the Donegal coast, where they were caught in 'enormous quantities' in sheltered bays and estuaries and were readily exploited by full-time and part-time fishermen alike.[14] Boats set out for the fishing grounds with crews of four men per boat, and on reaching the grounds around sunset they 'shot' their nets just as the light was disappearing. In an account of salmon fishing around Gola Island in the 1960s, Brody described fishing methods that had changed little since the nineteenth century.[15] Nets measuring up to 4,000 yards long were fed into the water at right angles to the shore and across the route of migrating salmon making their way to rivers along the north and west coasts. Between sunset and dawn, the crew waited and, depending on weather conditions, hauled their nets at dawn, after which the fishermen headed for shore to 'box the catch'. From the first of August onwards, the men turned their attention to potting for lobsters, and searched for edible crabs at low tide in rocks and crannies. Lobsters were generally caught off the side of small boats and close in to the shore, where the pots were laid in shallow water covered in ground seaweed. This was arduous work that involved 'shooting' and hauling

39 Launching a currach on the Aran Islands, Co. Galway, in the late nineteenth century. The ancestry of this craft dates back thousands of years and may have had its origins in prehistoric skin-covered huts used by early coastal settlers (from Mason, *Islands of Ireland* (1936)).

pots, the number of pots used being determined both by the time taken to 'shoot' them, and the amount of equipment fishermen were willing to risk. A 'string' of ten lobster pots, hauled and baited three times a day, could take a considerable length of time. Making of pots was a time-consuming and skilful occupation, and if swept away in a strong tide, they could take with them long lengths of valuable rope and floats. Right down to the start of the twentieth century, the inflated carcasses of dogs were used as 'marking buoys' in some stretches of Donegal coastline.

Along the coast and offshore islands of Donegal, it was not uncommon for lobster fishing to be conducted from home-made currachs. This method of fishing tended to limit the number of pots a boat could carry, for in addition to laying lobster pots, the men had to find fish with which to bait them. Bait consisted chiefly of pollock, mackerel and wrasse, all of which were caught with short 'bait nets' and cut into strips to be tied to the bottom of each pot. Donegal lobstermen frequently salted their bait, in the mistaken belief that this would deter conger eels from taking it. The latter were often more common than lobsters in many pots, and once inside a pot, they were extremely difficult, and dangerous, to remove. In bad weather conditions, lobster fishing, like night salmon fishing, was a highly dangerous activity. Currachs could not be allowed to drift too close to the shore when the sea was rough, or when tides were running. Since lobster fishing began around August, the length of the season was severely restricted by the onset of winter and the very real possibility of stormy weather. However, the relatively high prices commanded for only an average sized lobster ensured the continuation of lobster fishing well into the winter months. Around the coast of Donegal, Sligo and Mayo, fishermen sold lobsters by the dozen, rather than by weight, which meant that they often earned considerably less than east coast fishermen. The close of the lobster-fishing season also coincided with the onset of the winter herring season on these remote coasts. However, when the herring shoals failed to appear, this effectively marked the end of fishing season for salmon and lobster alike.

In the eighteenth and nineteenth centuries, huge shoals of herring made their way into the inshore waters that separated the islands of west Donegal from the mainland. Herring fishing on this stretch of coast could keep islanders and coastal fishing communities busy throughout much of the winter. The season for herring usually ended in the west of the county around January and had 'a triple value' for fishing communities on this stretch of coastline. Firstly, it extended the inshore lobster season well into the month of October, and sometimes even into November. Secondly, it extended the fishing season in general deep into the winter months, a time when work on the land was practically finished. Thirdly, it provided islanders and part-time fishermen who farmed marginal land with food and a valuable source of cash income that helped them survive throughout the year. In a good herring season, small fishing vessels in the mid-1780s made up to £54 profit from a few months' fishing alone. In 1785, for example, total exports of herring amounted to approximately 35,500 barrels. The herring exports to the West Indies were estimated at just over £7,000 in 1790, and there was also a brisk trade in mackerel, cod and ling in that year.[16] Towards the end of the nineteenth century, the Baseline Reports of the Congested Districts Board recorded that the average annual cash income per household in coastal areas around Donegal could be as low as £38 or £40. Here, as in several other 'congested districts' along Ireland's Atlantic coast, fishing alone accounted for as much as 50 per cent of a poor family's cash income. The difficulty confronting fishermen here was not the size and the saleability of fish catches, as many of the more remote communities were unable to preserve or market their fish. In Gweedore, for example, money from the sale of fish scarcely featured in the cash income of families in the 1890s, despite the fact that coastal communities here were strongly dependent upon the sea and shoreline for their very survival. Instead, families here earned money from knitting socks and other garments, which taken together with the 'Scotch earnings' and 'Laggan money' of 'hirelings' and seasonal workers, accounted for 60 per cent of cash income.[17] Nevertheless, Brody's account of expenses and income from fishing off the Rosses coast in the 1960s suggested that salmon fishing by then had become a major source of income. He calculated a total outlay of almost £70 for nets, engine fuel and licence, with earnings from salmon fishing alone amounting to around £2,000 for a season that lasted a mere thirty nights. Salmon were traditionally graded according to size, with small salmon under 8.5lbs (known as grawls from the seventeenth to the nineteenth century, and 'grilse' in more recent times) fetching 4s. per pound in the 1960s, while fish above that weight fetched 5s. 6d. per pound.[18]

In marginal agricultural districts all along the north and west coasts, fish famines, whether caused by the non-arrival of herring shoals, poor weather conditions or a bad 'run' of salmon, were more frequent than potato famines, and could have equally devastating consequences. This was particularly the case in island communities, and for those living on remote headlands that had little or no farmland. Fish famines were regular occurrences in these coastal districts in pre-Famine times. They happened when the herring or mackerel failed to turn up, or when the shoals stayed so far out to sea that fishermen were unable to reach them by rowing or sailing out from the shore in flimsy currachs. The regular occurrence of these famines meant that many remote coastal communities lived in constant dread of shoals not arriving at the start of the fishing season. Large numbers of the coastal poor lived highly precarious lives, and were equally dependent upon the vagaries of nature and the unpredictability of fish prices. Not surprisingly therefore, a succession of poor fishing seasons could contribute to the dissolution of close-knit nuclear families and communities alike. In coastal districts from Malin Head to the Mullet Peninsula in west Mayo, this meant that the seasonal migration of young men to the potato fields of Scotland could become a permanent phenomenon. The failure of fishing in these districts could thus have catastrophic effects on fishing families and could determine the future viability of coastal communities. The precarious nature of these impoverished fishing communities was well captured in Peadar O'Donnell's novella, *Islanders*, first published in 1928. This was equally the case for many families on the maritime fringes of Connaught and Munster throughout the latter half of the nineteenth century. O'Donnell's *Islanders* is an exceptional portrayal of coastal life, chiefly because it focuses on the life of a fishing community at a time when most Irish writers were concerned with rural themes and land issues. Indeed, it would require simply a change of the setting, names and characters to transform *Islanders* into a very realistic portrayal of the lives of many poor fishing communities in post-Famine coastal Ireland. Rather than romanticising their poverty and idealising their lives, O'Donnell rejoices in the heroism of poor islanders and fishermen off the west coast of Donegal. As Lynd also suggested, families here were compelled to 'force a living from the rocks, and live in charity with one another among the uncharitable stones'.[19] *Islanders* is a rich tapestry of social realism that captures the hardships of community life in a remote island community that was almost totally dependent on fishing. It is equally an example of heroic literature, set in an Irish context where impoverished coastal dwellers struggle to eke a living from among rocks and the sea. O'Donnell's main achievement was to write about 'the poor folk of the island without either kailyard sentimentality or the realists' overemphasis on dismal things'. He presents the Doogans, the family at the centre of the novel, 'as living human beings in the circumstances of their daily life … so that the very economy of the household is interesting, and the purchase of a bag of flour [bought with the meagre proceeds from a night spent fishing for herring] becomes as important even for us as it is for them'.[20]

For many coastal communities, and especially for islanders and small fishing villages around the Donegal, Mayo and Kerry coastline, fishing dominated the annual rhythms of family and social life, especially when the shoals 'were in' and the fishing was good. The traditional wealth of the more impoverished sectors of such communities depended in large part on what they could harvest from the sea and shoreline, supplemented by what they could grow on meagre plots of marginal land. Here, it was suggested that distance from market and lack of the 'commercial habit' prevented the coastal poor from exploiting the inshore and deep-sea fisheries. However, this was far from the case on the remote islands and isolated headlands of the north-west of Ireland, where fishermen were extremely inventive when it came to getting fish to the market. Yet the commercial acumen of fishermen has generally been ignored, due to the fact that the lives of fishermen provided writers with romantic and idealised images of coastal communities. Certainly on the islands and headlands around the north-west coast, fishermen found many ingenious ways of getting their fish to market. The 'commercial habit' was particularly well developed on the remote island of Inistrahull in the mid-nineteenth century. Lying five miles offshore from Malin Head, this island had a population of sixty-eight who, in 1851, lived on 114 acres of sandy, rock-strewn land.[21] The community survived primarily because the island was on the route taken by steamers travelling from Glasgow and Liverpool to Derry, and by transatlantic liners sailing between North America and the ports of Derry and Belfast. These ships passed sufficiently close for the island fishermen to sail out to meet them. The diary of a lighthouse-keeper, stationed here between 1870 and 1873, provided a detailed description of fishing and farming on Inistrahull some twenty years after the Great Famine.

> There were a few acres of tillage ground on the island, but it was by fishing that the islanders principally supported themselves. They got quantities of provisions, clothes etc. from passing vessels. There was no sailing vessel allowed to pass without being boarded by them. If fresh fish, fowl or eggs were to be had, a supply was hurriedly taken into the boat and a crew of six or seven men pulled or sailed as circumstances suited, from the mass of canvas which was looming in view many miles away in the distance. There was often a rival boat and after a long and exciting race, the beaten boat would return. The great vessel was boarded and the captain usually condescended to speak to them; they were the first people he had met since he left New York or Philadelphia some four or five weeks previously, and to converse with them. A doleful story was told him of their situation on the island; that they lived on what they could get from passing vessels; they were so many miles from the mainland, which they seldom visited, that they had no tea, sugar, tobacco etc. Most captains wished to clear out any surplus stores they had on board before going back to port, as it showed the owners that the captain was able to use good judgment in not taking unnecessary stores on board. Bread was first asked and a large quantity handed over the side into their boats, then beef, sugar, tea, tobacco, treacle and every imaginable thing, and last of all whiskey, which they always drank, none ever being brought ashore … The islanders also got clothes from the sailors who also cleared out anything they did not want as they were going to port.[22]

Another entry in the diary that illustrated the resourcefulness of the island fishermen, stated that

> Their principal fishing was turbot, for which they went off some thirty miles to a sandy bottom bank. They set their lines on this bank, and then let them lie an hour or so. Then they hauled them in and returned to the

island towards the evening, having sailed some sixty miles. One boat took on board all the fish of the other boats, went off some fifteen miles to meet the steamer leaving Derry for Liverpool, put the live turbot on board and at a late hour arrived back at the island. Their coarse lines were set along the rocks of the island for ling and conger eels, which were used for bating their lines next morning for their turbot fishing. Everyday while circumstances were suitable, they performed this long journey to the turbot-fishing ground. When a storm would intervene and prevent their going on shore with the turbot, they kept them alive by tethering them in the harbour by means of a line, one end of which was tied to the derrick on the landing, the other having a fishing hook fastened through the snout of a turbot. In this way the fish could live for several days swimming about in a small space. If an accident should happen to a turbot and it got killed, it was sent up to the lighthouse to us, and in this way many a fine turbot we got. The turbot caught off this island was the largest and best caught anywhere on the coast of Ireland. They were in Liverpool and Glasgow markets some twenty-four hours after they were caught.[23]

Fishermen living along the coast of Donegal, Kerry, Mayo and Galway also engaged in a form of 'island-hopping'. This was the maritime equivalent of transhumance practices that caused poor tenants on marginal land to send younger members of the family up onto mountain pastures to tend sheep and cattle in the summer months. Fishermen on remote islands and coastal headlands similarly moved between mainland and offshore islands in order to supplement the produce of the land by harvesting the seas during rich fishing seasons. The small fishing community on Inistrahull abandoned their summer homes on the island and moved to Glengad, on the Inishowen mainland, 'principally for the want of firing, and because fishing could not be carried on in the island as advantageously as the mainland'. In this nineteenth-century example of 'bi-location', the fishermen of Inistrahull were likened to 'poor castaways' who 'had their friends on the mainland as well as on the island'. The island lighthouse keeper described the 'heart-rending and pitiable scenes of great sorrow' that occurred when the fishermen had to leave their island homes for the mainland. However, when they returned at summertime 'to where their wives and families lived, the joyous scenes were indescribable'.[24]

We have already seen that coastal communities consumed large quantities of fish and shellfish, simply in order to survive in the decades before and immediately after the Famine. Here, as in marginal lowlands along the west coast in general,

40 Boating and fishing activity on the Causeway Coast, Co. Antrim, at the start of the nineteenth century. Fishing fleets from Scotland and England often operated in the deeper waters off the north coast, while local fishermen were largely confined to inshore waters (from Halls, *Ireland: its scenery, character etc.* (1841–3)).

fishing acquired a profound sense of urgency, and was sometimes considered more vital to the community's survival than farming. It dictated how a day was spent, how a season of the year was passed, how much money was earned, and how much was available to buy basic goods such as flour and tea. It profoundly influenced family life, not least in the aftermath of a boating disaster, and imposed its own order on the social and economic life of coastal communities. In coastal districts such as these, the routines of fishing were strict, and strictly observed, and the fishermen's days were carefully structured around the vagaries of tides and weather.[25] Taken together, therefore, the routines and structures of the fishing season reinforced the *primacy* of fishing, not least in coastal communities forced to eke out a living in some of the country's harshest environments.

In a statistical survey of Co. Derry in 1802, George Sampson stated that the principal salmon fisheries were 'those on the River Bann, and at Culmore on the coast side of the harbour of Derry', adding that there was also 'an inconsiderable one on the Roe'. The original right to these fisheries was vested in the ancient monasteries, within whose precincts they lay, and on the suppression of the monasteries, they were claimed by the bishop of Derry.[26] In coastal districts of Londonderry the full-grown salmon go up the river to breed in March. The young salmon, or grawls (grilse), follow for the same purpose in June; in November and December they rood in the fords or shallows. The ova, or pea, continue in the sand or gravel for three months. About March, the fry shoal downwards to the sea; at this time they are not larger than a small finger, yet in the following June, when they are taken at their return from the sea, some have increased to the weight of 19 pounds; the very least weigh two pounds.[27]

Sampson went on to state that

> The size of a full-grown salmon varies from six to 50lb; few exceed 30lb. The best size is, from 16 to 20lb; grawls are reckoned one penny a pound inferior to salmon. I have heard that 140 fishes were once caught in two draughts, which weighed 6 tons. As to price, in 1757, salmon sold at one penny per pound; for many years the price continued at one penny and one ha'penny; about twelve years ago it rose three pence, and since that to 3 and a halfpence.[28]

Where the Crannagh River ran through Buncrana, 'two sets of fishers were employed, night and day, during the season'. A total of seventy persons were engaged in this particular salmon fishery at the start of the nineteenth century. Considerable expense was incurred in the management of the fishery, with water bailiffs employed 'to watch the nightly depredators, who, with lights, which allured the fish, and, by means of nets and gaffs, contrived to kill vast numbers of salmon, even at the time of rooding'. George Hill, the proprietor of the fishery at the time of Sampson's survey, had established 'a communication with the Liverpool markets by means of fast-sailing smacks'. This enhanced the price of salmon, raising the price of fresh fish by 5*d.* per pound in 1800.[29] Sampson claimed that haddock were in 'plentiful supply', both from the coast of Derry, and Inishowen, the price of which varied from 6*d.* to 1*s.* Cod were 'extremely common' off the coast of Derry and Donegal in the early nineteenth century, and salted cod were consumed 'by the gentry and the country people' as part of their 'country store', especially around Christmas time. The poor, on the other hand, 'due to their want of butter', preferred herring, which were 'more abundant in oil'. As for turbot, Sampson believed that that nowhere was 'better supplied than Londonderry with this fish'. Lampreys, an ancient delicacy when eaten fresh from the water, were still being taken on a regular basis near the mouth of the Bann at the start of the nineteenth century. Some of these were 'potted for export', while fresh lampreys could fetch anything from 10*d.* to 10*s.* 6*d.* each.[30]

In his survey of Co. Antrim in 1812, John Dubourdieu described the summer 'run' of salmon through the River Bann and up into Lough Neagh as follows:

> The salmon, in their progress to Lough Neagh, make their appearance in the mouth of the Bann about March or April, sometimes sooner if the weather is fine, and return again, playing in the ebb. The full-grown fish ascend the river about the 20th of April, or the beginning of May; this is called the run of the fish, and continues until the end of the latter month. At this time, the fishery is slackened, and not carried on so briskly as about mid-summer; for then the graul, or young salmon, ascend, and continue to do so for several months. The Leap is situated in the river, about four miles from the sea, and a mile above the town of Coleraine, and is about twenty miles from Lough Neagh, so that the fish are obliged to ascend 24 miles, and overcome all the obstacles in their progress before they enter the lake, from whence they distribute themselves into numerous streams and rivers, which are discharged into it. To cross this lough, and obtain the shallows of the rivers, in many places is not less than the distance from the sea to it, so that 50 miles may be said to be traversed by these fish, from their leaving the sea until the time of spawning; for they are often taken in the branches of the Main Water, at a great distance from the lough, even above Broughshane.[31]

Eels were in 'great abundance' in the rivers throughout east Derry and north Antrim, while Lough Neagh was considered 'the great rendezvous of this fish'. Some idea of the value of the eel fishery in this part of Ulster can be gauged from its rental value, and Lord Donegall let it to a tenant for £400 per annum in the 1780s. Dubourdieu felt that similar valuable eel fisheries could, 'at little expense', be established 'in many rivers' throughout Ireland. 'All the rivers' of Antrim and Derry in particular, 'abounded' with eels, 'but from want of proper attention, and materials for taking those valuable fish, small advantage is made of the plenty with which they are distributed'. Herring, on then other hand, were seldom present 'in sufficient quantities' to become 'a commercial object'. Haddock, cod, whiting, ling, mackerel, gurnard, mullet were all 'widely taken' off the coast. Turbot were in 'constant supply', and were 'brought to Belfast by

41 Fishing boats at Carrickfergus, Co. Antrim (from Nicholl,
The northern coast of Ireland (1835)).

the coasters from the northern parts of the county, and from the county of
Derry'. Dubourdieu also felt that the sea fisheries off the Antrim and Down
coast could be 'extremely valuable were they properly attended to', but had
'never been turned to the best advantage'. This he attributed to 'want of
capital', 'want of skill' and lack of means for transporting fresh fish to the
markets in England. Boats from Rush and from Liverpool regularly trawled in
Dundrum Bay at this stage, and 'carried off great quantities of turbot, sole,
plaice, cod and haddock, whilst the inhabitants of the shore, from want of
apparatus, caught comparatively few'. At Bangor, Dubourdieu found 'a
considerable fishery of sole, plaice, a few turbot'; while cod were caught in
considerable numbers, and 'excellent oysters' were available throughout the
Lagan Estuary. Large quantities of herring were 'to be had the whole year
round' in Strangford Lough, 'but with respect of fatness and flavour, they were
much inferior to those taken on the coast of the main sea'. They occasionally
came close to the shore, which meant that they were easy to catch, but 'in
general they keep further to the east towards the Isle of Man'. Boats from
Newcastle pursued the herring shoals up and down the coast, and when
caught, herring were sold around coastal towns, with some being 'dispersed
through the countryside by fish carriers who attended upon the beach, and

purchased them from the boats as they arrived'. Before the completion of the
Lagan navigation in the 1790s, 'numbers of salmon frequented that river'.
However, at the time of Dubourdieu's survey, these fish 'were stopped by the
locks' and had largely deserted the River Lagan. Whiting, gurnard, sea trout,
mackerel, skate, lobsters, crabs, shrimps and prawns were all caught off the
Down coast at the start of the nineteenth century, while small red 'codlin' that
were 'much better than the cod' were taken around Copland Island.[32] In his
account of Ardglass, the 'common centre' of sea fishing on the coast of Down
in the 1830s, Samuel Lewis noted that 'the labouring classes were wholly
employed in the fisheries'.[33] At the height of the season, there were 'three
hundred to four hundred vessels in this harbour'. Fishing boats came here from
Donaghadee, Carlingford, Skerries, Dublin, Arklow and the Isle of Man, 'but
principally from Penzance, on the coast of Cornwall'. Those from outside the
immediate county regularly came ashore to dispose of their fish catches, which
were 'quickly purchased by carriers, who took them into the interior of the
country'. Huge quantities of herring were also bought up by local merchants,
and by 'the masters of sloops and small craft who waited in the harbour for the
arrival of the fishing boats, and proceeded directly to Dublin or Liverpool to
dispose of the herrings fresh'. Lewis found that the sloops which transported
fish to these markets 'usually performed two trips in the week, and the masters
frequently make from £20 to £50 by each cargo'. He described the harbour at
Ardglass as 'admirably adapted for trade and steam navigation'. The construction
of a new pier at a cost of £25,000 in 1834 meant that the port 'was sufficient to
accommodate steamers of any tonnage'. 'Vessels of 500 tons burden' were able
to enter the deep-water harbour 'in any state of the tide', while the inner
harbour at Ardglass was 'capable of accommodating a great number of fishing
boats'. Built of 'hewn and dressed' stone blocks from the Isle of Man, 'and
forming a safe breakwater for the harbour', the new pier and other installations
'afforded a beautiful promenade, embracing fine views of the Isle of Man and
the Calf of Man'.[34]

In a rare scholarly analysis of commercialised herring fishery in Irish waters,
Vivienne Pollock has shown that in the latter half of the nineteenth century,
boats gathered at the great herring fishery off the coast of Down from as far
south as Howth and Dublin, and some even travelled across to Scotland to sell
their fish.[35] Located midway between the east coast of Ulster and the south-
west of Scotland, the herring fishery on this coast was part of a much wider
enterprise and was never simply a local concern. At the height of the frenetic
summer herring season, for example, 'buying boats' from English and Scottish

42 Steam trawlers at Ardglass, Co. Down, *c.*1900. The thriving herring fishery off this coast attracted well-equipped fleets from Scotland and England, and from other ports along the east coast of Ireland (courtesy of the de Courcy Ireland collection).

ports accompanied the fishing fleets, bought up their catches and dispatched huge quantities of fish to markets in Ireland, Scotland and England. While this enabled fishermen to work for longer periods without having to leave the fishing grounds, it deprived onshore workers in the processing and handling sectors of employment. A fishery inspector, who visited Ardglass at the height of the summer season in 1868, reported that there was 'a large quantity of fish carried away from the fishing ground of which no account could be taken'. Two steamers from England, and one from Scotland, remained offshore for the greater part of the season 'for the purpose of conveying the fish away to Liverpool, to Holyhead, to Workington and to Glasgow'. With a coastline measuring around one hundred miles, Co. Down had abundant natural harbours and the tidal loughs of Strangford, Carlingford and Belfast formed part of the shallow Irish Sea. The sheer richness of these waters fostered economies of scale in the herring industry and facilitated specialisation, and the summer fishing season in particular was a cosmopolitan affair that attracted boats from both sides of the Irish Sea. Yet, despite the best efforts of fishery inspectors to have curing stations established here in the 1860s and 1870s, this did not happen until later in the century. The early curing stations were highly mobile and rudimentary affairs, requiring only poorly paid fish gutters, and coopers, to process and pack herring in barrels for the market. Offshore fleets from Scotland and England, not surprisingly, occasionally attracted young men from the surrounding countryside in search of employment. This was also the case on the south coast, where the crews of fishing vessels registered elsewhere were drawn from all over Great Britain and Ireland. For many local youths, a season of fishing on such vessels was a rite of passage. Once the fishing season ended, many of them moved with the fleet to England and Scotland in search of work. In the late 1850s, for example, 'about twenty young fishermen from Newcastle and Annalong' obtained employment 'for the months of June and July in Anstruther, in Scotland, to assist in the herring fishery'. They each received a one-twelfth share of the catch, a considerable sum to any young man raised in the relative poverty of rural county Down in the mid-nineteenth century.

The years from 1860 to the 1930s saw the strengthening of the herring fishery off the Down coast, as new steam links were established between local ports and the west coast of Britain. Road and rail links were also upgraded, harbours were improved, and a major effort was made to establish new markets and to strengthen existing ones.[36] The switchover from sail to power driven boats towards the end of the century also reinforced the herring fishery in this part of the Irish coast. These improvements provided the very conditions for the growth of small-scale operations *alongside* highly commercialised fishing operations. Indeed, as Pollack has suggested, the herring fishery off this coast of east Ulster had many of the characteristics of a post-modern economy, with flexible working patterns, an international workforce and a rich diversity of national, regional and local cultures.

Fishing here was a highly seasonal activity that often clashed with the rhythms of the farming year, causing part-time fishermen to make difficult choices about the priority of farming over fishing. At the height of the summer season, competition among fishermen often resulted in open conflict between 'insiders' and 'outsiders' engaged in the exploitation of a common fishing ground. At other times of the year, rivalry was avoided because local fishermen and overseas fleets were presented with a range of opportunities that operated to the benefit of all. There were three distinct herring seasons on the Down coast. In May and June, the herring gathered to spawn around Dundrum Bay and up and down the east coast of the county. At the beginning of September, the shoals often came so close to the southern shores of the county that they were within reach of part-time fishermen. In January and February, herring were occasionally fished in Strangford Lough, Carlingford Lough and Dundrum Bay.[37] Each of these fishing seasons tended to attract different types of fishing craft, and there were significant variations in levels of local involvement in the fishery at different times of the year. Pollock has argued that the autumn fishing for herring off the east coast in the 1860s was

> of considerable local significance, but was essentially a small-boat enterprise, exploited by south Down men in skiffs, many of whom were fishermen only when the herring were in the area. The summer fishery, however, was a cosmopolitan affair, patronised by travelling boats from the four corners of the British Isles and followed as part of a peripatetic fishery which circled the Atlantic, Irish and North Sea, and English Channel coasts.[38]

Finally, there was also a significant degree of variation in types of enterprises that fishermen were engaged in, and this could influence the degree to which local fleets could avail of the presence of visiting fleets. There was, for example, a considerable degree of specialisation within the fishing industry in the rich fishing grounds off the coasts of Down, Dublin, Waterford, Cork and Galway. Specialisation here was dependent on the wealth of offshore fisheries, the availability of transportation, the quality of onshore processing facilities, and the overall duration of fishing seasons.

THE WEST COAST

In his surveys of the more remote sea fisheries off the coast of Sligo and Mayo, James Mac Parlan stated that the former county had a 'considerable salmon fishery' that was privately run by its two proprietors at the start of the nineteenth century.[39] Up until the years 1783 or 1784, he argued, the herring fishery on the Sligo coast 'had been of very great importance'. Since then, however, it had 'failed entirely', with only 'a few herring' still being caught in the 'summer fishing'. Cod, turbot and haddock were 'caught on this coast in great abundance'. An estimated fifty fishing boats were then 'plying about Killala', where the fishery was said to be 'frequently a good one'. The salmon fishery at Newport was rented for £60 per annum, while the one at Killary Harbour produced 'an annual rent of £150 to the lessee of Lord Sligo'. By the start of the nineteenth century, herring fishing off Mayo had declined

43 Fishing scene in Killary Harbour, Co. Galway, in the pre-Famine period. Marine inlets and coastal estuaries were extensively fished by native fishermen using locally-constructed boats and fishing nets (from Halls, *Ireland: its scenery, character etc.* (1841–3)).

drastically, and the huge shoals that formerly frequented this coast simply abandoned it. There were two 'considerable salmon fisheries' in the county, namely at Belclare and Louisburg. Mac Parlan reckoned that 'all the rivers and lakes of the county' abounded 'with all sorts of fresh-water fish', and many of these rivers were 'depots' where salmon deposited their spawn. Clonlomley River was the chief nursery of the Ballina fishery, and this was in the care of 'bargers' or water bailiffs appointed to monitor local rivers during the spawning season. However, these men were 'extremely troublesome', and often entered 'the houses of peaceable inhabitants at late hours, abusing and beating them when not in bribe'. To improve local fisheries, Mac Parlan believed that the children of the poor should be 'instructed in fishing with hooks, lines and proper baits'. This, he argued, would tide them over in 'times of scarcity', giving them 'an abundance of fish' in the summer, and thereby reducing their dependence on meal and potatoes.[40]

Wallop Brabazon also visited this coast in the mid-nineteenth century and singled out Newport as a suitable centre for net-making, because 500 spinners and weavers were already working in this area for very low wages. Net-making, he added, would 'give work to children of fishermen from fourteen years and upwards' in what was then a very impoverished coastal district.[41] Another writer who commented on the fisheries around Mayo in the early years of nineteenth century was William Maxwell. His *Wild Sports of the West* appeared in 1832 and contained detailed accounts of customary fishing practices around Achill Island and other parts of the county. Mullet, which were consumed in large quantities around the Mediterranean, including the North African coast, were widely fished. Maxwell stated that

> The mullet are generally first seen here in the month of June ... [when they] are taken in draft nets like salmon, but on this coast a different mode of fishing is pursued. The shoals in hot weather run with the tide, and after remaining on the shores and estuaries during flood, they return with the ebbing water. The following method we employed in our fishing today. Being provided with a sufficient quantity of herring nets and a number of spars and poles, we selected at low water a sandy creek for our operations, and commenced erecting a line of poles across the entrance of the cove. The nets were then extended along these uprights, and also secured firmly to the bottom of the spars; the lower part of the net is kept upon the bottom by a row of stones, and the remainder laid flat upon the sands. With the flowing tide, the fish pass over the prostrate net, and run along the estuary; at high-water the buoy ropes are raised and secured to the upright poles – and, with the assistance of a boat, the whole is effected in a few minutes, and a net-work barrier effectually cuts off the retreat of all within. When the ebb of tide commences, the mullet begin to retire, and when they discover that their egress is obstructed, their attempts to effect a passage are both constant and curious – now running down the nets, trying for a broken mesh by which to force an aperture – now with a spring endeavouring to clear the buoy ropes, and even after repeated failures, leaping at it again and again. The last effort is directed to the bottom; but there the heavy stones resist every attempt to dislodge them, and deserted by the treacherous water, the mullet are left upon the bare sands.[42]

Achill Sound was so 'full of mackerel' that he and his fishing companions took 'above 500' of these fish on a two-hour fishing trip. The inshore waters and shoreline of Mayo also held 'a plentiful supply of shellfish, which were enumerated among the principal advantages which this wild coast offers to its

inhabitants'. Along the cliffs of the islands, and mainland, lobsters were 'found
in abundance'. However, commercial lobster fishing was under-developed on
this coast, due to the fact that the peasantry lacked 'the necessary means for
prosecuting the fishery'. Using the most rudimentary equipment, the local
inhabitants caught them 'by sinking pots and baskets in the deep sea'.
However, many of these were subsequently stolen 'by strangers', who come for
this purpose from a considerable distance. Those killed by the islanders were
only procurable at low springs, when the ebbing of the water beyond its
customary limits permitted caves and crannies in the rocks to be investigated.[43]
Maxwell reported that large numbers of crabs 'of considerable size' were also
found on this coast, and like lobsters, were 'only accidentally procured'. The
shellfish 'most prized by all Mayo fishermen' was the scallop, which in this part
of the west coast was 'of very superior size and flavour'. These were commonly
caught by oyster-dredgers in deep water, and were 'transferred' to the local
gentry in order to curry favour with local magistrates and other government
officials.[44] Oysters were said to be so plentiful in the bays and estuaries of Mayo
at this stage that 'a turf-basket large enough to contain six or seven hundred
oysters can be filled for sixpence. Here also 'a couple of men will easily, and in
a few hours, lift a horse-load; and, not withstanding the numbers carried away
by sailing boats from Clare and Munster, the stock appears to be little reduced
by the constant dredging'. These and other shellfish were said to be 'greatly
prized by the peasantry', as they made 'a welcome change in the otherwise
unvarying potato diet'. Better still, Maxwell argued, the oyster harvest
employed 'the idler members of the family, whose youth and age unfitted them
for more laborious exertions'.[45]

In a detailed historical account of aquaculture around Galway Bay and the
Mayo coast, Wilkins has shown that many of the oyster beds were in serious
decline in the early decades of the nineteenth century. In the early 1830s, there
were no native species in many coastal inlets that were renowned for their oysters
earlier in the century.[46] Small oysters dredged up on the coasts of Galway and
Mayo were subsequently fattened at a number of sites around Galway Bay, and
these were eventually sent off in great numbers to Dublin. By the time of Griffith's
valuation in the 1850s, there were only ten privately owned oyster beds in the
Muckinish inlet. Burton Bindon, a local landlord who carried out many
improvements in the Burren district, owned the Red Bank oyster bed at
Aughinish, which was said to be worth £260. John Whitty, a civil engineer who
visited this district in 1853, described these oyster beds as follows:

The beds, once stocked, are found capable of holding, on average, 3 and a half years consumption for the Dublin markets. Their produce for the last 15 years might be estimated at 42 baskets per week, each basket containing about 700 oysters, equal to 294 hundreds in the week, which for the season of nearly 38 weeks duration brings the amount consumption to 11,172 hundred, or 14 boat loads per year, and this for 3 and a half years amounts to nearly 50 boat loads. The proprietor to stock these banks should lay out probably £1,000 in the purchase of 50 boatloads of spawn oysters at about £20 per load.[47]

On this reckoning, the Dublin market consumed around 1.4 million oysters per annum in the mid-nineteenth century. In the mid-1860s, another visitor to the area around Galway Bay was 'exceedingly struck with the quantities of oysters upon the ground' in the vicinity of the Red Bank, where 'it was almost impossible to thrust the end of one's knife in to the ground without touching and disturbing some of them'.[48] These beds were worked by thirty-five to forty women of all ages, who were supervised by 'a local man who scolded them continually'. From 1845 onwards, the government granted exclusive licences to a number of local landlords and merchants in order to develop private oyster beds on the Galway coast. The bulk of these were dispatched by train to Dublin. The records of the Great Western Railway reveal that 3,400 tons of oysters were carried on this line alone from 1853 to 1865. This made for a total of approximately twenty million oysters for one thirteen-year period.

In a detailed survey of Galway's sea and freshwater fisheries in 1824, Hely Dutton referred to the fishermen of this coast as 'a mulish race'. He also insisted, however, that there were 'few subjects of more importance than the fisheries, whether we consider the home consumption, the supply for which is in general below demand, or the exportation of a redundancy which could be infinitely increased'.[49] Galway Bay was so renowned for hake fishing that it was called 'the bay of hakes'. Hely Dutton estimated that there were 'at least five hundred fishing boats belonging to Galway Bay, besides those that belong to the Claddagh fishermen who have between 200–250, employing upwards of 2,500 hands who live entirely by fishing of various kinds'.[50] The highly productive cod and ling fishery on this coast commenced around the first of February and was 'convenient to inshore fishermen, as it was located only seven or eight leagues from the land and extended along the north-west coast of Ireland'. It was generally reckoned that the huge fishing bank that stretched from Cleggan Bay on the coast of Connemara extended right across to

Newfoundland. The waters here, as off the coast of Canada, were abounded with cod, but unlike in the latter fishery, the boats used in the west of Ireland were 'too small to encounter that part of the sea where the best fish abound'. With proper boats and equipment, it was argued, the 'quantity of fish that might be killed on the bank, and convenient to the shore' were 'beyond calculation'. Ling were particularly plentiful on this coast, and their number was believed to 'exceed that of cod in the proportion of five to one'. When Connemara fishing boats managed to reach this fishing ground, they filled their currachs 'in a few hours', using only hand-lines. In March 1815, 'a boat from Connemara, with only two spillards or long lines, in one day brought in thirty-six dozen cod, all of which were caught near the land, and very few ling amongst them'. The hooks used by the fishermen, however, were 'so very small, and so unfit for heavy fish' that they lost one fourth of the catch. In 1815, also a single boat 'with one line and one hook brought in nineteen dozen fish, and would have killed more had they not, alas, lost their only hook'. In the same year, a number of Galway boats 'of seven or eight tons burden' returned from a four-day fishing trip off the west coast 'loaded with split cod and ling'. So large were their catches that they could not carry the quantity of fish they had caught, 'and anyway they had insufficient salt for curing them'. It was reckoned that a properly fitted rowing boat, with 'a well appointed' crew, would be able 'kill ten times as much as any of the common boats, and fish ten days for one that the Connemara boats do'. Each rowing boat, or wherry, it was argued, could 'kill and cure forty tons [of fish] for exportation'. The fish were sold locally, but sizeable quantities were also sent to the more lucrative Dublin market where prices were high in 'the spring of the year when fresh fish sold well'.[51]

Writing in the 1850s, George Hill described the inhabitants of the islands along the west and north-west coasts of Ireland as 'fearless boatmen, and skilful in their own way' in the use of a 'very ancient kind of substitute for a boat, called a Corragh'. As we have already seen, relations between these western fishermen and the owners of fishing smacks and wherries from the east coast were far from cordial. This was especially the case during the herring and mackerel seasons, when fishing communities along the north and west coasts faced stiff competition from better-equipped boats from the east coast. Discussing this rivalry, Hill stated that

> In the beginning of January, shoals of herring make their appearance
> upon this coast, when the people, clubbing their means to purchase boats
> and nets, make great exertions to avail themselves of this supposed source

of profit. No salt was to be had but at the distant towns before mentioned; and when the fish were abundant, an immense price was paid for salt. For want, however, of regularity and protection, the fishery, instead of proving a blessing and a source of profit, often turns out the reverse, especially as it has occasioned a fearful loss of life, for which there could be no compensation. Wherries from Rush, Balbriggan and Skerries, and other strange boats, come here and molest the poor natives, cutting their nets and otherwise annoying them. From the stormy and rugged character of the coast, the people are afraid to stay out all night by their nets in their small boats; and therefore, contrary to what should be the practice, they cast their nets by daylight, leave them there all night, and return in the morning to look for them. By such means, if a storm arises, the nets break adrift, get mixed together, and, floating about full of dead fish, scare the shoals from the coast – many hundreds of pounds' worth of nets are lost in this manner. Whereas, if the government sent a cutter to preserve order, much mischief would be prevented; its presence would give confidence to the fishermen, who would, under such circumstances, remain out with their nets, knowing that should it come on to blow, there would be assistance and a refuge at hand.[52]

The Galway coast also harboured a prosperous sunfish or basking shark fishery. These fish usually reached Irish waters in the spring. Hely Dutton described the waters beyond the Aran Islands as 'remarkable for sun-fish', adding that they were 'there in plenty, and of such value, that if a boat be out for two months and takes one sunfish, the owners think themselves repaid'.[53] The season for catching this valuable fish began around the middle of April and lasted to the start of June, when the Connemara fishermen would 'discontinue looking for them, and apply themselves to their country occupations'. Each sunfish produced from six to seven barrels of oil. The Connemara boats generally headed for harbour every night, which meant that they lost 'the beginning of every day' sailing to the fishing grounds. The sunfish came 'from the southward, and sweep along the north-west coast of Ireland northward, in the line of the Rosses, seldom close to the land, and from thence along to the west coast of Scotland'. On 4 and 5 May 1815, 'there were such quantities of sun fish about the direction of the bank aforementioned, that the Galway and Connemara boats killed between one and two hundred of them, with which they all returned to their respective homes quite content with what they had got'.[54] Brabazon was also impressed with the sun fishery off the Galway coast.

44 Hunting the sunfish off the west coast of Ireland. Sunfish, or basking sharks, were regularly hunted off the coast of Mayo and Galway in the nineteenth century, when their oil was a valuable export commodity (from Brabazon, *The deep-sea and coast fisheries of Ireland* (1848)).

In warm weather at the end of April, the fish began to show above the surface of the water far out to sea. Although Brabazon considered it an under-exploited fish, he was in no doubt that great quantities of basking shark were there for the taking.[55] The fishermen reckoned that it was a day's sail out of sight of land to the best sunfish grounds. Their huge dorsal fin could be seen from a great distance as it rose three or four feet out of the water. As they lay motionless on the surface, basking in the sun, 'they were easily approached and struck with a harpoon'. The fishermen usually allowed the harpooned fish 'an hour to tire out before they begin to haul on the harpoon line, and play him sometimes 8–9 hours before they can get him to come to the surface, and when he does they strike him with 2–3 more harpoons'. Basking sharks were also to 'be met with in large numbers off Tory Island, and along the north-west coast of Donegal'. Here, fishermen from Skerries 'found them at different times lying so thick over the ground where their cod lines were set, that they would not venture to put to sea in their open boats to lift the cod lines for fear of the sun fish striking their boats'.[56]

Hely Dutton felt that herring fishing off the Galway coast was 'not carried on to that extent that it ought to be' and was generally 'mismanaged'.[57] This was due to the fluctuations in prices and the perennial 'want of salt to meet the extraordinary take of this variable fish'. However, it was equally attributable to 'poorly-maintained nets', 'leaky boats' and lack of capital. The price of herring could also drop from as high as 'a guinea per thousand' to a low of 15s. for the same amount, when the fishing was good and salt was scarce. To effectively fish for herrings, it was necessary to have two sets of nets, as the nets used for the spring fishery were generally too large to capture fish in the summer season. The boats used in the winter and spring fishing seasons were often 'so small that the boatmen are afraid to venture where they are most likely to catch fish'. The fishermen believed that the quantity of fish caught off Galway had decreased at the end of the eighteenth century. This was attributed 'in some measure … to their not being aware that the fish are often to be found in great abundance below the usual depths at which they are generally looked for'. The approach of the herrings to the bay of Galway was 'indicated by the appearance of those fowls that feed on herrings, and their making an unusual noise; by a great take of cod, hake or black Pollock, who follow the herrings; by the luminous appearance of the sea at night, and other signs known to the fishermen'.[58]

There were strict regulations governing herring fishing in this stretch of coast throughout the nineteenth century. When the herring appeared in the bay, 'the admiral' of the Galway fishermen 'dispatched boats to prevent all the boats in the bay from going out until permission has been obtained'. Persons acting contrary to his orders were 'punished with the loss of boats and nets, and probably a sound drubbing'. At the admiral's command, an evening was appointed when 'upwards of 500 boats would assemble at the Claddagh … and all of these would sail out together, and preserve a profound silence until they arrived on the fishing ground'. Upon a signal from the admiral's boat, 'they all at once drop their nets'.[59]

The extensive list of fish regularly caught in the waters around Galway Bay included mullet, mackerel, bass, salmon, turbot, sole, John Dory, plaice, halibut, skate, cod, haddock, hake, ling, bream and gurnard. Conger and silver eels, together with lobster cockles, razor fish, scallops and edible crabs, were also plentiful in the bay. Boats working this coast in the 1790 were considered too small to be effective, 'but since that period, they have increased them to fourteen tons, with which they are now going to Limerick, Westport and Sligo'. Nets were 'always of hemp, tanned with oak bark', and it was customary for fishermen to fish with five or six hands per boat, and since they 'have had this fishery [since] time immemorial, they would not permit a stranger to settle amongst them'. From the late eighteenth century to the early 1820s, the

45 A wherry from Skerries, Co. Dublin. Wherries like this allowed east-coast
fishermen to extend their range around the north and northwest coasts,
where local fishermen regarded them as 'interlopers' (from Holdsworth,
Deep-sea fishing and fishing boats (1874)).

population of the Claddagh district increased from just over 500 inhabitants to
'to upwards of 3,000'. Prior to the enlargement of their boats, the Claddagh
men 'seldom ventured beyond the islands of Arran, and on the appearance of
a squall, ran into the first sheltered creek they could make, and frequently lost
their market'. Fishing vessels from England, Scotland, the Isle of Man, Cork,
Waterford and Dublin waited in the bay to collect 'great cargos' of herring
from these smaller boats. The fish were then cured and yielded a 'great profit'
to the fish merchants who bought them. Hely Dutton claimed that if the
Galway merchants 'possessed a proper spirit of enterprise, this profit should
centre in their pockets, and they would have long since formed an extensive
fishing company, and not seen themselves disgraced by frequent advertisement
of 'Scotch herrings just arrived'.

Turbot were 'in great plenty at some seasons' around the Connemara coast,
and at the start of the nineteenth century these were sent by mail coaches to
Dublin. Lobsters were plentiful all around the coast, and in some parts the

local people put smaller lobsters 'into holes in the rocks that are covered at half ebb, and feed them to a large size with fish and other food'. Oysters 'of very superior quality' were 'in season almost the whole year', and 'pearls of great beauty, but not very large', were found in a number of rivers throughout Connemara. Mussels were 'much used' in the surrounding countryside for 'making soup on fasting days, and if well-made, this is a delicious dish'. Cockles were also used to make fish sauces, but 'unlike those used in Dublin', they were 'a very insipid addition, because they were brought to market ready dressed, and the liquor, the best of sauce, was thrown away'. In the first three days of Lent, 'upwards of five hundred guineas' worth of cod and other fish were sold in Galway alone in the opening years of the nineteenth century. The city also had one of the wealthiest salmon fisheries in the country. Salmon were then 'frequently speared from the battlement of the bridge, a very curious but dangerous practice, which has been time immemorial in one family'. 'Excellent salmon' were also to be had 'in abundance in every river on the coast of Connemara, especially at Ballynahinch', while in Lough Corrib there were 'a great variety of trout'.[60]

While the freshwater fisheries of Galway were widely recognised as a valuable resource in the eighteenth and nineteenth centuries, the fisheries on the bay were considerably more so. In 1762, it was stated in the Irish House of Commons that 'the fishery in the bay and harbour of Galway is remarkably good, that there is the best herring and cod fishery there in the kingdom, and a cod bank near Bophin, about a night's draft from the shore'. At this time also, the fishermen of Galway supplied saltwater fish to Limerick city 'and to a greater part of the inland county'. An estimated 200 boats were employed during the fishing season, 'of which about 160 belong to the town, and the rest to the county of Clare side of the harbour'.[61] In a statistical survey of Co. Clare in 1808, also conducted by Hely Dutton, it was stated that there were 'not more fish caught than what supplies the markets of Limerick, Kilrush, Miltown and the southern and western parts of the county; the northern and eastern parts being mostly supplied from Galway'.[62] The author went on to state that

> Though the numerous bays and creeks from Loop Head to Kilrush are admirably well adapted for the fitting out and safe lying of fishing-boats, from the poverty and laziness of those who are capable of pursuing the fishing business, it is not carried on with the spirit that such undertakings require.

46 Charles Whymper's sketch *Blessing the Waters*, showing a Dominican monk
and submissive fishermen in Galway Bay. Published in Richard Lovett's
Irish Pictures in 1888, it shows the church's efforts to bring unruly fishermen
into the fold of 'respectable' Irish society.

Around 200 boats were engaged in fishing for herring, but this fishery was
'uncertain', and one bad season was capable of 'completely ruining these poor
men, who have expended all upon their boats and fishing apparatus'. There
was also 'a very productive turbot fishery that might be carried on in the

mouth of the Shannon', yet 'no exertions' were made to develop this fishery. This was because 'few if any of the fishermen' were in a position to 'expend fifteen or twenty guineas for a trawl'. 'Owing to boisterous weather', it was argued, the inhabitants of the Clare coast often went 'without fish of any kind for several months at a time'. At such times, the men engaged in the 'more agreeable employment of carrying goods ashore from smuggling vessels'. As many as 500 French vessels fished the extensive fishing banks off the Clare coast at the start of the nineteenth century, while English fishing fleets 'explored only the western banks'. Due to its distance from the shoreline, the centre of this great fishing ground was under-exploited, even though it was 'likely to afford large quantities of fish'. Oysters were taken in large quantities on various parts of the coast, and those taken at Pouldoody in the bay of Galway had 'a high reputation for flavour; lately however, from want of stocking the bed, they have become scarce'. An 'inferior sort' of oyster was sold by fish hawkers and street sellers throughout Clare, Galway and Limerick, while 'Burrin oysters', and 'fine Pouldoody oysters' were sold directly from boats at George's Quay in Dublin. Huge crabs and lobsters were 'caught in great plenty on the shores of the bay of Galway, and in every creek from Blackhead to Ardfry'. These were generally sold locally 'at a very reasonable price', while those dispatched to Dublin 'fetched as much as seven shillings', compared to the 'mere six pence, and sometimes less' that they commanded at local markets in Clare and Limerick. The quantity of salmon caught in the inshore waters and estuaries of Clare was 'considerable', with 'a few being taken in all the rivers that communicate with the sea'. The salmon fishery at Limerick was in decline at the start of the nineteenth century, due 'in good measure to the illegal practice of destroying the fish at night by lights in Adair'. Salmon stocks were also depleted, due chiefly to poaching during the spawning season and 'the very general practice of watering flax in the Shannon, in full view of the magistrates of Killaloe, and in violation of an Act of Parliament against such practices'. Eels, on the other hand, formed 'another very material article of consumption' around this coast, and were said to 'abound in every river and rivulet'. The author felt that 'it would be a very desirable thing, if they could be caught without obstructing the passage of the water, as ell-weirs are the chief cause of very great damage to lands on the banks of rivers'. At Liscannor Bay, a considerable quantity of small turbot was regularly landed, and these were sold 'at a reasonable price' to a 'person who has lived in Dublin'. The fishing grounds that produced the largest fish were 'too far from shore to permit the small boats in use for this purpose to avail themselves of it'. However, mullet

47 A 'pusha net' being landed in the west of Ireland, in a sketch taken from Halls, *Ireland: its scenery, character etc.* (1841–3).

and bass were 'sometimes caught at the mouth of some rivers', while 'many kinds of flat fish, with mackerel, herrings and whitings in their proper season, were 'caught in abundance', and were 'a great relief to the poor of Limerick and other towns'.

O'Brien's brief account of Kerry's sea fisheries in 1804 stated that there were 'around 120 substantial fishing boats, weighing from ten to fifteen tons burden' operating out of Dingle alone.[63] These were partly engaged in summer trading in turf and farm produce, and partly in the herring fishing during the autumn months. Wherries from Rush, and hookers from Kinsale and Galway, regularly fished for herring, mackerel and pilchards in the waters off Kerry. O'Brien estimated that there were almost 800 such small fishing boats and currachs operating on this stretch of coastline. With only two harbours, one at Dingle and the other at Valentia, boats had to be beached well back from the shore in stormy weather. He estimated that there were just over 3,000 fishermen in the county, not counting those employed in gutting and processing fish. Valentia was deemed 'perhaps the safest harbour in the world', and was of 'great importance if ever the fishery on this coast were to meet encouragement'. O'Brien urged the construction of a lighthouse on the island, 'to improve navigation' and contribute to the development of the local maritime economy.

His report, which was dispatched to the Dublin Society, paints a picture of fishing in this part of Munster as 'struggling doggedly' to survive without any support from either local landlords, merchants or central government.

THE SOUTH COAST

In the 1750s, Charles Smith described the sea and freshwater fisheries around Co. Cork in considerable detail and, in so doing, set himself apart from most of his contemporary historians, who concentrated chiefly on the history of rural distress and the ways and means for redressing it.[64] At Lough Allua, on the upper reaches of the Lee, he found salmon, and 'trout that were almost as large as salmon', as well as small river trout, and charr or alpine trout. Lough Hyne, near Skibbereen, 'abounded in various kinds of sea fish', and 'excellent oysters, crabs, escalops and small deep oysters'. The lake was the property of Sir John Freke, who had 'the opportunity of having excellent sea fish from it, even in the most stormy weather'.[65] A few miles to the west of Lough Hyne lay Baltimore, 'formerly called Dunashad, an ancient corporation and an excellent harbour'. Further along this coast lay Bantry, which he described as a 'thriving town' when pilchards frequented the bay, but for want of employment it had once again 'fallen into decay'. In many creeks and estuaries around this coast, fish palaces had been built to preserve and salt pilchards. When the pilchard fishery was at its height, 'several thousand pounds worth' of fish had 'been sent hence to Spain, Portugal and Italy, but of late years not a single pilchard appeared on the coast'. Pilchard fishing around Bantry 'began generally about St James' day', i.e. during the 'first dark' of July. In the first three months of the season, the catch consisted of fish that were 'large, fat and full of oil'. These were preserved 'with considerable difficulty' and were darker than those taken in the winter months. They were also 'less prized in foreign markets, notwithstanding the fact that they afforded more profit, having a much greater quantity of oil'. Smith also commented that Kenmare Bay was 'frequented by numerous shoals of … hake, mackerel and ling', which were annually 'taken by boats from Kinsale and other places'.[66] He believed that 'many more vessels might be employed, to good purpose, in fishing on this coast'. The creeks and harbours around Kenmare 'abounded with large lobsters, crabs, escalops, oysters, and other shellfish, while the rivulets contained plenty of salmon'. The latter, he argued, 'would be more numerous, were they not destroyed by seals or sea-dogs, which breed here in great abundance'. The chief obstacle in the development the fishing industry on this coast was that 'its inhabitants were

48 Impoverished fish-workers processing fish at Portmagee in Co. Kerry. Women
and children in coastal communities all around Ireland were regularly employed in
this poorly paid work throughout the nineteenth and early twentieth centuries
(courtesy of the de Courcy Ireland collection).

very remote from any market'. 'Great numbers of herring' also passed off
Kenmare and Tralee in August and September, and these were generally caught
for local consumption, although many were also dispatched to markets around
the coast. Dingle and Ventry were particularly famous for 'excellent oysters',
while Valentia was 'renowned for these and other kinds of shellfish'. Those who
harvested the 'fine beds of oysters' at the mouth of the Shannon were able to
dredge up 'some thousands per day in one boat', for which they received only
2*d.* per hundred. Shellfish were 'greatly prized by the country people, as were
crabs and lobsters' and many contemporary accounts emphasise their place in
the diet of rural communities and coastal dwellers alike.[67] Being cheap and
easily transported, they were hawked around the streets, consumed in home
and tavern alike, where they 'reached appetites far down the social scale'.[68]
What made shellfish and crabs all the more attractive was the fact that they
were easily procurable at low spring tides, and required only local skill and the
most rudimentary of tools in order to harvest them.

In his detailed account of fishing around the Cork coast, Colman
O'Mahony has shown that Kinsale was considered the most important fishing

port in the country throughout most of the nineteenth century.[69] The coastline around Kinsale, like great herring fishery off the coast of Co. Down, had all the characteristics of a maritime enclave economy. In addition to the highly productive spring and autumn mackerel fisheries, this stretch of Cork coastline also benefited from a lengthy 'long-line' fishing season, when fishermen from Kinsale, Youghal, Dungarvan and Dunmore East caught a wide range of other saltwater fish. The offshore waters were particularly noted for mackerel, and these attracted large numbers of French and British boats in springtime. Complaints about the number of French herring boats off the Cork and Kerry coastline were being made throughout the mid-eighteenth century. In 1757, a Cork newspaper reported the presence 'of fifty vessels fishing for mackerel near Bantry Bay without interruption'.[70] In 1770, there were 'upwards of 300 sail of French fishing vessels, some of 200 tons, on the coasts of Ireland, where they met with great success in the mackerel fishery'. In that same year, 'large numbers' of French boats were operating off the coast and these were 'not only abetted but encouraged by the native Irish'. However, the presence of such large numbers of foreign fishing vessels was 'thought to be the cause of the great scarcity of fish experienced at this time'. In 1786, the captain of a revenue cruiser estimated that no fewer than 200 French vessels were fishing for mackerel near Baltimore and Crookhaven, each of which was manned 'by thirty men and used up to 2 miles of netting'. The 'depredations' caused by this degree of over-fishing by foreign vessels caused 'poor fishermen to be satisfied with the few straggling fish which might happen to escape them'.[71] In 1793, local fishermen were still complaining of the number of French fishermen 'resorting to the fishing grounds off Kinsale'. At this stage, there were 'as many as 200–300 French boats of from 60–80 ton burthen … fishing there on a regular basis from the 17th of March to the end of May'.

Kinsale's major fishing banks lay only thirty-five miles offshore, and were fished from Monday to Friday during the fishing season. In 1808, concerns about over-fishing by foreign vessels were once again expressed, and the burgesses of the town sought to introduce regulations 'to prevent trawling and to regulate the fisheries and dredging for oysters within the harbour'.[72] An estimated fifty single-mast hookers, weighing between twenty and twenty five tons, fished out of the town at that time. Hook and line were still the principal method of fishing used by most smaller fishing vessels, and attempts to introduce trammel nets were rigorously resisted on the grounds that they were depleting stocks of fish. The town's population was highly dependent on fishing, and in years when fishing was poor, destitution was rife. Kinsale had a population of around 7,500 in the early 1820s, at least 500 of whom were unemployed.[73] When the fishing season opened in 1865, there were an estimated thiry-one Manx, four Howth and four Scottish boats in Kinsale Harbour. The Manx craft were reputed to be the best available. Weighing around thirty tons, they were built especially for fishing. On a particularly good night, one Cornish boat took 4,000 to 6,000 mackerel. Throughout most of the nineteenth century, open decked hookers with large sails were the most common craft in use on the Cork coastline. Fishermen earned between 9s. and 12s. per week, but their 'intemperate habits' caused them to be 'more destitute than … any class of labourers'.[74] The local Ladies' Society provided classes in net-making for poor girls in the town, and in 1830 over 5,000 yards of seine cloth, 6,000 yards of flannel and frieze, and forty-four mackerel and herring nets had been manufactured. George Dawson, one of the major employers in Kinsale, engaged a steamer to convey fish to the markets in Cork, and by the mid-1840s, Kinsale fishermen constituted 'a separate community of around 300 families' within the overall population of the town.

The presence of such large numbers of foreign fishermen off the south coast of Cork benefited local businesses and services in Kinsale in particular. It was pointed out that 'their outlay at the butcher's stall for the best meat and mutton is considerable, the grocer and baker largely benefit from them, while the house of prayer is full of devout worshipers, and resounds with the noise of praise and thanksgiving, both on Sabbath and other occasions, when not engaged in their vocation'.[75]

According to a census conducted at the start of the 1870s, there were an estimated 1,534 fishermen in Kinsale and a total of 253 boats. Ten years later, these numbers had declined to 637 men and forty boats. Despite the strength of fishing in the area, it was reported that 'in inland places, not many miles from Kinsale, the scarcity of fresh fish is such as to have placed it beyond the reach of the working people'. In the 1880s, Church of Ireland ministers in the area were criticising fish-buyers for 'taking advantage of the state of the market to exact an undue profit from the men who are working for them'. By then, however, fish catches were down all along the coast, east and west of Kinsale, even though improvements were noted in boats and equipment. The town had no ice-house, its two curing stations were roofless, and lack of commitment was evident among many of the skippers of the hundred or so boats still engaged in sea fishing. A report from Commissioners of the Deep Sea and Coast Fisheries of Ireland left no doubt about the real cause of decline when it stated that

49 Kinsale Harbour, Co. Cork, at the start of the twentieth century. This town was associated with the commercial exploitation of fish from as early as the sixteenth century. During the herring and mackerel seasons, it attracted large fishing fleets from Britain and mainland Europe (courtesy of the de Courcy Ireland collection).

The fishermen are now the main obstacles to success. Drunkenness and laziness prevent them availing themselves of good takes, and want of energy prevents them following fish into strange waters, even when the owners have capital to embark in proper size boats. The shores of Kinsale, Oysterhaven and Courtmacsherry are disfigured by wrecks of fishing boats of unknown ages, which but for the marvellous laziness of the inhabitants, would have been broken up twenty years ago.[76]

This criticism of the Kinsale fishermen was later qualified by a Commissioner of the Deep Sea Fisheries, who stated that they could not be relied upon to act on their own initiative, due mainly to the 'bad habits they developed during periods of idleness'.[77] Hickey described the majority of fishermen in his study as men whose 'moral habits were good', but whose circumstances were 'miserable', while a local fisheries inspector argued that only 'under good leadership, restraint and constant supervision could they be entrusted with money, boats and fishing gear'. Otherwise, he added, the habits of 'excessive drinking' that they and their wives had contracted would probably result in 'the unauthorised sale of boats and equipment to feed the whiskey and pawnbrokers' shops and increase the demoralisation'.[78] One of the main causes of the decline in the Kinsale fishery was the discovery of huge shoals of mackerel out to sea further westward from the town. While this impacted adversely on the fortunes of fishermen from east Cork to Waterford, it fostered the development of fishing stations at smaller centres such as Glandore, Castletownbere, Baltimore and Castletownsend. In the 1880s, the fishermen of Baltimore and Cape Clear received considerable support from Baroness Coutts. With encouragement from the parish priest of Baltimore, she provided a fleet of boats for their use, 'contenting herself magnanimously by receiving payment for the men in easy instalments, all of which were repaid religiously, and on time'.[79] Another factor in the relative decline of Kinsale was the appearance of huge shoals of mackerel off the western shores of England, which caused many English boats to remain at home to fish these waters.

While the sea fisheries off Kinsale and east Cork were intensely exploited, those in the west of the county were far less developed. Poor fishermen in ill-equipped boats on this stretch of coast struggled to meet local demand, and improvements in fishing were 'painfully slow'. Throughout the first half of the century, fish were reported to be 'abundant', but fishermen could not catch them for 'want of apparatus'. Most people here struggled to make a living from the land, while the 'poorer sort' struggled to eke a living from the sea. A local fishery inspector provided the following picture of the sheer resourcefulness of the poorer sort of fisherman as he struggled to mend his boat in the Mizen Head area in the early 1820s:

> He will repair his crazy bark … if he can get his boat once on the stocks and have a few pieces of timber and plank, his ingenuity will suggest a thousand little devices for the supply of materials. If he can give the carpenter subsistence he will get credit for the wages, the smith will afford the same accommodation; the houses of his neighbours are searched for pieces of old timber; so that between a small sum on hand, and a little credit, some kindly feeling on the part of his friends, and a great deal of ingenuity and perseverance, the boat is afloat once more.[80]

Hickey has shown that the first initiative to improve inshore fishing in this part of the coast did not occur until the early 1820s. He argued that

> In 1823, the London Tavern Committee granted two hundred pounds for fishing lines and a supply of hooks was sent from Bristol. It also gave five

thousand pounds of its remaining funds to the Fishery Board to be given out as loans to distressed fishermen. This board set up a committee from among themselves to administer it, which consisted of Lord Carbery, a Colonel Hodder and James Redmond, who was also struggling to promote fisheries. The local committee for Roaringwater Bay to Mizen Head … painfully realised that fishing was not established on a commercial basis. The Reverend Horace Townsend recommended to J.R. Barry that a fish-curing station be established a Baltimore and curing houses in Crookhaven. The fishermen were curing the fish in their own smoky cabins with poor results as regards quality. There were four boats at Crookhaven whose crews were full-time fishermen and the rest were fishermen/farmers/labourers.[81]

Commercial fishing for pilchard declined rapidly in west Cork in the first half of the nineteenth century.[82] In 1818, J.R. Barry of Glandore founded the Southern Fishery Association, and when the Fisheries Board was established in the following year, he was appointed Commissioner for Fisheries for the maritime district from Schull to Shannon. In this extensive stretch of coastline there were then an estimated forty-eight decked vessels, 127 half-decked vessels, 536 'open sail' boats, and just over 2,000 rowing boats employing around 15,000 boys and men. By 1830, the number of small rowing boats had increased to 25,000.[83] Trawling represented an improved method of deep-sea fishing off the south-west coast in the decades before the Famine. However, the 'outsiders' who controlled this fishery transported huge catches of herring and other species to markets outside the region. In so doing, the new trawlers caused a considerable degree of hardship for local fishing communities, contributed to over-fishing and added to the general destruction of herring and mackerel spawns. Hickey found that it was 'usually strangers who came trawling, and the local fishermen complained about them, but did not attack them as fishermen did in Dingle and Galway'. The use of seine nets on this stretch did lead to violent breaches of the peace, however. Borrowed originally from Denmark, where it was ideally suited to the inshore waters of the Kattegat and the North Sea, 'seining' was one of the most common fishing methods in rivers and lakes in Western Europe from the seventeenth century onwards.[84] In the south-west of Ireland, seine netting competed with trawl nets, particularly in the latter half of the nineteenth century, and required less engine power than the more expensive, capital-intensive trawlers. Right from the start, therefore, vessels using seine netting was more economic on fuel than were trawlers, and with

the difficulties facing the herring industry, this provided an alternative source
of employment to many fishermen along the south and south-west coast. Seine
netting also came at a time when improved road transport was beginning to
complement rail as the principal means of getting fresh fish to market. This
meant that isolated coastal districts throughout Cork and Kerry could now
engage in the commercial exploitation of offshore fisheries. 'Seining' was
particularly popular in sheltered bays and estuaries in the autumn and winter
seasons when fish were concentrated in deep water. The chief disadvantage of
seine nets was that they were non-selective, and many under-sized fish that
should have been preserved did not escape from the nets. This method of
fishing meant that upwards of 600 barrels of fish could be enclosed together in
one net. Seine netting was probably first introduced into the south-west of
Ireland in the mid-seventeenth century to improve the commercial fishing for
pilchards.[85] Writing in 1672, William Petty referred to 'about twenty gentlemen'
who were engaged in pilchard fishing and who had 'among them about 160
saynes wherewith they take about 400 hogsheads of pilchard worth about ten
thousand pounds'.[86] Seining was still the most important method for catching
pilchards in the nineteenth century, and when pilchard fishing declined, seine
nets were adapted for herring and mackerel fishing, particularly in inshore
waters. Seine netting was extremely arduous and labour intensive; it involved
the use of two large rowing boats and up to 400 yards of nets. Went has given
the following description of 'seining' as it was practised in the calmer waters off
west Cork and Kerry in the nineteenth century:

> Two boats, the seine and the so-called 'follower', were used in the fishery.
> The seine boat, a large boat pulled by perhaps a dozen or more oars,
> carried the net … An experienced fisherman acted as 'huer' (hewer) by
> directing fishing operations from suitable points of vantage. From high
> land the huer could see the shoals of pilchards clearly and directed the
> 'skipper' of the seine boat by suitable signs to the location of a likely
> shoal. On the given sign, the net was shot around the shoal by the seine
> boat, every muscle of the oarsmen being exerted to speed the boat thru
> the water and complete the circle. In the meantime, the free end of the
> net was picked up by the 'follower', and the two ends of the net were
> brought together. Stones or weighted pieces of timber, on ropes of
> suitable length, were splashed in the gap between the two vends of the
> net to prevent the fish from escaping. The weighted foot-ropes of the net
> were gradually drawn up until the fish were completely enclosed in a

purse net. By means of baskets, the fish were then gradually transferred from the net to the boat and fishing continued until no more fish could be managed, or if the catches were poor, until darkness descended. Sometimes fishing was done by night, when the fish were identified by the phosphorescence they caused in the water.[87]

While seine sets were widely used even into the twentieth century, local fishermen around west Cork also used long lines and short hand-lines in the pre-Famine period. Long lines were mounted with between 2,000 and 3,000 baited hooks, and were widely used to catch cod, haddock, conger and turbot. Most of the fish caught by local part-time fishermen were sold to dealers, and little of the catches were sold locally, as people either had boats of their own, 'or were too poor to buy fish, although they needed them'.[88] Not as comfortably off as tradesmen, most fishermen of this coast were on the same level as farm labourers and, prior to the Famine, almost all had little plots of land. Special facilities were sometimes available for those seeking small loans for boats and gear, and for the improvement of piers, while national schools near the coast provided basic practical education on fishing methods.[89] Typical of these new fishing towns was Baltimore, which, in the 1830s, had a population of around 500, and was a 'great resort of foreign fishermen'. Although small, the town was said to be 'rapidly increasing in size and importance', and 'several large and handsome houses' had recently been erected, while others were 'in progress'. In 1833, a substantial pier was constructed at the joint expense of the Fishery Board and Lord Carbery.[90] Further along the coast, Cape Clear was 'well known to mariners' and had a 'good harbour' and 'a neat pier constructed on the south side of the island at the joint expense of Sir William Becher and the late Fishery Board'. The male inhabitants of the island were 'wholly employed in fishing, for which the island is admirably adapted: they leave every Monday or Tuesday morning during the summer season, and return on Friday evening or Saturday morning'. Their boats and tackle had improved throughout the 1820s, when men travelled up to thirty leagues out to sea in hookers and half-decked boats. On their return, the fish were given to the women of the island for curing, while the men generally spent their time 'in leisure and recreation until the day of their next departure'. When cured, the fish were sold to visiting merchants, and were sent to the fish market in Cork. Cape Clear fishermen were reputed to be 'expert and resolute seamen, and the best pilots on the coast'. They were also 'remarkable for discerning land at a distance in snowy or foggy weather, possess an uncommon sagacity in discovering the approach of bad weather, and are exceedingly skilful in the management of their vessels'.[91]

We have already seen that the sea fisheries off the south-east coast in the sixteenth and seventeenth centuries were among the most cosmopolitan in the entire country. For centuries, boats from Britain and continental Europe fished for hake, cod, herring and mackerel, and disposed of their catches in port cities on Britain, France and Spain in particular. In addition to its close ties with Britain and continental Europe, the maritime region around Waterford also had powerful social and economic connections with the Newfoundland cod fisheries. The south-east was especially noted for its hake fisheries, and for the long-line men who fished them. In the mid-eighteenth century, there were two seasons in which hake were 'taken in plenty'. The first coincided with the commencement of the mackerel season in June, when these fish were widely used as bait for catching hake. Fish caught at the start of the summer season tended to be larger than those taken during the autumn fishing season that coincided with the arrival of herring around September. Smith found that hake taken on this coast were 'salted and dried for exportation', but 'great quantities' of fresh and salted fish were also consumed throughout the countryside.[92]

We know that hake were a most important fish in the late Middle Ages, and together with salmon, herring and cod, were exported in considerable quantities to continental Europe and England. Large catches of hake caught off the south-east coast were already being dispatched to France in the sixteenth century. They were the staple diet of many coastal dwellers along the south and west coasts. The small port of Youghal was a prominent exporter of salted hake and salmon in the seventeenth century. Went estimated that 116,000 hake were taken in Irish waters in 1664 alone, most of which were caught on the south coast and subsequently exported to Spain.[93] Dungarvan's hake fishery continued to prosper throughout most of the seventeenth century, and in 1669 Thomas Burrow reported that four vessels had come into Kinsale laden with hake from Dungarvan and destined for Bilbao. While most fish were caught on hand-lines baited with mackerel, smaller quantities were taken in seine nets. Considered a 'remarkably cheap town', Dungarvan in the 1830s was a substantial port for the hake fishery and large numbers of women were employed gutting and packing fish. In 1824, the town 'supplied a great part of the interior of Munster with fresh fish'.[94] Trawling for hake in Irish waters was

50 Dunmore Harbour, Co. Waterford, at the beginning of the twentieth century, showing boats from Arklow, the Isle of Man and Scotland. Historically, this corner of maritime Ireland had close links with the south-east of England and the north-west of France (courtesy of the de Courcy Ireland collection).

not introduced until the 1830s, and was then confined mostly to the seas around Waterford. In a description of sea fishing on the Waterford coast at the start of the nineteenth century, Ryland claimed that 'more than one hundred and sixty boats', employing 'about one thousand one hundred men', were engaged in fishing on the Nymph bank off the coast of Dungarvan.[95] In 1823 alone, this fishing ground yielded 'more than one thousand tons of excellent fish … and as the wives and children of the fishermen were engaged in cleaning and salting the fish, the total number of persons that derived employment was not less than 3,000'. In the mid-1830s, Samuel Lewis calculated that there were eighty hookers representing 'an aggregate burthen of 1,600 tons' on this coast. There were an additional ninety-three smaller fishing boats and thirty four 'coasting vessels' attached to the port of Dungarvan. The people of the town were 'very expert at salting, saving and drying hake, and most other sorts of fish, taking great care to cure them exceedingly well, which gives their flesh a great reputation in foreign markets'.[96] Relatively small investments resulted in significant improvements in quays harbours and docking facilities in Cork, Dungarvan, Youghal and Kinsale in the late eighteenth and early nineteenth

century. Local capital, private as well as corporate, underwrote quay development in these and other Munster towns, while a number of smaller harbours
in less favoured sites along the coast also benefited from loans and grants from
the Irish Fishery Board in the 1820s.[97] In terms of urban structure and harbour
development, Dungarvan and Lismore benefited most from landlord investment
in the fisheries, with hundreds of artisanal houses and a number of new streets
being constructed in each of these towns. Assessing the effect of investment on
towns in the Devonshire estate in the early nineteenth century, Dickson has
argued that

> The crowing achievement was at Dungarvan, where a massive single-arch
> bridge was erected across the Colligan River that linked Abbeyside with
> the old town, a project that in 1804 had been reckoned too costly for the
> county grand jury to contemplate. But it was the smaller Lismore which
> saw the greatest physical change among the Devonshire towns: little more
> than an estate village in 1800, its population had trebled by 1831, energised
> by the extraordinary flow of spending that was lavished on the castle,
> gardens and woodlands and on the town itself by the sixth duke after his
> succession in 1811.[98]

At this stage also, the short-lived Fishery Board helped to modernise sea fishing
all along the south coast, breathing new life into towns such as Dungarvan,
Kinsale, Baltimore and Youghal. While much of the increased fish catches was
salted for export, a considerable volume was carried inland on carts drawn by
donkeys, a form of transport that extended the market for fresh fish and gave
added flexibility to small fish merchants on the coast. Writing in 1824, Ryland
argued that

> the fisheries of the southern coast of Ireland, whether considered as a
> source of national wealth, as a nursery for seamen, as affording employment
> to a superabundant population, and at the same time yielding an ample
> supply of nutritious food, present to the enlightened statesman a wide
> field for the exercise of political sagacity.[99]

The Nymph bank stretched 'along the whole of the southern coast, at a
distance of about seven leagues from its eastern part at Dungarvan, to a
distance of from 14–20 leagues from its western part at Cape Clear and the
Mizen Head'. These grounds contained 'an inexhaustible supply of cod, ling

51 The port of New Ross in the 1870s. Small estuarine ports such as this played an important role in trade to the New World in the eighteenth century, but only a few developed into prosperous fishing ports in the nineteenth century (from the Cavanagh Collection, National Library of Ireland).

and other fish' and represented 'a great accession to the wealth of the country'. However, the wealth of these fisheries could only be realised with improvements to piers and harbours, and after 'capital was afforded to the fishermen to enable them to equip their boats'. Ryland estimated that 5,000 people depended 'for their support on this branch of national industry'. He pointed out that 'the fostering care of government' had already 'produced many beneficial results … infusing 'a spirit of life and vigour into the minds of the people … and calling into action a portion of capital that would otherwise have lain dormant'. Nevertheless, he insisted, the Dungarvan fishery was still 'in its infancy', and would 'for some time require encouragement and support'.[100]

In his survey of Co. Wicklow in 1807, Robert Fraser estimated that there were approximately forty-five boats 'employed in the herring fishing every season', with each boat employing six men.[101] The rent of the fishermen's cabins on this coast ranged from £3 to £5. Some paid 1s. per year 'for the ground on which to build a hut with their own labour'. Large numbers of women and children were employed during the 'dead season' in making nets. Commenting on the state of sea fishing along the south-east coast some forty years before the Famine, he reported that

Along the whole of the maritime coastline of Co. Wexford ... a very
considerable number of people are constantly employed in the fishing
business solely. On the southern and eastern coasts, there are numerous
assemblages of people at every creek, where there is shelter for a boat,
who derive their subsistence partly from little holdings of land, but
chiefly from the seas; all that is needed to raise these poor people to
prosperity and wealth, is to form small harbours to shelter their boats,
and afford the means of a safe retreat in the event of sudden storms.[102]

Pointing out that there was 'a small harbour at the Bay of Ballyteigue', he
added that

Inadequate as this little harbour is, yet it has enabled the fishermen to
extend the size and number of their boats from five and six, to twelve and
fifteen tons, of which there are about twenty chiefly employed in catching
lobsters, which the large boats carry to Dublin. The fishery is carried on
in summer, in which season they take considerable quantities of cod and
ling, mullet, gurnard and other small fish. The winter fishery, which would
afford them much employment, both in pursuit of the cod fishery, and of
the herring fishery, they are unable to follow, from the want of a harbour
sufficient to shelter their boats. Indeed, we have not seen any situation on
this coast where a little money could be of so much importance in
extending the fisheries, as the formation of a harbour at or near this
place. It would not only be of great advantage to the fishermen adjacent,
but to those from the harbour at Waterford and other parts of the coast
resorting to this fishing ground.[103]

When the herring season ended on this coast, fishing boats dredged for oysters.
These were sent to Liverpool, and the boats carried back coal and earthenware
on their return journey. An estimated thirty oyster boats operated off the coast
at Arklow in the 1830s, when catches were worth around £100 per boat.
Oysters from Wexford and Wicklow were then sold at 8*d.* per hundred and 6*s.*
by the thousand.[104] When the herring season 'proved boisterous', the profits
were said to be 'very considerable'. However, fishermen were plagued by
damages done to their boats due to 'the wretched state of the harbour', which,
it was argued, 'at a very small expense, might be made both safe and
convenient for boats'.[105] The coast of Wexford did a thriving trade in herring,
cod and oysters in the late eighteenth and early nineteenth centuries. With a

total of seven fairs per year, the highest number in the county, New Ross 'was made by its waterways'. Prior to the construction of a bridge at Waterford in 1794, this town was the focal point of much of the commerce of south Kilkenny. Despite this, New Ross remained a plebeian town, and never had a substantial merchant class of any size or influence. This was partially because of the close links between neighbouring Waterford and the Newfoundland fisheries, which left New Ross drawing goods and men chiefly from the its immediate hinterland.[106] Nevertheless, it acted as a significant centre for the provision trade in the south-east, and exported considerable quantities of beef, butter, pork, fish and hides to the colonies. A meat market was established in the town in 1749, with a corn market being added in 1818. However, from the 1820s onwards, the bulk of the region's trade passed through Waterford, and the volume going through New Ross dropped off dramatically.[107]

In 1816, H.L. Bayly described the herring fishery on the Wicklow coast as 'an object of considerable consequence'. In outlining the state of the fishery here, he went on to state that

> There are two seasons in the year: one commencing in May, and continuing six weeks; the other in November, lasting an equal time. From 100 to 130 boats are generally collected, from different parts of the coast, including Dublin and Wexford; some likewise from the Isle of Man and the Welsh coast, during the summer fishery, when vessels from Dublin lie in the bay and purchase for their respective markets; but much the greater quantity of fish is distributed through the interior of the counties of Wicklow, Wexford, Carlow and Kilkenny, by carriers, who find a ready sale, and make a good profit … It is a circumstance worthy of observation, that the herring fishery in the bay of Arklow is considered, next to that of Galway, as the best on the coast of Ireland. And as the numerous advantages to be derived from its increase become more manifest, it will probably be considered, in the not very distant period, as an object of national importance.[108]

In the 1830s, Arklow was described as 'the headquarters of the entire of the whole coast fishery of the county of Wicklow'. Even then, however, onshore facilities were quite rudimentary, and according to one commentator

> The natural harbour formed by the Avoca within its tide-bar is the only retreat for boats, and is unprovided with either pier or any artificial improvement. All vessels that frequent it are built to suit its peculiarities,

52 A typical French mackerel boat of the late nineteenth century. Boats such as these ranged all around the south and south-west, especially during the mackerel season (from Green, 'The sea fisheries' (1902)).

and even they must all lighten on the outside of the bar. The very fishing boats are obliged to lie off, and watch an opportunity of passing the bar on a rise of the wave; they seldom if ever enter without striking; and they are occasionally compelled to run to Wicklow, or Dungarvan. Even at high water of spring tides, the depth over the bar seldom exceeds from four to five feet.[109]

Despite these disadvantages, the sea fisheries off Wicklow employed an estimated 1,380 men on thirty-nine decked vessels and 153 half-decked vessels. An additional 246 men were employed on fifty-seven open sailing boats, with another forty-eight men on rowing boats. It was said that the Arklow fishermen were so industrious and enterprising that

They not only contrive the enormous disadvantage of wanting an accessible harbour, but succeed in keeping themselves constantly employed in some one or other of a series of fisheries. They fish for herring and hake between Mizen Head and Cahore Point, but for the last fourteen years have had little success in that fishery; they frequent the Isle of Man when there is a fishery there; and, when they are not better engaged, they pursue the oyster fishery from January till September, and find it not only an unfailing employment, but a succedanum for the agriculture alternative on which most other fishermen in Ireland rely. They load their boats with oysters and proceed to Beaumaris in Anglesey; and having there laid the oysters on the banks, they afterwards, at periods when they are in season and most in demand, draw supplies for the markets of Liverpool and Manchester. All materials for boats and fishing-gear are procured from Dublin; sails are purchased in Whitehaven; and, in 1836, boat-building was so brisk that, though four shillings and four pence was paid, a sufficient number of shipwrights could not be obtained.[110]

At this time also, several small coastal villages on the Wexford coast were engaged in deep-sea fishing and trading, with the tiny village of Ballyhack on the River Suir being 'chiefly supported by the shipping anchored in the estuary'. Fish and shellfish certainly featured prominently in the economy of coastal communities around Wexford in the late eighteenth century. In the 1770s, Arthur Young described a 'considerable herring fishery' in Bargy and Forth, with 'every creek' having 'four or five boats'. Most of the fish caught along the coast were sent to Wexford for curing and export.[111] The 1851 census recorded no less than 448 registered vessels, employing just over 2,000 men and boys in the county as a whole. This figure excluded the large number of boats owned by small farmers and others for whom fishing was a subsidiary activity that supplemented farming.[112] The rental income from fishing on this coast also augmented land rentals, albeit to a slight degree. Thus, for example, one local landlord earned between £10 and £20 in 1833 from the small fishing villages of Ballyhack, Blackhile, Nuke and Saltmills. There were extensive oyster beds on this coast, with those located in the north coast of the county being regularly poached by 'rapacious Arklow men'. Large numbers of local boats carried huge catches of herring, lobster and shellfish to the Dublin market. It has been suggested that the waters off Wexford may well have been over-fished in the mid-nineteenth century and a ban was imposed on trawling in the summer herring season of 1857.[113]

53 The Arklow mackerel fleet at the end of the nineteenth century, when its offshore fishing grounds attracted large fleets from around the south coast of Ireland and the west coast of Britain (from Green, 'The sea fisheries' (1902)).

We have already seen that the south-east of Ireland had strong connections with continental Europe and Britain since at least the fifteenth century. De Courcy Ireland has argued that fishermen and seamen from the south and south-east joined the navy of revolutionary France in the closing decades of the eighteenth century.[114] Others from this region were joined the British navy, while many more accompanied the exodus of landless labourers and impoverished fishermen who left for Newfoundland in the latter half the eighteenth century. Fishing vessels from the south-east of Ireland regularly put ashore at Plymouth and Poole on the English coast prior to their departure for the Newfoundland cod fisheries.[115] As far back as the sixteenth century, a number of Dublin-sponsored fishing fleets were already operating off Newfoundland, the most notable of which were those organised by Nicholas Weston in the 1590s. The number of Irish vessels engaged in the Newfoundland fisheries in the mid-eighteenth century was comparable to the number of boats leaving London for Newfoundland.[116] Indeed, the links between this region and the east coast of Canada were so strong in the latter half of the eighteenth century that Newfoundland, or *Talamh na hEisc* (the 'Land of the Fish'), was occasionally known as 'the fifth province of Ireland'. Similarly, the road networks in Labrador and Newfoundland were so poor right up until the start of the twentieth century that many coastal settlements in this corner of Canada had closer ties with Ireland than they did with their Canadian neighbours.[117] In a number of pioneering studies of Irish involvement in international fisheries in the eighteenth century, John Mannion has shown that merchants and fishermen from Waterford and Wexford were involved in many aspects of the Newfoundland cod industry.[118] English fishing vessels calling at Waterford on their way to Newfoundland provided passage for thousands young men and, in the eighteenth century, the international cod trade spawned a mass movement of farm labourers and migrant workers from the south-east of Ireland. The fact that so many undertook such as a hazardous journey is an indication of the intolerable social and economic conditions prevailing in this corner of coastal Ireland.[119] In the mid-1770s, an estimated 5,000 men returned each year at the end of the cod-fishing season in Newfoundland. Large numbers of the emigrants found employment with fish merchants and their agents in Newfoundland, many of whom hailed from the same counties as their employees. Debarred from a wide range of employment in colonial Ireland, and unwilling to invest in Ireland's less profitable sea fisheries, a number of Catholic merchants from Waterford and Wexford found lucrative outlets for investment in Newfoundland. Some of these accumulated great wealth as a result of their overseas fishing enterprises and went on to dominate the political landscape of Newfoundland well into the nineteenth century. Richard Welsh of New Ross established a very successful fishing firm at Placentia in Newfoundland in the 1730s, and subsequently became a very influential figure in the cod trade in the 1750s. 'At its peak', Mannion states, 'this house owned a dozen ocean-going vessels, employed or supplied several hundred men and shipped over 25,000 pounds of dried cod in a season to markets around the North Atlantic'.[120] By the start of the nineteenth century, his company was responsible for settling 'scores of Irish immigrants' in and around Placentia. The Sweetmans of Newbawn, Co. Wexford, were another important Irish family who invested heavily in the Newfoundland cod fishery. Having been deprived of their lands in the Cromwellian wars, they moved to Newfoundland in the latter half of the seventeenth century. By the end of the century, they 'owned more than a dozen deep-sea fishing vessels that linked together Spain, Ireland and Newfoundland in a triangular network of a trade based primarily on cod that lasted down to the early nineteenth century'.[121] The export of high quality dried cod to Catholic Spain and Italy constituted the mainstay of their business. In the 1780s, the Sweetmans and the Saunders dominated what Mannion aptly termed the 'Irish cod industry'. Employing approximately 500 fishermen, most of them Irish or of Irish descent, they also provided additional employment to some 250 male and female workers in a wide variety of onshore operations. At the height of their influence, these firms shipped almost 40,000 hundredweight of cod from Placentia alone, and accounted for roughly 4 per cent of the island's total catch of cod.[122] The movement of such large numbers of fishermen and farm workers from the east of Ireland to Newfoundland was a highly organised and comparatively successful affair. Many of the inhabitants of the maritime counties of Wexford and Waterford probably had closer ties with coastal Canada than with rural counties in the interior of Ireland. Straddling these two 'watery' worlds, they were as much at home in the wide amphibian world of trans-Atlantic fishing, as they were in the much narrower parochial world of Waterford city and county. Certainly, their movement to Newfoundland was a major factor in the creation of a trans-national community and in the development of a very important transient fishery on this stretch of Canadian coastline. The initial transfers seem to have commenced around the end of the sixteenth century and developed into a sophisticated and commercially successful operation by the start of the eighteenth century. The flow of poor Irish emigrants to parts of Newfoundland at the start of the eighteenth century was so great that at least one English naval officer complained that boats 'bought over every year from Bristol, Bideford and Barnstaple great numbers of Irish Roman Catholic servants, who all settle to the southward in our plantations'. English authorities also complained of the number of unlicensed Irish fishing vessels operating out of Placentia.[123]

While fishermen from Waterford and Wexford played a very important role in the development of the Newfoundland fisheries, those from around Dublin Bay operated in a much narrower sphere. Dublin at this stage was a major consumer, rather than a producer of fish, and, as we have already seen, fishing boats from Rush, Skerries and Howth regularly fished off the north and west

54 A dramatic image of shipping and fishing activity at South Wall lighthouse, Dublin, in the late eighteenth century (courtesy of the de Courcy Ireland collection).

coasts. The city was also the most profitable market for unloading fish, and visitors regularly commented on the differences in prices for fish and shellfish in Dublin, compared to those in coastal towns and cities on the south and west coasts. Boats up and down the east coast brought sizeable quantities of oysters, lobsters and other shellfish into the city. Herring were brought down from the coast of Co. Down and up from Arklow, Wexford and Waterford, while cod, whiting, mackerel, salmon and hake were drawn from all over the Irish coast. In a statistical survey of the county in 1801, Joseph Archer estimated that ninety fishing wherries, employing over 600 men, were operating out of fishing ports near the city. Thirty of these fished out of Skerries, each of which carried between seven and eight men and received a parliamentary bounty of 20s. per ton of fish landed. Besides wherries, there were twenty fishing smacks chiefly employed in salmon fishing at the start of the nineteenth century. Eleven fishing yawls fished out of Dun Laoghaire for whiting, pollock and herring, and a further seven operated out of Bullock Island.[124] By the early 1830s, there were twenty fishing yawls registered in Dun Laoghaire alone. The fishing then was considered so good around the Dublin coast that it drew in large numbers of fishermen from Cornwall and the Isle of Man. De Courcy Ireland estimated that herring exports from Ireland between 1801 and 1810 were worth £2,000 per

55 A fishing trawler with its nets down in the pre-Famine period. On some stretches of coast, the exploits of trawlers such as these were considered a threat to local fishing communities (from Brabazon, *The deep-sea and coast fisheries of Ireland* (1848)).

year on average, and this represented a 50 per cent decrease on the previous decade.[125] A considerable salmon fishery extended from the weir at Island Bridge to the Lighthouse at Poolbeg and employed some eighteen men. This was managed by Sir William Worthington and lasted from the first of January to the end of September. Archer maintained that this fishery yielded ninety to 200 fish per week, with each fish fetching between 15*s*. and 18*s*. The Sutton and Clontarf oyster beds at this stage were regularly stocked with French and American oysters, and the arrival of large numbers of English buyers in the 1840s provided 'a great stimulus' to the oyster trade in and around Dublin, Wexford and Wicklow. An estimated one million oysters were taken from the Irish oyster beds in 1843 alone, and this was said to represent 'a great drain' on local stocks.[126]

The introduction of trawl-nets carried on a wide beam brought about a revolution in fishing around the coast of Britain and Ireland in the mid-nineteenth century. The initial breakthrough in trawling occurred with the introduction of sailing trawlers in the southern waters of the North Sea in the early part of the nineteenth century. The more economical, power-driven trawlers did not appear in Irish waters until the 1880s. The early attempts at trawling with cumbersome, sail-powered 'smacks' had already commenced in the North Sea in the late 1830s. New techniques involving mid-water trawling were first developed in south Devon, where they caused the rapid expansion of an existing small fishery and attracted fishermen from along the south coast of England. Trawling on the east coast of Ireland was initially introduced at Ringsend by a group of Devonshire fishermen earlier in the nineteenth century. This contributed to the expansion of fishing and meant that fishermen from around Dublin were able to venture further out to sea. Fishermen from Torbay in Devon were fishing in and around Dublin Bay in 1818, and a small group of the city's merchants then embarked on a project to build a fleet of trawlers capable of supplying fish to the Dublin market.[127] The company appointed Captain James Steward as superintendent of the Pigeon House Dock at Ringsend, instructing him to visit Brixham in England in order 'to purchase seven new fishing smacks and to recruit crews to man them'. The new boats were 'fine, cutter-rigged vessels of from forty to forty five tons' which could operate in almost all weather conditions. Fitted with patented winches, and operated by only three men and a boy, they were quite capable of doing the work of eight to ten men. They were especially adept at taking large catches of sole, turbot and other deep-sea species that were beyond the reach of other poorly equipped boats. Not surprisingly, therefore, conflicts often broke out between the more traditional fishermen and the owners of new trawlers, as the local men feared that the latter would put them out of business.[128] In July 1819, several of the Dublin company's smacks 'were stalked at sea by some 18 local fishing wherries off Howth Head'. In this case, however, the superior sailing power of the company's smacks saved them from destruction. The fishing grounds covered by the Dublin trawlers ranged over the entire length of the Irish Sea, and extended from Carlingford Lough to Dungarvan. Commenting on the damage caused to fish stocks by the new trawlers, one commentator in 1848 stated that

> The distress among the fishermen on the east coast is caused by the spawn on the fishing banks being destroyed, along with the small fish, by the trawlers, which has made a great scarcity of fish, and its effects have been severely felt by the poor fishermen who supported themselves by line-fishing out of the small shore boats; and on the west coast of Ireland the very great poverty of the fishermen arises from the want of markets or other demand for fish.[129]

56 An early nineteenth-century schooner of the type recommended for deep
sea fishing off the west coast of Ireland in the nineteenth century
(from Brabazon, *The deep-sea and coast fisheries of Ireland* (1848)).

In the 1850s, the Dublin trawlers began fishing off Galway, but they encountered such strong opposition from the Claddagh fishermen that they 'had to leave their trawl nets on deck and return home'.[130] Nevertheless, Torbay fishermen continued to fish off Dublin right up to the 1840s, when the Dublin Fishing Company became a victim of its own success. With increased competition, poor management and a decline in the price of fish, the company was subsequently dissolved and its boats were sold off.

We can conclude that the first twenty years of the nineteenth century witnessed a substantial increase in the fish-trade in Ireland, as significant amounts of capital were invested in new boats and equipment, while much smaller sums of money circulated among the fishermen and fish-curers. However, by the mid-1830s, subsidies and other supports for fishing came to an end, and this was followed by a rapid decline in the ability of many Irish fishermen to exploit the country's sea fisheries on an expanding commercial basis. By the standards of most European countries, Ireland's offshore fishing grounds harboured huge populations and a highly diversified range of sea fish whose populations and distribution were influenced by a number of ecological factors. These included the depth, temperature and salinity of seawater; the seasonal availability of phytoplankton and other micro-organisms in Ireland's offshore waters; the physical properties of the Irish seabed; the extent of the continental shelf; the seasonality of rhythms of fish reproduction; and the migratory behaviour of species such as herring, salmon and mackerel.[131] However, the economic and commercial potential of these fisheries did not depend solely upon the volume, variety and value of the species they contained. Other factors clearly influenced the degree to which local communities could successfully exploit the rich sea fisheries off the coast of Ireland. These included the nature and extent of the coastline; the relative location of fishing grounds and their distance from land; the ability of fish merchants to access fishing ports; the timing of seasonal migrations of pelagic species such as herring and mackerel; the nature of the marine environment; competition between 'foreigners' and 'natives' in coastal waters; and the nature and extent of onshore facilities for the exploitation of offshore resources.

The following chapter focuses on developmental problems confronting fishermen in Ireland the nineteenth century. While recognising the existence of a number of enclaves of commercially successful fishing around the east and south coasts in particular, it suggests that sea fishing in general was in a pre-capitalist, under-developed state throughout most of the nineteenth century. This, it is argued, was partially attributable to lack of government and private investment in boats, harbours, transportation, fishing tackle, curing stations and other supports necessary for the transformation of fishing from a local, often rudimentary enterprise, into a national industry in its own right.

CHAPTER NINE

Developmental issues in Irish sea fishing: the nineteenth-century heritage

THE ROYAL DUBLIN SOCIETY AND IRELAND'S SEA FISHERIES

Founded in 1731 to help foster scientific improvements in husbandry and the 'useful arts', the Dublin Society was a comparatively efficient channel for promoting technical education in Ireland throughout the latter half of the eighteenth. This work continued throughout the nineteenth century as the Society acquired royal patronage to become the Royal Dublin Society in 1820. The Society was extensively patronised by the Irish parliament and maintained a strong interest in Irish fisheries and marine ecology. In one of its earliest ventures in promoting fishing, it offered a premium of £25 for salting and curing fish. In an effort to stamp out fishing 'irregularities' off the north-west coast in the 1780s, it sought to have an overseer appointed to monitor fishing operations between Lough Swilly and Horn Head. Then, in an effort to reduce the seal population on the north-west coast in the mid-1780s, the Society allocated almost £40 to three firms for culling almost 400 seals.[1] In 1890, it conducted surveys of the coast of Galway and Mayo, and concluded that the Aran Islands 'were admirably suited' for sea fishing. Between 1861 and 1877, William Andrews, a founder member of the Natural History Society of Dublin, published a number of influential papers on fisheries, and fish science, in the journal of the Royal Dublin Society. Andrews' work was chiefly important for drawing scientific attention to the country's rich cod, ling, herring and salmon fisheries at a time when land matters monopolised public debate on economic development in Ireland. His studies of marine life did much to dispel many of the misconceptions about fish reproduction in Ireland's offshore waters, while simultaneously drawing attention to the wealth of the country's sea and freshwater fisheries. It is arguable that the chief contribution of pioneering work such as this lay in its practical applications. Between 1887 and 1889, the Royal Dublin Society commissioned a valuable comparative study of the Atlantic coast of Ireland and North America. As a result of this, W.S. Green travelled to the United States on one of the earliest and most successful trade missions from nineteenth-century Ireland in order to establish a major export trade in salt mackerel.[2] In the aftermath of this visit, the Society called for the development of fish-curing facilities to improve the quality, and increase the quantity, of fish exports from Ireland. In 1884, the Society set up a fisheries committee to develop scientific programmes on various aspects of marine ecology. In the late 1880s, it commissioned Green, a native of Cork, to conduct a regional study of the fishing potential of the waters off the south-west of the country. To develop the commercial potential of sea fisheries off this coast, Green demanded government support for a 'cured brand' of Irish mackerel to compete with the huge quantities of cured fish entering Ireland from Norway, Scotland and Newfoundland.[3] Like other commentators on the state of Irish fisheries at this stage, Green pointed out that facilities for preserving and transporting fish to market were at their worst where the economic potential of offshore fisheries was greatest. Suggesting that Ireland should become a major supplier of fresh fish and shellfish to the UK, one commentator argued that

> If the approaches to the English markets were widened and the railway rates reduced, three times the quantity of fish could be sent to the London market. In the event, too much fish went to Liverpool and northern towns, where prices were lower and demand less. Herring caught off Ireland are sent to Liverpool for curing then shipped back to Ireland for consumption. Fresh herring sold in Cork for a shilling a hundred, while smoked and imported herring go for sixpence per pound. Two railway companies held a monopoly of fish transportation. They control the price of fish, and thereby the price of food.[4]

In his a statistical survey of east Ulster in 1812, John Dubourdieu similarly argued that the 'natural advantages' of the Irish had 'been turned to the best advantage'. As he saw it, this 'proceeded from many causes, in some case from want of capital, in others from want of skill'. As an instance of what was 'lost by want of skill', he pointed out that the Liverpool market was never well supplied with fish from the coast 'until fishermen were brought from Torbay who were better instructed in business'.[5] Lack of curing facilities was a perennial problem for fishing communities in the more isolated districts. While properly constructed curing stations were beyond the reach of poor fishermen, individual landlords and merchants invested in them in the late eighteenth and early nineteenth centuries. Prior to this, fishermen simply smoked fish inside their cabins. However, the inferior quality of the finished products reduced their saleability. Young noted that merchants from Derry constructed 'a complete salting house' at Inch Island in 1776. This was a substantial affair that consisted of 'a range of houses for all operations' associated with the preservation and packing of herring for export. The new building was 'divided into four apartments, one of 20 feet by 18, a store room for coarse salt, which will hold 150 to 200 tons; another of the same dimensions for fine salt; a third for receiving herring from the boats and gutting them, of the same size; and a fourth for a cooper's shop'.[6] At Inverbay in south Donegal, two other landlords who invested in curing facilities were rewarded with a significant expansion of herring fishing in the 1770s. In the 1840s, the agent on the Martin estate in Ballynahinch, Co. Galway, had 'done much good' by giving 'considerable employment in his salmon fishery, and also in his extensive establishment for preserving provisions'. In 1846, the honourable David Plunkett acquired permission to build a smoking house at the head of Killary Harbour. Other landlords who received grants from the Board of Works to improve piers, wharves and boat slips on the coast of Connaught included F.J. Graham of Ballynakil, J.A. O'Neill of Bunowen, A. Thompson of Rosroe and Thomas Martin of Roundstone.[7] In some districts, fishermen were prohibited from hauling their nets onto the shores of landed estates and, in order to redress this particular problem, the Dublin Society issued a number of lawsuits to give local fishermen legal access to private shorelines. The Society also contributed towards the construction of curing stations and houses for coopers in remote districts. Alexander Montgomery of Donegal, for example, received £125 to help construct a house for salting and curing fish in 1775.[8]

Through their systematic studies of marine life in Irish waters in the nineteenth century, William Andrews, John Templeton and William Thompson laid the basis for the scientific study of Ireland's sea fisheries. The rapid development of fish farming and the artificial cultivation of molluscs were logical extensions of this type of research. The commercial potential of sea fisheries was also highlighted by the publication and distribution of guidebooks on Irish marine by the Irish Commissioners of Fisheries. The Dublin Society was also responsible for translating and publishing a number of foreign treatises on fish and the fishing industry, and four such papers were published in 1800 alone. These included one scientific paper by a Dutch scientist on the herring fishery, two works on freshwater salmon and trout, and one study on modern methods for catching salmon, herring and cod.[9] Disregarding the security implications of its actions, the Society made admiralty sea-charts available to fishermen and in 1771 arranged for the copying of charts of the relatively unchartered waters from Lough Swilly to Broadhaven. On a more practical level, it placed advertisements in local newspapers advising fishermen to 'crimp' or 'score' cod in order to lengthen their 'shelf life'.[10] Despite this, however, the commercial exploitation of Ireland's sea fisheries, at least by Irish fishermen, lagged well behind their English, Scottish and continental counterparts. Irish fishermen were considered 'backward' compared to their overseas neighbours, while their boats were said to be 'ill-equipped' and their nets deemed unsuitable for deep-sea fishing in particular. Outside the major ports, most of those engaged in fishing worked on a part-time basis, with the result that their currachs and fishing smacks were no match for the well-equipped clinker-built decked vessels used by foreign deep-sea fishermen. Even in a substantial port like Galway, in 1829 there were around 300 boats 'lined up in the quay daily', but most of these were small fishing craft that, despite their size, were capable of landing up to 20,000 herring.[11] The difficulties fishermen encountered in getting them to market meant that species such as herring and mackerel fetched as little as 6s. to 10s. per 1,000 in many districts along the west and north coasts. Many part-time fishermen had no option but to dispose of their surplus catches by feeding them to pigs, or using them to fertilise their potato plots.

THE UNDER-DEVELOPMENT OF IRELAND'S SEA FISHERIES

At the start of the nineteenth century, therefore, Ireland's sea fisheries were, as John de Courcy Ireland put it, quite simply 'in a sad state'. Deep-sea fishing was the victim of 'government high-handedness and laissez faire economic theory'. Herring to the value of almost £60,000 were actually imported into the country in 1818.[12] Pilchard fishing, one of the most successful commercial fishing ventures in seventeenth-century Ireland, continued to operate right up to the nineteenth century, but then went into serious decline. On the eve of the Great Famine, Irish fishing was described as 'a backward and neglected industry' and the limited efforts to transform it into a viable industry in the first half of the century had not succeeded. Cecil Woodham Smith concluded that

> The difficulties, which had prevented a fishing industry from developing in Ireland, remained: the poverty of the country, the want of proper boats, the remoteness from a market, and the dangers of the 'tremendous coast' in the west. In many places, trawling was declared impossible, owing to the rocky and foul nature of the sea bottom; in others … for part of the season the fishermen had to row twenty-five miles to the

fishing grounds; the weather was unreliable, and small boats, currachs especially, laden with their catch were difficult to bring in when a squall blew up. Fish-curing stations could not operate economically when the supply of fish was not regular, or did not prove easy to dispose of the finished product; a number of stations had cured fish left on their hands.[13]

Some felt that the country's sea fisheries were intentionally maintained in an under-developed state so that Irish fishermen might not compete with their Scottish or English counterparts. In a statement to the Devon Commission in 1844, the Earl of Glengall stated that the 'intrigue to destroy the Irish deep-sea fisheries was too successful, in order that ... the Scotch fisheries might not be interfered with'.[14] There were many who concurred with his interpretation of the declining importance of fishing in Ireland after the Union. James Bowles-Daly argued that the 'government in Ireland suppressed fishing, and the Cromwellian parliament was inundated with petitions that the Irish fishermen might be suppressed, in consequence of competition with the English'. As a result, he added, 'many of these fishermen were banished to Connaught, and others were transplanted to the West Indian Islands'. He then went on to point out that

> All authorities unite in proclaiming that the Irish coast continues to be the resort of vast shoals of fish. For the last 30 years, the history of the Irish Fisheries is a record of almost continuous decline in the number of boats and crew. In the Isle of Man, with its small population, one out of every 19 is a fisherman while, in Ireland, there is only one in every 200 of the population. The decline is not due to the scarcity of fish. Cornish, Scotch, Manx and French boats habitually visit the Irish coast, while the native boats are not 29 per cent of those at work on purely Irish waters. The best stations are Howth, Ardglass and Kinsale. At Ardglass station the Irish boats are less than 14 per cent, and in the mackerel fishing at Kinsale, only a small proportion of the total number of craft which come from the various ports and share the spoil are Irish.[15]

Fishermen in the west of Ireland were able to 'see the creeks along the west coast crammed with fish, when they could take tons of them at a haul ... with a deep seine or drift net, but when caught they would be useless to them, as they could not either salt or sell them'.[16] Some have suggested that locational factors alone accounted for the under-development of Ireland's fisheries in the first half of the nineteenth century. O'Grada has argued that *coastal geography* gave the east and south-east of the country a comparative advantage over the west and north-west of the country, where seas were rougher and the weather was harsher.[17] Unlike in the west of the country, the man-made harbours on the east coast were also within easy reach of sizeable urban markets. Reminiscing on a life spent fishing off the south-west of Ireland, Tomás Ó Criomhthain, who was born on the Blaskets in 1856, described conditions all too familiar to fishermen in many western coastal districts throughout the late nineteenth and early twentieth century. He stated that

> All along the coast, every canoe was up to the chin with mackerel. In Smerwick Harbour the seine-nets were down to the seabed with fish. The sight of all the fish on its way to Dingle was a marvel to behold. A good part of it was bought at a shilling a hundred. That was not enough to pay the cartage; it was sixpence short. The man who had caught the fish did not get even that shilling – no, not a penny of it. Not a single sixpence came into the island for that day's fishing, though the boats were down to the gunwale. The carters used to take it; there was too much of it; it wouldn't pay. It couldn't be salted either. The salt dealers had been charging a crown a hundred, but when they saw the people's plight, they charged fifteen shillings. So there was nothing left for it but to pick the fishes out of the nets and throw them back dead into the sea.[18]

In calling for the more investment in sea fisheries in the 1880s, Bowles-Daly claimed that the fishing industry was

> more easily developed than any other, as no large plant is necessary, there are no customers to solicit, and no connections to make. The wealth is all at our own doors; the foreigner has hitherto come and gathered the harvest, while Ireland looks on unmoved. It is high time that the country should wake up to its opportunities and drop forever the beggar's whine.[19]

Attributing the under-development of Irish fishing to 'English misrule', he went on to assert that

> For years the land of Ireland has been locked against the industry of the people, and for the most part confined to the possession of a few who wanted the capital, skill and, it may be, inclination, to develop its

resources ... The west of Ireland might be made a great training establishment, both for sailors and fishermen, if only some of the ships, now
rotting in the dockyards of England, were applied to this purpose; the
cost of the experiment would be contemptible. Trained sailors and
thoroughly equipped smaller craft, not unwieldy machines, will secure
the empire of the sea.[20]

A number of attempts were made to resuscitate sea fishing at a regional level,
one example of which was the Southern Fishery Association established in
Kinsale in 1818. When the Irish Fisheries Board was set up in the following
year, J.H. Barry was appointed Commissioner for Fisheries for the maritime
district extending from Schull in west Cork to the Shannon Estuary. One of
the chief architects of Irish fishery policy in the 1820s, Barry was an energetic
fisheries inspector and a local landowner. He built the estate village of
Glandore around the fishing industry by installing new quays, boatyards and a
fish-curing plant in its immediate vicinity.[21] The pier-building work of the
Fisheries Board, together with local initiatives of landlords, had a catalysing
effect on the development of fisheries at Waterford, Dungarvan, the Ring
Peninsula, Baltimore and Valentia Island at this stage. At the dissolution of the
board in 1829, there were an estimated 869 sailing vessels and approximately
25,000 people engaged in fishing and allied trades between Dungarvan and
Dingle. This represented almost one third of total employment in these trades
in the entire country. The new Board had made bounties payable to fishermen
according to tonnage of their boats and quantity and species of fish landed.
Premiums for catching and curing fish were given to fishermen around the
Cork and Kerry coast, where large catches of mackerel, herring, shad, ling and
hake were regularly reported.[22] Much of the money that went on premiums to
fishermen was collected on levies on imported herring, and some argued that
the liberal distribution of premiums was not entirely beneficial as it made
fishermen over-dependent on government support. That said, however, the
premium system did contribute to a substantial increase in the number of
fishing vessels, particularly in poorer districts, where it encouraged fishermen
to move into commercial fishing. However, premiums were only a temporary
expedient for the alleviation of coastal poverty, and when they were discontinued in the 1830s, the fish-trade fell 'into languor and exhaustion'. Some
argued that the premiums ended too abruptly, while others believed they
provided 'an excess of stimulation' and contributed to fraudulent claims.[23]
Government agencies regarded poor-law legislation as more acceptable than

57 Burtonport, south Donegal, in the early twentieth century. The coast from Lough Foyle to Galway Bay had remarkably few fishing ports and those that managed to survive to the end of the nineteenth century often lacked basic processing facilities (courtesy of Seán Beattie).

government support for fishermen to alleviate coastal poverty in pre-Famine Ireland. This was in marked contrast to the continuation of the bounty system in Scotland, which promoted the commercialisation of fishing in some of that country's more remote coastal areas. Not surprisingly, therefore, the more organised Irish fishermen alleged that 'the Scottish interest in parliament had worked against the Irish fisheries'. Thereafter, many boats were withdrawn from fishing and 'were suffered to rot on the beach, while the men sought other employment or sunk into mendicancy'.[24]

Pointing out that the country had 'a coastline of about 2,000 miles, broken into an exceptionally large number of excellent harbours', and 'waters teeming with fish, many of them being among the very best of their kind', Robert Dennis insisted that 'all the natural advantages for carrying on a great fishing industry clearly existed in Ireland'. In a veritable 'eulogy' in praise of the 'natural advantages' of maritime Ireland, he added that

As if to mark the island out as a special field for gathering in the harvest of the sea, Nature has placed her best harbours where there are most fish. The eastern coast, with Strangford Lough as the only good harbour between Belfast and Waterford, comes far behind the western in its yield; while all round the south-west, west and northern coasts, where the sea makes deep incisions into the land every few miles, the waters swarm with cod, hake, ling, mackerel and herring. The south-west coast is especially prolific, and occasionally there is almost what one might call a 'miraculous draught'. On the west coast there is also an abundance of fish. Outside Arran Island there are magnificent banks; nearer land, in Galway Bay, the fish would be plentiful if trawling, which destroys the 'cover' and which ought to be practised only in deep water, were prohibited; off the coast of Connemara there is so much fish (and so bad a market for it) that tons are annually thrown upon the land for manure; round the island of Bofin the sea has often been actually 'roughened with fish'; Clew Bay is a perfect 'stew'; Broadhaven and Blacksod Bays, in Co. Mayo, are so landlocked that boats could go out and make a haul every day in the year; Carew might have referred to Donegal Bay when he wrote of his 'fishful pond'. In the end, however, the advantages that Ireland possessed as a maritime nation were 'thrown away'. Scotland, which had a coastline only 500 miles longer than that of Ireland, 'but with fewer harbours and ... less fruitful and more tempestuous seas, supported by her fisheries one-seventh of her entire population. Ireland, on the other hand, had plenty of open mouths ready to receive fish, but the means of catching the fish – boats, nets and piers – were wanting'.[25]

He also pointed out that Scotland's sea fisheries supported 'one in seven of the entire population', while the corresponding figure for Ireland was 'one in two hundred and fifty'.[26] In yet another tribute to the seas around Ireland, a different commentator stated that

The Atlantic sends in its shoals of mackerel with fair regularity twice every year. Herrings, too, appear in varying numbers. Pilchards used to come, but have not done so for many years and ... dogfish follow the pelagic fish in millions. The fishing grounds around Ireland produce sole, turbot, plaice, cod, ling, hake, haddock, conger and ray, with a sprinkling of halibut, and in the deeper waters tusk. Owing to the contour of the submarine plateau on which Ireland stands, these fishing grounds on the west coast extend to only a short distance from the shore, whereas on the south, north and east they extend as far as the boats can go. The water that bathes the Irish shores is brought thither by the great drift from the ocean known as the Gulf Stream, and, being replete with living organisms, an abundance of food is always coming from in from outside the fishing area.[27]

Notwithstanding these highly favourable environmental conditions, and despite the best efforts of individual landlords to improve sea fisheries, Ireland failed to develop the commercial potential of its sea fisheries in the nineteenth century. For most coastal communities, fishing remained a marginal, albeit vital component of a coastal economy characterised by limited degrees of specialisation and commercialisation on the one hand, and primitive methods for catching, curing and distributing fish on the other. Sea fishing was unevenly developed, as the labour-intensive fishing operations of part-time fishermen co-existed alongside regionally concentrated and highly commercialised sea fisheries off the south and east. The achievements of commercially successful fishermen have, to an extent, been recognised, while local historians are only now uncovering the historical experiences of poorer fishermen. This neglect of the coastal poor was in part due to their weaker political organisation and their inability to match the socio-economic achievements of substantial tenant farmers and the petty bourgeoisie. This contributed to their marginalisation and socio-political exclusion, as fishing became so closely associated with poverty and hardship that political leaders looked to farming and industry as the only *proper* basis for the country's economic and political progress in nineteenth-century Ireland. Evolutionary theories of social progress throughout the Darwinian half of that century suggested that those whose subsistence was based on pre-capitalist hunting and gathering were at a lower stage of social evolution than progressive farmers and captains of industry.[28] For that reason, the issue of land ownership and the politics of nation-building, so dominated public discourse that the needs of coastal communities and the concerns of fishermen were scarcely considered. Thus, despite the obvious wealth of the country's deep-sea and inshore fisheries, rural fundamentalism had such a firm grasp even on *progressive* thinkers that most political leaders committed *la trahison des clercs* by turning their backs on the sea and its resources.[29] Unlike the farming community, fishermen never developed political leaders or an organic intelligentsia of their own, people who could champion the cause of fishing communities in the same way that priests, politicians and farming organisations defended the cause of rural Ireland. English, Scottish and French fleets were the chief exploiters of Ireland's deep-sea fisheries, while, with a few notable exceptions, freshwater fishing remained a sporting affair largely associated with 'upper crust' privilege and the Anglo-Irish aristocracy. For some, the cause of this neglect lay in the social structure of rural Ireland and the reluctance of landed elites to diversify the rural economy of coastal Ireland. Quite clearly, there was a strong element of anti-landlordism in this line of argument, which tended to Anglicise the causes of economic under-development of Ireland's coastal communities and nationalise their solutions. For others, the paltry state of sea fishing was due to its association with poverty and hardship and the unstated assumption that maritime Ireland failed to fully support rural Ireland in the worst years of the Famine. Some thirty years after the in the Great Famine, one commentator could still ask:

> Why is it that the sea, which is open to all, should be powerless to alleviate the perpetual cry of distress, which, like a wind from the cross, moans over that unhappy country? It is not for want of material opportunity, for there is probably no part of the globe where the sea offers so much support to an adventurous population. Among the many industries of Ireland which could be rendered available towards increased comfort and the prosperity of the empire, the fisheries are entitled to the first attention. The geographical character of the island would alone be sufficient to confirm this position. Ireland is surrounded by an ocean teeming with fish of every description to gratify the most fastidious palate; her whole coast is indented with deep and spacious bays, creeks and havens, in which smaller craft can find shelter in stormy weather. The expenditure of a few thousands would enhance the value of those national capacities.[30]

The real causes for the under-development of Ireland's fisheries at this stage were attributable to regional under-development, rural isolation, lack of investment in infrastructure, the unrealistically low price of fish and shellfish, the high price of salt, the low level of effective demand for fish, and the fact that unscrupulous fish merchants could control local markets by driving the price of fish down at the height of the fishing season. Anything beyond the most rudimentary level of sea fishing was literally beyond the reach of most coastal dwellers. Despite this, however, fishing accounted for a very considerable proportion of the income of households in districts that had access to markets for fish and shellfish. Tomás Ó Criomhthain's description of the close-knit community on the Blasket islands at the end of the nineteenth century could equally be applied to many out-of-the-way coastal communities around the Atlantic fringe of Ireland. Here, he wrote, 'were poor, simple people, living from hand to mouth. I fancy we should have been better off if we had been misers. We were apt and willing to live, without repining, the life of the Blessed Master who made us, often and again ploughing the sea with our only hope in God to bring us through'.[31] The poor in districts such as these were connected to the world beyond their parish through their boats, and through the emigrant trails that linked them to the urban centres of Britain and North America. These linkages were often more important, and more profitable, than the far weaker trade-links that tied coastal communities to the emerging nation-state. If there were any doubts that much of coastal Ireland was on the verge of collapse in the latter half of the century, they were dispelled by census figures from the period of post-Famine readjustment. In 1841, for example, the population of Donegal was just under 300,000. Forty years later, and following a rural exodus that witnessed the radical depletion of coastal communities, that figure was almost halved. As in other coastal counties, this emptying of the countryside facilitated the emergence of a rural petty bourgeoisie who took control of institutions of local government and went on to occupy the socially strategic positions in rural and coastal Ireland alike.[32] In many western and northern districts, fishing did not advance beyond pre-capitalist levels of resource exploitation. For some, the answer to these problems lay in the extension of capitalist relations of production, and in the development of 'fisheries companies' capable of solving the problems of the west of Ireland. It was suggested that these companies would reduce the price of fish by adopting more efficient means for exploiting the country's sea fisheries. In his statistical survey of Co. Clare in 1808, Hely Dutton pointed out that 'no part of Ireland ... is so well situated for carrying on a lucrative fishery; but, as only the weak and small fish keep near the shore, it must be mere peddling, until companies are formed that will be able to fit out vessels large enough to navigate the sea as far as the banks of Newfoundland'.[33] No sooner were fishing companies formed, however, than they ran into conflicts with smaller fishermen who regarded them as 'interlopers' in 'their' waters. As we have already seen, the Claddagh fishermen of Galway organised themselves in a highly effective social movement to protect the moral economy and customary rights of poorer fishermen in and around Galway Bay. Similarly, fishermen from villages along the coast of Dublin 'attacked the boats of the

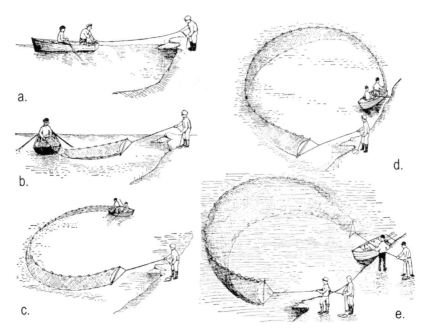

58 Methods of fishing with draft nets in major rivers and marine estuaries (from Went, 'The pursuit of salmon in Ireland' (1964)).

Dublin Fishing Company' because they threatened fish stocks and livelihoods on the east coast.[34]

OF BOATS, NETS AND FISHING GEAR

The commonest vessels in many western and northern districts were simple currachs, or *naomogs*, made from animal hides stretched over rods taken from beech, hazel and holly trees. While these craft could operate very effectively in inshore waters, especially in summertime and during the harvest season, they were difficult to manage in the hazardous conditions off the west and south-west coasts in late autumn and winter months. Foul weather and the rocky nature of the sea floor made it impossible for trawlers to operate along entire stretches of this coast. Fishermen often had to row fragile currachs and cumbersome fishing yawls great distances out to sea simply in order to reach the fishing grounds. Some commentators found it surprising that these boats could 'catch half the quantity of fish they do, and were it not for the dense shoals they fish amongst, their take would be very limited'. In the late eighteenth century, it was said that the fishing currachs on the Clare coast had 'changed little from the remotest period of history'. They were described as 'wicker-work affairs covered with either horse or cow hides' and were believed to be the only type of craft that 'could live a moment in the violent surf that generally beats on this shore'.[35] While the larger rowing currachs could measure up to twenty-five feet, the smaller 'paddle curracks' of the north-west coast measured only eight to ten feet in length. The latter were somewhere between the ancient river baskets used for fishing in medieval times, and the sharp pointed rowing currachs found elsewhere on the Irish coast in the nineteenth century. 'Paddle currachs' covered with horsehide were the typical fishing vessels used by many poor fishermen off the coast of Mayo in the decades before the Famine. Despite their agility and the undoubted skill of their handlers, fisheries inspectors on the west coast repeatedly stressed the unsuitability of currachs for deep-sea fishing. Irish fishermen, they suggested, 'preferred to wait ashore until fish came to them, instead of going out to sea to catch them'. In arguing thus, these commentators failed to appreciate the fact that the currach, with all its defects, was well adapted to the multiple needs of coastal dwellers on the Atlantic fringe of Ireland. They not only allowed the coastal poor to combine fishing with farming; they were extremely flexible, multi-functional and entirely appropriate to the needs of part-time fishermen and farmers alike. Coastal dwellers used them to fish in inshore waters, put down lobster pots, set long lines, gather kelp and sea wrack, transport people and livestock, and hunt for basking shark off the north and west coasts. In addition to fishing, 'paddle currachs' on the north coast were also used to harvest sea wrack and, here, women and young girls dragged vast quantities of the wet and heavy weed ashore.[36] The most remarkable area for seaweed cultivation was at the mouth of Carlingford Lough, where wrack was harvested as long ago as the sixteenth century. In the second half of the nineteenth century, there were over a thousand seaweed beds in this district alone. Extensive beds of seaweed were also harvested in Clew Bay, Lough Swilly and Achill Sound, while elsewhere in the country wrack and other forms of seaweed were used to raise the fertility of acid soils and to fertilise potato plots. In some parts of the north-west coast, seaweed beds were the necessary adjuncts to arable land, and smallholders sometimes paid more rent for seaweed-covered rocks than they did for the sandy fields where they grew potatoes. In the Mourne district of Co. Down, men 'would walk three miles to be present at the division of the wrack and were content to take back a single creelful on their backs'.[37]

In south Donegal, currachs were also used to gather huge quantities of mussels, and together with seashells and shellfish, these were carried up to

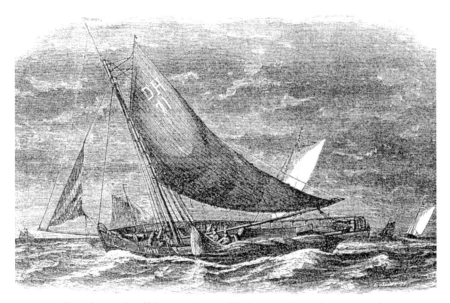

59 Hauling the catch off the east coast of Ireland in the early nineteenth century, when fishermen from the port of Torbay, in south Devon, were regular visitors to Dublin Bay (courtesy of E.P. Symes).

thirty miles inland. All along the north-west coast, currachs were used to catch vast quantities of sprats as they came close to the shore in the late summer. In the pre-Famine period, sprats constituted the chief food of the peasantry for three to four months of the year, while on the Waterford coast, they were trapped in specially designed weirs.

Currach fishermen were skilful interpreters of the signs that heralded the seasonal comings and goings of mid-water species such as herring and mackerel. They were also accustomed to keeping a net or two at hand, in preparation for the arrival of the herring shoals. They had their own look-out points from which they could detect the arrival of herring, mackerel, salmon, basking sharks and pilchards. Here 'huers' would shout out directions to offshore fishermen, guiding them towards their prey. With the arrival of 'harvest herring' in September and October, currachs and fishing yawls that were used to transport seaweed, turf and farm animals would erupt into a frenzy of fishing as the coastal poor took to the sea en masse. Herring and mackerel were caught in trammel nets and seine nets, and preserved as 'winter kitchen' to be consumed locally along the coast throughout the winter months. George Hill described the natives of west Donegal as 'very fearless boatmen, and skilful in their own way'. While commentators in the past, like boating enthusiasts today, have commented on the agility of currachs and the dexterity of their handlers, these light-weight vessels were no match for the foreign vessels that continued to take the bulk of commercial catches of fish in Irish waters. In the Gweedore area, currachs were usually two feet deep and three feet wide, and measured only nine feet from stern to stem. Hill considered these to be 'most handy little things' and described their construction as follows:

> In 'building' currachs, a flat oval frame, or gunwale, with holes at regular distances, from which the ribs are to start, is laid down in the first instance, and secured to the ground. The ribs, which consist of stout sallows, are planted in the gunwale holes; and the sides are basket-work for about six inches wide, above the flooring (as a skirting), all round; the ribs (being intertwined at their junction) are crossed by traverse laths, extending from stern to stern, and which are lashed together where they cross each other, with cords made of horse hair. The frame is, therefore, very strong and elastic; it is then 'skinned' with a hide or tarred canvas. A very good one that would last for four years perfect, may be made at a cost of thirty shillings; seven score of sallows are required, and a man would make one entirely, including 'skinning' and tarring, in four days. There is no beam or seat in a corragh, but the 'crew' sit down on the floor, and must remain there perfectly steady, as a very little lateral motion (there being no keel) would capsize them. Short paddles are used to propel them; and when one person only works a corragh, he kneels at the bow, and with alternate strokes, from side to side, guides the frail barque.[38]

Like other commentators in his day and since then, Hill was in awe of the 'wonderful sight' that currachs presented 'as they darted from island to island' through the surf, landing on rocky beaches 'where no other boat could land in safety'. However, he admitted that they were also 'very "ticklish" things', and 'great skill and caution ... was necessary for their safe management'. Not everyone shared such romantic images of working currachs and their handlers. Unimpressed by the fishing village of Claddagh, one commentator stated that 'the language and manners of this singular colony has undergone no change since the days of St Endius, now 1,400 years ago'. The traditional fishing craft here was 'actually inferior to the currach used 2,000 years ago'. Unlike currachs of old, they were without masts and were generally constructed from 'timber and hides suspended by osiers and canvas'.[39]

Aside from currachs, fishing 'hookers' and 'luggers' were probably the next most common fishing craft off the south and west coasts. The 'lugger', an Irish

60 Cape Clear Harbour, Co. Cork, in the late nineteenth century. The men of
the island were expert and resolute seamen, and were among the best pilots on the
south coast. For much of the nineteenth century, they fished from hookers or
half-decked boats, leaving home on Mondays and returning on Fridays
(courtesy of the Cape Clear Museum).

adaptation of Cornish herring boats, was used extensively in offshore waters
around the country. In the waters around Galway Bay, 'hookers' were used
both in fishing, and in the transportation of turf and other produce. Boats here
were regularly 'out of order' or 'leaky', and 'want of salt' meant that 'huge
quantities' of fish were 'thrown on the seashore and left to rot'. At other times
of the year, entire boatloads of herring were 'sold for eighteen pence'.[40]
Inadequate boats and lack of proper netting were regularly evoked as the main
causes for comparatively poor catches of fish. On the coasts of Cork, Kerry,
Clare, Mayo and Donegal, boats constructed from animal hides and bog oak,
with tillers made from whin-roots, were still being used well into the
nineteenth century.[41] Fishing craft employed in the winter and spring fishery
off the Galway coast were said to be 'so small, that the boatmen were afraid to
venture where they were most likely to catch fish'.[42] In his statistical survey of
Clare, Hely Dutton declared that

> The boats in general use are such as have been used from the remotest
> period of history, wicker-work covered with either horse or cow hides;

they are the only kind that could live a moment in the violent surf that generally beats on this shore; it is astonishing what a sea they will venture to encounter, one where a ship's boat would immediately founder, but these boats mount with every wave. It is nothing uncommon for a man to put his foot through the skin, when much worn; if he has nothing at hand to cram the hole, he must keep his leg there until he reaches the shore, but frequently he takes off his wig, which answers the purpose; these accidents happen so often that he is seldom at a loss and as little concerned. The small boats, generally used on the Shannon, are about three feet broad, flat-bottomed, and cost about 4 guineas; many are much smaller, for attending the weirs and for angling, and some are much larger; it is astonishing to see the number of people that these unsteady boats will carry across the Shannon at Castle-Connel, and other places, even in rapids, where one would think such narrow boats would be overset; yet they are managed so skilfully, that few accidents ever happen.[43]

Writing in the 1880s, Dennis pointed out that Ireland had plenty of suitable craft for 'near-shore' fishing, and added that

each family has at least one boat; some families have three or four. They are called third-class boats; very few of them are decked; and they are quite incapable of facing the tumult of the best fishing waters 30 or 40 miles off the coasts. For deep-sea fishing, 'decked boats of at least 30 tonnage were required. These cost from two hundred to four hundred pounds each, and the lack of them meant that the deep-sea fisheries of the west coast of Ireland have practically to be abandoned to the English, Scotch, Norwegian and Dutch fishermen … who annually flock to the enormous shoals which extend in an almost unbroken line from Bantry Bay to Bloody Foreland'.[44]

This author also insisted that the 'homemade' currachs were excellent fishing vessels.[45] However, such 'ill-equipped' boats could not compete with 'well-appointed' boats from Scotland, Cornwall and the Isle of Man that were able to

Follow the shoals of herring (in company with its many enemies, namely small whales, porpoises, herring hogs, and numberless seabirds who follow) with unerring precision, and fix the course pursued by the herring from the time they leave the icebergs until they take refuge there again. One part of this great shoal (and by far the largest) strikes out into the Atlantic and ... comes down along the west coast, striking in at some point generally in the north of Donegal, coasting down along the shore to Galway, but often not coming in from the deep sea till they get down as low as Galway Bay. This shoal of herrings, travelling through a rougher sea and along a much wilder coast where boats have not the number of small harbours to run into for shelter ... is seldom or never fished for by the coast fishermen until they run into some of the numerous creeks or bays along the coast.[46]

Currachs were by no means the only boats used off the Irish coast in the decades before the Famine. The herring fisheries on the north and west coasts also attracted fishermen from Scotland and England, and sail-driven fishing vessels were drawn to these waters from Dublin, Skerries, Balbriggan and Clogher. These 'interlopers' brought their own cargo of salt for preserving fish, and bought up the surplus catches of local fishermen at rock bottom prices. Their vessels ranged from forty to sixty ton burthen, carried a much larger cargo than flimsy currachs, and transported large quantities of fish to market. However, by the start of the nineteenth century, many of these had ceased fishing due to

the uncertainty as to where they had to go to purchase their cargo, and they had to leave the east coast at the most inclement season of the year, generally the beginning of December, and work round the north of Ireland, keeping at sea the whole of December, January and February, collecting part of their cargo at different points of the coast. The great effort was to get back in time to meet the Easter demand for fish in the towns along the east coast.[47]

Aside from 'ill-equipped' boats, poor netting and lack of salt for preserving their catches were considered by many to be a major problem in many western and northern districts. Irish nets were said to be 'so narrow that the fish can easily pass under them in large shoals, even in a very moderate depth of water, whereas a Scottish net would stop the passage until the quantity of fish meshed would sink to the bottom with the buoys or corks'. These nets trapped fish 'only by chance, even when they are in the middle of a shoal, whereas the St Ives men are certain of a good take as soon as they find where the shoal is, as they can adapt their nets to the depth of water at which fish are swimming'.

61 A two-man rowing currach from Sheepshaven Bay, Co. Donegal, in the 1920s. Although they largely disappeared from the east coast in the aftermath of the Viking raids, boats such as these continued in use along the west and northwest coast until well into the twentieth century (courtesy of the Ulster Folk and Transport Museum).

On many stretches of coast, fishing, although important, was haphazard and under-valued. Maxwell described how crabs and lobsters 'of considerable size' were 'accidentally procured' on the coast of Mayo. He maintained that 'the most prized fish of all the shellfish-tribe' were scallops, which were 'commonly found by the oyster-dredgers in deep water'. These, he added, were 'esteemed so highly as a luxury as to cause their being transferred to the next gentleman who may have been serviceable to the peasant who finds them, or whose favour it may be advisable to propitiate'.[48] Evans has shown that in nineteenth-century Ireland, crabs and lobsters were regularly taken, either by hand or with an iron hook or wooden rod, from the rock holes where they sheltered. He described how in parts of Kerry, 'one man would hold another under the water while he searched the holes' for crabs and lobster. Lobstermen, he added, were 'a hardy breed', many of whom readily switched from long-line to lobster fishing, but continued to keep up 'the feuds and rivalries to which long-liners were addicted' throughout the latter half of the nineteenth century.[49] The intensification of lobster fishing was also accompanied by an expansion in the manufacture of pots and creels that showed marked regional variations. As more and more coastal districts were drawn into the orbit of expanding urban

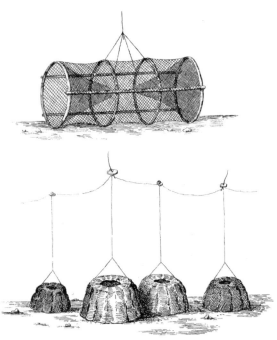

62 Standardised lobster traps and pots that were recommended for the development of lobster fishing at the start of the nineteenth century. Above: 'English lobster trap'; below: 'Irish lobster pots' (from Brabazon, *The deep-sea and coast fisheries of Ireland* (1848)).

markets, it became common practice for individual lobstermen to deploy dozens of pots at the one time. In the 1840s, Brabazon described how herring shoals in the west coast of Ireland were 'followed by boats very imperfectly found in every respect, especially in the small size of their train of nets'.[50] In the 1880s, 'the coast and creeks of Connemara swarmed with herring for three months', but despite the fact that shoals came 'up quite close to the land where they had never been seen before', the lack of nets meant that the fishermen 'could not catch them'.[51] Yet, even then, many fishermen along the west and north-west coast were able to land large quantities of fish by using a combination of long lines, seine nets and rudimentary drift nets. Fishing nets were considered to be a particularly serious problem for many of the country's poor inshore fishermen. In order to 'fish with the full effect for herrings', some suggested that those on the west coast needed 'to have two sets of nets, as the meshes of those used for the spring fishery would be too large for those used in summer, and the fish would almost all go through, whilst those not using the summer fishery would be too small to mesh them in spring'. It was claimed that fishermen on entire stretches of coast simply 'let down the nets', and hoped that the fish would 'mesh themselves'. On the west coast of Scotland, on the other hand, nets were 'drawn against the shoals of herrings, by which means a boat was immediately loaded'. On enquiring why this 'beneficial practice' was not adopted in Irish waters, one commentator was told that 'it would disturb the fish, and they would leave the bay'. On the Shannon Estuary, it was thought that this would 'disturb' the herring, thereby causing them to 'retire' entirely'.[52]

The herring season around Gweedore usually commenced around the beginning of January. When the herring arrived off the coast of west Donegal, local fishermen and small-holders, 'clubbing their means to purchase boats and nets, made great exertions to avail themselves of this supposed source of profit'. However, as no salt was to be had in the immediate vicinity, fishermen here often had to pay 'an immense price' for salt brought in from towns in the interior of the county. Fishermen here faced another problem, namely 'want of protection', which meant that the herring fishery, 'instead of proving a blessing and a source of profit, often turned out the reverse, especially as it occasioned a fearful loss of life, for which there could be no compensation'. Moreover, wherries from Rush, Balbriggan and Skerries, and other 'strange boats' regularly 'molested the poor natives of this coast, cutting their nets and otherwise annoying them'.[53] In the 1840s, distress among the fishermen on the east coast was 'caused by the spawn on the fishing banks being destroyed, along with the small fish, by the trawlers, which has made a great scarcity of fish, and its effects have been severely felt by the poor fishermen who supported themselves by line-fishing out of the small shore boats'. The trawlers in question were mostly from Scotland, Cornwall and the Isle of Man. Similarly, rough seas, poor weather and the rugged character of the coastline, meant that many small fishermen were forced to 'cast their nets by daylight and leave them there all night, and then return in the morning to look for them'. If a storm happened to arise, the nets drifted from their original markings or became 'mixed together' with other nets and 'floated about full of dead fish'. Not surprisingly, 'many hundreds of pounds' worth of nets were lost in this manner. In the 1850s, Hill called on the government to have 'cutters' stationed in the more remote stretches of the Irish coast to 'preserve order' and prevent 'much mischief' between 'interlopers' and local fishermen. This, he suggested, would 'give confidence to the fishermen, who would, under such circumstances, remain out with their nets, knowing that should it come on to blow, there would be assistance and a refuge at hand'.[54] Even in the 1880s, it was argued that net-making was 'but little understood or practised among the fishing population of Ireland'. In Scottish fishing communities, on the other hand, it was widely known that the womenfolk of coastal communities made 'nearly all

63 Sketch of the Greencastle yawl from Holdsworth's *Deep-sea fishing and fishing boats*. This was a hybrid fishing craft from the north coast of Ireland that had its origins in the Trondheim district in the southwest coast of Norway.

the nets', with the result that their fishermen were far better equipped than many of their Irish counterparts. In Ireland, however, the men had 'to buy all their gear', and could 'only afford a very inferior quality, or gear which was quite inadequate to the needs of the Irish fisheries'. Fishing also had to compete with kelp-gathering in many coastal districts. When the price of kelp 'happened to rise from £5 to £7 a ton, then they stopped fishing, neglected their boats and their gear, and fell out of the habit of fishing'. However, when the price dropped to around £3 per ton, the fishermen 'were without the means of recovering the ground they had lost' by abandoning fishing for the less lucrative kelp harvest.

With so much emphasis placed on the poor quality of boats and netting as factors in the under-development of sea fishing in Ireland, it is important to stress that fishermen were by no means completely dependent upon well-equipped boats and high-quality netting in order to land large quantities of fish. Long-line fishing for cod, hake, skate, ling, turbot, dogfish and other large fish was commonly practiced all around the coast of Ireland. This highly effective method of fishing satisfied the needs of local markets prior to the large-scale exploitation of herring and mackerel fisheries of the late nineteenth century. On the north coast, long-line fishing from 'drontheims' or clinker-built fishing yawls dated back at least to the closing years of eighteenth century.[55] Elsewhere on the Irish coast, currachs, hookers, skiffs and other small craft were used to transport long-line fishermen to deep-sea fishing banks. In many parts of the coast, these long-linemen had to row up to thirty miles to reach the best fishing banks, and then row back with their cargo of fish. In coastal districts in Galway, Antrim and Down, specially woven and highly ornate baskets made from unpeeled willow rods were used for holding hooks and long lines. Floats for long lines were made from sealskins, and not infrequently from dog skins, while 'sinkers', or fishing weights, were little more than grooved stones gathered from the beach. The long-line season on Cape Clear lasted from four to six weeks during the months of July and August, while around Malin Head it could extend right through the winter and on into May and the start of the salmon season. Before the arrival of large trawlers in the late nineteenth century, long-line fishermen were often considered the aristocrats of sea fishing on these stretches of coast. Reputed to be exceptionally hardy, they 'were regarded with awe and respect among the inshore fishermen-farmers'. Even in close-knit fishing communities, their intimate knowledge of deep-sea fishing banks was shrouded in secrecy, and was passed down from father to son. So also was their knowledge of the onshore 'markings' that allowed them to locate their position while fishing offshore. In a number of the larger Scottish islands, long-line fishermen cast lots for the best fishing banks, a practice that helped reduce tensions and prevented the outbreak of fighting among the fishermen. In the Hebrides, the casting of lots took place on Bride's Day. There, and possibly also on the coast of Ireland, fishing banks were actually rotated 'in a kind of marine rundale' to prevent the monopolisation of prime fishing grounds by a few fishermen.[56] Brabazon noted that 'spillards' or long lines were commonly used along the west coast in the pre-Famine period. Long lines were primarily used to catch, ling, hake, dogfish, haddock and conger eels over stony fishing grounds, and in waters too deep for trawling. Great numbers of cod were also caught with long lines off Clogher Head, Skerries, Balbriggan and Howth. The 'spillard line' measured around '210–220 fathoms long, with a hook fastened to it by a snouding line 2 fathoms or a fathom and a half long at a distance of a fathom between each snouding'. This meant that there were approximately 200 baited hooks to each spillard, with each rowing boat having up to five lines, thus making for a total of approximately one thousand hooks per boat. The line was set by manoeuvring the boat along the fishing ground, allowing the baited hooks to drop over the side of the boat as the lines were fed out. Baited hooks were laid in specially designed baskets 'so that they fall into the sea without entangling as the line veers out'. The 'spillards' were kept floating in the water by crude buoys made from dog-skins filled with air, which the fishermen called 'watchmen'. Rush fishermen were reported to have had eighteen score of hooks to each man's share of lines, with two a length of fathoms separating the hook from the main long line.[57]

Visitors to coastal Ireland in the opening decades of the nineteenth century were regularly impressed by the frenzy of activity that accompanied each

64 Baiting lines for night fishing on Rathlin Island, Co. Antrim, in the late nineteenth or early twentieth century. Long-line fishermen such as these were the aristocrats of the sea, who passed their sea-lore from father to son (courtesy of the de Courcy Ireland collection).

fishing season. When the herring season commenced around Galway Bay, almost the entire male population of the neighbouring villages would run to the shore to assist in the fishing. Each man had a certain share, amounting to a guinea or more, for a night's work. The small rowboats used in inshore waters could now take 'upwards of 20,000 herrings in a night, which sometimes sell for £1 7s. per thousand, and they often make two trips if the fish are in abundance, and near the shore'. At the height of the season, 5,000 herring were reckoned as 'a middling night's take of herring for one boat'. Herring fetched between 16d. and 2s. per hundred, although prices were 'sometimes much higher, though often less'.[58] The great years of the herring fishery were undoubtedly the final decades of the nineteenth century. In Ireland as elsewhere in Europe, the herring fishery was hugely volatile. Baltic herring, which were smaller and matured earlier than Atlantic herring, had formed the original basis and strength of the Hanseatic League. These Baltic stocks mysteriously declined around 1420 and the supremacy of the Hanseatic League declined with them. Tradition has it that the herring migrated to the North Sea, and Dutch fishermen dominated the herring fishery in the seventeenth and eighteenth centuries. Herring were considered to be so plentiful in these waters that it was widely believed that it would be impossible to fish out the North Sea. Yet, the North Sea herring fishery became a classic example of man failing to realise that a natural resource could be exhaustible until the damage was practically irreparable.[59] Similarly in Ireland, W.B. Yeats' poem 'The Meditation of the Old Fisherman' captured the dramatic decline of herring off the west of the west coast of Ireland since he was a boy:

> The herring are not in the tides as they were of old;
> My sorrow! For many a creak gave the creel in the cart
> That carried the take to Sligo town to be sold,
> When I was a boy with never a crack in my heart.[60]

One of the most productive Irish fisheries lay off the coast of Co. Down. This was fished both by local boats and larger trawlers drawn from elsewhere in Ireland, and from Scotland and the west coast of England. In 1802, Dubourdieu described how 'boats from Rush, and formerly from Liverpool, come to trawl in Dundrum Bay, and carry off great quantities of turbot, sole, plaice, cod and haddock, whilst the inhabitants of the shore, from want of apparatus, get comparatively few'. At Bangor, he reported, there was 'a considerable fishery of sole, plaice, a few turbot and in winter of cod and excellent oysters'.[61] Describing the state of the herring fishery in this section of the Irish coast in the last quarter of the nineteenth century, Pollock stated that

> These fisheries were of enormous productivity and value for a concern that was pursued at most for only five or six months of the year. According to official figures, between 1864 and 1919 over 225,000 tons of herring, worth more than 1,500,000 pounds in quayside sales alone, were landed at Co. Down ports, giving an average annual return for the fishery of over 4,000 tons of fish worth over 30,000 pounds in quayside value. The prominence of the Down herring fisheries in national terms is also indicated in the official records, which reveal that during these years one-quarter of all the herring landed in Ireland and almost one-third of the total Irish revenue from herring sales was won from the county's ports.[62]

Viewed thus, Ireland's sea fisheries in the nineteenth century were highly developed, but development was spatially uneven and largely confined to a handful of coastal regions. It may have appeared that the country had a dual fisheries economy, characterised by subsistence fishing in many western and

65 Herring boats from Scotland ranged around the north-east coast of Ireland at
the height of the herring boom in the late nineteenth century
(courtesy of Aberdeen University Library).

northern districts, with far more commercialised fishing taking place along the
south and east coasts. However, closer examination reveals that these geographical
dichotomies were far too simplistic to account for the complex interconnections
between so-called 'subsistence' fishing on the one hand, and 'commercial
fishing' on the other. They particularly fail to account for the high levels of
interdependence between subsistence fishermen and their commercial counterparts throughout the nineteenth century. Commercial fishermen were highly
dependent upon the subsistence sector for the use of ports all around the Irish
coast. They also relied on cheap and abundant supplies of labour from poor
fishing communities to fill the crews of trawlers and to process huge quantities
of fish at local ports at the height of the fishing season. Subsistence fishermen,
for their part, disposed of surpluses that could not be sold or preserved locally.
However, they regularly complained when the uncontrolled competition of
commercial fishermen threatened to destroy local fish stocks and undermine
the moral economy of indigenous fishing communities. Thus, far from
representing different phases or separate stages in the evolution of the country's
sea fisheries, commercial and subsistence fishing co-existed side-by-side in what
was sometimes an acrimonious relationship, and at other times a relatively
harmonious one that profited both sectors, albeit in a highly uneven manner.

FISHING IN THE FAMINE YEARS

While much more research is required to establish the precise impact of the potato famine on Irish fishing communities, it would appear that the fishermen who were arguably worst off during the Great Famine were, paradoxically, those who were most dependent upon fishing. This was especially true of those living along the Atlantic coast, who were forced to trade boats and fishing gear for meal and other food when famine struck in the 1840s. Writing a few years before the Famine, the Halls complained of the over-dependence of the rural poor on potatoes and their neglect of sea fisheries in the following terms:

It is notorious that the teeming wealth conveyed by the ocean around their shores – easily rendered as productive as their soil – is neglected by the people, who cleave to old prejudices and customs with unaccountable bigotry; the consequence is that the Irish are the worst fishermen to be found anywhere; and that, not infrequently, even the markets of large towns are supplied by the activity and industry of their Scottish neighbours – the fish being caught a stone's throw away of the Irish strands.[63]

Finding it difficult to understand why the Irish, 'thousands of whom lived near the coast', did not eat fish during the 'Hungry Forties', Cecil Woodham Smith pointed out that the starving poor in coastal Kerry and Mayo ate 'old cabbage leaves, roadside weeds, rotten turnips, while on the coast itself the population lived on dilisk (edible seaweed) and raw limpets'. Yet, she added, 'fine fish abounded, especially along the west coast, where distress was most severe'.[64] However, Tim Robinson has shown that 'shore-food such as limpets and seaweed called *sleabhcan* made the difference between death and survival for the Aran folk and the Connemara refugees … During the Famine, and even in the earlier decades of the twentieth century, some poor families depended on it'. A survey of the state of sea fishing along the western seaboard in the 1830s found that localised famines were a 'regular occurrence', and that

the means of the fisherman are most completely inadequate to the profitable pursuit of his avocation. Here it is that the country offers the fewest auxiliaries to the philanthropist in his plans of improvement; and that the Commissioners have found the greatest difficulty in discovering any satisfactory or applicable measure of relief. Along the greater line of the coast, the boats, both in size in and construction, are unfitted for encountering the uncertain and turbulent ocean; while the remoteness of

66 Fishing boat from the Scottish coast in the late nineteenth century. Open boats such as these operated in the Irish Sea, particularly during the rich herring season, when they often topped up their catches by buying fish from local fishermen (courtesy of the Wick Society, Scotland).

the great towns leaves the fisherman (excepting those near Galway and Sligo) without a sufficient accessible supply of salt and of the means of curing the fish, should they arrive in great abundance on the shore.[65]

When Henry Inglis travelled around coastal Galway and Connemara in the early 1830s, he found the cabins of fishermen to be 'very far superior to those of any country labourers … an air of decency was visible about them … none were without chairs and bedsteads, and [many had] a respectable display of crockery'.[66] However, the sight of coastal poverty shocked Reynolds Hole, another visitor to this area in the decade after the Great Famine. He observed that fishermen in the Claddagh lived in 'miserable cabins, the walls made of mud and stone, and for the most part windowless, the floors damp and dirty and the roofs a mass of rotten straw and weeds'.[67] Other visitors found the outward manifestations of poverty in more remote coastal stretches of Connaught to be quite deceptive. Richard Lovett, who visited the coast around Galway some four decades after the Great Famine, wrote:

The appearance of the village of Claddagh is dirty, but the houses are clean enough inside; and be it known that before the Famine their houses were models of cleanliness; and we must recollect that those manure heaps which frequently offend the eye in Irish villages have no offensive odour, on account of the deodorising power of the peat which forms a large part of the compost. The men and women have generally clean linen, although often covered with rags. It is a general fact worthy of note that in Ireland a dirty outside generally covers a clean heart.[68]

Not everyone was uncritical of the state of the country's poor fishing communities in the mid-nineteenth century. O'Dowd has shown that the number of occupied houses in Claddagh slumped from the 500 recorded in 1812, and by the time of Griffith's Valuation in the mid-1850s, 'Fairhill Road had 133 houses and ten ruins, while the rest of the Claddagh contained 329 thatched homes, of which forty-five were already derelict'.[69] Standing on the cliffs at Achill in the winter of 1846, the Quaker philanthropist James Hack Tuke reported on scenes of great coastal poverty, with 'poor starving creatures' everywhere to be seen, and entire coastal communities that 'made no use of the inexhaustible supply of food from the sea'. Here also, he gazed down at 'the clear Atlantic' and observed 'shoals of herring and mackerel in immense quantities, while further out, in the deeper waters, were cod, ling, sole, turbot and haddock'.[70] Commenting on the general effects of famine on the country's sea fisheries, the author of a report of the Commissioners of Public Works stated that

No branch of the industrial resources of Ireland suffered more severely, in the first instances, from the famine and distress of 1846–7 than the fisheries, both deep-sea and inland … This extraordinary state of things resulted partly from a prejudice against the use of fish as a dietary, but mainly from the fact that the fisheries of this country, however valuable or important, were not fixed on the solid basis of an established trade, nor were they followed or maintained as a real commercial undertaking for the profit which the would directly yield.[71]

Notwithstanding the numbers engaged in part-time fishing on the Atlantic fringes of Cork, Galway, Mayo, Clare and Donegal, fishing and the harvest of the shoreline provided coastal communities with the means of subsistence, if not a major source of income, in the decades prior to the Great Famine.

Despite the length of this coastline, whole stretches were entirely devoid of landing facilities and fish-curing stations. Unsafe piers, a general lack of slipways and a series of poor fishing seasons added to the problems of these coastal dwellers. In Galway, piers were constructed at Cleggan, Ballynakill and Derryinver to provide employment in times of distress in the first half of the century.[72] After 1832, the Board of Works supervised the construction of piers in a number of districts along the west and south-west coasts, but in many cases they took so long to complete that they were still unfinished at the start of the Famine. Indeed, the slow pace of pier construction and harbour development was in marked contrast to the speed with which work-houses for the poor were built in the 1830s and 1840s.[73] In many parts of the west and north-west coasts, the construction of piers did not get under way until the interventions of the Congested Districts Board in the 1890s. Lack of storage facilities and the absence of readily accessible markets meant that in the mid-1840s, 'quantities of fish were allowed to rot on the shore, or were spread on the adjacent fields for manure'.[74] Commenting on the state of fishing around Skibbereen in the run up to the Famine, one government official reported that 'this coast abounded with the finest fish in the world', but the 'want of suitable boats' meant that local fishermen were unable to catch them. Another visitor to the west of Ireland stated that 'the poor cottier had a simple currach, fished for his family or neighbours and got paid in potatoes'.[75] At the height of the famine on Achill Island, the local fishing fleet consisted of four currachs and one fishing-boat. The finest fishing grounds around Mayo at this time were off Erris Head. Cod and ling were particularly plentiful here in the winter season, but weather conditions made it impossible or perilous to fish them. The only land-link between this area and the outside world was 'over a high and boggy mountain, so wet and swampy that it [was] difficult to reach even in summer'.[76] Needless to add, this rendered it extremely difficult for local fishermen to transport fish inland, or to obtain salt to preserve them, in towns in the interior of the country.

In some parts of the west coast, fishermen operated their own version of *mare clausum* (that is to say, 'closed sea'), which effectively prevented 'transplanters' or outsiders from fishing in 'their waters'. Thus, despite the huge supplies of fish off the coast of Galway, it was reported that the 'incorrigible' Claddagh men would not allow the waters around the bay to be fished by anyone other than themselves. When a representative from the Society of Friends visited the area in the mid-1840s, he found that the fishermen would only go to sea at specified times, and then only on certain days of the week. If other boats 'dared' to fish outside these restricted times, 'their crews would be beaten and their nets destroyed'. Referring to the state of boats and fishing tackle in the Claddagh, he stated that it was 'really awful to observe the waste of their property from want of attention and care'. He estimated that, if properly equipped and manned, 'one sixth the number of boats ... would take a much greater amount of fish'. He went on to state that 'nothing could be more vexatious than to see many boats ruined from the circumstances of allowing large stones to drop from the quays and boats to rest on them as the tide ebbed'.[77] The onset of famine, here as elsewhere in many impoverished coastal districts, caused small fishermen to sell or pawn their boats and fishing gear in order to buy food. At the Claddagh on 9 January 1847, 'all the boats were drawn up to the quay wall, stripped to the bare poles, not a sign of tackle or sail remaining ... not a fish to be had in the town, not a boat was at sea'. Similarly, on Achill Island, the offshore waters went unfished because nets and tackle were sold to 'buy a little meal'. Similar reports from Belmullet, Killybegs and the fishing ports of Cos Clare and Kerry suggest that this was common practice at the height of the Famine. A fishery inspector who visited Killybegs in the exceptionally severe winter of 1846–7 reported that weather conditions rendered it impossible for men to fish. Fishermen here were on public works, and were afraid to leave them until they could 'be sure that the weather will allow them to fish continuously'.[78] The failure of the potato crop could also cause a chain reaction in some coastal communities. This was because those affected by famine were not simply those whose potatoes were destroyed. In some of the worst affected areas, the 'entire fabric of society was dissolved', as fishermen pawned their boats and gear, and large numbers of people were thrown out of work and farmers and other employers discharged their servants and labourers. With 'sea manure' (kelp) no longer in demand, those engaged in gathering it were also forced to seek relief from local agencies.[79] The Society of Friends set up fishing stations near Clifden in Galway, at Achill Sound in Mayo, and at Belmullet in Erris to help to encourage fishing off the Mayo coast. In west Cork, a fish-curing plant was established at Castletownbere, and a trawler was hired to accompany rowing boats and currachs to their fishing grounds. In an effort to support fishermen in their time of need, the government appointed a member of the Board of Works to the position of commissioner for the fishery department. The new commissioner called for £100,000 to be spent immediately on the improvement of piers, harbours and boat slips, with an additional £10,000 per year to be spent on upgrading boats 'to make up for past neglect'. In the event, commissioner Mulvany's proposals were largely ignored. With the introduction of a limited relief scheme January 1847, a mere £5,000 per year was to be spent on fishing. Mulvany's call for small loans to be paid to poor fishermen to enable them to improve tackle and carry out repairs to boats was similarly ignored.[80] Charles Trevelyan, the assistant secretary to the treasury, with responsibility for famine relief, cautioned against offering assistance to fishermen on the grounds that it would damage the men's morale. Motivated by an evangelical dogmatism that sought to minimise state intervention and compel greater independence among the coastal poor, Trevelyan believed that experience had shown that any reliance of fishermen on state aid or charity would cause them to acquire 'habits of chicanery and bad faith in their struggle to avoid payment of loans'.[81] In the event, the Society of Friends, operating through local agencies on the ground, arguably did more than most government agencies to alleviate distress among impoverished fishermen. The local vicar in Arklow 'estimated that 161 families were kept alive through the winter of 1847 because the Friends lent them money to redeem their boats and nets'. Similarly, in the vicinity of the Ring Peninsula in Co. Waterford, aid from the Society of Friends enabled local fishermen to support themselves without Poor Law relief, while in Galway the clothing provisions granted to the Claddagh men meant that they were able to stay at sea in cold weather conditions.[82]

In his regional study of the effects of famine on fishing communities in west Cork, Hickey has pointed out that 'the fishermen and labourers of Crookhaven petitioned the lord lieutenant on 4 September 1846, stating that over 500 of the town's 600 people were in 'actual distress and want' as a result of the failure of the potato crop. Almost all of these were dependent on fishing and on their potato plots, with a number also engaged as pilots by local trading vessels. It was, they pointed out, only as a result of 'great struggle' that they endeavoured 'to scrape a poor subsistence, not having cattle or any other subsistence except a few fishing boats which they could not dispose of to meet their present wants'.[83] The potato blight struck the livelihoods of these petitioners as heavily as that of poor tenant farmers further inland. This was because the vast majority were not full-time fishermen equipped with good boats and fishing gear who had ready access to curing facilities. They were, instead, part-time fishermen, labourers and tenant farmers who were as dependent upon the sea and the shoreline as they were on their own potato plots. The plight of these fishermen deteriorated significantly when they were forced to sell their boats and fishing gear in order to buy food and other necessities. In his report to the Commissioners of Public Works in 1850, Francis Herbert Hore demanded that

67 Scottish and English boats at Killybegs, Co. Donegal, during a busy herring season in the 1920s. A thriving fishing town from 1970 to the early 1990s, Killybegs in the nineteenth century was notoriously underdeveloped, with the result that local fishermen found it difficult to preserve fish, or to transport them to market (courtesy of Donald Martin).

lessons should be learned from the anomalous experience of famine in a maritime nation whose sea fisheries were largely untapped by the country's coastal dwellers. He concluded that

> The fact of great numbers of persons dying from want of food (or such profitable employment as would enable them to buy it), along the shores of a sea abounding in fish and which was calculated to afford remunerative employment in its production, has established beyond all controversy the necessity for permanently developing and relying upon its fisheries in this country as a source of industry and trade, and consequently of food.[84]

After the Famine, it was widely agreed in some maritime districts in the west and south of the country that the resources of the sea should be more thoroughly exploited in order to alleviate poverty in the future. Even at the height of the Famine, resolutions were passed which stressed the impossibility of supporting the coastal destitute on public relief schemes that were financed by subscriptions from the relatively small number of rate-payers living in such impoverished coastal districts. In response to one such resolution, passed at a meeting held in Ballydehob, William Fagan, the Member of Parliament for Cork, urged the government to develop the sea fisheries in the west of the county, pointing out that 'the country imported 200,000 pounds worth of fish each year'. A medical doctor who visited some of the worst affected areas of coastal Ireland during the Famine maintained that 'cultivating the waste-lands of the country, and exploring the circling wastes of the seas, would be found to be more efficient sanitary measures than placing hospitals in every townland and doctors in every hamlet'.[85]

POST-FAMINE ADJUSTMENTS

Despite the effects of famine distress, the last quarter of the nineteenth century did see a substantial re-organisation of Ireland's sea fisheries. Developments in road and rail transport, and the introduction of steam trawlers, contributed to an expansion of the market for fresh fish such as mackerel, herring and salmon. Improvements in transport also helped lobster fishermen, and brought many isolated coastal communities in the west and north-west into greater contact with expanding urban markets. Crabs, lobsters and scallops, which were widely consumed in pre-Famine rural Ireland, were now caught on a commercial basis and dispatched to urban centres around the country. By the final decade of the nineteenth century, lobster fishing was of considerable importance to many small farmers and poor fishermen all along the south and west coasts. Capital requirements for this type of fishing were small to negligible. Because lobster fishing was confined to inshore waters, it was easy for part-time fishermen to spend part of the day fishing in small four-oared boats measuring twenty-four feet, while spending the remainder of the day attending to work on the land. Levis has shown that in the early 1890s, the waters off west Cork were fished by 'a well-established fleet of lobster boats concentrated in the corner of Roaring Water Bay'.[86] However, the existence of highly localised fleets specialising in lobster fishing was quite unusual on the south coast, where mackerel was by far the dominant fishery, and where 'lobstering was not pursued with the same long-term commitment and single-mindedness'. When a Congested Districts Board inspector visited the thriving port of Castletownbere in the 1890s, only twenty boats were 'occasionally employed' in lobster fishing, which 'did not seem to be pursued in a regular manner'. It has also been shown that a mere thirteen of the 113 registered boats in the extensive Congested District of Schull (an area that encompassed the entire Mizen Peninsula) were engaged in commercial fishing for lobsters at the end of the nineteenth century. In isolated coastal districts such as this, fishermen faced the added difficulty of marketing the lobsters that they caught. Like other shellfish, they deteriorated rapidly if they could not be delivered alive, which meant that fishermen were dependent on fast and efficient sailing smacks, and other means of transportation, to carry their catches to the market. Poor rail facilities were still a problem for fishermen in the country's more isolated fishing communities in the 1880s. Towards the end of the decade, it was reported that the Irish railway companies had generally not catered to the needs of the fish-trade. According to one commentator, the railway companies

> provided no facilities beyond running a few fish-vans with their ordinary goods trains. This is no encouragement whatever. Fish-vans ought to be run with passenger trains, and branch lines, or tramways at least, should be run to a number of points along the coast. A railway from Clifden in Connemara to Galway would drain all the fisheries of the Connemara coast. Its length would be about 49 English miles, and it could be constructed for less than £180,000. The necessity for better means of transport is proved by the fact that, with the exception of oysters (which can be sent alive), no fish from Connemara is sent even to Galway![87]

Lack of proper sea-charts was considered another major problem in the last quarter of the nineteenth century. Dennis argued that

> There did not exist a single chart on which either the inshore fishery banks, to say nothing of the deep-sea banks, are laid down. The consequence is that the men do not know where to go for fish. The Irish fisheries, in every branch of them, from oysters to periwinkles, and from salmon to pilchards, need reforming from the beginning to the end. The natural resources are there; but everything else is lacking. One might say as much in this respect of New Guinea as of Ireland. Indeed, the only difference is that New Guinea is farther from us and is inhabited by savages.[88]

As the nineteenth century drew to a close, many inshore fishermen, part-time fishermen and islanders gradually abandoned traditional sailing smacks operated with crews of six to eight men, in favour of fishing yawls and canvas-covered currachs manned by two to four men. Despite the fact that currachs

68 Multi-tasking fishermen in south Donegal transporting turf across Loughross Bay around 1910. Visitors to the west coast of Ireland regularly commented on the dexterity of currach men and the multiple uses to which they put their craft (courtesy of the de Courcy Ireland collection).

were no match for the larger trawlers now competing fiercely among themselves in an uncontrolled expansion of deep-sea fishing, they were the often considered the ideal craft for these poorer fishermen who were engaged in herring and mackerel fishing. This was due to the fact that, being light and easy to handle and repair, currachs were particularly well suited to the needs of lobster fishermen. However, the relative prosperity of the currach fishermen was short-lived, and it was not long before larger boats and fleets of trawlers appeared in the inshore waters, scouring the shallow waters of coastal bays and ranging progressively further out to sea as inshore stocks of fish were depleted. This growing commercialisation of sea fishing in the early decades of the twentieth century inevitably affected large numbers of inshore fishermen. In one district to the west of Dingle, the number of *naomhogs*, or currachs, declined from an estimated 400 in 1921, to a mere eighty in the mid-1930s.[89] The hazards confronting poor fishermen who put to sea in yawls and currachs were captured well by the Blasket islander, Tomás Ó Criomhthain, when he recalled that

Often we put out to sea in fair weather at dawn, and when we returned the people were keening for us, the day had turned so foul. Often we had to be out at night, and the misery of that kind of fishing cannot be described. I count it the worst of all trades that ever I set hand or foot to: the rollers towering overhead and shutting out the sight of land; a long, cold night battling against heavy seas, and often with little profit, just praying from one moment to the next for the help of God. It is seldom we got a haul sufficient for our needs, and even then we might have to cut the nets, which we had bought so dear, and leave them, fish and all, to drift away with the tide. On other nights, the boats would be nicely full after all our toil, but then we could not make harbour or land with the swell rising up over the green grass in a north-westerly gale and the surf sweeping over the rocks in every stretch of the sea. We would then have to run under sail before the wind, some of us to Crooked Creek, others to Ventry Harbour or Dingle; then home in the teeth of the storm, then out again the next night on the bank where our livelihood was.[90]

Elsewhere on the south coast, the commercialisation of deep-sea fishing continued to draw in fleets form Scotland, England and France. Manx fishermen took such huge catches of herring off Kinsale that the boat-building industry in the Isle of Man experienced boom conditions in the last quarter of the nineteenth century. It would appear that the Manx boats first visited Irish waters in search of mackerel in the early 1860s. The Reverend Green described how their thirty-ton yawls subsequently became the model for most first-class Irish fishing vessels on the south and south-west coasts. By the late 1880s, most of these had been fitted with the fore-and-aft rigging that was considered more efficient in Irish waters. When E.W.H. Holdsworth, Secretary to the Royal Sea Fisheries Commission, visited Kinsale in the 1870s, he was far from impressed with the local fishermen. He noted that Manx fishermen accounted for the bulk of the mackerel caught off this coast. Stating that he 'would be glad if he could commend the Kinsale fishermen for their industry', he went on to report that it was

difficult to do so when we have ourselves seen almost all their boats lying idle in the harbour in the middle of the mackerel season, whilst Manx boats were bringing in their cargoes of fish. On inquiring the reason for this, we heard that the Kinsale boats had had three large takes of mackerel two days before and the men had been occupied in drinking their money. We then went among the fishermen, and after a little conversation here and there about what sort fishing they were making, ascertained that a good many mackerel had been lately caught, and the boats were going out again. A little tobacco is generally very effective in opening a fisherman's heart, but in more than one instance in Kinsale our inquiries were interrupted by the request for 'the price of a glass of whiskey'. The almost irresistible attraction to whiskey of these men when they have money to spend is unfortunately not a matter for question; but better reports of them have been given recently, and it is to be hoped that examples of temperance and industry among themselves will not be without effect on the rest of the fishermen.[91]

When he travelled on to Bantry Bay, Holdsworth found that the local sea fisheries there had been in decline for many years. Large numbers of boats lay abandoned after fishermen and small farmers emigrated in large numbers to the United States and Britain. Moving onwards to Galway, he attributed the slow progress of fishing off the coast of Connaught to 'the lawless activity of the Claddagh fishermen, who for many years had virtually decided when and how the fisheries should be carried out'. Only when he arrived off the Donegal coast did Holdsworth notice any improvement in the condition of Ireland's sea fisheries. This he attributed to the reappearance of the herring shoals after several years' absence, rather than to the industry of local fishermen. The fishermen around Inverbay caught considerable quantities of mackerel on long lines, while seine nets were only used when the shoals came close inshore. At the end of his visit to Donegal, Holdsworth concluded that

> It was very difficult to speak with any degree of certainty of the capabilities of Donegal Bay as a fishing ground; the poverty and doubtless to some extent the ignorance of the fishermen have interfered with justice being done to its fisheries; but there is abundant evidence that even under the present adverse circumstances, a great quantity of fish of various kinds is taken. Yet the fishermen continue to live merely from hand to mouth, and subscriptions to provide them with what is requisite for their fishing seem to have done them little permanent good.[92]

A report on the state of mackerel fishing in Ireland in the spring of 1890 found that this fishery relied heavily on the English market, as distinct from the autumn fishery, which was almost totally dependent upon the export of cured fish for the United States.[93] Boats engaged in the mackerel fishery in that year were classified as follows:

English and Isle of Man: 322 All first-class (40–50ft)
Scottish: 23 All first-class
French: 58 All first-class
Irish: 385 First-class (with 2,695 men and boys)
Irish: 224 Second-class (18–40ft) with 1,103 men and boys
Irish: 246 Currachs with 748 men

At the end of the nineteenth century, Green put the size of the fleet off the south-west coast at 350 Irish, 160 Manx, fifty English and Scottish, and seventy French. Large numbers of smaller fishing craft fished alongside well-equipped boats drawn from the east-coast ports of Arklow and Ardglass, and from England, Scotland, France and the Isle of Man. In the 1870s, there were 'as many as 700 boats with nets worth £600 each' in Kinsale Harbour at the height of the herring season. Around this time also, the small fishing ports of Bearhaven, Bantry, Baltimore and Valentia acquired national prominence, as the presence of a large numbers of English, French and Irish fishing vessels made these the principal centres for mackerel fishing off the south-west coast. Still, it was reported, the 'great swarms of herring' off the coast from Bearhaven to Bantry often went 'unfished because of the unorganised nature or the fisheries there'.[94] Hookers from Kinsale and other Cork ports travelled round the south-west coast to fish off Achill Island. In the final decades of the nineteenth century, fishing off the coast of Cork was in a 'vibrant' condition. Levis has argued that

> By 1890, Baltimore had become one of the most important fishing ports in Ireland for the mackerel fishery, and large volumes of mackerel were being landed by a huge fleet of mackerel 'drifters' from the Isle of Man, England, Scotland, France and the east coast of Ireland. Smaller but very significant amounts of mackerel were also landed at Castletownbere, Crookhaven and Schull. The total number of mackerel boats fishing off the south coast in the spring of 1880 was estimated at around 740.[95]

In 1891, the forty-five boats that fished out of Valentia Island and the adjoining mainland, landed an estimated 375,000 mackerel and 190,000 herring in a twelve-month period. Small fishing communities like Beginish Island and

69 A rare portrait of a group of seine fishermen from Dursey Island on the Beara Peninsula, Co. Cork, in 1905 (courtesy of Críostóir Mac Cárthaigh).

Coonana, near Cahirciveen in south Kerry, had their complement of seine boats. In the 1920s, mackerel were processed at these locations and sent to America. As late as 1927, over 7,000 barrels of fish left Valentia, but mackerel fishing by seine boats declined massively after World War II, with the introduction of motorised craft. This era also saw the end of the all-important rail-link that had been used to transport large quantities of fish from the south-west of Ireland. In areas with good rail networks, a certain amount of the west-coast catches went to the English market, and large quantities of mackerel were dispatched to the United States. West-coast herring were considered to be of very high quality and often took top prices in German and American markets.

All along the east coast, clinker-built boats were widely used to dredge for oyster and mussels. Went has shown that more than thirty boats dredged for oysters for eight months of the year off the coast at Arklow. The oysters were then 'boated' to Anglesey, where they were stacked on banks prior to being sent onwards to the fish markets at Liverpool. Oyster dredging in this stretch of coast was reported to have received 'a great stimulus' in the 1840s, 'due to fact that English buyers arrived in large numbers and bought up large numbers of oysters to restock the Essex and Kent beds'. Went estimated that one million oysters, 'which constituted a great drain on local stocks', were taken off

Wexford and Wicklow alone in 1843. In the 1860s, there were around one hundred boats dredging for oysters on this coast, and these were sold mainly to French buyers.[96] Right down to the end of the nineteenth century, large quantities of ling were caught on the long line, using either herring or 'lugworm' as bait. Where access to outside markets existed, most of these fish were cured locally and dispatched to Dublin, Liverpool and Glasgow. In the 1870s, the coast from Ardglass to Dublin was considered to be prime herring ground. Once renowned chiefly for line fishing, Kinsale was transformed into an important mackerel station and it had no less than seven steamers for transporting fish to the English markets in the 1870s. At that time, mackerel were packed in boxes of 120, and in one year alone as many as 121,533 boxes were dispatched from the port. Dublin then was considered the Irish headquarters of deep-sea trawling. Yet there were only around fifty fishing smacks operating all year round off this coast at the century's end.

In many of the fishing ports on the east and south coasts, and in a number of the larger western ports, sailing smacks were gradually being replaced by steam trawlers in the closing decades of the nineteenth century. This period also witnessed significant changes in the size and type of boats used by fishermen, and in the amount of netting they were able to carry. In an account of fishing life on Cape Clear, Ó Síocháin recalled that there were rumours abroad in the 1890s 'that there were big boats fishing out of Kinsale and that they were catching mackerel; the earnings from them were big, for there was great demand entirely for that fish in the market on the other side, that is the English market'.[97] These boats, he added, 'couldn't be got anywhere except in the Isle of Man at that time; and it was difficult to obtain them for they cost far too much'. At the same time, there was 'another kind of boat available, which was far from newly-built and was far cheaper: with all the gear included, the price was a couple of hundred pounds'. Two islanders from Cape Clear went into partnership to buy one of these boats, 'and fished for a season with her and did so well that the island wasn't dependent on one only but actually had four of them'.[98] Altogether, there were twenty-five of these boats on the island at the end of the nineteenth century, when fish merchants from elsewhere in Ireland, and from England and Scotland, regularly visited small fishing ports on the south-west coast to buy up large quantities of mackerel and herring. In addition to the new boats that were 'bought into' Cape Clear, there were 400 to 500 boats fishing out of nearby Baltimore at the height of the mackerel season. O'Siochain recalled how he 'often saw three steamers being filled in a single day for the English market, which is proof that fish were in great demand over there'. The islanders, he added, 'used to start preparations for this kind of fishing in the beginning of March, and it took two weeks to get the boats ready for sea'. There were around twelve companies from Irish and English fish merchants represented in Baltimore by buyers who purchased the fish directly from the boats. Indeed, supplies of fish were so great then that the buyers brought in ice from Norway in order to preserve them.

By the end of June, the mackerel season around Cape Clear and the south-west coast had finished, and the nets were landed, dried and brought home. It was then that fishermen prepared for fishing with long lines, catching ling, hake, eels, skate and halibut. The long-line season on this part of the coast generally lasted for three or four weeks, during which the fishermen would come home once a week with the catch in order to salt it while it was still fresh. After three or four voyages spent in this kind of fishing, the season for the 'big boats' ended for the year. With the long-line season over, August was spent preparing for the autumn fishing, which was often considered more profitable to small fishermen than fishing with large boats around the south-west coast. It was said that the bays around the south-west coast 'filled up' with mackerel during the autumn season. When the autumn fishing began, each of the Cape Clear boats put down six wooden anchors 'of their own design and making' in order to mark their berths. The demand for cured fish was so great in this market that buyers used to outbid each other 'until the very last boat arrived laden with fish'. When the fish were put ashore from the boats, each buyer ordered his team of 'handlers' to set to work cutting the fish open with knives and gutting them, after which they would be thrown into a vat full of water for washing prior to being pickled in large vats. One week later, the fish were salted for a second time and packed in airtight barrels for export. In the last two decades of the nineteenth century, the processing and packing of fish provided employment for large numbers of women and young girls all around the west and north-west coasts. Ó Síocháin claimed that 'there wasn't a woman, a girl or a child' on Cape Clear in the 1880s and 1890s 'who couldn't earn something in those days'. Indeed, there was often so much to do at the height of the mackerel season then 'that the very fishermen themselves had to lend a helping hand when there were large landings of fish, for the sake of finishing the day's work'.[99]

In the 1880s and 1890s, the important sea fishery off the coast from Malin Head to Greencastle was carried out in twenty-four foot yawls and decked 'otterers' measuring about thirty feet, that were fitted with standing rigging. Unlike currachs, these were very substantial vessels that had been locally built

70 Tory Island in the 1940s. Tory lacked even the most basic infrastructure for developing its rich sea fisheries. Like the inhabitants of Inistrahull Island off Malin Head, fishermen here were often obliged to sell their catch at rock-bottom prices, or dispose of them to passing trans-Atlantic liners (courtesy of Seán Beattie).

at Moville since the late eighteenth century. They were widely used to fish for cod, haddock, halibut, herring, ling, plaice, pollock, sole, turbot and salmon. There were an estimated 685 men and 109 boats engaged in this fishing in the 1890s. Boats were usually laid up for the winter and the trawling season extended from February right through to the end of September. Facilities for the sale of fish along this part of the Irish coast scarcely existed in the closing decades of the nineteenth century. In 1894, an inspector for the Congested Districts Board found that most fish caught off Malin Head had 'to be carted twenty miles to Moville if they are to be sold as fresh; or they must be first cured and then sent by boats or carts, at great loss of fishing time, to distant markets'.[100] Fishermen from around Culdaff, a tiny fishing port on the north coast of the Inishowen Peninsula, had to 'boat' their fish catches either to Greencastle or to Magilligan Point, 'a sail and pull of twenty miles each way at the end of their day's or night's fishing'. The quantity of fish bought for export at Moville, Greencastle and Magilligan Point in 1893 amounted to 'upwards of 8,000 boxes of over 600 tons weight and consisted chiefly of turbot, flat fish, cod, crabs and lobsters'. Most of the fishermen on this coast used 'spillets' and the 'best of the cod off Malin Head' were caught with baited hand-lines. In a report that emphasised the huge difficulties experienced by fishermen in bringing fresh fish to market, the inspector went on to point out that although Moville was over twenty miles from Malin Head, it was considered 'the surest market inasmuch as fish could be sold there for shipment every week day'. At Carndonagh, there was a weekly market each Monday, and here 'a great weight of cured fish' was sold throughout the year. Fish were either transported by horse and cart over very long distances, or were carried along the coast by boat to the nearest market town. At Carndonagh, the number of cart-loads brought in on market days was 'never less than from ten to twenty' and often reached from fifty to one hundred in the spring months. On the Monday before Easter, up to forty cartloads of 'mild cured' pollock, amounting to approximately 500 dozen fish, were sold. The prices paid at Moville were generally in line with those in Scottish and English markets and varied according to species. The major problems confronting fishermen here were not the proverbial 'inadequate boats' or 'poor tackle', but the great difficulty in preserving and transporting fresh fish to markets that were often only twenty to thirty miles away. Thus, long-line fishermen at Malin Head, Moville, Greencastle and Culdaff all reported that they had no trouble in catching fish, and that 'the boats could then be filled several times over if there were the means of getting rid of the fish as they are caught'. When fish were plentiful, and when the weather allowed for a full load to be brought ashore, a single share of the catch could amount to four dozen fish per day for each crewmember. The fish were sometimes decapitated to save stowage room and weight in the boats, and in calm weather, when the boats were full and fish still remained on the long line, fish were often 'lashed together and towed to the landing place'. The fishermen also believed that if the fishing 'could be carried on in vessels which would accommodate the crews, and they were able to remain by the fish in ordinary weather, the aggregate take would be many times larger than it is under present conditions'. Weather permitting, the season for taking cod and pollock off Malin Head was from November to May. Salmon and flat fish were caught in May and June, while *glasson* or small pollock were taken in June and July. From Malin Head to Culdaff, the boats were described as 'imperfectly equipped with nets', and the men fished chiefly with hand-lines. The fishing grounds lay up to thirty miles off the coast and small piers around Malin Head sheltered most of the boats, although large numbers of drontheims or fishing yawls were simply beached on the shore. The main pier at Malin Head was completed in 1888 with money raised both from the rates and from private subscriptions. The fishermen considered it 'a matter of great importance … that steamers should be enabled and induced to call as regularly as the weather permits, as such calls imply a direct, cheap and rapid communication with Glasgow for passengers, fish, produce, meal and goods, and might be expected to exercise a generally enlightening and awakening influence'.

Regarding the developmental potential of sea fisheries around the coast of Inishowen in the early 1890s, W.P Gaskell stated that

> It is not to be expected that the present generation of fishermen would readily adopt new methods, even if they had the opportunity of doing so; but looking only at the loss of time and labour involved in fishing from open boats at long distances from land, it would seem worth consideration whether improvement could not be gradually introduced. There is reason to believe that if shelter were provided at Greencastle or Moville, either substantial security would be offered for loans to fishermen, or private capital would be forthcoming to build and equip decked vessels with or without tanks. At present at Moville, even in the summer, the boats must be emptied and hauled high and dry on their return to shore. In the case of the 'otterers', which carry a ton or more of ballast, this takes time as well as labour. It is said, and it is probably the truth, that fish are more bruised in the cartage to Moville, and must on that account be sold at a disadvantage in British markets as compared with fish carried by sea. Minor and inexpensive improvements, of the first consequence to scores of individuals, of the fine race of boatmen and fishermen which this district boasts, would consist in clearing the entrances to the boat-harbours of rocks, and in facilitating the beaching of boats whenever that can be done easily.[101]

In the event, fishermen, farmers and workers in the garment industry in Inishowen were not 'awakened' by the 'enlightening influence' that contact with Glasgow was supposed to bring about. As coastal Ireland entered the new century, the rising nationalist intelligentsia and the new social collectivities in rural Ireland insisted that the family farm, and rural industry, were to be the basis for the country's future prosperity. Fishing, so long associated with poverty and hardship, became even more marginalised in the new nationalist Ireland, as fishermen found themselves practically voiceless in a nation-state from which they were radically excluded.

The chapter that follows examines social and cultural attitudes to the fishermen and sea fisheries of Ireland in the post-Famine decades, when this

New Ireland was in the making. It argues that social and economic factors alone do not explain the under-development of the country's sea fisheries at the end of the nineteenth century. A whole set of strongly-held political and cultural beliefs were also brought to debates about the role of fishing and coastal districts in nation-building Ireland throughout the latter half of the nineteenth century. In the end, it is argued, the social values expressed in the rural fundamentalism of this New Ireland meant that fishermen, and fishing communities, were to remain at the political, and not just the geographical margins of the Irish nation-state.

CHAPTER TEN

Rural fundamentalism and the marginalisation of Ireland's sea fisheries

THE PERIPHERALISATION OF COASTAL IRELAND

Quite apart from the socio-economic and developmental problems preventing Ireland from competing with overseas fleets and fostering a vibrant fishing industry, a whole series of political and cultural factors influenced attitudes towards the country's seafaring coastal communities in the latter half of the nineteenth and the first half of the twentieth century. These, I have argued, largely sealed the fate of the industry in post-Famine and post-independence Ireland. The rise of agrarian nationalism, coupled with a growing insensitivity to the problems of impoverished coastal communities, meant that fishing as an industry, and fishermen as a social group, were marginalised to the outer edges of nation-building Ireland. Cultural nationalists tended to dignify all that was authentic, settled, noble and creative about Irish society and Irish history. In so doing, they denigrated that which was 'uncouth', 'unsettling', 'backward' and 'poverty-stricken', at least from the perspective of the new hegemonic social collectivities emerging in late nineteenth-century Ireland. When the coastal poor intruded upon the consciousness of these cultural nationalists, they did so as the romantic 'other' of a passing Ireland, or as the social inferiors, and rarely the equals of substantial farmers and the town-based bourgeoisie. As such, they were the shadowy remnants of an impoverished, pre-modern past that had to be suppressed, even 'consumed', in order for the process of urban and rural modernisation to proceed unobstructed. Aside from their occasional eulogising as 'noble warriors' struggling to make a living from inhospitable seas, fishermen were more commonly characterised as 'the people of the rocks'.[1] As a social group, fishermen had no claim on Irish land, or on Irish history, and were noticeable by their absence in the historic struggles for agrarian reform and national independence. For that reason, many felt that fishermen were un-deserving of the same political status as land-holders, industrialists and the new professional classes. If impoverished fishermen were to have any place within the material and moral structures of a progressive Irish nation, they were to become economic wards, rather than rightful citizens of

71 Boys and young men at Baltimore Fishery School in the 1890s. The school was established in 1887 in an effort to disseminate new fishing skills and an entrepreneurial spirit to coastal communities around the south and west of the country in particular (courtesy of the *Irish Examiner* archives).

that nation. Thus, unlike their urban and rural counterparts, they were subjects of state power and were very rarely power-holders in the local and national institutions of the state. This was partially because in the Darwinian, post-Famine environment of nation-building Ireland, the historical struggles of fishermen to wrest a living from sea and shoreline were rarely considered as historical in any meaningful or *evolutionary* sense. Instead, it was argued, the history of fishing was an endless story of aimless hardship and unrelenting struggle, a history that lacked its own narrators, and even lacked its own audience.[2]

While social Darwinian ideas have long been recognised as having a powerful role in providing quasi-scientific justifications for the subordination of colonial peoples in the nineteenth-century world order, their implications for social and economic minorities in developing nation states have received far less attention. Yet, social Darwinism often combined with nationalism to justify the marginalisation of minority groups within European society throughout the latter half of the nineteenth and well into the twentieth century. Given the racist character of much of his ethnographic writings on nomadic and pre-capitalist communities, it is not surprising that Friedrich Ratzel's social Darwinian writings on ethnic and racial minorities found their way into German geopolitics in the 1930s. Ratzel (1857–1902), was a German political geographer whose writings on geopolitics were widely used to justify the coercive domination of indigenous peoples in the colonial world, and the containment of 'lower orders' in nineteenth-century nation-building Europe.[3] However, he also devised a profoundly nationalistic, ethnocentric and 'stageist' theory of social progress that prioritised sedentarism over nomadism and ranked the advanced industrial nations of western Europe at the apex of an international social order dominated by the White colonial powers.[4] Other societies, especially those still engaged in fishing and rudimentary forms of pastoralism in the nineteenth century, were placed lower down the social hierarchy, either because they 'mismanaged' their relationship with the environment, or otherwise 'under-utilised' the earth's resources. Added to this was the fact that pre-industrial societies were militarily weak, which was no asset at all in an age when nations had to assert themselves on the world stage. Writing in a late nineteenth-century context that witnessed the western bourgeoisie appropriating more and more of the earth's surface, Ratzel legitimised the takeover of the lands of nomadic people on the grounds that advanced sedentary societies, especially the expansionist capitalist nations of Western Europe, should have first claim on global resources. This was because, he argued, their approach to environmental management was infinitely superior to the environmental practices of nomadic and pre-capitalist societies. Ratzel's ideas, and the pervasive social Darwinism of other nineteenth-century social thinkers, were also evident in nationalist thinking, not least in relation to subordinate social groups such as fishermen, disappearing craft workers, domestic servants, farm workers and the travelling poor. Indeed, these ideas were frequently refracted through social class lenses in such a way as to suggest that such groups were social anachronisms in an age of modernity. In nation-building Ireland, social class attitudes towards landless labourers, fishermen, the itinerant poor and migrant workers were strongly influenced by evolutionary theory in general, and by bourgeois nationalist ideals in particular. The unconscious fusion of such attitudes with the territorial imperatives of nation-builders clearly had implications for these and other groups. Once again, this was clearly articulated in Ratzel's writings where he argued that

> The struggle for existence means a struggle for space. A superior people, invading the territory of its weaker savage neighbours, robs them of their

land, forces them back into corners too small for their support, and continues to encroach even upon this meagre possession, till the weaker finally loses the last remnants of its domain, and is literally crowded off the earth.[5]

Thus for Ratzel, and for most nation-builders in the Darwinian half of the nineteenth century, the superiority of a people could be measured primarily in terms of their ability to appropriate, populate and thoroughly utilise *territory*. Writing at a time when the European bourgeoisie were appropriating an increasing amount of the earth's surface, social Darwinists implied that this was a perfectly natural process. Arguing from deep nationalist convictions, Ratzel claimed that rural sedentary and industrial societies were more superior to nomadic societies because *their* utilisation of the natural environment was considered vastly superior to the environmental practices of fragile groups whose very existence depended on their ability to eke out a precarious living from land, sea and shoreline. To some people indeed, fishermen, landless labourers, the travelling poor and the urban under-class were considered 'superfluous', even 'dirty' people who were not entitled to participation in the institutions that constituted the material and moral structures of the modern nation state.[6] In nineteenth-century nationalist Ireland, the social inferiority of the poor could occasionally take on racial undertones. In a letter to his friend P.V. Fitzpatrick, in 1839, Daniel O'Connell expressed his attitude towards the role of these sectors of Irish society in his struggle for Catholic emancipation as follows:

> I will never get half credit enough for carrying Emancipation, because posterity never can believe *the species of animals* with which I had to carry my warfare with the common enemy. It is crawling slaves like them that prevent our being a nation (emphasis added).[7]

Having accepted their lot with a Brechtian sense of resignation, fishermen were also assumed to be devoid of the romantic ideals of 'primitive rebellion' that periodically, and sporadically, brought the poorest of the rural poor crashing onto the stage of nineteenth-century Irish history. Instead, they inhabited a rootless and amphibious world that was literally beyond the reach, and the comprehension of most Irish people. As coastal dwellers and seafarers, they mimicked neither peasant nor worker. Their location at the outer edges of the geographical nation was replicated in their marginal status in national consciousness. To petty bourgeois sectors of Irish society, it seemed as though the very survival of impoverished fishing communities on the Atlantic fringes of post-Famine Ireland was itself a source of wonder, even sometimes a source of shock. To these 'rising' sectors of a petty bourgeois national society, there was much about the culture of fishing communities that 'intimidated' their sensibilities. It was not just that the amphibious nature of the fisherman's world made it difficult for rural and urban Ireland to accommodate it in the rural Irish nation. Their poverty, superstitions and rootlessness, together with their so-called 'ribald manners' and 'fearlessness', seemed to place them beyond the pale of middle-class gentility and respectability, including the respect of property-owners for precise laws and good order. All of this suggested a 'geography of development' and a 'geography of knowing' that implied that those located furthest from the heartlands of modern Ireland were the most under-developed and least sophisticated sectors of Irish society.[8] Not surprisingly, for some writers, nationalists and artists, fishermen were as mysterious and elusive as the world they inhabited. Thus, as part of a relic cultural landscape that was literally, metaphorically and precariously attached to the maritime fringe of an Atlantic world, coastal Ireland was widely considered as a place apart from the economic heartlands of progressive Ireland. For some, indeed, this part of Ireland was little more than a barren wasteland, a place still clouded by the shadow of Famine in an otherwise 'thriving country'.[9]

There clearly was a high degree of overlap between neglect of the maritime, particularly the maritime poor in Irish history, and the social class implications of bourgeois nationalism. This went back to the conditions in which the nation in post-Famine Ireland was conceived as a cradle of modernity and petty bourgeois rural respectability. Nineteenth-century Irish nationalism, simply considered as an expression of hegemonic conflicts over power and political *space*, regularly sought to construct the 'Irish people' as a successful, cohesive, political community. Whole sections of Irish society were excluded from these constructs of the nation as the embodiment of social and economic success. This was partially because the nation in Ireland, as indeed elsewhere in Europe and the Americas, was regularly conceived of as an historical system of exclusions and dominations from which the socially, as well as the racially 'inferior' were to be radically excluded. Urban capitalism, rural fundamentalism, patriarchal property rights and all the moral and cultural capital that accompanied these, held pride of place in the nineteenth-century modern nation. In Ireland's case also, nationalism conjured up images of the Irish as a capable people – a people able to manage their own affairs, and capable of 'holding their own' among the nations of the world. This in turn emphasised the powerful 'organic' links between 'the people' or *volk* on the one hand, and their 'natural' homeland or *heimat* on the other. Thus, nationalist hegemony in nineteenth-century Ireland had quite distinctive geographical correlates. The nation-state was arguably more representative of some socio-spatial regions than others, while other parts of the country, notably the western seaboard and the under-developed north-west of the country, were absorbed into the nation on highly unfavourable terms. Prosperous farmers in the midlands and south of the country were the favoured sectors of this nation-building Ireland, and the policies that favoured the development of agriculture here largely ignored the needs of small farmers and fishermen on the maritime fringe. In addition, the very idea of a 'people deserving of nationhood' conjured up images of successful *settled* societies. The latter were imbued with a strong sense of 'blood and soil' nationalism that linked people to their homeland in such a way as to render it a quasi-sacred entity. From the start, therefore, the historical categories of the 'people' and the 'nation' in nineteenth-century Ireland were both inclusive and exclusive. Here again, as elsewhere in nation-building Europe, attitudes towards the rural poor and coastal-dwellers were shaped by prevailing attitudes towards Ireland's place in the international community of nations. Many felt that the disintegration of fishing communities steeped in ribaldry and clinging to their own plebeian culture was a small price to pay for the modernisation of an increasingly puritanical Catholic Ireland. Thus, while nationalism sought to anchor the substantial 'rural stock' to the land of Ireland, it did not have the same 'anchoring' or 'territorialising' function for the rural and urban poor, or for fishermen, fish workers, seasonal migrants and a whole host of other marginalised groups.[10] As in the late nineteenth century, so also in the early post-independence period, the state remained particularly silent about the plight of the coastal poor, many of whom flooded out of Ireland to work in Britain, North America and Australia. The New Ireland that was to be constructed out of the social inequalities that characterised the early post-Famine decades was to be built not only by, but also for the 'stalwart, muscular, dauntless young braves' of rural Ireland. Unlike impoverished coastal communities on the fringes of nation-building Ireland, the sons of substantial farmers, successful businessmen and urban professionals were said to be 'royally-endowed with every attribute that goes to make up a peerless and magnificent manhood'.[11] *Their* disappearance through emigration was to be prevented at all costs because it would deprive Ireland of the very 'bone and sinew' needed in the construction of a healthy and viable nation. The coastal and rural poor on the other hand, not least the 'sad, weeping and melancholy emigrants' from the west of Ireland, and all those who had 'cast off all allegiance to the land', deserved to emigrate because they had nothing substantial to offer the Irish nation.[12] Fishermen and fish workers were often deemed inferior to the poorest sections of the settled rural poor. For that very reason, they were looked upon as a people without land or history in an age when land and history were on the side of nation-builders. Impoverished fishermen and fish-workers were also denied a role in the nation-building project because their amphibious geography failed to reinforce any claim to national legitimacy. The amphibious nature of their world seemed to place them beyond the boundary of the nation. For nationalists, the historic re-conquest and repossession of the land of Ireland was the very basis of their claims to nationhood. Coastal communities that made their living from the sea and shoreline, and who did not conceive of territory in terms of personal, proprietorial allegiances, were difficult to accommodate in the nation-state. The amphibious realms within which they moved and worked, were at once infirm and anomalous. For that reason, nationalists argued, the political artifice that was the nation could not be constructed on such 'unsound' foundations. State sovereignty, it was insisted, could not be constructed on sand, sea or silt. From at least the seventeenth century onwards, it was argued that those who dwelt in such watery realms were condemned to an ignoble existence. Thus, for example, in a deeply racist poem by Andrew Marvell written in 1651, Dutch seafarers, fishermen and all those who depended on the resources of the sea were deemed to have no right to nationhood because they were 'the indigested vomit of the seas'.[13] Similarly in Ireland, the social attitudes of nation-builders towards themselves as a people deserving of nationhood must be analysed against a background that prioritised sedentarism over nomadism, and legitimised the cultural values of the propertied while ignoring the position of the propertyless.

Just as the desolate coastal stretches and watery wastes of Atlantic Europe could not confer the attributes of a true *patria* in the eighteenth century, it was felt that those who still dwelt in such amphibian habitats in the nineteenth century were politically unmanageable and economically backward. Land and industry were what chiefly mattered, as only land provided the nation with a dwelling place and 'yielded bread to eat and wood and stone to build with'.[14] As such, land alone was fit for men's habitations, and those who flouted this strict nationalist stricture were mocked as 'usurpers who deprived fish of their dwelling places'. To most nationalists, with the notable exception of those in the Dutch Republic in the seventeenth and eighteenth centuries, the amphibian habitat of fishermen was an uncharted and unmanageable world that bred poverty, coarseness, danger and 'ungracious' social habits. It was as if the very metabolism that made fishermen so adaptable to sea life also rendered them intractable subjects of state authority. Their 'spontaneity', 'lawlessness' and anarchic customs were difficult to contain within the increasingly refined moral geography of the modern surveillance state. In matters of rank and respect for authority, fishermen and fishing communities in general were considered casual at best, and indifferent at worst. Others considered the social levelling and egalitarianism that were such fundamentally important features of coastal communities as proof of their incorrigible character and their lack of respect for social distinctions and the ethos of individualism. Just as it was inconceivable that state sanction should be extended to smugglers, pirates and the 'enemies of good order' in colonial Ireland, it appeared equally implausible that the impoverished inhabitants of the country's amphibian habitats in the nineteenth century could ever become the social equals of urban and rural nation-builders. This attitude towards marginalised communities on the periphery of a nation-building society was in no way peculiar to nineteenth-century Irish nationalists. It had much deeper roots in European discourses on race and development dating back at least to the seventeenth century. In his *Mare Liberum*, published in 1609, the Dutch-born jurist and theologian Hugo Grotius (1583–1645) justified Dutch claims to trade with whatever countries to which they could sail.[15] In so doing, he laid the basis for an international law of the sea that suggested that the development of laws, culture and civilisation was intimately linked to the evolution of complex man-land relationships over time and space. Quoting from sacred history, Grotius suggested that the 'primitive', common ownership of moveable items of personal property, technically known as *chattel*, was gradually abandoned when 'men were not content to feed on the spontaneous products of the earth, to dwell in caves, to have the body either naked or clothed in … the skin of wild animals, but chose a more refined mode of life; this gives rise to industry'.[16] John Locke (1632–1704) also contributed to this prioritisation of property rights based on toil or 'industry' on the one hand, and the marginalisation of what we may call hunters, gathers and propertyless people on the other. For Locke, 'primitive' groups approached 'enlightenment' the more they abandoned communal ownership of goods and services, showed respect for private property, and espoused the rights of individuals over and above those of the community. Moreover, Locke, unlike many of his predecessors, did not trace the origins of private property to any social pact or covenant. He linked it instead to the adoption of 'settled' conditions and the abandonment of 'primitive' nomadic lifestyles, including primitive communism. In an interesting passage revealing his preference for the settled life of the 'industrious' over the unsettled and spontaneous life of 'hunters and gathers', Locke further suggested that private property emerged when men invested their labour or 'industry' in the natural resources of the world around them. This *transformative* power of labour meant that the privatisation of property was legitimised in terms of the amount of labour invested in it. This, in turn, meant that entire sections of society who made no claims on landed property, and who did not accumulate wealth as the private product of human labour, had correspondingly fewer political and social rights in class-structured and hierarchical societies. Like most Enlightenment thinkers, Locke regarded 'primitive' peoples, including those he considered to be 'primitive' within the confines of otherwise Enlightened societies, as lacking in the necessary attributes needed for the advancement of healthy civilisation. For these thinkers, as for many nineteenth-century nationalists, those social groups whose way of life was dependent upon rudimentary forms of agriculture and the preservation of nomadic practices, were not only different from 'settled society'. In a nineteenth-century world of militarily powerful and economically competitive nations, they were perceived as social obstacles that could prevent poor, struggling nations from acquiring statehood. For that reason, they had to be treated as wards of the state that belonged to an earlier stage of social evolution. Adam Smith, one of the earliest exponents of a stageist theory of social progress, used resource-utilisation as a basis for classifying societies in a hierarchical social order. Writing as early as the 1760s, Semyon Desnitsky, a Russian student of Smith, outlined four distinctive stages in the evolution of developed societies. Starting with 'primordial' societies of 'noble savages', Desnitsky argued that nomadic hunters, primitive agriculturalists and fishermen represented the most primitive stage of development because theirs was the condition of 'people living by hunting animals and feeding on the spontaneous fruits of the earth'.[17] The next stage was 'the condition of people living as shepherds', which he labelled the pastoral stage. Sedentary agriculturalists represented the third stage, and these were considered more advanced than mere pastoralists because they made a stronger impact on the environment. These were followed by those societies that engaged in industry, commerce and international trade. Like all stageist theories of social development, those of Desnitsky, Grotius, Locke and Smith were based on the premise that each stage of social evolution was characterised by distinct forms of social

72 In a scene reminiscent of Brain Friel's 1990 play, *Dancing at Lughnasa*, two women are engaged in the collection of 'shore food' on the Blaskets in the 1920s (from Stagles, *The Blasket Islands: next parish America* (1980)).

and political organisation. What is important to note here, however, is that their writings were subsequently used by nineteenth-century nation-builders to sanction the marginalisation of a whole range of socially subordinate groups within metropolitan society.

COASTAL COMMUNITIES: IRELAND'S PEOPLE WITHOUT HISTORY?

Even before the coastal districts of the west of Ireland featured in the works of nationalist writers, its inhabitants, and habitats, had been 'written up' in the 'fabulous geographies' of visitors to the west of the country from the sixteenth to the nineteenth century. Well into the nineteenth century, they also featured in romantic caricatures of the 'wild' but 'scenic' coastline of Atlantic Ireland. The 'primitive' inhabitants of this part of nineteenth-century Ireland were, it was suggested, still engaged in ancient, rudimentary forms of fishing and agriculture that had scarcely changed with the passage of centuries. Those who visited the 'highways and byways' of this 'hidden Ireland' were either enchanted by its wild scenery or 'revolted' by the poverty and backwardness of its inhabitants. However, for nationalist writers such as Daniel Corkery and Stephen Gwynn, the western seaboard and marginal uplands of Ireland were a cherished stretch of a disappearing world that was accessible only to those who travelled the offbeat 'highways and byways' out along the Atlantic fringe of the country.[18] The very remoteness of the western seaboard seemed to render this part of Ireland safe from the forces of modernity. Moreover, they insisted, its peripherality maintained much of Atlantic Ireland in a pristine state of geographical isolation and rendered it a precious 'bastion of Gaeldom' right down to the beginning of the twentieth century. Corkery described the 'wild seaboard of the West' and 'the hard mountain lands' in the 'back places' of Cork, Kerry, Mayo, Galway and Donegal, as a world where 'the Gael was not put upon'.[19] For Swift, on the other hand, these were the places where 'the savage old Irish' were to be found. Writing in 1720, he added that 'whoever travels through this country and observes the face of nature, or the faces and habits and dwellings of the natives, would hardly think himself in a land where either religion, or common humanity was professed'.[20] Bishop Berkeley described the inhabitants of this 'other Ireland' as a place where people grew up 'in a cynical content in dirt and beggary to a degree beyond any other people in Christendom'. For Corkery, on the other hand, the 'hidden Ireland' of the west coast was 'the true face of Irish Ireland – that hidden land whose story had never been told'. 'Poverty', he added, was 'its only wear – poverty in the town, the cabin, the person, the gear and the landscape'. Civic life here was said to be non-existent, just as the 'institutions, public edifices, ceremonies and arts' of 'home-centred countries' had ceased to exist. For Corkery, life here 'did no more than crawl along, without enough to eat, unclothed, fever-stricken, slow'. Here indeed was a place where there was no thought 'for anything beyond mere existence from day to day'. To penetrate the amphibian world and upland regions of this other Ireland 'one must venture among the bogs and hills, far into the mountains, where the native Irish … still lurked'.[21] To 'develop' the fragile outposts of this Gaelic-speaking Ireland was to utterly change them, and this ran counter to the mindset of cultural nationalists and all those who defended the Gaelic language.

Writing at the dusk of the nineteenth century, Stephen Gwynn considered places such as post-Famine Kerry, Mayo and Donegal as little more than 'worthless appendages of the Empire' that could never become 'thriving counties'. Echoing twentieth-century Nazi ideas on the role of wilderness in the revival of the human spirit, Gwynn also believed that the 'lonely regions' of these maritime counties would become the playgrounds 'of our laborious Irish race'.[22] As such, they were to be the outdoor lungs of an invigorated nation, providing urban dwellers with *lebensraum*, or 'breathing space', and a place where they could breathe-in the clean salty air of a less contaminated Ireland. The more cultural nationalists rooted Irish identity in the wild and 'pure' landscapes of the Atlantic coast, the more they looked on Gaelic-speaking communities in Donegal, Kerry, Cork, Clare, Galway and Mayo as cultural role-models for citizens of the new nation. Instead of proffering solutions to the economic difficulties of this part of coastal Ireland, they presented it instead as an antidote to the secularised versions of modernity to be found in Irish cities, and in industrial Britain. Here in this 'other Ireland', they insisted, people 'knew their place' and possessed a strong sense of place that was forged out of an intimate relationship with land and sea that was at once resilient and timeless. Viewed thus, the cultural nationalist construct of the west coast was both a political artifice and a social construct. This part of the country represented a cultural mind-set and an amalgam of flattering, and oftentimes patronising images that frequently had little connection with the realities of coastal communities struggling to eke out an existence in some of the country's harshest environments. Perhaps more than any other part of the country, the identity of these counties on the Atlantic seaboard of nineteenth-century Ireland was also a product of comparisons with other parts of Ireland and Great Britain. Like the Highlands of Scotland, the valleys of Wales, the American West, and the south of Italy, the western seaboard of Ireland was as much a geographical metaphor as a 'real place'. Depending on the perspective of the viewer, it was a 'dream-space', a 'place apart' from the modern world, and a precious part of nation-building Ireland that was clearly also set apart from the rest of the country. It was also perceived as an outpost of Gaeldom, a borderland between landed Ireland and amphibian Ireland, a natural wilderness, an enchanted place, an emblem of backwardness, a problem region, a soulful place and a soft place of quiet retreat. For centuries, this part of Ireland was subjected to the gaze of the curious traveller, the 'improving' landlord, the social reformer, the proselytising clergyman and the government official. Well before the nineteenth century, it also featured in English-language official documents, travelogues, paintings, novels, poetry and song. The inhabitants and habitats of this Ireland were described in considerable detail in the 'fabulous geographies' compiled by travellers to the west of Ireland in the seventeenth and eighteenth centuries. Right down to the nineteenth century, they also featured in the fantastic tales told by travellers about Ireland's 'wild landscapes', 'desolate coastline' and 'ferocious people'.[23] When Thomas Carlyle visited the western edge of Donegal in the 1840s, he found nothing but 'black, dim, lonely valleys, some stony beyond measure' whose inhabitants were 'sprinkled in ragged clusters here and there'. Here also were poor 'deludit craiturs' and 'dark barbarians' who were 'lazy, superstitious and hungry', and who struggled to survive on a diet of fish and endless helpings of 'stirabout'.[24] Somewhat similar to visitors to the Pyrenees in the mid-nineteenth century, those 'outsiders' who ventured here sought the sublime in the mountains and the exotic in the local population.

In order to conjure up political capital from the neglect of Atlantic Ireland's inshore fisheries and marginal uplands, cultural nationalists were often compelled to ignore the structuring roles of rural poverty and emigration in clearing a space for viable family farms in isolated pockets of Ireland's maritime fringe. Attributing regional malaise and emigration to 'landlord neglect' and 'rancherism', they Anglicised the causes and nationalised the solutions to the social and economic problems of the western seaboard.[25] In other words, they failed to offer *specific* solutions to the social ills besetting maritime Ireland, and simply suggested that this 'hidden Ireland' was an indispensable component of the nation's cultural landscape. According to this narrow nationalist perspective, *landlord* neglect was directly and indirectly responsible for the plight of poor tenant farmers and fishermen on the country's Atlantic fringe. Insisting that English political economy and 'rancherism' had no place in a modernising Irish society, they argued that landlord rule should give way to a system of *petit culture* initially centred on tenant holdings and subsequently based on family-run farms. Pointing out that whole sections of Irish society were being driven overseas when they were most needed to build a strong nation at home, most nationalists failed to outline a programme for the rejuvenation of coastal Ireland. While the Catholic Church might decry emigration as 'a kind of self-defacement' that contributed to the destruction of the country's coastal communities, business and political leaders, and strong farmers in particular, looked on emigration as an acceptable solution to the intractable problems of maritime Ireland. 'New Ireland', it was suggested, held little room for the 'pale and panic-stricken' poor from the western seaboard.[26] Population pressure in the nineteenth century had pushed people onto marginal lands, and out into the coastal areas, causing a significant increase in the number of part-time fishermen between 1800 and 1845. The outflow of harvest migrants also increased from a few thousand per year in the early part of the century, to around 80,000 in 1841. In 1819, a fishery board was set up, comprising unpaid commissioners appointed by the lord lieutenant. It had a small staff, a number of local inspectors and four general inspectors. It paid bounties for boat-building, as well as on actual fish catches, made loans for boat purchases and the construction and repair of small piers, and employed an engineer to survey the Irish coast. All of this showed that the board, loosely defined as it was, believed that the fishing industry had great potential, and that it could and should be developed. By 1829, the number of fishermen in the country had almost doubled. Nevertheless, the board was abolished a year later, amid accusations that the country was overrun with aid agencies that were squandering public money. As Prime Minister Peel argued, 'everyone in Ireland, instead of setting about improvement as people do elsewhere, pester government about boards and public aid. Why cannot people in Ireland fish without a board, if fishing be, as Lord Glengall declares it to be, so profitable?'

Not all of those who visited the Atlantic fringe of Ireland were overwhelmed by its poverty or stunned by its 'wild' and 'wonderful' coastal scenery. As we have already seen, romantic images of fishermen and poor peasants featured strongly in the works of a number of Irish and Anglo-Irish writers and artists. However, such romanticisation of the 'wandering Irish' was in sharp contrast to their marginalisation in political and economic accounts of conditions in the west of Ireland. For most nineteenth-century modernisers, the push towards modernity meant that the poverty associated with fishing and farming on the Atlantic fringe of Ireland was presented as the opposite to development and progress found elsewhere in the country. This, in turn, meant that the concerns of the rural and coastal poor were frequently considered inimical to political progress because they presented an unacceptable image of the nation to the world at large. It was as if the sheer trauma of 'settling down', involving as it did the appropriation and privatisation of property and the adoption of petty bourgeois sedentary life-styles, separated out fishermen, fish-workers, travellers and the landless poor from the more successful elements of national society. For fishing communities and the travelling poor, this presentation of nomadism and sedentarism in stark oppositional terms meant that they were separated from the 'sedentary Irish', who in turn found themselves more and more detached from their own maritime past. The entire process of social distancing and historical amnesia that ensued from this also enabled strong tenant-farmers and the town-based bourgeoisie to dissociate themselves from the 'the wretched' of the Irish earth. This was not dissimilar from the bouts of 'communal amnesia' that Declan Kiberd and others have identified in other post-colonial societies in the nineteenth and twentieth centuries. Quoting Friedrich Nietzsche, Kiberd suggests that 'post-colonial amnesiacs' often had very good strategic reasons for their forgetfulness of the historic past.[27] In the run-up to independence, Ireland's more conservative political leaders, fixated on the project of rural and industrial modernisation, suggested that it was time to 'forget' Ireland's colonial past, and all those who did not fit into their image of a progressive Irish nation. Like the anarchist peasantry of southern Italy so well described in Carlo Levi's novel, *Christ Stopped at Eboli*, the fishing communities of nineteenth-century Ireland were assumed to exist outside the framework of Irish historical time, being confined instead to that which was 'changeless and eternal'.[28] Like Levi's Italian peasantry, Ireland's fishing communities had to resign themselves to being dominated, rather than actively participating in the making of the new state. In so doing, they rarely felt as their own the glories and undertakings of a bourgeois and petty bourgeois Ireland from which they were increasingly distanced. Almost like the Mexican Indian peasantry in Traven's novel *Government*, they were, to all intents and purposes, a people 'without a country to belong to, without the right to call themselves members of the nation'; a people who were 'driven hither and thither by every pull of the wind'.[29]

As we have already seen, the roots of this 'turning away' from maritime Ireland were to be found in a 'common sense' social Darwinism that overlapped with nationalism in the post-Famine period. Nationalism in Ireland and other European countries caused the nation to be perceived as an historical system of exclusions and dominations. In Ireland's case, this meant that the nation became a place where rural fundamentalism and the patriarchal property values of the bourgeoisie occupied pride of place. Moreover, while the social distance between 'progressive' and 'backward' Ireland tended to increase the closer the nation came to statehood, for conservative nationalists, the social distinctions within the world of the poor had all but collapsed by the end of the nineteenth century. The poor in general were perceived as an undifferentiated social amalgam. The subtle distinctions of poverty that mattered immensely to its victims were, by then, of little concern to the hegemonic sectors of a society that almost regarded the poor as their racial inferiors. This marginalisation of the poor is particularly noticeable in J.B. Keane's play *The Field*, which is concerned with the struggle for land in an impoverished parish in rural Kerry in the middle of the twentieth century.[30] Unlike Merimee's portrayal of the Gypsy, and the Gypsy woman especially, as the sexually attractive and exotic 'other' in bourgeois society who flaunts her sexuality to shatter the norms of middle-class respectability, Keane presents the poor 'tinker' woman here in far darker colours. Ultimately, she is seen as a threat to the patriarchal authority of a fundamentally rural society. Like Van Gogh, who painted the peasants of the Brabant region of the Netherlands in colours so dark that they were indistinguishable from the soil they worked and the potatoes they ate, Keane also portrayed the wandering Irish in his corner of Kerry in strong, earthy colours. Thus in the *Potato Eaters* (1885), Van Gogh set out to devise a 'real peasant picture' that 'would teach something'. As such, his intimate image of the rural destitute represented what he celebrated as the 'redemptive burden and sanctification of lowly labour'.[31] As in other paintings from this period, the Dutch artist set out to develop an ambitious programme of painting and drawing that would sympathetically represent the full cycle of production of marginal groups such as handloom weavers and potato gatherers. He depicted the latter in activities of planting, bending and digging their crop, and then partaking of the fruits of their honestly earned labour. However, unlike Van Gogh's sympathetic portrayals of landless labourers and poor handloom weavers in the last quarter of the nineteenth century, the rural Kerryman Keane has little sympathy for 'tinkers', the most impoverished section of the Irish rural poor in the first half of the twentieth century. Thus, in *The Field*, the 'tinker woman' is at once a 'dirty tinker' and a 'dirty whore'. In Jim Sheridan's film adaptation of the play, she is portrayed in more provocative and attractive colours. She is the red-haired girl who uses her sexuality to entice the only son of the patriarch, Bull McCabe, off the land in order to encourage him to 'take to the road'. In so doing, she begs him to reject the puritanical Hiberno-Victorian values of the landed Irish poor, in favour of an open life on the road, far from the narrow confines of small farming life. Her success here would represent not only a triumph of love and sexuality over love of the land and filial piety, it would constitute an affront to all the patriarchal values associated with family farming. Thus, the travelling woman in Keane's play threatens to cause the seed of the patriarch to fall by the wayside, rather than allowing it to take root in Irish soil.

The marginalisation of fishermen in post-Famine maritime Ireland, therefore, coincided with the emergence of rural capitalism, the disintegration of colonialism and the transformation of Irish peasant society. More importantly still, however, the latter half of the nineteenth century witnessed the emergence of an ethnic intelligentsia among the rural population. This contributed to the growth of a new and articulate leadership, capable of voicing the concerns of rural Ireland, and capable also of raising the political consciousness of the farming population. With remarkably few exceptions, this did not occur in Irish fishing communities. Since they failed to develop an articulate grassroots leadership of their own, the voices of fishermen were scarcely heard in the run up to political independence. The radical disavowal of the country's coastal communities that ensued from this combination of forces exacerbated the decline of coastal communities. This in turn forced the country's rich maritime culture to the outer edges of the national psyche, causing fishing communities to respond to the needs of an increasingly rural, host society. Rather than articulating their identity as a socio-economic group with a right to special treatment, and a right to their own way of life and living, fishermen were forced into silence in a New Ireland that was forged on the anvil of land wars.

Historically, distinctions between the travelling Irish poor and impoverished fishing communities on the one hand, and the 'settled' population of the rural heartlands of Ireland on the other, were complicated by a number of factors. In the first place, colonial 'settlers' from the sixteenth to the eighteenth century were practically synonymous with the colonial population in early modern Ireland. Colonial conquest caused massive 'shake-outs' within the Gaelic population, and this meant that entire sections of the native population fell through the ranks of the indigenous class structure, to end up among the country's more traditional vagrant groups. Unlike in Elizabethan England, where the enclosure system also transformed entire sections of the rural poor into 'sturdy beggars' and 'vagrants', those forced from prestigious positions in Gaelic Ireland into vagrancy and mendicancy in colonial Ireland often retained the respect of the native dispossessed well into the eighteenth century.[32] Secondly, large sections of the so-called 'settled' population were highly mobile. This was especially noticeable in the case of the rural and coastal poor in the late nineteenth century, when large numbers of migrant workers from rural and coastal communities were moving between Ireland and mainland Britain in search of work. In England and Scotland, these seasonal migrants from coastal regions in Ireland were often indistinguishable from conventional Irish 'tinkers'. In the third place, large sections of the so-called 'settled population' in coastal Ireland had been extremely mobile for centuries, and this was particularly true of the coastal poor. As 'an emigrant nursery', coastal Ireland was linked to the outer edges of an expanding world economy from at least the seventeenth century. In the nineteenth, and for much of the twentieth century, large numbers of young adults from small farming and fishing communities in this part of the country were raised alongside well-established 'emigrant trails' that led to Britain, the United States, Canada, Australia and South Africa. They also forged new trails to the expanding frontiers of the world economy by 'peopling' its outer edges, from a very early age. Similarly, in sending cash 'remittances' back home, the emigrant sons and daughters of coastal Ireland contributed to the very survival of small farming and fishing communities on the Atlantic fringe of the country well into the twentieth century. The 'Scottish money', or 'emigrant remittances', which seasonal migrants sent home, could account for as much as 20 per cent of the cash income of poor families in impoverished mixed farming and fishing communities throughout the west and north-west of Ireland right up to the eve of World War I.[33] Handley has estimated that almost 38,000 'seasonal migrants' were annually moving between Ireland and England in the closing decades of the nineteenth century. Many of these engaged in 'tattie-hoking' and other unskilled harvest work in Scotland and England during the autumn and winter months.[34] Their destinations abroad often reflected a need to locate in regions that provided seasonal employment, while also allowing them ready access to home at harvest time, and at the all-important spring and summer fishing seasons. These so-called 'settled', seasonal migrants from coastal Ireland may well have regarded seasonal work in lowland Scotland and the north of England as a geographical extension of 'hiring out' practices that were customary among impoverished coastal communities throughout nineteenth and early twentieth centuries. The latter 'hired out' children, some as young as ten years old, to local farmers and other employers in an effort to supplement meagre family incomes in coastal and upland districts where opportunities for paid-employment for grown adults were few and far between. Their poverty, like their survival strategies, tended to identify them with the travelling poor, who similarly looked on a nomadic way of life as a strategy for survival that was infinitely preferable to a sedentary life of the impoverishment in urban and rural Ireland.

Writing shortly before World War I, Arthur Griffith stated that 'the number of public men in Ireland who realise that the sea fisheries of this country could be an industry second only to agriculture might be counted on one hand'. He went on outline his vision of a national government that would make Ireland's sea fisheries 'and other dependent industries' yield £3 million in the space of ten years. Griffith also affirmed that 'a hundred thousand people would find employment in connection with our sea fisheries, and four thousand people would gain a comfortable livelihood through them'.[35] In the event, of course, Griffith, who was President of Dáil Éireann for the short period from January 1922 until his death on 12 August of the same year, never lived long enough to see his vision of a vibrant maritime Ireland come to fruition. Yet he was unique among Irish statesmen in his appreciation of the role that sea fishing and related industries could contribute to the national wealth. As John de Courcy Ireland rather simplistically put it, 'had he survived, fishing would surely not have been allowed to slip back again from the crested years of hope' that characterised the opening decade of the century, to 'the trough of depression where it was to lie inert for so long'. When the new state was founded, a minister of fisheries was indeed appointed, but his duties were purely administrative. He devoted his early years in power uniting under one government department the two bodies that had been concerned with fisheries, namely the fishery wing of the Congested Districts Board, which was dissolved in 1923, and the fishery branch of the Department of Agriculture and Technical Instruction. When the Department of Fisheries emerged in June 1924, it had a much less important role than that envisaged by Griffith. In the event, it was charged with the administration of rural industries, 'an early sign that the government of the day was not concerned to inaugurate a single-minded campaign of fishery development'.[36] The country's sea fisheries were subsequently downgraded, and for decades afterwards 'they were shuffled between the Departments of Lands and Agriculture as a minor appendage of one or the other'. As far as the leaders of the new Ireland were concerned, sea fisheries 'had as their chief apparent function the provision of a parliamentary secretaryship, to be held for a short period by ambitious politicians serving their junior apprenticeship on the lowest rung of the hierarchical ladder'. In 1929, the vocational classes in elementary fishery training were actually discontinued. This was followed by the ending of the subsidies paid to a select number of industrial schools for instruction in boat-building. Apprenticeships to encourage young men from fish-curing districts to learn skills of coopering (useful in the manufacture of fish barrels) were also abolished. By the late 1920s, scientific research on Ireland's teeming sea fisheries had come to an end. As de Courcy Ireland also pointed out, the Fisheries Branch of the Department of Lands and Fisheries did not even possess a laboratory until 1950.[37] In 1934, the May issue of the *Catholic Bulletin* reported that Ireland's sea fisheries were 'in a most lamentable plight' and showed 'little or no sign of recovery, still less of progress'. In attributing this solely to 'foreign' exploitation of the country's resources, it went on to state that 'our seas are despoiled by foreign craft, systematically, even recklessly'.[38] Describing the late 1920s through to the mid-1970s as the 'rock-bottom years' for the Irish mackerel fishery, Molloy has argued that these years were

> barren for many sectors of the fishing industry, with the mackerel fishery being particularly affected. Export markets had disappeared, the home market was very limited and the entire mackerel fishery appeared to be

almost non-existent. Apart from catch statistics, the mackerel fishery was not even mentioned in many of the annual reports of the Department. Between 1928 and 1934, mackerel landings declined from almost 9,500 tons to less than 900 tons. There was little or no prospect of selling mackerel in the US because of heavy landings by the local fleet, an emerging taste for mackerel fillets, and the imposition of a two-dollar tariff per barrel on imported fish. In 1934, the main port for the autumn mackerel fishery was Loughshinny, Co. Dublin. Although no longer a fishing port, Loughshinny was once home to many famous boats and fishing families. The annual report for 1935 states that despite a slight improvement in the landings in 1935, prices had collapsed completely. In the west-Kerry strongholds of the mackerel fishery, the fishermen were only paid about ten old pennies per hundred and this was very little after they had met the charges for cartage of the fish to Dingle ... The situation was so bad that later in the season a bounty of 25 per cent *ad valorem* was paid on consignments of cured mackerel that were sent to markets other than Britain, together with a bounty of 10 per cent *ad valorem* of fresh mackerel dispatched to British markets ... During the 1950s, the mackerel fishery continued in a very poor state and was at rock bottom. Catches fluctuated between 600 tons in 1955 and about 1,700 tons in 1958. The shoals remained offshore out of reach of the local boats, and the entire fishery was hit by a lack of markets, boats and fish.[39]

Writing on the missed opportunities resulting from lack of state investment in sea fisheries in the early years of independence, de Courcy Ireland also stated that

> In the 1920s, Irish sea-fishermen concentrated on the fluctuating herring and mackerel shoals, and only a small minority kept a tiny inshore fishery alive based on plaice, cod, haddock and whiting, and on the traditional shell fisheries. Had these men had the backing of up-to-date research, and had new entrants into the industry had full training, the foundations would have been laid of a fishing industry so prosperous that today we would probably be able to play a leading role in developing a Common Market fisheries policy.[40]

In the event, the numbers engaged in fishing declined steadily throughout the 1930s and 1940s. In 1936, there were an estimated 1,815 full-time fishermen and

5,920 'occasional fishermen' in the twenty-six counties. By 1938, these figures had dropped to 1,463 and 5,888 respectively. In 1936, the country's fishing fleet consisted of a mere ninety vessels of fifteen tons and upward, and 1,551 fishing craft under fifteen tons weight. By 1938, there were only eighty-one vessels in the fifteen tons or more category, and 1,409 boats of under fifteen tons. At the outbreak of World War II, there was no clearly defined government policy on sea fisheries in Ireland. Despite the high prices paid for fish in the war years, the number of full-time fishermen increased only slightly, to reach 1,925 in 1944, and fell off to 1,888 in the following year. By 1945, however, those designated as 'occasionals' or part-time fishermen numbered 8,191, an increase of around 40 per cent on the immediate pre-War figures. Writing in the *Journal of the Marine Institute* in 1946, a member of the Sea Fisheries Association, founded in 1925, summed up the wartime achievements of the country's fishermen as follows:

> Our people are willing and anxious to increase production so long as there is a reasonable prospect of securing a fair return on their labours. The attainment of such conditions, save as a temporary consequence of two world wars, has, unfortunately, not proved feasible in our times; but this should not be so.[41]

This pretty much reflected the status of the Irish fishing industry throughout the first half of the twentieth century, and quite clearly any proper analysis of developments since then would require much more space than is available here. Nevertheless, we can draw a number of conclusions about the comparative under-development of the industry since the foundation of the state. We can begin by recognising that governments clearly are large investors and important regulators of social and economic activity in all state-centred societies. Consequently, their regional policies have considerable impact upon spatial variations in levels of social and economic well-being. This raises intriguing questions regarding the role of the state in the spatial redistribution of income and employment. In Ireland, as in a number of other western democracies, politicians have frequently been elected by territorial constituencies and are often held accountable to them at election times. This, in turn, suggests that political parties and governments also *legitimise* their control over states in *regional* as well as social and political contexts.[42] Thus, they are frequently compelled to consider their political futures and the wishes of their electorate when formulating and implementing policies that have overt regional and social consequences. Few are willing to implement policies that can be justified solely on the grounds of economic rationality, if such policies meet with opposition from crucial sectors of their electorate. The symbiotic and volatile relationship that binds political parties to their electorates in societies experiencing regional decline or growth often makes the task of creating harmony between different sectors an imperative one. Consequently, there has been a tendency to see the state either as a referee seeking to resolve conflicting interests between opposing parties (the pluralist perspective), or as representative of the conscious effort of powerful economic interests to redistribute and accumulate resources in their favour (the elitist perspective). It is possible to propose an alternative perspective that regards the state as the propagator and enforcer of socially based hegemonies and specific sets of dominant practices that provide the rules governing the operation of social and economic life, including economic decision-making. In Ireland's case, this has meant that successive governments in the past have been able to prioritise industry, agriculture, tourism and the financial sector without having to worry about the level of opposition that this would engender in marginalised fishing communities. For a whole range of historical reasons already discussed in this study, fishing communities were pushed to the political as well as the geographical margins of the nation state.

Notes

CHAPTER ONE *The neglect of the maritime in Irish history*

1 Basil Greenhill, *The archaeology of boats and ships* (London, 1995), p. 19.
2 Jim Mac Laughlin, *Re-imagining the nation state: the contested terrains of nation-building* (London, 2001); Ethel Crowley, *Land matters: power struggles in rural Ireland* (Dublin, 2006).
3 Cecil Woodham-Smith, *The Great Hunger* (London, 1974), p. 285.
4 Ibid., p. 289.
5 Hely Dutton, *A statistical survey of County Galway* (Dublin, 1824), p. 390.
6 Ibid., p. 392.
7 Wallop Brabazon, *The deep-sea and coast fisheries of Ireland, with suggestions for the working of a fishing company* (London, 1848), p. 28.
8 John Bowles-Daly, *Glimpses of Irish industry* (London, 1889), p. 34.
9 Ibid., p. 45.   10 Ibid., p. 47.
11 J.P. Doyle, *Old Ireland improved and made new* (London, 1881), p. 233.
12 George O'Brien, *An economic history of Ireland in the seventeenth century* (Dublin, 1918), p. 82.
13 W.E.H. Lecky, *Ireland in the eighteenth century* (London, 1829), vol. i, pp 339–40.
14 Emyr Estyn Evans, *Irish folk ways* (London, 1967), p. 218.
15 Ibid., p. 242.   16 Ibid., p. 221.
17 Sam Hanna Bell, *The December Bride* (Belfast, 1975).
18 John Derricke, *The Image of Irelande, with a discoverie of woodkarne*, ed. John Small (Belfast, 1985).
19 D.B. Quinn, *The Elizabethans and the Irish* (Ithaca, NY, 1966), p. 104; Fintan Cullen, *Visual politics: the representation of Ireland, 1750–1930* (Cork, 1997), pp 5–11.
20 Mac Laughlin, *Re-imagining the nation state*, p. 60.
21 David Richards, *Masks of difference: cultural representation in literature, anthropology and art* (Cambridge, 1994), p. 134.
22 Jim Mac Laughlin, 'The gypsy as "other" in European society', *The European legacy*, 4 (1999), p. 40.
23 Jim Mac Laughlin, 'European gypsies and the historical geography of loathing', *Review Journal of the Fernand Braudel Center*, 22 (1999), p. 33.
24 J.B. Hochstrasser, *Still life and trade in the Dutch Golden Age* (New Haven, 2007), p. 37.
25 Peter Murray, 'Representations of Ireland in *The Illustrated London News*' in Peter Murray (ed.), *Whipping the herring: survival and celebration in nineteenth century Irish art* (Cork, 2006), pp 230–56; Tom Dunne, 'The dark side of the Irish landscape: depictions of the rural poor, 1760–1850' in Murray (ed.), *Whipping the herring* (2006), pp 46–61.
26 Máire de Paor, 'Irish antiquarian artists' in Adele Dalsimer (ed.), *Visualizing Ireland: national identity and the pictorial tradition* (Winchester, MA, 1993), p. 120.
27 Kevin O'Neill, 'Looking at pictures: art and artfulness in colonial Ireland' in Dalsimer (ed.), *Visualizing Ireland*, p. 56.
28 Ibid., p. 57.
29 Raymond Gillespie, 'Describing Dublin: Francis Place's visit, 1698–1699' in Dalsimer (ed.), *Visualizing Ireland*, p. 99.
30 Fintan Cullen, *The Irish face* (London, 2004), pp 33–51.
31 L.P. Curtis, *Apes and angels: the Irishman in Victorian caricature* (Newton Abbot, Devon, 1971), pp 29–57.
32 Martin McLoone, *Irish film: the emergence of a contemporary cinema* (London, 2000), p. 20.
33 Julie A. Stevens, *The Irish scene in Somerville and Ross* (Dublin, 2007), pp 171–85; Gifford Lewis, *Somerville and Ross: the world of the Irish R.M.* (London, 1987), pp 162–9.

34 Kevin Rockett, Luke Gibbons and John Hill, *Cinema in Ireland* (London, 1988), p. 230.
35 Jim Mac Laughlin, 'Looking at landscapes' in Jim Mac Laughlin (ed.), *Donegal: the making of a northern county* (Dublin, 2007), p. 22.
36 Peadar O'Donnell, *Islanders* (Dublin, 1928); Peadar O'Donnell, *Proud island* (Dublin, 1988).
37 Peter Hegarty, *Peadar O'Donnell* (Cork, 1999), p. 23.
38 Robert Lynd in O'Donnell, *Islanders* (Cork, 1977), p. 6.
39 Hegarty, *Peadar O'Donnell*, p. 45.
40 Julian Campbell, 'Frederick William Burton' in Murray, *Whipping the herring*, p. 154.
41 Julian Campbell, 'Aloysius O'Kelly' in Murray, *Whipping the herring*, p. 218.
42 Julian Campbell, 'Samuel Lover' in Murray, *Whipping the herring*, p. 214.
43 Bruce Arnold, *Jack Yeats* (New York, 1998), p. 129.
44 Paul Henry, *An Irish portrait* (London, 1951), p. 34.
45 Arnold, *Jack Yeats*, pp 192–6.
46 Ibid., p. 198.   47 Ibid., p. 185.
48 J.M. Synge, *The playboy of the western world* (Dublin, 1907); J.M. Synge, *The tinker's wedding* (Dublin, 1904); J.M. Synge, *In Wicklow, west Kerry and Connemara* (Dublin, 1980).
49 J.F. Knapp, 'Primitivism and empire: John Synge and Paul Gauguin', *Comparative Literature*, 12 (1983), p. 59.
50 J.M. Synge, *The vagrants of County Wicklow* (Dublin, 1910).
51 Frank Keogh, 'In Gorumna Island', *The New Ireland Review*, 9 (1898), p. 38.
52 J.M. Synge, *Collected works: prose* (London, 1982), pp 166–88.
53 Ibid., p. 173.
54 Daniel Corkery, *Hidden Ireland: a study of Gaelic Munster in the eighteenth century* (Dublin, 1924).
55 Mac Laughlin, *Re-imagining the nation state*, pp 84–8.
56 Friedrich Ratzel, *Politische geographie* (Munich, 1897); Friedrich Ratzel, 'The laws of the spatial growth of states' in R.E. Kasperson and J.V. Minghi (eds), *The structure of political geography* (Chicago, 1969); Ellen Churchill Semple, *Influences of geographical environment on the basis of Ratzel's system of anthropo-geography* (New York, 1911); Jim Mac Laughlin, 'State-centred social science and the anarchist critique: ideology in political geography', *Antipode*, 18:1 (1986), pp 11–38.
57 Victor Kiernan, *The lords of humankind* (London, 1972).
58 Eric Wolf, *Europe and the peoples without history* (Berkeley, CA, 1982).
59 Mac Laughlin, 'State-centred social science', pp 14–21.

CHAPTER TWO *'Marauding seafarers' versus 'settled farmers': the archaeology of Irish fishing*

1 Jonathan Adams and Katherine Holman, *Scandinavia and Europe, 800–1350: contact, conflict and coexistence* (Turnhout, Belgium, 2004); Anne Norgard Jorgensen et al. (eds), *Marine warfare in northern Europe: technology, organisation, logistics and administration, 500BC–1500AD* (Copenhagen, 2002); James Hines, Alan Lane and Michael Redknap (eds), *Land, sea and home* (London, 2004).
2 Edward W. Fox, *History in geographic perspective: the other France* (New York, 1975), pp 33–9.
3 Eric Wolf, *Sons of the shaking earth* (New York, 1972), pp 23–45; Maurice Dobb, *Studies in the development of capitalism* (London, 1975), pp 3–12.
4 J.P. Doyle, *Old Ireland improved and made new* (London, 1881), p. 91.
5 Christopher Moriarty, 'Fish and fisheries' in J.W. Wilson (ed.), *Nature in Ireland: a scientific and cultural history* (Dublin, 1997), p. 283.
6 Laurence Flanagan, *Ancient Ireland* (Dublin, 1998), p. 20.
7 Brian Lacey, 'Prehistoric and Early Christian settlement in Donegal' in William Nolan et al. (eds), *Donegal: history and society* (Dublin, 1995), p. 16.
8 Geraldine Stout, 'Wexford in prehistory' in Kevin Whelan and William Nolan (eds), *Wexford: history and society* (Dublin, 1987), p. 3.
9 Peter Woodman, 'Mount Sandel' in Brian Lalor (ed.), *Encyclopaedia of Ireland* (Dublin, 2003), p. 745.

10 J.P. Mallory and T.E. McNeill, *The archaeology of Ulster* (Belfast, 1991), p. 49.

11 Lacey, 'Prehistoric and Early Christian Donegal', p. 4.

12 Peter Woodman, 'The exploitation of Ireland's coastal resources: a marginal resource through time?' in Manuel Gonzalez Morales and G.A. Clark (eds), *The Mesolithic of the Atlantic facade* (Tempe, AZ, 2004), p. 45.

13 Ibid., p. 47.

14 Margaret McCarthy 'Archaeozoological studies of early medieval Munster' in Michael Monk and John Sheehan (eds), *Early Medieval Munster: archaeology, history and society* (Cork, 1998), p. 61.

15 Frank Mitchell, *The Irish landscape* (London, 1976), pp 100–5.

16 G.F. Mitchell, 'Further early kitchen middens in Co. Louth', *Journal of the County Louth Archaeological and Historical Society,* 12 (1949), pp 14–20.

17 Mitchell, *Irish landscape*, p. 101.

18 Peter Woodman, *Excavations at Ferriter's Cove, 1983–1995: last foragers, first farmers in the Dingle Peninsula* (Bray, 1999).

19 Mitchell, *Irish landscape*, p. 104.

20 Ibid., p. 103. 21 Ibid., p. 104.

22 Regina Sexton, *A short history of Irish food* (Cork, 2001), p. 26.

23 S.P. Ó Ríordáin, *Antiquities of the Irish countryside* (London, 1953); S.P. Ó Ríordáin, 'Lough Gur excavations: Neolithic and Bronze-Age houses on Knockadoon', *Proceedings of the Royal Irish Academy,* 51 (Dublin, 1954).

24 Fergus Kelly, *Early Irish farming* (Dundalk, 2000), pp 287–8.

25 A.E.J. Went, 'Irish fishing spears', *Journal of the Royal Society of Antiquaries of Ireland,* 82 (1952), p. 111.

26 Aidan O'Sullivan, 'Last foragers or first farmers?', *Archaeology Ireland,* 11:2 (1997), pp 14–16.

27 P. Mellars, 'Excavation and economic analysis of Mesolithic shell middens on the Island of Oronsay' in L.M. Thoms (ed.), *Early man in the Scottish landscape* (Edinburgh, 1978), pp 43–61.

28 Moriarty, 'Fish and fisheries', pp 283–4.

29 Peter Woodman, 'A narrow blade Mesolithic site at Glynn, Co. Antrim', *Ulster Journal of Archaeology,* 40 (1977), pp 12–20.

30 James Fairley, *Irish whales and whaling* (Belfast, 1984), pp 96–7.

31 Ibid., p. 99.

32 William O'Brien, 'Prehistoric human settlement in Killarney' in Jim Larner (ed.), *Killarney: history and heritage* (Cork, 2005), pp 3.

33 Woodman, *Excavations at Ferriter's Cove*, p. 15.

34 O'Brien, 'Prehistoric human settlement in Killarney', pp 2–5.

35 Adam Lynch, 'Man and environment in south-west Ireland', *British Archaeological Reports,* 85 (London, 1981).

36 Elizabeth Shee Twohig and Margaret Ronayne (eds), *Past perceptions: the prehistoric archaeology of south-west Ireland* (Cork, 1993).

37 James R. Coull, *The sea fisheries of Europe: an economic geography* (London, 1972), pp 29–37.

38 Kelly, *Early Irish farming*, pp 287–90.

39 A.E.J. Went, 'An ancient fish-weir at Ballynatray, Co. Waterford, Ireland', *Antiquity,* 25 (1951), pp 32–5.

40 Went, 'Irish fishing spears'; A.E.J. Went, 'Fish weirs of River Erne', *Journal of the Royal Society of Antiquaries of Ireland,* 75 (1945), pp 213–23.

41 Kelly, *Early Irish farming*, p. 288.

42 Melanie McQuade 'Gone fishing', *Archaeology Ireland,* 22:1 (2008), pp 8–11.

43 Maria FitzGerald, 'Catch of the day at Clowanstown, Co. Meath', *Archaeology Ireland,* 21:4 (2007), pp 12–15.

44 Evans, *Irish folk ways*, pp 233–40; Flanagan, *Ancient Ireland*, pp 19–22.

45 James Hornell, *British coracles and Irish curraghs* (London, 1938), p. 213.

46 Phillip Marsden, 'Ships of the Roman period and after in Britain' in G.F. Bass (ed.), *History of seafaring* (London, 1972), pp 129–78.

47 John de Courcy Ireland, *Ireland's sea fisheries* (Dublin, 1981), p. 9.
48 Michael McCaughan, 'Irish vernacular boats and their European connections', *Ulster Folklife*, 24 (1978), p. 5.
49 Ibid., p. 11.
50 John O'Donovan (ed.), *Annals of the kingdom of Ireland* (1856), p. 267.
51 John Sheehan et al., 'A Viking-Age maritime haven: a reassessment of the island settlement at Beginish, Co. Kerry', *Journal of Irish Archaeology*, 10 (2001), p. 108.
52 McCarthy, 'Early Medieval Munster', p. 62.
53 Jenny White Marshall and Claire Walsh, 'Illaunloughan: life and death on a small Early Medieval monastic site', *Archaeology Ireland*, 8:4 (1994), pp 25–8.
54 Manus O'Donnell, *The life of Colum Cille* (Dublin, 1994), pp 89–91.
55 McCaughan, 'Irish vernacular boats', pp 3–4.
56 Earl of Belmore, 'Ancient maps of Enniskillen and its environs', *Ulster Journal of Archaeology*, ser. 2, vol. 2 (1896), pp 218–43.
57 James Hornell, *British coracles and Irish curraghs* (London, 1938).
58 J.T. Gilbert, *Facsimiles of national manuscripts of Ireland* (Dublin, 1874–84).
59 James Coull, *Sea fisheries of Scotland* (Edinburgh, 1996), pp 33–41.
60 R.M. Black (ed.), *Society of free fishermen* (Edinburgh, 1951).
61 H.B. Clarke, Máire Ní Mhaonaigh and Raghnall Ó Floinn (eds), *Ireland and Scandinavia in the early Viking Age* (Dublin, 1998).
62 Aidan O'Sullivan, 'Harvesting the waters', *Archaeology Ireland*, 8:1 (1996), pp 10–12.
63 Aidan O'Sullivan et al., 'Medieval fish-traps in Strangford Lough, Co. Down', *Archaeology Ireland*, 11:1 (1997), pp 36–8.
64 Maurice Lenihan, *The history of Limerick* (Cork, 1886), p. 231.
65 Belmore, 'Ancient maps of Enniskillen', p. 220.
66 O'Sullivan, 'Last foragers or first farmers?', p. 15.
67 O'Sullivan et al., 'Medieval fish-traps', pp 36–8.
68 Oliver Rackham, *Woodlands* (London, 2007), p. 64.
69 O'Sullivan et al., 'Medieval fish-traps', p. 37.
70 Colmán Ó Clabaigh, 'Cistercians' in Lalor (ed.), *Encyclopaedia of Ireland*, p. 200.
71 O'Sullivan, 'Harvesting the waters'; A.E.J. Went, 'The pursuit of salmon in Ireland', *Proceedings of the Royal Irish Academy* 63C6 (1962–4), pp 191–244.
72 Eoin Mac Neill, *Early Irish laws and institutions* (Dublin, 1934), pp 36–41; Eoin MacNeill *Celtic Ireland* (Dublin, 1921), pp 67–71.
73 Mac Neill, *Early Irish laws*, p. 34.
74 Joseph Brady and Anngret Simms, *Dublin through space and time* (Dublin, 2001), pp 46–8.
75 J.D. Richards, *The Vikings* (Oxford, 2005), pp 1–7; J.D. Richards, *Viking-Age England* (London, 2000); Edmund Christiansen, *The Norsemen in the Viking Age* (London, 2002).
76 Norgard Jorgensen et al. (eds), *Maritime warfare*; Hines et al. (eds), *Land, sea and home*.
77 Billy Colfer, 'Medieval Wexford', *Journal of Wexford Historical Society*, 13 (1990–1), pp 5–29; Edward Culleton, 'The rise and fall of Norse Wexford', *Journal of the Wexford Historical Society*, 14 (1992), pp 151–9.
78 Dáibhí Ó Cróinín, *Early Medieval Ireland, 400–1200* (London, 1992), pp 260–71.
79 Linzi Simpson, 'Excavations on the southern side of the medieval town at Ship Street little, Dublin' in Seán Duffy (ed.), *Medieval Dublin* (Dublin, 2004), pp 9–51; see also John de Courcy Ireland, 'The Liffey banks in Dublin: early works of the private developers', *Dublin Historical Record*, 57:2 (2004), pp 146–51; H.B. Clarke (ed.), *Medieval Dublin* (Dublin, 1990); Charles Halliday, *The Scandinavian kingdom of Dublin* (Dublin, 1881).
80 H.B. Clarke, 'The early development of Dublin' in Christine Casey (ed.), *The buildings of Ireland* (London, 2005), pp 13–17.
81 A.J. Otway-Ruthven, 'The character of Norman settlement in Ireland', *Historical Studies*, 5 (1965), pp 75–84.
82 V.A. Hurley, *The early church in the south-west of Ireland: settlement and organisation* (Oxford, 1982).

83 Roy Tomlinson, 'Forests and woodland' in F.H.A. Aalen et al. (eds), *Atlas of the Irish rural landscape* (Cork, 1997), pp 122–33.

84 Colfer, 'Medieval Wexford', p. 7; Billy Colfer, 'Anglo-Norman settlement in Co. Wexford' in Kevin Whelan and William Nolan (eds), *Wexford: history and society* (1987), pp 65–101.

85 Brady and Simms, *Dublin through space and time*, p. 46

86 A.P. Smyth, *Scandinavian York and Dublin* (Dublin, 1979), p. 208.

87 Ibid., p. 210.

88 Colin Breen, 'The archaeology of early harbours and landing places in County Down, 800–1700AD', *Ulster Local Studies,* 19:2 (1998), pp 11–26.

89 Colfer, 'Anglo-Norman settlement in Co. Wexford', pp 89–92.

90 Breen, 'Archaeology of early harbours', pp 16–20.

91 R.H. Buchanan, 'Lecale Peninsula, Co. Down' in Aalen et al. (eds), *Atlas of Irish rural landscape*, p. 281.

92 W. Harris, *The ancient and present state of the County of Down* (Dublin, 1744), pp 34–65.

93 de Courcy Ireland, *Ireland's sea fisheries*, p. 9.

94 Lenihan, *History of Limerick*, p. 34.

95 Ibid., p. 52.

96 Richards, *The Vikings*, p. 72.

97 Ibid., p. 57.

98 de Courcy Ireland, *Ireland's sea fisheries*, p. 27.

99 Seán McGrail, *Ancient boats in north-western Europe* (London, 1998), p. 207.

CHAPTER THREE *Fishing and fish consumption in medieval Ireland*

1 Kelly, *Early Irish farming*, p. 286.

2 Ibid., p. 287. 3 Ibid., p. 289.

4 K.W. Nicholls, *Gaelic and Gaelicised Ireland in the Middle Ages* (Dublin, 1972); Patrick Heraughty, *Inishmurray: an ancient monastic island* (Dublin, 1982); Colmán Etchingham, *Church organisation in Ireland* (Maynooth, 1999).

5 Isabel Colegate, *A pelican in the wilderness: hermits, solitaries and recluses* (London, 2002), p. 104.

6 Ibid., p. 525. 7 Ibid., p. 162.

8 Ó Cróinín, *Early Medieval Ireland*, p. 264; A. Walsh, *Scandinavian relations with Ireland during the Viking period* (Dublin, 1922), pp 14–16.

9 Ó Cróinín, *Early Medieval Ireland*, p. 264.

10 See Carl Sauer, *Northern mists* (Berkeley, CA, 1968), pp 6–9.

11 Fridtjof Nansen, *Farthest north, being a record of a voyage of discovery of the ship 'Fram', 1893–6* (Westminster, 1897), p. 187.

12 Sauer, *Northern mists*, p. 160.

13 Tim Robinson, *Stones of Aran* (London, 1990), p. 173.

14 Colfer, *Hook Peninsula*, p. 81.

15 H.A. Jefferies, *Cork: historical perspectives* (Dublin, 2004), p. 87.

16 Buchan, 'Lecale', p. 281.

17 Theodora Fitzgibbon, *A taste of Ireland: Irish traditional food* (London, 1968), p. 56.

18 Sarah Paston-Williams, *The art of dining* (London, 1989), p. 104.

19 James Joyce, *Ulysses* (1992), p. 516.

20 Fitzgibbon, *Taste of Ireland*, p. 96.

21 Kelly, *Early Irish farming*, p. 291.

22 Ibid., p. 302. 23 Ibid., pp 291–3.

24 P.W. Joyce, *Social history of ancient Ireland from earliest times to 1608* (London, 1893), pp 133–4.

25 Bill Irish, *Shipbuilding in Waterford* (Bray, 2005), pp 1–2.

26 Ibid., pp 2–5.

27 O'Sullivan, 'Harvesting the waters', p. 11.

28 Went, 'Galway fishery', pp 205–17.

29 Joyce, *Social history of ancient Ireland.*

30 Hugh Hencken, 'Lagore crannog: an Irish royal residence of the seventh to tenth centuries AD', *Proceedings of the Royal Irish Academy*, 53C1 (1950), p. 238.

31 Went, 'Galway fishery', pp 200–4; 'Irish fishing spears', pp 109–34.

32 Went, 'Fishing weirs of the River Erne', pp 214–15.

33 Went 'Eel fishing at Athlone', p. 151.

34 A.E.J. Went, 'Irish monastic fisheries', *Journal of the Cork Historical and Archaeological Society*, ser. 2, vol. 60 (1955), p. 50.

35 Kelly, *Early Irish farming*, p. 296.

36 Ibid., p. 289.

37 Went, 'Eel fishing at Athlone', pp 146–54.

38 Went, 'Irish monastic fisheries', p. 50.

39 Went, 'Fishing weirs of the River Erne', p. 219.

40 O'Neill, *Merchants and mariners*, p. 38.

41 H.D. Smith, *Shetland life and trade, 1550–1914* (Edinburgh, 1984); E.P. Thompson, *Albion's fatal tree* (London, 1977).

42 Lenihan, *History of Limerick*, p. 207.

43 Ibid., p. 53.   44 Ibid., p. 51.

45 L.M. Cullen, *The emergence of modern Ireland, 1600–1900* (London, 1981), p. 19.

46 James Lydon, *The lordship of Ireland in the Middle Ages* (Dublin, 1972), pp 19–21.

47 Ibid., p. 20.

48 Ibid., p. 47.

49 Cathal Cowan and Regina Sexton, *Ireland's traditional foods: an exploration of Irish local and typical food and drinks* (Dublin, 1997), p. 45.

50 Tom Fort, 'Fish in English history', *The Guardian*, 4 February 2004.

51 Kelly, *Early Irish farming*, p. 297.

52 Ibid., p. 286.

53 O'Neill, *Merchants and mariners*, pp 31–7.

54 Charles Doherty, *Exchange and trade in Early Medieval Ireland* (Dublin, 1980).

55 Colegate, *Pelican in the wilderness*, p. 102.

56 Peter Woodman, Robert Devoy and David Sleeman, *Occasional Publications of Irish Biogeography Society* (1986), pp 1–7.

57 J.J. O'Meara (ed.), *The topography of Ireland by Giraldus Cambrensis* (Dubin, 1951), p. 45.

58 Bríd Mahon, *Land of milk and honey* (Cork, 1991), pp 45–6.

59 David Cabot, *Ireland* (London, 1999), pp 211–15.

60 Fairley, *Irish whales and whaling*, pp 97–8.

61 Nichola Fletcher, *Charlemagne's tablecloth: a piquant history of feasting* (London, 2004), p. 47.

62 Lydon, *Ireland in the later Middle Ages*, p. 19.

63 Paston-Williams, *Art of dining*, p. 205.

64 Ibid., p. 174.

65 Fletcher, *Charlemagne's tablecloth*, pp 50–1.

66 Anne Chambers, *Eleanor, Countess of Desmond* (Dublin, 2000), p. 41.

67 Cullen, *Emergence of modern Ireland*, p. 155.

68 Ibid., pp 153–6.

69 Trevelyan, *English social history*, pp 204–5.

70 George Hill, *Plantation papers: a summary sketch of the great Ulster plantation in the year 1610* (Dublin, 1889), p. 307.

71 Paston-Williams, *Art of dining*, p. 111.

72 Mahon, *Land of milk and honey*, pp 2–3.

73 Fletcher, *Charlemagne's tablecloth*, pp 51–4.

74 Halliday, *Scandinavian kingdom of Dublin*, p. 244.

75 Moriarty, 'Fish and fisheries', p. 285.

76 Kelly, *Early Irish farming*, 287.
77 Ibid., pp 289–90.
78 Longfield, *Anglo-Irish trade*, p. 193.
79 Joyce, *Social history of ancient Ireland*, p. 430.
80 Ibid., p. 523.

CHAPTER FOUR *Exploitation of the marine and freshwater fisheries of pre-colonial Ireland*

1 Críostóir Mac Cárthaigh (ed.), *Traditional boats in Ireland: history, folklore and construction* (Cork, 2008); John Molloy, *The Irish mackerel fishery: the making of an industry* (Killarney, Co. Kerry, 2004); John Molloy, *Herring fisheries of Ireland* (Oranmore, Co. Galway, 2006); Fairley, *Irish whales and whaling*; Seamus Fitzgerald, *Mackerel and the making of Baltimore* (Dublin, 2002); Michael McCaughan and John Appleby (eds), *The Irish Sea* (Belfast, 1989).
2 McCaughan and Appleby (eds), *The Irish Sea*, p. 11.
3 de Courcy Ireland, *Ireland's sea fisheries*, p. 15.
4 T.J. Westropp, 'Early Italian maps of Ireland from 1300 to 1600, with notes on foreign settlers and trade', *Proceedings of the Royal Irish Academy*, 30C (1913), pp 361–428.
5 Buchanan, 'The Lecale Peninsula', p. 280.
6 Darren Mac Eiteagain, 'The Renaissance and the late medieval lordship of Tír Chonaill, 1461–1555' in William Nolan et al. (eds), *Donegal: history and society* (Dublin, 1995), pp 203–28.
7 Breen, 'Archaeology of early harbours', pp 17–19.
8 Des Ekin, *The stolen village* (Dublin, 2006), p. 240.
9 Quoted in Ekin, *Stolen village*, p. 55; see also W.F.T. Butler, *Gleanings from Irish history* (Dublin, 1925), pp 166–8.
10 Henri Pirenne, 'Stages in the social history of capitalism', *American Historical Review*, 19:3 (1914), pp 494–95.
11 Fairley, *Irish whales and whaling*, pp 38–9, 118–19.
12 Nicholls, *Gaelic and Gaelicised Ireland*, p. 144.
13 de Courcy Ireland, *Ireland's sea fisheries*, p. 19.
14 Diarmuid Ó Drisceoil and Donal Ó Drisceoil, *Serving a city: the story of Cork's English market* (Cork, 2005), pp 2–3.
15 Ekin, *Stolen village*, pp 54–64.
16 Brian Dornan, *Mayo's lost islands: the Inishkeas* (Dublin, 2000), p. 15.
17 Went, 'Galway fishery', p. 199.
18 de Courcy Ireland, *Ireland's sea fisheries*, p. 26.
19 M.D. O'Sullivan, 'Glimpses of the life of Galway merchants and mariners', *Journal of the Galway Archaeological and Historical Society*, 15 (1933), p. 131.
20 M.D. O'Sullivan, *Old Galway: history of a Norman colony in Ireland* (Cambridge, 1942), pp 399–405; O'Sullivan, 'Glimpses of life of Galway merchants', pp 129–33.
21 Went, 'Foreign fishing fleets', p. 21.
22 T.W. Fulton quoted in Molloy, *Irish mackerel fishery*, pp 31–2.
23 Molloy, *Irish mackerel fishery*, p. 32.
24 Terence O'Rorke, *History of Sligo: town and county* (Dublin, [1890]), p. 210.
25 Ibid., p. 35.
26 McGettigan, 'Tír Chonaill', pp 216–21.
27 O'Rorke, *Sligo*, p. 217.
28 Quoted in Moriarty, 'Fish and fisheries', pp 284–5.
29 Longfield, *Anglo-Irish trade*, pp 34–7.
30 Went, 'Irish hake fishery', p. 44.
31 Smith, *History of Cork*, p. 232.
32 Went, 'Irish hake fishery', p. 47.
33 Ibid., p. 48. 34 Ibid., p. 49. 35 Ibid., p. 43.

36 H.F. Hore, *An inquiry into the legislation, control and improvement of salmon and sea fisheries of Ireland* (London, 1850), p. 3.
37 Went, 'Foreign fishing fleets', p. 18.
38 Smith, *History of Cork*, p. 36.
39 Eamon Lankford, *Cape Clear Island: its people and landscape* (Cork, 1999), pp 36–7.
40 Henry Gilbard, *Discourse of Ireland* (London, 1572), p. 78.
41 Francis B. Head, *A fortnight in Ireland* (London, 1852), p. 96.
42 Longfield, *Anglo-Irish trade*, p. 58.
43 Molloy, *Herring fisheries*, pp 34–9.
44 O'Neill, *Merchants and mariners*, p. 26; Went, 'Foreign fishing fleets', p. 18.
45 O'Neill, *Merchants and mariners*, p. 36.
46 McGettigan, 'Tír Chonaill', p. 220.
47 Ibid., pp 214–16.
48 *Carew MSS, 1515–74*, p. 181.
49 Colin Breen, *The Gaelic lordship of the O'Sullivan Beare: a landscape cultural history* (Dublin, 2005), p. 117.
50 Went, 'Foreign fishing fleets', pp 17–18.
51 Lenihan, *History of Limerick*, p. 67.
52 Longfield, *Anglo-Irish trade*, p. 126.
53 Irish, *Shipbuilding in Waterford*, p. 4.
54 Ibid., p. 3.
55 O'Neill, *Merchants and mariners*, p. 34.
56 Went, 'Foreign fishing fleets', p. 25.
57 Walter Coppinger, *History of the Coppingers of Co. Cork* (London, 1884), pp 37–45; Ekin, *Stolen village*, p. 28.
58 Ibid., p. 34.
59 Smith, *County and city of Cork*, p. 262.
60 Lankford, *Cape Clear*, p. 52.
61 O'Rorke, *Sligo*, p. 119.
62 C.W.P. MacArthur, *Dunfanaghy's Presbyterian congregation and its times* (Dunfanaghy, Co. Donegal, 1978), p. 18.
63 Went, 'Foreign fishing fleets', p. 17.
64 O'Neill, *Merchants and mariners*, p. 38.
65 T.W. Moody, *The Londonderry Plantation, 1609–14* (Dublin, 1939), p. 44.
66 Hilary Kelleher, *An archaeological study of fish palaces of west Cork*, MA, UCC, 1995, p. 23.
67 Patrick O'Flanagan, 'Three hundred years of urban life: villages and towns in County Cork' in Patrick O'Flanagan and Neil Buttimer (eds), *Cork: history and society* (Dublin, 1993), pp 394–8.
68 Kelleher, *Fish palaces of west Cork*, p. 32.
69 Ekin, *Stolen village*, pp 32–4.
70 Jane H. Ohlmeyer, 'The Dunkirk of Ireland: Wexford privateers during the 1640s', *Journal of Wexford Historical Society*, 12 (1988–9), pp 23–49.
71 Nicholls, *Gaelic and Gaelicised Ireland*, p. 47.
72 Ibid., p. 145.
73 Colin Breen, 'Archaeology of early Harbours', pp 21–3; Breen, *Gaelic lordship of the O'Sullivan Beare*, pp 113–21; de Courcy Ireland, *Ireland's sea fisheries*, pp 16–27; O'Flanagan, 'Three hundred years of urban life', pp 398–9.
74 Seamus Fitzgerald, *Mackerel and the making of Baltimore* (Dublin, 1999), pp 23–32; Ekin, *Stolen village*, pp 19–23.
75 Breen, *Gaelic lordship of the O'Sullivan Beare* (Dublin, 2007), pp 92–6.
76 Mark Kurlansky, *Cod: a biography of the fish that changed the world* (London, 1998), pp 28–9.
77 Ibid., p. 54.
78 John Mannion, 'A transatlantic merchant fishery: Richard Welsh of New Ross and the Sweetmans of Newbawn in Newfoundland, 1734–1862' in Kevin Whelan and William Nolan (eds), *Wexford: history and society* (Dublin, 1987), pp 373–421.

79 Ibid., pp 374–5. 80 Ibid., 376. 81 Ibid., p. 375.
82 O'Brien, *Ireland in the seventeenth century*, pp 93–4.
83 David B. Quinn, *The Irish parliamentary subsidy in the fifteenth and sixteenth centuries* (Dublin, 1935), p. 139.
84 Went, 'Foreign fishing fleets', p. 28.
85 O'Neill, *Merchants and mariners*, p. 32.
86 Gilbard, *Discourse of Ireland*, p. 56.
87 Butler, *Gleanings from Irish History*, p. 167.
88 O'Brien, *Ireland in the seventeenth century*, p. 49.
89 Kelleher, *Fish palaces of west Cork*, p. 39.
90 Quoted in O'Brien (ed.), *Advertisements for Ireland*, p. 32.
91 O'Brien, *Ireland in the seventeenth century*, p. 52.
92 Dobb, *Studies in the development of capitalism*, p. 90.

CHAPTER FIVE *Imposing order on the maritime fringe*

1 Rose-Marie Hagen and Rainer Hagen, 'The merchants of Venice' in *Fifteenth-century paintings* (Koln, 2001), pp 175–6.
2 Cullen, *Emergence of modern Ireland*, pp 153–5.
3 Norbert Elias, *The civilizing process* (Oxford, 1985), p. 3.
4 Fernand Braudel, *The structures of everyday life* (London, 1985), p. 54.
5 Alain Corbin, *The foul and the fragrant* (New York, 1986), pp 93–100.
6 Patrick Suskind, *Perfume* (London, 1986), p. 3.
7 Maria Kelly, *The great dying: the Black Death in Dublin* (Dublin, 2003), pp 28–9.
8 Ibid., p. 33.
9 Corbin, *Foul and fragrant*, pp 43–5.
10 Ibid., p. 62.
11 Ó Drisceoil and Ó Drisceoil, *Serving a city*, pp 12–13.
12 A.F. O'Brien, 'Politics, economy and society: the development of Cork and the Irish south coast region, *c.*1170 to 1583' in Flanagan and Buttimer (eds), *Cork*, pp 93–4.
13 Christine Casey, *Buildings of Ireland: Dublin* (London, 2005), pp 316, 371–2.
14 Edmund Curtis, *Irish historical documents* (London, 1943), p. 205.
15 Longfield, *Anglo-Irish trade*, p. 163.
16 Smith, *History of Cork*, p. 143.
17 Ibid., p. 149.
18 Smith, *History of Cork*, p. 301.
19 Edmund Downey, *The story of Waterford* (Waterford, 1914), p. 107.
20 Ibid., p. 112. 21 Ibid., p. 114. 22 Ibid., p. 119. 23 Ibid., p. 121.
24 Longfield, *Anglo-Irish trade*, p. 78.
25 Kelly, *Early Irish farming*, pp 288–91.
26 O'Sullivan, *History of Cork*, p. 101.
27 O'Sullivan, *Old Galway*, pp 401–9; O'Sullivan, 'Life of Galway merchants and mariners', pp 134–6.
28 James Hardiman, *The history of the town and county of Galway* (Galway, 1958), p. 93.
29 Ibid., p. 218.
30 Downey, *Waterford*, pp 102–4.
31 Corbin, *Foul and fragrant*, pp 92–3; see also Jim Mac Laughlin, 'Pestilence on their backs, famine in their stomachs: the racial construction of Irishness in the Victorian Britain' in Colin Graham and Richard Kirkland (eds), *Cultural theory and Ireland* (London, 1999), pp 50–76.
32 Casey, *Dublin*, pp 371–2.
33 Clark, 'Early development of Dublin' in Craig, *Dublin*, pp 11–12.
34 Colfer, 'Medieval Wexford', pp 9–10.
35 Lydon, *Ireland in the later Middle Ages*, pp 15–17.

36 Ibid., p. 16.   37 Ibid., p. 17.   38 Ibid., pp 15–20.

39 T.K. Moylan, 'Poverty, pigs and pestilence in medieval Dublin', *Dublin Historical Record*, 7 (1956), p. 155.

40 David McNally, 'Tudor Dublin's dung problem', *Dublin Historical Record*, 16 (1992), p. 66.

41 Ibid., p. 35.

42 Corbin, *Foul and fragrant*, p. 117.

43 Moylan, 'Poverty, pigs and pestilence', p. 157.

44 Ibid., p. 33.

45 Quoted in Moody, *The Londonderry Plantation*, p. 253.

46 Corbin, *Foul and fragrant*, p. 110.

47 Ekin, *Stolen village*, p. 3.

48 Moylan, 'Poverty, pigs and pestilence', p. 156.

49 O'Sullivan, *Old Galway*, p. 405.

50 N.J.G. Pounds, 'Cornish fish cellars', *Antiquity*, 18 (1944), p. 38.

51 Dawn Williams, 'Whipping the herring out of town' in Peter Murray (ed.), *Whipping the herring*, p. 68.

52 Furlong, 'Life in Wexford', p. 151.

53 Ibid., pp 17–18.

54 Lydon, *Ireland in the later Middle Ages*, pp 23–5.

55 Corbin, *Foul and fragrant*, p. 132.

56 Ibid., pp 34–76.

57 Quoted in Jim Rees, *Arklow: the story of a town* (Arklow, 2004), p. 307.

58 J.H. Tuke, *A visit to Connacht in the autumn of 1848* (Dublin, 1848).

59 Hardiman, *Galway*, p. 304.

60 Head, *A fortnight in Ireland*, p. 92.

61 Ibid., p. 282.

62 Lenihan, *Limerick*, p. 34.

63 McGettigan, 'Tír Chonaill', pp 206–8.

64 Phillip Robinson, *The plantation of Ulster* (Dublin, 1984), p. 175.

65 Anne Chambers, *Granuaile: Ireland's pirate queen* (Dublin, 2003), p. 112.

66 Marcus Rediker, *Villains of all nations: Atlantic pirates in the Golden Age* (London, 2004), pp 104–22.

67 Chambers, *Granuaile*, p. 132.

68 Ibid., p. 96.

69 O'Sullivan, *Old Galway*, pp 408–11.

70 Ibid., pp 58–60.   71 Ibid., p. 56.

72 Ekin, *Stolen village*, p. 29.

73 Ibid., p. 31.

74 Ohlmeyer, 'Dunkirk of Ireland', p. 28.

75 Ibid., p. 25.   76 Ibid., p. 29.   77 Ibid., p. 28.

78 Rediker, *Between the devil and the deep blue sea* (Cambridge, 1992), p. 112.

79 Ibid., p. 117.

80 Colman O'Mahony, 'Press-gangs off the Cork Coast, 1755–1812', *Journal of the Cork Historical and Archaeological Society*, 21 (1996), p. 14; see also Eoghan Ó hAnnacháin, 'Men of the west in the galleys of France', *Journal of the Galway Historical and Archaeological Society*, 59 (2007), pp 37–45.

81 O'Mahony, *Press-gangs*, p. 17.

CHAPTER SIX *The maritime world of fishermen*

1 Robin Lane Fox, *The classical world* (London, 2005), pp 142–3.

2 Andrew Dalby, *Empires of pleasure: luxury and indulgence in the Roman world* (London, 2000), pp 15–17.

3 de Courcy Ireland, *Ireland's sea fisheries*, p. 9.

4 Sauer, *Northern mists*, p. 4.

5 Kelly, *Early Irish farming*, p. 292.

6 Sauer, *Northern mists*, pp 161–3.

7 Charles Boxer, *The Dutch seaborne empire* (London, 1965), p. 6.

8 Buchanan, 'Lecale'.

9 Sauer, *Northern mists*, p. 6.

10 Herbert Heaton, *Economic history of Europe* (London, 1964), pp 233–45; Hochstrasser, *Still life and trade*, pp 37–42.

11 Heaton, *Economic history*, pp 274–5; James Coull, *Fisheries of Europe* (London, 1972), pp 66–72; H.A. Innis, *Cod fisheries* (Toronto, 1978), pp 236–42; Kurlansky, *Cod*, pp 48–61.

12 Fernand Braudel, *The Mediterranean and the Mediterranean world in the age of Phillip II* (London, 1972), vol. i, pp 144–5.

13 Furlong, 'Life in Wexford port, 1600–1800', p. 150.

14 de Courcy Ireland, *Ireland's sea fisheries*, p. 25.

15 Buchanan, 'Lecale', p. 281; Breen, 'Archaeology of early harbours', p. 19.

16 Breen, 'Archaeology of early harbours', p. 14.

17 Westropp, 'Early Italian maps of Ireland', p. 365.

18 Breen, 'Archaeology of early harbours', p. 21.

19 Smith, *Dalkey*, pp 18–19.

20 *Preliminary survey of the ancient monuments of Northern Ireland* (Belfast, 1940), pp 40–2.

21 Longfield, *Anglo-Irish trade*, pp 35, 52; O'Brien, *Ireland in the seventeenth century*, pp 105–6.

22 Lenihan, *History of Limerick*, p. 215.

23 Ibid., p. 231.

24 O'Sullivan, *Old Galway*, p. 402.

25 Hardiman, *Galway*, p. 302.

26 Henry Inglis, *A journey throughout Ireland, during the spring, summer and autumn of 1834* (London, 1836), pp 214–15.

27 Mr and Mrs S.C. Hall, *Ireland: scenery, character etc* (London, 1841–3), p. 42.

28 Hardiman, *Galway*, p. 305.

29 *The Illustrated London News*, 31 January 1880.

30 *Black's guide to Galway, Clare and the west of Ireland* (London, 1888), p. 136.

31 Hardiman, *Galway*, pp 302–4; O'Dowd, *Down by the Claddagh*, p. 14.

32 Peadar O'Dowd, *Down by the Claddagh* (Galway, 1993), pp 15–16.

33 Ibid., p. 40.

34 Hardiman, *Galway*, p. 304.

35 Quoted in O'Dowd, *Down by the Claddagh*, p. 41.

36 An Oxonian, *A little tour in Ireland* (London, 1859), p. 116.

37 Anonymous, *A Frenchman's walk through Ireland* (Dublin, n.d.), p. 151.

38 H.L. Bayly, 'Statistical survey of Arklow', quoted in Rees, *Arklow*, p. 308.

39 Mannion, 'A transatlantic merchant fishery', pp 373–81.

40 Rediker, *Devil and the deep blue sea*, p. 164.

41 Ibid., p. 168.   42 Ibid., p. 178.

43 C. Levis, *Towelsail yawls: the lobsterboats of Heir Island and Roaringwater Bay* (Ardfield, Co. Cork, 2002), pp 23–5.

44 Hardiman, *Galway*, p. 304.

45 Robert Hughes, *Barcelona* (London, 1992), p. 161.

46 Ibid., p. 68.

47 Joseph Tomelty, *Red is the harbour light* (Belfast, 1983), p. 5.

48 Ibid., p. 158.

49 W.S. Green, *The sea fisheries of the south and south-west of Ireland* (Dublin, 1888), p. 45.

50 Rediker, *Devil and the deep blue sea*, p. 77.

51 Ibid., p. 43.

52 Arnold, *Jack Yeats*, p. 196.

53 Ibid., p. 153.

54 Strauss, *Petty*, p. 133.

55 Rediker, *Devil and the deep blue sea*, pp 193–7.
56 Robin Fox, *The Tory Islanders* (Cambridge, 1978), p. 130.
57 Hughes, *Barcelona*, p. 164.
58 Ibid., pp 163, 166.
59 Levis, *Towel sail yawls*, p. 18.
60 Hardiman, *Galway*, pp 306–7.
61 F.H.A. Aalen and Hugh Brody, *Gola: life and last days of an island community* (Cork, 1969), p. 97.
62 Neil Gunn, *The silver darlings* (London, 1999), pp 444–5.
63 O'Donnell, *Islanders*, p. 12.
64 O'Donnell, *Proud Island*, p. 8.
65 Kelleher, *Fish palaces of west Cork*, pp 71–5.
66 Rediker, *Villains of all nations*, p. 176.

CHAPTER SEVEN *Ireland's sea fisheries in the age of colonial expansion*

1   George Boyce, *Nationalism in Ireland* (London, 1991), pp 58–60.
2   R.J. Hunter, 'Sir Ralph Bingley: Ulster planter' in Peter Roebuck (ed.), *Plantation to partition* (Belfast, 1981), pp 14–16; William Macafee and V.I. Morgan, 'Population in Ulster, 1660–1760' in Peter Roebuck, *Plantation to partition*, pp 46–63.
3   Peter Gibbon, *The origins of Ulster Unionism* (Manchester, 1979), pp 13–17.
4   Colm Regan, 'Economic development in Ireland: the historical dimension', *Antipode*, 12:1 (1980), pp 3–4.
5   Kevin Whelan, 'Pre- and post-Famine landscape change' in Cathal Poirteir (ed.), *The Great Irish Famine* (Cork, 1995), p. 22.
6   Ibid., p. 24.
7   Evans, *Irish folk ways*, p. 46.
8   George Hill, *Facts from Gweedore* (Dublin, 1887), p. 16.
9   Donal MacPolin, *The Drontheim: forgotten sailing boat of the north Irish coast* (Dublin, 1992).
10 Timothy Collins, 'From hoekers to hookers: a survey of the literature and annotated bibliography on the origins of the Galway hooker', *Journal of the Galway Historical and Archaeological Society*, 53 (2001), pp 66–83.
11 K.H. Connell, 'Population of Ireland in the eighteenth century', *Economic History Review*, 15 (1946), pp 111–24.
12 Fernand Braudel, *The wheels of commerce* (London, 1982), pp 514–16.
13 Jim Mac Laughlin, 'The making of a northern county' in Mac Laughlin (ed.), *Donegal*, pp 1–21; Desmond Mc Court, 'Infield and outfield in Ireland', *Economic History Review*, 9 (1954–5), pp 369–76.
14 Buchanan, 'Lecale', pp 277–86.
15 Fairley, *Irish whales and whaling*, pp 122–30; A.E.J. Went, 'Pilchards in the south of Ireland', *Journal of the Cork Historical and Archaeological Society*, ser. 2, vol. 51 (1946), p. 138.
16 Louis Cullen, 'The port of New Ross: a comparative historical profile' in J. Dunne (ed.), *New Ross* (Ardvan, Co. Wexford, 2007), p. 243.
17 Ibid., p. 174.
18 Jim Mac Laughlin, 'Political arithmetic and the early origins of ethnic minorities' in Mac Laughlin, *Re-imagining the nation state*, pp 70–90.
19 Mac Laughlin, 'European gypsies', pp 31–60.
20 O'Dowd, *Down by the Claddagh*, p. 38.
21 Samuel Lewis, 'Cape Clear' in *Topographical Dictionary of Ireland* (London, 1837), vol. i, p. 249.
22 O'Dowd, *Down by the Claddagh*, p. 37.
23 O'Sullivan, *Economic history of Cork*, p. 128.
24 Ibid.
25 Quoted in Green, 'Sea fisheries', p. 374.

26 O'Neill, 'Trade and shipping in Irish Sea', p. 28.
27 Went, 'Foreign fishing fleets', p. 17.
28 Ekin, *Stolen island*, p. 60; Breen, *Gaelic lordship of O'Sullivan Beare*, pp 117–21.
29 *Carew MSS, 1515–74*, pp 422–3.
30 Went, 'Foreign fishing fleets', p. 20.
31 Longfield, *Anglo-Irish trade*, p. 44.
32 Ibid., p. 103.
33 George Hill, *An historical account of the plantation in Ulster* (Shannon, 1970), p. 130.
34 Mac Eiteagain, 'Tír Chonaill', pp 207–8.
35 Ibid., p. 210.
36 Hill, *Plantation in Ulster*, p. 62.
37 Ibid., pp 362, 374–7.
38 *Carew MSS, 1603–14*, p. 150.
39 Hill, *Plantation in Ulster*, p. 376.
40 Mac Laughlin, *Re-imagining the nation state*, p. 147.
41 Ibid., p. 100.
42 Florence O'Sullivan, *The history of Kinsale* (Cork, 1916), p. 112.
43 O'Brien, *Ireland in the seventeenth century*, p. 80.
44 Ibid., pp 193–4.
45 Cahal Dallat, 'Ice-houses', *Ulster Local Studies*, 13:2 (1991), pp 37–41.
46 Elizabeth David, *Harvest of the cold months: the social history of ice and ices* (London, 1994), p. xv.
47 Ibid., p. 184.
48 Richard Pococke, *A tour in Ireland in 1752* (London, 1891), p. 98.
49 *Ordnance survey memoirs of Ireland: parishes of County Londonderry* (Belfast, 1990), p. 112.
50 John Appleby, 'Merchants and mariners, pirates and privateers' in McCaughan and Appleby (eds), *Irish Sea*, p. 47.
51 Went, 'Irish fishing spears', p. 125.
52 Ibid.
53 A.E.J. Went, 'Historical notes on the oyster fisheries of Ireland', *Proceedings of the Royal Irish Academy*, 62c7 (1962), pp 197–8.
54 Mac Eiteagain, 'Tír Chonaill', p. 216.
54 Ekin, *Stolen village*, pp 31–6.
55 Kelleher, *Fish palaces of west Cork*, pp 12–14.
56 Went, 'Foreign fishing fleets', p. 21.
57 Ibid., p. 19.
58 *Carew MSS*, Description of Ireland (1614).
60 *Calendar of state papers, Ireland, 1666–9*, p. 132.
61 David Dickson, *Old World colony: Cork and south Munster, 1630–1830* (Cork, 2005), pp 19–21.
62 Dorothea Townsend, *The life and letters of the great earl of Cork* (London, 1904), p. vii.
63 Dickson, *Old World colony*, p. 21.
64 Mac Laughlin, 'Evolution of modern demography', pp 324–32.
65 Allesandro Roncaglia, *Petty: the origins of political economy* (Cardiff, 1985), p. 5.
66 D.B. Quinn, *The Elizabethans in Ireland* (Cornell, 1966), p. 126.
67 Eric Strauss, *Sir William Petty* (London, 1954), p. 25.
68 William Petty, *The political anatomy of Ireland* (Dublin, 1970), p. 117.
69 Ibid., p. 109.
70 E. Fitzmaurice, *The life of Sir William Petty* (London, 1895), pp 126–7.
71 Ibid., p. 133.
72 Smith, *History of Cork*, p. 219.
73 Quoted in Went, 'Pilchards in the south of Ireland', p. 141.
74 Smith, *History of Cork*, p. 206.
75 Moriarty, 'Fish and fisheries', pp 286–7.
76 Gerard Boate, *A natural history of Ireland* (Dublin, 1726), p. 41.

77 Ibid., p. 46.
78 Cullen, *Emergence of modern Ireland*, pp 140–5.
79 E.M. Crawford, 'Food and famine: diet in County Londonderry, 1820–1860' in G. O'Brien and W. Nolan (eds), *Derry and Londonderry: history and society* (Dublin, 1999), pp 519–36.
80 Mac Laughlin, 'Pestilence on their backs', pp 50–5.
81 Cullen, *Emergence of modern Ireland*, pp 147–51.
82 Mahon, *Land of milk and honey* (Cork, 1998), p. 43.
83 Joyce, *Ancient Ireland*, p. 103.
84 Went, 'Irish fishing spears', p. III.
85 Evans, *Irish folk ways*, pp 243–6.
86 Went, 'Irish fishing spears', pp 109–12.
87 Evans, *Irish folk ways*, p. 226.
88 Cullen, *Emergence of Modern Ireland*, p. 156.
89 Went, 'Oyster fisheries of Ireland', p. 196.
90 Pococke, *Tour*, p. 214.
91 Ibid., p. 198.
92 J.C. Walker, *An historical essay on the dress of the ancient and modern Irish* (Dublin, 1788), p. 20.
93 Arthur Young, *A tour in Ireland* (London, 1892), pp 80–2.
94 Cullen, *Emergence of modern Ireland*, pp 154–5.
95 Ibid.
96 Cullen, *Emergence of modern Ireland*, p. 155.
97 Anthony Marmion, *Ancient and modern history of maritime ports of Ireland* (London, 1855).
98 Went, 'The pursuit of salmon in Ireland', pp 191–244.
99 Smith, *History of Cork*, p. 257.
100 Cullen, *Emergence of modern Ireland*, pp 153–6.
101 Quoted in Mahon, *Land of milk and honey*, p. 44.
102 Longfield, *Anglo-Irish trade*, p. 41.
103 Lydon, *Ireland in later Middle Ages*, pp 15–19.
104 Síle Ní Chinneidhe, 'A view of Kilkenny city and county in 1790', *Journal of the Royal Society of Antiquaries of Ireland*, 114 (1976), p. 29.
105 Cullen, *Emergence of modern Ireland*, p. 146.
106 *The Folklore Journal* (1888), p. 47.
107 E.M. Crawford, 'Food and famine' in Pórtéir (ed.), *Great Irish Famine*, p. 60.

CHAPTER EIGHT *The coastal geography of sea fishing, 1750–1880*

1 *Southern reporter*, July 1823.
2 *Tenth report of the commissioners of the Irish fishery office* (Dublin, 1829), pp 55–6.
3 James Mac Parlan, *A statistical survey of County Donegal* (Dublin, 1802), p. 71.
4 R.J. Berry, *Islands* (London, 2009), p. 199.
5 Young, *Tour in Ireland*, vol. i, p. 168.
6 Ibid., p. 170.   7 Ibid., p. 177.   8 Ibid., p. 182.   9 Ibid., p. 183.
10 Cullen, *Emergence of modern Ireland*, p. 154.
11 Hill, *Plantation in Ulster*, p. 105.
12 Brabazon, *Deep-sea fisheries*, p. 56.
13 Ibid., p. 39.
14 Cullen, *Emergence of modern Ireland*, p. 155; Went, 'Pursuit of salmon in Ireland', pp 228–32.
15 Aalen and Brody, *Gola*, pp 88–92.
16 de Courcy Ireland, *Ireland's sea fisheries*, p. 45.
17 Desmond Murphy, *Donegal, Derry and modern Ulster, 1790–1921* (Culmore, Co. Derry, 1981), pp 224–6.
18 Aalen and Brody, *Gola*, pp 88–9.

19 Robert Lynd, 'Introduction' in O'Donnell, *Islanders*, p. 6.

20 Ibid., p. 7.

21 Sean Beattie, *The book of Inistrahull* (Culdaff, Co. Donegal, 1997), p. 17.

22 Ibid., p. 8.   23 Ibid., p. 9.   24 Ibid., p. 12.

25 Aalen and Brody, *Gola*, p. 92.

26 Ibid., p. 327.   27 Ibid., p. 331.   28 Ibid., pp 330–1.   29 Ibid., pp 331–2.   30 Ibid., pp 334–5.

31 John Dubourdieu, *Statistical survey of County Antrim* (Dublin, 1812), pp 113–14.

32 Ibid., p. 116.

33 Lewis, *Topographical dictionary of Ireland*, vol. i, p. 52.

34 Ibid., p. 53.

35 Vivienne Pollock, 'Herring fishery in County Down' in Lindsay Proudfoot and William Nolan (eds), *Down: society and history* (Dublin, 1997), pp 405–30 at pp 409–10.

36 Ibid., pp 410–12; Pollock, 'The introduction of engine power in the County Down sea fisheries', *Ulster Folklife*, 37 (1991), pp 1–12.

37 Pollock, 'Herring fishery in County Down', pp 408–10.

38 Ibid., p. 412.

39 James Mac Parlan, *Statistical survey of County Sligo* (Dublin, 1801), p. 87.

40 Ibid., p. 112.

41 Brabazon, *Deep-sea fisheries*, p. 24.

42 William Maxwell, *Wild sports of the west* (London, 1892), p. 61.

43 Ibid., pp 140–1.   44 Ibid., p. 143.   45 Ibid., p. 145.

46 Noel Wilkins, *Oysters and oystering in Galway Bay* (Galway, 2001), p. 29.

47 Quoted in Wilkins, p. 30.

48 Ibid., p. 32.

49 Dutton, *Statistical survey of County Galway*, p. 383.

50 Ibid., p. 396.   51 Ibid., pp 387–9.

52 Hill, *Facts from Gweedore*, p. 56.

53 Dutton, *Statistical survey of County Galway*, p. 392.

54 Hill, *Facts from Gweedore*, p. 58.

55 Brabazon, *Deep-sea fisheries*, p. 51.

56 Ibid., p. 49.

57 Dutton, *Statistical survey of County Galway*, p. 400.

58 Ibid., p. 397.   59 Ibid., p. 395.   60 Ibid., pp 396–8.   61 Ibid., p. 392.

62 Hely Dutton, *A statistical survey of the County of Clare* (Dublin, 1808), p. 227.

63 O'Brien, *A statistical survey of the County of Kerry* (Dublin, 1804), p. 233.

64 Smith, *History of Cork*, p. 216.

65 Ibid., p. 218.   66 Ibid., p. 305.

67 Cullen, *Emergence of modern Ireland*, p. 155.

68 Ibid., p. 156.

69 Colman O'Mahony, 'Fishing in nineteenth-century Kinsale', *Journal of the Cork Historical and Archaeological Society*, 98 (1993), pp 113–32.

70 *Cork Constitution*, 27 January 1757.

71 O'Mahony, 'Fishing in nineteenth-century Kinsale', p. 113.

72 Ibid., p. 114.   73 Ibid., p. 113.   74 Ibid., p. 115.

75 *Cork Constitution*, 25 March 1868.

76 *Cork Constitution*, 23 July 1868.

77 O'Mahony, 'Fishing in nineteenth-century Kinsale', p. 117.

78 *Cork Constitution*, 31 August 1868.

79 O'Sullivan, *History of Kinsale*, p. 116.

80 *Report of the committee for the relief of the distressed districts in Ireland* (London, 1823), p. 9.

81 Patrick Hickey, *Famine in west Cork* (Cork, 2002), p. 48.

82 Ibid., p. 14.   83 Ibid., pp 123–4.

84 Coull, *Sea fisheries of Europe*, pp 121–35.

85 Went, 'Pilchards in the south of Ireland', p. 141.
86 Quoted in Kelleher, *Fish palaces of west Cork*, p. 25.
87 Went, 'Pilchards in the south of Ireland', p. 140.
88 Hickey, *Famine in west Cork*, p. 124.
89 Ibid., p. 125.
90 Lewis, *Topographical dictionary of Ireland*, vol. i, pp 249–50.
91 Ibid., p. 172.
92 Smith, *History of Cork*, p. 198.
93 Went, 'Irish hake fishery', p. 46.
94 Mannion, 'Vessels, masters and seafaring: patterns in Waterford voyages' in W. Nolan and T.P. Power (eds), *Waterford: history and society* (Dublin, 1992), p. 374.
95 R.H. Ryland, *The history, topography and antiquities of the county and city of Waterford* (London, 1824), p. 309.
96 Lewis, *Topographical dictionary of Ireland*, vol. i, p. 579.
97 Dickson, *Old World colony*, p. 434.
98 Ibid., p. 435.
99 Ryland, *Waterford*, p. 310.
100 Ibid., pp 311–12.
101 Robert Fraser, *A statistical survey of the County of Wexford* (Dublin, 1807), pp 22–3.
102 Ibid., p. 22.   103 Ibid., pp 23–4.
104 Went, 'Oyster fisheries of Ireland', p. 210.
105 Rees, *Arklow*, pp 150–1.
106 Cullen, 'The port of New Ross', p. 246.
107 Ibid., p. 244.
108 H.L. Bayly, quoted in Rees, *Arklow*, p. 306.
109 Rees, *Arklow*, p. 305.
110 Ibid., pp 150–1.
111 Young, *Tour in Ireland*, vol. i, p. 89.
112 Mary Gwinnell, 'Some aspects of the economic life of County Wexford in the nineteenth century', *Journal of the Wexford Historical Society*, 10 (1984–5), pp 5–24.
113 Ibid., p. 18.
114 de Courcy Ireland, *Ireland's sea fisheries*, p. 47.
115 John Appleby, 'The fishing ventures of Nicholas Weston of Dublin', *Dublin Historical Record*, 39:4, (1986), pp 152–3.
116 Ibid., p. 153.
117 John Gimlette, *Theatre of fish* (London, 2005), p. 4.
118 Mannion, 'Vessels, masters and shipping', pp 373–5.
119 Irish, *Shipbuilding in Waterford*, p. 6.
120 Mannion, 'A transatlantic merchant fishery', pp 375–81.
121 Ibid., p. 380.   122 Ibid., pp 385–94.   123 Ibid., p. 375.
124 Joseph Archer, *A statistical survey of County Dublin* (Dublin, 1801), pp 119–20.
125 de Courcy Ireland, *Ireland's sea fisheries*, p. 51.
126 Went, 'Oyster fisheries of Ireland', p. 201.
127 E.P. Stymes, 'The Torbay fishermen in Ringsend', *Dublin Historical Record*, 53:4 (2000), p. 140.
128 Ibid., pp 142–4.
129 Brabazon, *Deep-sea fisheries*, p. 56.
130 Stymes, 'Torbay fishermen in Ringsend', p. 142.
131 Pollock, 'Herring fishery in County Down', pp 409–10.

CHAPTER NINE *Developmental issues in Irish sea fishing: the nineteenth-century heritage*

1 A.E.J. Went, 'Fisheries' in James Meenan and Desmond Clarke (eds), *The Royal Dublin Society, 1731–1981* (Dublin, 1981), pp 143–5.
2 Moriarty, 'Fish and fisheries', p. 292.
3 W.S. Green, *The sea fisheries of the south and south-west of Ireland: second report of the fisheries committee of the RDS* (Dublin, 1888), p. 376.
4 Bowles-Daly, *Glimpses of Irish industry*, p. 209.
5 Dubourdieu, *Statistical survey of County Antrim*, p. 186.
6 Young, *Tour in Ireland*, vol. i, p. 168.
7 Eiblín Ní Scannlain, *Land and people: land use and population change in north-west Connemara in the nineteenth century* (Connemara, Co. Galway, 1999), pp 30–1.
8 Jim Mac Laughlin, 'Regional social history, the nationalist and the Famine', *Journal of Northwest Historical and Archaeological Society*, 1:1 (1984), pp 26–37.
9 Moriarty, 'Fish and fisheries', p. 289.
10 Molloy, *Irish mackerel fishery*, pp 40–3.
11 O'Dowd, *Down by the Claddagh*, p. 90.
12 de Courcy Ireland, *Ireland's sea fisheries*, pp 47–8.
13 Woodham-Smith, *Great hunger*, p. 289.
14 *Digest of evidence taken before her majesty's commissioners of inquiry into the state of the law and practice in respect of the occupation of the land* (Dublin, 1847–8), p. 384.
15 Bowles-Daly, *Glimpses of Irish industry*, p. 203.
16 Brabazon, *Deep-sea fisheries*, p. 23.
17 Cormac O'Grada, *Ireland: a new economic history* (Oxford, 1994), p. 149.
18 Tomás Ó Criomhthain, *Allagair na hInise* (Dublin, 1928), p. 92.
19 Bowles-Daly, *Glimpses of Irish industry*, p. 186.
20 Ibid., p. 185.
21 Dickson, *Old World colony*, p. 435.
22 Hickey, *Famine in west Cork*, pp 124–5.
23 *Cork Mercantile Chronicle*, 21 August 1838.
24 Hickey, *Famine in west Cork*, p. 124.
25 Robert Dennis, *Industrial Ireland* (Dublin, 1887), pp 44–5.
26 Ibid., p. 46.
27 W.S. Green, 'Sea fisheries' in *Ireland: industrial and agricultural. Handbook for the Glasgow international exhibition* (Dublin, 1902), pp 369–86.
28 Mac Laughlin, *Re-imagining the nation state*, pp 178–84.
29 de Courcy Ireland, *Ireland's sea fisheries*, p. 47.
30 Bowles-Daly, *Glimpses of Irish Industry*, p. 186.
31 Tomás O'Crohan, *The islandman* (Oxford, 1951), p. 187.
32 Jim Mac Laughlin, 'Displacement and dislocation' in Mac Laughlin, *Donegal*, pp 206–12.
33 Dutton, *Statistical survey of County Clare*, p. 229.
34 *Faulkner's Journal*, 16 September 1820.
35 Dutton, *Statistical survey of County Clare*, p. 231.
36 Ibid., pp 219–21.
37 Evans, *Irish folk ways*, pp 221–3.
38 Hill, *Facts from Gweedore*, pp 30–1.
39 Hornell, *British coracles and Irish curraghs*, p. 208.
40 Dutton, *Statistical survey of County Galway*, p. 396.
41 Hornell, *British coracles and Irish curraghs*, p. 234.
42 Dutton, *Statistical survey of County Galway*, p. 393.
43 Ibid., p. 231.
44 Dennis, *Industrial Ireland*, p. 46.

45 Ibid., p. 47.
46 Dutton, *Statistical survey of County Galway*, p. 395.
47 Woodham-Smith, *Great hunger*, p. 287.
48 Maxwell, *Wild sports of the west*, p. 147.
49 Evans, *Irish folk ways*, pp 251–2.
50 Brabazon, *Deep-sea fisheries*, p. 15.
51 Dennis, *Industrial Ireland*, p. 47.
52 Dutton, *Statistical survey of County Clare*, p. 228.
53 Mac Parlan, *Statistical survey of County Donegal*, p. 73.
54 Hill, *Facts from Gweedore*, p. 32.
55 Mac Polin, *Drontheim*, pp 5–7.
56 Evans, *Irish folk ways*, pp 251–2.
57 Brabazon, *Deep-sea fisheries*, p. 33.
58 Dutton, *Statistical survey of County Galway*, p. 393.
59 Coull, *Fisheries of Europe*, p. 138.
60 W.B. Yeats, *The poems* (London, 1994), p. 47.
61 Dubourdieu, *Statistical survey of County Down*, p. 117.
62 Pollock, *Herring fishery in County Down*, p. 409.
63 S.C. Hall, *Ireland: its scenery and character*, vol. i, p. 132.
64 Woodham-Smith, *Great hunger*, p. 285.
65 *First report of the commission of inquiry into the state of Irish fisheries* (1836), p. iv.
66 Inglis, *A journey throughout Ireland*, pp 214–15.
67 Hole, *A little tour in Ireland*, p. 114.
68 Richard Lovett, *Irish pictures* (London, 1888), p. 115.
69 O'Dowd, *Down by the Claddagh*, pp 13–14.
70 Quoted in Woodham-Smith, *Great hunger*, p. 285.
71 *Annual Report of the Commissioners of public works in Ireland, 1847–8* (London, 1849), p. xxiii.
72 Ní Scannlain, *Land and people*, pp 30–1.
73 Mac Laughlin, 'Regional social history, pp 26–37.
74 T.W. Freeman, *Pre-Famine Ireland* (Manchester, 1957), pp 92–4.
75 Woodham-Smith, *Great hunger*, p. 286.
76 Robert Webb, *Report of the central relief committee of the Society of Friends* (1850), p. 32.
77 Ibid., p. 26.
78 Woodham-Smith, *Great hunger*, pp 287–8.
79 L.S. Fleming, *Head or harp* (London, 1965), p. 128; Hickey, *Famine in west Cork*, pp 147–8.
80 Hickey, *Famine in west Cork*, pp 125–7.
81 Ibid., p. 200.
82 Woodham-Smith, *Great hunger*, p. 289.
83 Hickey, *Famine in west Cork*, p. 124.
84 F.H. Hore, *An inquiry into the legislation, control and improvement of the salmon and sea fisheries of Ireland* (Dublin, 1850), p. 327.
85 Donal Donovan, 'Observations on the peculiar diseases to which the famine of last year gave origin, and on the morbid effects of insufficient nourishment', *Dublin Medical Express*, 19 (1848), pp 67–8.
86 Levis, *Towel sail yawls*, pp 3–5.
87 Dennis, *Industrial Ireland*, p. 48.
88 Ibid., p. 55.
89 George Thomson, *Island home: the Blasket heritage* (Dingle, Co. Kerry, 1988), p. 19.
90 Ibid., p. 20.
91 E.W.H. Holdsworth, *Deep sea fishing and fishing boats* (London, 1874), p. 209.
92 Ibid., p. 197.
93 Molloy, *Irish mackerel fishery*, p. 37.

94 O'Sullivan, *History of Kinsale*, p. 126.
95 Fitzgerald, *Mackerel and the making of Baltimore*, pp 13–15.
96 Went, 'Oyster fisheries of Ireland', p. 195.
97 Conchúr Ó Síocháin, *The man from Cape Clear* (Dublin, 1940), p. 134.
98 Ibid., p. 136.   99 Ibid., p. 146.
100 W.P. Gaskell, *Report of congested district board inspector* (Dublin, 1894), p. 19.
101 Ibid., p. 22.

CHAPTER TEN *Rural fundamentalism and the marginalisation of Ireland's sea fisheries*

1 Patrick Gallagher, *My story* (Dunglow, Co. Donegal, n.d.), p. 67.
2 Jim Mac Laughlin, *Travellers and Ireland* (Cork, 1995), p. 28.
3 Peter Taylor, *Political geography* (Harlow, 1998), p. 85.
4 Victor Kiernan, *The lords of humankind* (London, 1974).
5 Ellen Churchill Semple, *Influences of geographic environment: on the basis of Ratzel's system of anthropo-geography* (London, 1911), p. 71.
6 Mac Laughlin, *Re-imagining the nation state*, p. 81.
7 Sean O'Faolain, *King of the beggars* (Dublin, 1980), p. 10.
8 Mac Laughlin, 'The gypsy as "other"', p. 37.
9 Stephen Gwynn, *Highways and byways in Donegal and Antrim* (London, 1899), p. 109.
10 Mac Laughlin, *Re-imagining the nation state*, p. 260.
11 Barbara Kerr, 'Irish seasonal migration to Great Britain, 1800–38', *Irish Historical Studies*, 3:12 (1943), pp 365–80.
12 G.R.C. Keep, 'Official opinion on Irish emigration in the later nineteenth century', *Irish Ecclesiastical Record*, 81 (1931), pp 412–21.
13 Simon Schama, *Embarrassment of riches* (Berkeley, CA, 1988), pp 262–3.
14 Ibid., p. 266.
15 Boxer, *Dutch seaborne empire*, pp 88–112.
16 Hugo Grotius, *On the origin of the native races of America* (Edinburgh, 1884), pp 57–9.
17 Jacob Bronowski and B.J. Mazlish, *The western intellectual tradition: from Leonardo to Hegel* (London, 1972), pp 243–51.
18 Corkery, *Hidden Ireland*, pp 17–24; Gwynn, *Highways and byways*, pp 19–25.
19 Corkery, *Hidden Ireland*, p. 30.
20 Ibid., p. 34.   21 Ibid., p. 36.
22 Mac Laughlin, 'Making of a northern county', p. 6.
23 Ibid., pp 7–10.
24 Thomas Carlyle, *Reminiscences of my Irish journey* (London, 1882), p. 86.
25 Clive Dewey, 'Celtic agrarian legislation and the Celtic revival', *Past and Present* (1974), pp 30–69.
26 Jim Mac Laughlin, *Ireland: the emigrant nursery and the world economy* (Cork, 1994), pp 23–31.
27 Declan Kiberd, *Inventing Ireland* (London, 1995), p. 421.
28 Carlo Levi, *Christ stopped at Eboli* (London, 1982), pp 35–7.
29 B. Traven, *Government* (Berkeley, CA, 1993), p. 23.
30 See Mac Laughlin, *Travellers and Ireland*, pp 33–5.
31 Debora Silverman, *Van Gogh and Gauguin: the search for sacred art* (New York, 2000), p. 9.
32 Jim Mac Laughlin, 'Emigration and the construction of nationalist hegemony in Ireland' in Jim Mac Laughlin (ed.), *Location and dislocation in contemporary Irish society* (Cork, 1997), pp 8–12.
33 Murphy, *Derry and Donegal*, pp 127–35.
34 J.E. Handley, *The Irish in modern Scotland* (Cork, 1947), p. 213.
35 See Molloy, *Mackerel fisheries*, pp 7–9; de Courcy Ireland, *Ireland's sea fisheries*, pp 27–9.
36 de Courcy Ireland, *Ireland's sea fisheries*, p. 32.

37 Ibid., p. 34.
38 *Catholic Bulletin* (1943), p. 167.
39 Molloy, *Mackerel fisheries*, p. 33.
40 de Courcy Ireland, *Ireland's sea fisheries*, p. 36.
41 Ibid., pp 37–9.
42 Jim Mac Laughlin and John Agnew, 'Hegemony and the regional question: the political geography of regional industrial policy in northern Ireland, 1945–72', *Annals of the Association of American Geographers*, 76:2 (1986), pp 247–61.

Bibliography

'An Oxonian', *A little tour in Ireland* (London, 1859).

Aalen, F.H.A. and Hugh Brody, *Gola: life and last days of an island community* (Cork, 1969).

Aalen, F.H.A., Kevin Whelan and Matthew Stout (eds), *Atlas of the Irish rural landscape* (Cork, 1997).

Adams, Jonathan and Katherine Holman (eds), *Scandinavia and Europe, 800–1350: contact, conflict and coexistence* (Turnhout, Belgium, 2004).

Appleby, John, 'Merchants and mariners, pirates and privateers' in John Appleby and Michael McCaughan (eds), *The Irish Sea: aspects of maritime history* (Belfast, 1989), pp 47–60.

Appleby, John, 'The fishing ventures of Nicholas Weston of Dublin', *Dublin Historical Record,* 39:4 (1986), 150–5.

Archer, Joseph, *A statistical survey of County Dublin* (Dublin, 1801).

Arnold, Bruce, *Jack Yeats* (New York, 1998).

Atkinson, Robert (ed.), *The Book of Ballymote* (Dublin, 1887).

Barry, R.J., *Islands* (London, 2009).

Bayly, H.L., 'Statistical survey of Arklow', appendix A in Jim Rees, *Arklow: the story of a town* (Arklow, Co. Wicklow, 2004), pp 303–11.

Beattie, Seán, *The book of Inistrahull* (Culdaff, Co. Donegal, 1997).

Bell, Sam Hanna, *The December bride* (Belfast, 1975).

Black, R.M. (ed.), *Society of free fishermen* (Edinburgh, 1951).

Black's Guide to Galway, Clare and the west of Ireland (London, 1888).

Boate, Gerard, *A natural history of Ireland* (Dublin, 1726).

Bowles-Daly, John, *Glimpses of Irish industry* (London, 1889).

Boxer, Charles, *The Dutch seaborne empire, 1600–1900* (London, 1965).

Boyce, George, *Nationalism in Ireland* (London, 1991).

Brabazon, Wallop, *The deep sea and coast fisheries of Ireland: with suggestions for the working of a fishing company* (London, 1848).

Brady, Joseph and Anngret Simms, *Dublin through space and time* (Dublin, 2001).

Brady, Karl, Fionnbarr Moore and Tom Condit, 'Newhaven: a forgotten harbour in Fingal', *Archaeology Ireland,* 21:4 (2007), 8–11.

Braudel, Fernand, *The Mediterranean and the Mediterranean world in the age of Phillip II* (London, 1972).

Braudel, Fernand, *The structures of everyday life* (London, 1985).

Braudel, Fernand, *The wheels of commerce* (London, 1982).

Breen, Colin, 'Archaeology of early harbours and landing places in County Down, 800–1700', *Ulster Local Studies*, 19:2 (1998), 11–26.

Breen, Colin, *The Gaelic lordship of the O'Sullivan Beare: a landscape cultural history* (Dublin, 2005).

Bronowski, Jacob and Bruce Mazlish, *The western intellectual tradition: from Leonardo to Hegel* (London, 1972).

Buchanan, R.H., 'Lecale Peninsula, County Down' in Aalen et al., (eds), *Atlas of the Irish rural landscape*, pp 277–86.

Buchanan, R.H., 'The Irish Sea' in Appleby and McCaughan (eds), *Irish Sea*, pp 1–12.

Butler, W.F.T., *Gleanings from Irish history* (Dublin, 1925).

Cabot, David, *Ireland* (London, 1999).

Campbell, Julian, 'Frederick William Burton' in Peter Murray (ed.), *Whipping the herring: survival and celebration in nineteenth-century Irish art* (Cork, 2006).

Carlyle, Thomas, *Reminiscences of my Irish journey* (London, 1882).

Chambers, Anne, *Eleanor, Countess of Desmond* (Dublin, 2000).

Chambers, Anne, *Granuaile: Ireland's Pirate Queen* (Dublin, 2003).

Christiansen, Edmund, *The Norsemen in the Viking Age* (London, 2002).

Clarke, H.B., Máire Ní Mhaonaigh and Raghnall Ó Floinn (eds), *Ireland and Scandinavia in the early Viking Age* (Dublin, 1998).

Clarke, H.B., 'The early development of Dublin' in Christine Casey (ed.), *The buildings of Ireland: Dublin* (London, 2005), pp 10–18.

Colegate, Isabel, *A pelican in the wilderness: hermits, solitaries and recluses* (London, 2002).

Colfer, Billy, 'Anglo-Norman settlement in County Wexford' in Whelan and Nolan (eds), *Wexford: history and society*, pp 65–101.

Colfer, Billy, 'Medieval Wexford', *Journal of Wexford Historical Society*, 13 (1990–1), 5–29.

Colfer, Billy, *The Hook Peninsula, County Wexford* (Cork, 2004).

Collins, Timothy, 'Fishing in nineteenth-century Kinsale', *Journal of the Cork Historical and Archaeological Society*, 98 (1993), 113–32.

Collins, Timothy, 'From *hoekers* to hookers: a survey of literature on the origins of the Galway hooker', *Journal of Galway Historical and Archaeological Society*, 97 (2000), 66–83.

Connell, K.H., 'Population of Ireland in the eighteenth century', *Economic History Review* (1946), 111–24.

Coppinger, Walter, *History of the Coppingers, Co. Cork* (London, 1884).

Corbin, Alain, *The foul and the fragrant* (New York, 1986).

Corkery, Daniel, *Hidden Ireland: a study of Gaelic Munster in the eighteenth century* (Dublin, 1924).

Coull, James R., *The sea fisheries of Scotland: an historical geography* (Edinburgh, 1996).

Coull, James R., *The sea fisheries of Europe: an economic geography* (London, 1972).

Cowan, Cathal and Regina Sexton, *Ireland's traditional foods: an exploration of Irish local and typical food and drinks* (Dublin, 1997).

Coyne, J.S. and N.P. Willis, *Scenery and antiquities of Ireland* (London, 1842).

Crawford, E.M., 'Food and famine: diet in County Londonderry, 1820–1860' in Gerard O'Brien (ed.), *Derry and Londonderry: history and society* (Dublin, 1999), pp 519–36.

Crawford, E.M., 'Food and famine' in Cathal Pórtéir (ed.), *The Great Irish Famine* (Cork, 1995), pp 60–73.

Crowley, Ethel, *Land matters: power struggles in rural Ireland* (Dublin, 2006).

Cullen, Fintan, *The Irish face: redefining the Irish portrait* (London, 2004).

Cullen, Fintan, *Visual politics: the representation of Ireland, 1750–1930* (Cork, 1997).

Cullen, L.M., 'The port of New Ross: a comparative historical profile' in J. Dunne (ed.), *New Ross* (Ardvan, Co. Wexford, 2007), pp 243–52.

Cullen, L.M., *The emergence of modern Ireland, 1600–1900* (London, 1981).

Culleton, Edward, 'Rise and fall of Norse Wexford', *Journal of Wexford Historical Society*, 14 (1992), 151–9.

Curtis, Edmund, *Irish historical documents* (London, 1943).

Curtis, L.P., *Apes and angels: the Irishman in Victorian caricature* (Newton Abbot, Devon, 1971).

Dalby, Andrew, *Empires of pleasure: luxury and indulgence in the Roman world* (London, 2000).

Dallat, Cahal, 'Ice-houses', *Ulster Local Studies*, 13:2 (1991), 37–43.

Dalsimer, Adele (ed.), *Visualizing Ireland: national identity and the pictorial tradition* (Winchester, MA, 1993).

David, Elizabeth, *Harvest of the cold months: the social history of ice and ices* (London, 1994).

de Bourgrenet, Jacques Louis, *A Frenchman's walk through Ireland, 1796–7* (Dublin, 1917).

de Courcy Ireland, John, 'The Liffey banks in Dublin: early works of the private developers', *Dublin Historical Record*, 57:2 (2004), 146–51.

de Courcy Ireland, John, *Ireland's sea fisheries* (Dublin, 1981).

de Paor, Máire, 'Irish antiquarian artists' in Dalsimer (ed.), *Visualizing Ireland*, pp 119–32.

Dennis, Robert, *Industrial Ireland: a practical and non-political view of 'Ireland for the Irish'* (Dublin, 1887).

Derricke, John, *The image of Irelande, with a discoverie of woodkerne*, ed. John Small (Belfast, 1985).

Dewey, Clive, 'Celtic agrarian legislation and the Celtic revival', *Past and Present*, 64 (1974), 31–71.

Dickson, David, *Old world colony: Cork and south Munster, 1630–1830* (Cork, 2005).

Digest of evidence taken before her majesty's commissioners of inquiry into the state of the law and practice in respect of the occupation of the land (Dublin, 1847–8).

Dobb, Maurice, *Studies in the development of capitalism* (London, 1975).

Doherty, Charles, 'Exchange and trade in early medieval Ireland', *Journal of the Royal Society of Antiquaries of Ireland*, 110 (1980), 67–89.

Donovan, Donal, 'Observations on the peculiar diseases to which the famine of last year gave origin', *Dublin Medical Express*, 19 (1848), 67–8.

Dornan, Brian, *Mayo's lost islands: the Inishkeas* (Dublin, 2000).

Downey, Edmund, *The story of Waterford* (Waterford, 1914).

Doyle, J.P., *Old Ireland improved and made new* (London, 1881).

Dubourdieu, John, *A statistical survey of County Antrim* (Dublin, 1812).

Dunne, Tom, 'The dark side of the Irish landscape' in Murray (ed.), *Whipping the herring*, pp 46–61.

Dutton, Hely, *A statistical survey of County Clare* (Dublin, 1808).

Dutton, Hely, *A statistical survey of County Galway* (Dublin, 1824).

Belmore, Earl of, 'Ancient maps of Enniskillen and its environs', *Ulster Journal of Archaeology*, 2:2 (1896), 218–43.

Ekin, Des, *The stolen village: Baltimore and the Barbary pirates* (Dublin, 2007).

Elias, Norbert, *The civilizing process: sociogenetic and psychogenetic investigations* (Oxford, 1985).

Etchingham, Colmán, *Church organization in Ireland, AD650–1000* (Maynooth, 1999).

Evans, E.E., *Irish folkways* (London, 1967).

Fairley, James, *Irish whales and whaling* (Belfast, 1984).

Fitzgerald, Maria, 'Catch of the day at Clowanstown, Co. Meath', *Archaeology Ireland*, 21:4 (2007), 12–17.

Fitzgerald, Seamus, *Mackerel and the making of Baltimore* (Dublin, 1999).

Fitzgibbon, Theodora, *A taste of Ireland: Irish traditional food* (London, 1968).

Fitzmaurice, Edmund, *The life of Sir William Petty* (London, 1895).

Flanagan, Laurence, *Ancient Ireland: life before the Celts* (Dublin, 1998).

Fleming, L.S., *Head or harp* (London, 1965).

Fletcher, Nichola, *Charlemagne's tablecloth: a piquant history of feasting* (London, 2004).

Fort, Tom, 'Fish in English history', *The Guardian*, 4 February 2004.

Fox, Edward W., *History in geographic perspective: the other France* (New York, 1975).

Fox, Robin Lane, *The classical world* (London, 2005).

Fox, Robin, *The Tory Islanders* (Cambridge, 1978).

Fraser, Robert, *A statistical survey of the county of Wexford* (Dublin, 1807).

Freeman, T.W., *Pre-Famine Ireland* (Manchester, 1957).

Furlong, Nicholas, 'Life in Wexford port' in Whelan and Nolan (eds), *Wexford: history and society*, pp 150–72.

Gallagher, Pat 'The Cope', *My story* (Dungloe, Co. Donegal [n.d.]).

Gaskell, W.P., *Report of a congested districts board inspector* (Dublin, 1984).

Gibbon, Peter, *The origins of Ulster unionism* (Manchester, 1979).

Gilbard, Henry, *Discourse of Ireland* (London, 1572).

Gilbert, J.T., *Facsimiles of national manuscripts of Ireland* (Dublin, 1874).

Gillespie, Raymond, 'Describing Dublin: Francis Place's visit, 1698–99' in Dalsimer (ed.), *Visualizing Ireland*, pp 99–118.

Gimlette, John, *Theatre of fish* (London, 2005).

Green, W.S., 'The sea fisheries' in *Ireland, industrial and agricultural* (Department of Agriculture, Dublin, 1902), pp 369–86.

Green, W.S., *The sea fisheries of the south and south-west of Ireland: second report of the fisheries committee of the RDS* (Dublin, 1888).

Greenhill, Basil, *The archaeology of boats and ships* (London, 1995).

Grotius, Hugo, *On the origins of the native races of America* (Edinburgh, 1884).

Gunn, Neil, *Silver darlings* (London, 1999).

Gwinnell, Mary, 'Some aspects of the economic life of County Wexford in the nineteenth century', *Journal of the Wexford Historical Society*, 10 (1984–5), 5–24.

Gwynn, Stephen, *Highways and byways in Donegal and Antrim* (London, 1899).

Hagen, Rose-Marie and Rainer Hagen, *Fifteenth-century paintings* (Köln, 2001).

Haliday, Charles, *The Scandinavian kingdom of Dublin* (Dublin, 1884).

Hall, Mr and Mrs S.C., *Ireland: its scenery and character etc.* (London, 1841–3).

Handley, J.H., *The Irish in modern Scotland* (Cork, 1947).

Hardiman, James, *The history of the town and county of Galway: from the earliest period to the present time* (Galway, 1958).

Harris, Walter, *The ancient and present state of the county of Down* (Dublin, 1744).

Head, Francis B., *A fortnight in Ireland* (London, 1852).

Heaton, Herbert, *Economic history of Europe* (London, 1964).

Hegarty, Peter, *Peadar O'Donnell* (Cork, 1999).

Hencken, Hugh, 'Lagore crannog: an Irish royal residence of the seventh and eighth centuries AD', *Proceedings of the Royal Irish Academy*, 53C (1950), 1–248.

Henry, Paul, *An Irish portrait* (London, 1951).

Heraughty, Patrick, *Inishmurray: an ancient monastic island* (Dublin, 1982).

Hickey, Patrick, *Famine in west Cork: the Mizen Peninsula, land and people, 1800–1852* (Cork, 2002).

Hill, George, *An historical account of the plantation in Ulster* (Shannon, 1970).

Hill, George, *Facts from Gweedore* (Dublin, 1887).

Hill, George, *Plantation papers: a summary of the great Ulster plantation in the year 1610* (Dublin, 1889).

Hines, James, Allen Lane and Mark Redknap (eds), *Land, sea and home* (London, 2004).

Hochstrasser, Julie, *Still life and trade in the Dutch Golden Age* (New Haven, 2007).

Holdsworth, E.W.H., *Deep-sea fishing and fishing boats* (London, 1874).

Hore, H.F., *An inquiry into the legislation, control and improvement of salmon and sea fisheries of Ireland* (London, 1850).

Hornell, James, *British coracles and Irish curraghs* (London, 1938).

Hughes, Robert, *Barcelona* (London, 1992).

Hunter, R.J., 'Sir Ralph Bingley: Ulster planter' in Peter Roebuck (ed.), *Plantation to partition* (Belfast, 1981), pp 14–28.

Hurley, Vincent, *The early church in the south-west of Ireland: settlement and organization* (Oxford, 1982).

Inglis, Henry, *Journey throughout Ireland during the spring, summer and autumn of 1834* (London, 1836).

Innis, H.A., *The cod fisheries: history of an international economy* (Toronto, 1978).

Irish, Bill, *Shipbuilding in Waterford* (Bray, 2005).

Jefferies, Henry Allen, *Cork: historical perspectives* (Dublin, 2004).

Joyce, James, *Ulysses* (London, 1992).

Joyce, P.W., *Social history of ancient Ireland from the earliest times to 1608* (London, 1893).

Keep, G.R.C., 'Official opinion on Irish emigration in the later nineteenth century', *Irish Ecclesiastical Record*, 81 (1931), 412–21.

Kelleher, Hilary, 'An archaeological study of fish palaces in west Cork' (MA, Department of Archaeology, UCC, 1995).

Kelly, Fergus, *Early Irish farming* (Dublin, 2000).

Kelly, Maria, *The great dying: the Black Death in Dublin* (Dublin, 2003).

Keogh, Frank, 'In Gorumna Island', *New Ireland Review*, 19 (1898), 36–41.

Kerr, Barbara A., 'Irish seasonal migration to Great Britain, 1800–38', *Irish Historical Studies*, 3:12 (1943), 365–80.

Kiberd, Declan, *Inventing Ireland* (London, 1995).

Kieran, Victor, *Lords of humankind: European attitudes to the outside world in the imperial age* (London, 1972).

Knapp, J.F., 'Primitivism and empire: John Synge and Paul Gaugin', *Comparative Literature*, 12 (1983), 56–63.

Kurlansky, Karl, *Cod: a biography of the fish that changed the world* (London, 1998).

Lacy, Brian, 'Prehistoric and Early Christian settlement in Donegal' in Nolan et al. (eds), *Donegal: history and society*, pp 1–24

Lalor, Brian (ed.), *Encyclopedia of Ireland* (Dublin, 2003).

Lankford, Eamon, *Cape Clear: its people and landscape* (Cape Clear, Cork, 1999).

Lecky, W.E.H., *Ireland in the eighteenth century* (London, 1829).

Lenihan, Maurice, *The history of Limerick* (Cork, 1886).

Levi, Carlo, *Christ stopped at Eboli* (London, 1982).

Levis, Cormac, *Towelsail yawls: the lobsterboats of Hare Island and Roaringwater Bay* (Ardfield, Co. Cork, 2002).

Lewis, Gifford, *Sommerville and Ross: the world of the Irish R.M.* (London, 1987).

Lewis, Samuel, *Topographical dictionary of Ireland* (London, 1837).

Longfield, A.K., *Anglo-Irish trade in the sixteenth century* (London, 1929).

Loone, Martin, *Irish film: the emergence of contemporary cinema* (London, 2000).

Lovett, Richard, *Irish pictures* (London, 1888).

Lydon, James, *The lordship of Ireland in the Middle Ages* (Dublin, 1972).

Lynch, Adam, 'Man and environment in south-west Ireland', *British Archaeological Reports*, 85 (London, 1981).

Macafee, William and Valerie Morgan, 'Population in Ulster' in Roebuck (ed.), *Plantation to partition*, pp 46–63.

MacArthur, C.W.P., *Dunfanaghy's Presbyterian congregation and its times* (Dunfanaghy, Co. Donegal, 1978).

Mac Cárthaigh, Críostóir, *Traditional boats in Ireland: history, folklore and construction* (Cork, 2008).

Mac Eiteagain, Darren, 'The renaissance and the late medieval lordship of Tir Chonaill' in Nolan et al. (eds), *Donegal: history and society*, pp 203–28.

Mac Grail, Seán, *Ancient boats in north western Europe* (New York, 1998).

Mac Laughlin, Jim and John Agnew, 'Hegemony and the regional question', *Annals of the Association of American Geographers*, 76:2 (1986), 247–61.

Mac Laughlin, Jim, 'Displacement and dislocation' in Mac Laughlin (ed.), *Donegal*, pp 206–12.

Mac Laughlin, Jim, 'Emigration and the construction of nationalist hegemony in Ireland' in Jim Mac Laughlin (ed.), *Location and dislocation in contemporary Irish society* (Cork, 1997), pp 5–35.

Mac Laughlin, Jim, 'European gypsies and the historical geography of loathing', *Review Journal of the Fernand Braudel Center*, 22 (1999), 31–61.

Mac Laughlin, Jim, 'Looking at landscapes' in Jim Mac Laughlin (ed.), *Donegal: the making of a northern county* (Dublin, 2007), pp 22–8.

Mac Laughlin, Jim, 'Pestilence on their backs, famine in their stomachs: the racial construction of Irishness in Victorian Britain' in Colin Graham and Richard Kirkland (eds), *Ireland and cultural theory* (London, 1999), pp 50–76.

Mac Laughlin, Jim, 'Regional social history, the nationalist and the famine', *Journal of Northwest Historical and Archaeological Society*, 1:1 (1985), 26–37.

Mac Laughlin, Jim, 'State-centred social science and the anarchist critique: ideology in political geography', *Antipode: a radical journal of geography*, 18:1 (1986), 11–38.

Mac Laughlin, Jim, 'The gypsy as "other" in European society: towards a political geography of hate', *The European Legacy*, 4 (1999), 35–50.

Mac Laughlin, Jim, 'The making of a northern county' in Mac Laughlin (ed.), *Donegal*, pp 1–21.

Mac Laughlin, Jim, *Ireland: the emigrant nursery and the world economy* (Cork, 1994).

Mac Laughlin, Jim, *Re-imagining the nation-state: the contested terrains of nation-building* (London, 2001).

Mac Laughlin, Jim, *Travellers and Ireland: whose country, whose history?* (Cork, 1995).

Mac Neill, Eoin, *Celtic Ireland* (Dublin, 1921).

Mac Neill, Eoin, *Early Irish laws and institutions* (Dublin, 1934).

Mac Parlan, James, *A statistical survey of County Donegal* (Dublin, 1802).

Mac Parlan, James, *A statistical survey of County Sligo* (Dublin, 1801).

Mac Polin, Donal, *Donegal currach* (Donaghadee, Co. Down, 2007).

Mac Polin, Donal, *Drontheim: a forgotten sailing boat of the north Irish coast* (Dublin, 1992).

Mahon, Brid, *Land of milk and honey* (Cork, 1991).

Mallory, J.P. and T.E. McNeill, *The archaeology of Ulster* (Belfast, 1991).

Mannion, John, 'A transatlantic merchant fishery: Richard Welsh of New Ross and the Sweetmans of Newbawn in Newfoundland, 1734–1862' in Whelan and Nolan (eds), *Wexford: history and society*, pp 373–421.

Mannion, John, 'Vessels, masters and seafaring: patterns in Waterford voyages' in William Nolan and T.P. Power (eds), *Waterford: history and society* (Dublin, 1992), pp 373–402.

Marmion, Anthony, *Ancient and modern history of maritime ports of Ireland* (London, 1855).

Marsden, Phillip, 'Ships of the Roman period and after in Britain' in G.F. Bass (ed.), *History of seafaring* (London, 1972), pp 129–78.

Marshall, Jenny White and Claire Walsh, 'Illaunloughan: life and death on a small early monastic site', *Archaeology Ireland*, 8:4 (1994), 25–8.

Martin, Donald, *Killybegs then and now* (Dublin, 1998).

Mason, T.H., *Islands of Ireland* (London, 1936).

Maxwell, William H., *Wild sports of the west: also legendary tales, folk-lore, local customs and natural history* (London, 1892).

McCarthy, Margaret, 'Archaeozoological studies of early medieval Munster' in Michael Monk and John Sheehan (eds), *Early Medieval Munster: archaeology, history and society* (Cork, 1998), pp 56–63.

McCaughan, Michael and John Appleby (eds), *The Irish Sea* (Belfast, 1989).

McCaughan, Michael, 'Irish vernacular boats and their European connections', *Ulster Folklife*, 24 (1978), 1–23.

McCourt, Desmond, 'Infield and outfield in Ireland', *Economic History Review*, 9 (1954–5), 396–76.

McLoone, Martin, *Irish film: the emergence of a contemporary cinema* (London, 2000).

McNally, David, 'Tudor Dublin's dung problem', *Dublin Historical Record*, 16:1 (1992), 65–8.

McQuade, Melanie, 'Gone fishin'', *Archaeology Ireland*, 22:1 (2008), 8–11.

Mitchell, Frank, *The Irish landscape* (London, 1976).

Mitchell, G.F., 'Further early kitchen middens in Co. Louth', *Journal of the County Louth Archaeological and Historical Society*, 12 (1949), 14–20.

Molloy, John, *Herring fisheries of Ireland* (Oranmore, Co. Galway, 2006).

Molloy, John, *The Irish mackerel fishery: the making of an industry* (Killarney, Co. Kerry, 2004).

Moody, T.W., *The Londonderry Plantation, 1609–14* (Dublin, 1939).

Moriarty, Christopher, 'Fish and fisheries' in J.W. Wilson (ed.), *Nature in Ireland: a scientific and cultural history* (Dublin, 1997), pp 283–97.

Moylan, Thomas, 'Poverty, pigs and pestilence in medieval Dublin', *Dublin Historical Record*, 7 (1956), 155–8.

Murphy, Desmond, *Donegal, Derry and modern Ulster, 1790–1921* (Culmore, Co. Derry, 1981).

Murray, Peter, 'Representations of Ireland in *The Illustrated London News*' in Peter Murray (ed.), *Whipping the herring: survival and celebration in nineteenth-century Irish art* (Cork, 2006), pp 230–56.

Nansen, Fridtjof, *Farthest north: being a record of a voyage of discovery of the ship 'Fram', 1893–96* (Westminster, London, 1897).

Ní Chinnéide, Síle, 'A view of Kilkenny, city and county, in 1790', *Journal of the Royal Society of Antiquaries of Ireland*, 114 (1974), 25–37.

Ní Scannlain, Eibhlín, *Land and people: land use and population in north west Connemara in the nineteenth century* (Connemara, Co. Galway, 1999).

Nicholl, Alexander, *Twelve drawings from the northern coast of Ireland* (London, 1835).

Nicholls, Kenneth, *Gaelic and Gaelicised Ireland in the Middle Ages* (Dublin, 1972).

Nolan, William, Liam Ronayne and Máiread Dunlevy (eds), *Donegal: history and society* (Dublin, 1995), pp 203–28.

Nørgård Jørgensen, Anne, *Maritime warfare in northern Europe* (Copenhagen, 2002).

O'Brien, A.F., 'Politics, economy and society: the development of Cork and the Irish south coast region, *c*.1700 to 1583' in Patrick O'Flanagan and Cornelius Buttimer (eds), *Cork: history and society* (Dublin, 1993), pp 83–156.

O'Brien, George, *An economic history of Ireland in the eighteenth century* (Dublin, 1919).

O'Brien, George, *An economic history of Ireland in the seventeenth century* (Dublin, 1918).

O'Brien, William, 'Prehistoric human settlement in Killarney' in Jim Larner (ed.), *Killarney: history and heritage* (Cork, 2005), pp 1–12.

O'Brien, William, *A statistical survey of the county of Kerry* (Dublin, 1804).

Ó Clabaigh, Colmán, 'Cistercians' in Brian Lalor (ed.), *Encyclopedia of Ireland* (Dublin, 2003), p. 200.

Ó Criomhthain, Tomás, *Allagair na hInise* (Dublin, 1928).

O'Crothan, Tomás, *The islandman* (Oxford, 1951).

Ó Cróinín, Dáibhí, *Early Medieval Ireland, 400–1200* (London, 1992).

O'Donnell, Manus, *Life of Colum Cille* (Dublin, 1994).

O'Donnell, Peadar, *Islanders* (Dublin, 1928).

O'Donnell, Peadar, *The proud island* (Dublin, 1988).

O'Donovan, John (ed.), *Annals of the kingdom of Ireland* (Dublin, 1856).

O'Dowd, Peadar, *Down by the Claddagh* (Galway, 1993).

Ó Drisceoil, Diarmuid and Donal Ó Drisceoil, *Serving a city: the story of Cork's English Market* (Cork, 2005).

O'Faolain, Seán, *King of the beggars* (Dublin, 1980).

O'Flanagan, Patrick, 'Three hundred years of urban life: villages and towns in County Cork' in O'Flanagan and Buttimer (eds), *Cork: history and society*, pp 391–68.

O'Grada, Cormac, *Ireland: a new economic history* (Oxford, 1994).

Ó hAnnacháin, Eoghan, 'Men of the west in the galleys of France', *Journal of the Galway Historical and Archaeological Society*, 59 (2007), 37–45.

O'Mahony, Colman, 'Fishing in nineteenth-century Kinsale', *Journal of the Cork Historical and Archaeological Society*, 98 (1993), 113–32.

O'Mahony, Colmán, 'Press-gangs off the Cork coast, 1755–1812', *Journal of the Cork Historical and Archaeological Society*, 101 (1996), 14–17.

O'Meara, J.J., *The topography of Ireland by Giraldus Cambrensis* (Dublin, 1951).

O'Neill, Kevin, 'Looking at pictures: art and artfulness in colonial Ireland' in Dalsimer, (ed.), *Visualizing Ireland*, pp 55–76.

O'Neill, Timothy, *Merchants and mariners in medieval Ireland* (Dublin, 1987).

Ó Ríordáin, S.P., 'Lough Gur excavations: Neolithic and Bronze-Age houses on Knockdoon', *Proceedings of the Royal Irish Academy*, 51C (1954), 299–459.

Ó Ríordáin, S.P., *Antiquities of the Irish countryside* (London, 1953).

O'Rorke, Terence, *History of Sligo: town and county* (Dublin, 1890).

Ó Síocháin, Conchur, *The man from Cape Clear* (Dublin, 1940).

O'Sullivan, Aidan, 'Harvesting the waters', *Archaeology Ireland*, 8:1 (1996), 10–12.

O'Sullivan, Aidan, 'Last foragers or first farmers?', *Archaeology Ireland*, 11:2 (1997), 14–16.

O'Sullivan, Aidan, et al., 'Medieval fishtraps in Strangford Lough, Co. Down', *Archaeology Ireland*, 11:1 (1997), 36–8.

O'Sullivan, Florence, *History of Kinsale* (Cork, 1916).

O'Sullivan, M.D., 'Glimpses of the life of Galway merchants and mariners in the early seventeenth century', *Journal of the Galway Archaeological and Historical Society*, 25 (1933), 129–40.

O'Sullivan, M.D., *Old Galway: history of a Norman colony in Ireland* (Cambridge, 1942).

Ohlmeyer, Jane H., 'Dunkirk of Ireland: Wexford privateers during the 1640s', *Journal of Wexford Historical Society*, 12 (1988), 23–49.

Otway Ruthven, A.J., 'The character of Norman settlement in Ireland', *Historical Studies*, 5 (1965), 75–84.

Petty, William, *The political anatomy of Ireland* (Dublin, 1970).

Pirenne, Henri, 'Stages in the social history of capitalism', *American Historical Review*, 19:3 (1914), 490–521.

Pococke, Richard, *A tour in Ireland in 1752* (London, 1891).

Pollock, Vivienne, 'The introduction of engine power in County Down sea fisheries', *Ulster Folklife*, 37 (1991), 1–12.

Pollock, Vivienne, 'Herring fishery in County Down' in Lindsay Proudfoot and William Nolan (eds), *Down: history and society* (Dublin, 1997), pp 405–30.

Pounds, N.J.G., 'Cornish fish cellars', *Antiquity*, 18 (1944), 36–41.

Quinn, D.B., *The Elizabethans in Ireland* (Cornell, NY, 1966).

Quinn, D.B., *The Irish parliamentary subsidy in the fifteenth and sixteenth centuries* (Dublin, 1935).

Rackham, Oliver, *Woodlands* (London, 2007).

Ratzel, Friedrich, 'The laws of spatial growth of states' in R.E. Kasperson and J.V. Minghi (eds), *The structure of political geography* (Chicago, IL, 1969), pp 57–65.

Ratzel, Friedrich, *Politsche geographie* (Munich, 1897).

Rediker, Marcus, *Between the devil and the deep blue sea* (Cambridge, 1992).

Rediker, Marcus, *Villains of all nations: Atlantic pirates in the Golden Age* (London, 2002).

Rees, Jim, *Arklow: the story of a town* (Arklow, Co. Wicklow, 2004).

Regan, Colm, 'Economic development in Ireland: the historical dimension', *Antipode: a Radical Journal of Geography*, 11:2 (1980), 1–14.

Richards, David, *Masks of difference: cultural representation in literature, anthropology and art* (Cambridge, 1994).

Richards, J.D., *The Vikings* (Oxford, 2005).

Richards, J.D., *Viking-Age England* (London, 2000).

Robinson, Phillip, *The plantation of Ulster* (Dublin, 1984).

Robinson, Tim, *Stones of Aran* (London, 1990).

Rockett, Kevin, Luke Gibbons and John Hill, *Cinema in Ireland* (London, 1988).

Roncaglia, Allesandro, *Petty: the origins of political economy* (Cardiff, 1985).

Ryland, R.H., *History, topography and antiquities of the county and city of Waterford* (London, 1824).

Sauer, Carl, *Northern mists* (Berkeley, CA, 1968).

Schama, Simon, *The embarrassment of riches: an interpretation of Dutch culture in the Golden Age* (London, 1991).

Semple, Ellen Churchill, *Influences of geographical environment on the basis of Ratzel's system of anthro-geography* (New York, 1911).

Sexton, Regina, *A short history of Irish food* (Cork, 2001).

Shee Twohig, Elizabeth and Margaret Ronayne (eds), *Past perceptions: the prehistoric archaeology of south-west Ireland* (Cork, 1993).

Sheehan, John, Steffen Stummann Hansen & Donnchadh Ó Corráin, 'A Viking-Age maritime haven: a reassessment of the island settlement at Beginish, Co. Kerry', *Journal of Irish Archaeology*, 10 (2001), 93–119.

Silverman, Debora, *Van Gogh and Gaugin: the search for sacred art* (New York, 2000).

Simpson, Linzi, 'Excavations on the southern side the medieval town at Ship Street Little, Dublin' in Seán Duffy (ed.), *Medieval Dublin V* (Dublin, 2004), pp 260–71.

Smith, C.V., *Dalkey: history and economy in a small medieval Irish town* (Dublin, 1996).

Smith, Charles, *Ancient and present state of the county and city of Cork* (Cork, 1894).

Smith, Charles, *Ancient and present state of the county of Kerry* (Dublin, 1969).

Smith, H.D., *Shetland life and trade, 1550–1914* (Edinburgh, 1984).

Smyth, A.P., *Scandinavian York and Dublin: the history and archaeology of two related Viking kingdoms* (Dublin, 1979).

Stafford, Thomas, *Pacata Hibernia, or a history of the wars in Ireland* (London, 1633).

Stevens, Julie A., *The Irish scene in Somerville and Ross* (Dublin, 2007).

Stout, Geraldine, 'Wexford in prehistory' in Whelan and Nolan (eds), *Wexford: history and society*, pp 1–39.

Strauss, Eric, *Sir William Petty* (London, 1951).

Stymes, E.P., 'Torbay fishermen in Ringsend', *Dublin Historical Record*, 53:4 (2000), 139–49.

Suskind, Patrick, *Perfume* (London, 1986).

Synge, J.M., *Collected works: prose* (London, 1982).

Synge, J.M., *In Wicklow, west Kerry and Connemara* (Dublin, 1980).

Synge, J.M., *The playboy of the western world* (Dublin, 1907).

Synge, J.M., *The tinker's wedding* (Dublin, 1904).

Synge, J.M., *Vagrants of County Wicklow* (Dublin, 1910).

Taylor, Peter, *Political geography: world economy, nation-state and locality* (Harlow, 1998).

Thompson, Edward P., *Albion's fatal tree* (London, 1977).

Thompson, George, *Island home* (Dingle, Co. Kerry, 1988).

Thoms, L.M., *Early man in the Scottish landscape* (Edinburgh, 1978).

Tomelty, Joseph, *Red is the harbour light* (Belfast, 1983).

Tomlinson, Roy, 'Forests and woodlands' in Aalen et al. (eds), *Atlas of the Irish rural landscape*, pp 122–33.

Townsend, Dorothea, *Life and letters of the great earl of Cork* (London, 1904).

Traven, B., *Government* (New York, 1992).

Trevelyan, G.M., *English social history* (London, 1974).

Tuke, J.H., *A visit to Connacht in the autumn of 1848* (Dublin, 1848).

Wakeman, W.F., *Handbook of Irish antiquities, pagan and Christian* (Dublin, 1891).

Walker, J.C., *An historical essay on the dress of the ancient and modern Irish* (Dublin, 1788).

Walsh, A., *Scandinavian relations with Ireland during the Viking period* (Dublin, 1922).

Webb, R., *Report of the central committee of the Society of Friends* (Dublin, 1850).

Went, A.E.J., 'An ancient fish-weir at Ballynatray, County Waterford', *Antiquity*, 25 (1951), 32–5.

Went, A.E.J., 'Eel fishing at Athlone, past and present', *Journal of the Royal Society of Antiquaries of Ireland*, 80 (1950), 146–54.

Went, A.E.J., 'Fisheries' in James Meenan and Desmond Clarke (eds), *The Royal Dublin Society, 1731–1981* (Dublin, 1981), pp 142–53.

Went, A.E.J., 'Fishing scenes from Irish topographical prints', *Journal of the Royal Society of Antiquaries of Ireland*, 81 (1951), 156–60.

Went, A.E.J., 'Fish-weirs of river Erne', *Journal of the Royal Society of Antiquaries of Ireland*, 75 (1945), 213–23.

Went, A.E.J., 'Foreign fishing fleets along the Irish coasts', *Journal of the Cork Historical and Archaeological Society*, 54 (1949), 17–24.

Went, A.E.J., 'Historical notes on the oyster fisheries of Ireland', *Proceedings of the Royal Irish Academy*, 62 (1962), 195–223.

Went, A.E.J., 'Irish fishing spears', *Journal of the Royal Society of Antiquaries of Ireland*, 82 (1952), 109–34.

Went, A.E.J., 'Irish monastic fisheries', *Journal of the Cork Historical and Archaeological Society*, 60 (1955), 47–56.

Went, A.E.J., 'Pilchards in the south of Ireland', *Journal of the Cork Historical and Archaeological Society*, 51 (1946), 137–57.

Went, A.E.J., 'The Galway fishery', *Proceedings of the Royal Irish Academy*, 48 (1942–3), 233–53.

Went, A.E.J., 'The Irish hake fishery, 1504–1824', *Journal of the Cork Historical and Archaeological Society*, 51 (1946), 41–51.

Went, A.E.J., 'The pursuit of salmon in Ireland', *Proceedings of the Royal Irish Academy*, 63:6 (1964), 191–244.

Westropp, T.J., 'Early Italian maps of Ireland from 1300 to 1400, with notes on foreign settlers and trade', *Proceedings of the Royal Irish Academy*, 30C, (1913), 361–428.

Whelan, Kevin, 'Pre- and post-Famine landscape change' in Pórtéir (ed.), *Great Irish Famine*, pp 19–33.

Whelan, Kevin and William Nolan (eds), *Wexford: history and society* (Dublin, 1987).

Wilkins, Noel, *Oysters and oystering in Galway Bay* (Galway, 2001).

Williams, Dawn, 'Whipping the herring out of town' in Murray (ed.), *Whipping the herring*, p. 68.

Williams, Sarah Paston, *The art of dining* (London, 1989).

Wolf, Eric, *Europe and the peoples without history* (Berkeley, CA, 1982).

Wolf, Eric, *Sons of the shaking earth* (New York, 1972).

Woodham-Smith, Cecil, *The great hunger* (London, 1974).

Woodman, Peter, 'A narrow blade Mesolithic site at Glynn, Co. Antrim', *Ulster Journal of Archaeology*, 40 (1977), 12–20.

Woodman, Peter, 'Mount Sandel' in Lalor (ed.), *Encyclopedia of Ireland*, p. 745.

Woodman, Peter, 'The exploitation of Ireland's coastal resources: a marginal resource through time?' in Manuel Gonzalez Morales and G.A. Clark (eds), *The Mesolithic of the Atlantic façade* (Tempe, AZ, 2004), pp 37–55.

Woodman, Peter, *Excavations at Ferriter's Cove, 1983–95: last foragers, first farmers in the Dingle Peninsula* (Bray, 1999).

Woodman, Peter, Robert Devoy and David Sleeman, *Occasional publications of Irish Biogeography Society* (1986).

Yeats, W.B., *The poems* (London, 1994).

Young, Arthur, *A tour in Ireland*, ed. A.W. Hutton (London, 1892).

Index

Abbey Theatre, Dublin, 26
aboriginal fishermen, 37–43, 45–8
Achill, Co. Mayo, 21, 23, 41, 196, 249,
    299, 317
Act of Union, 290
ancient sea lore, 65–70
Andrews, William, 286–8
Anglesey, Wales, 326
Anglo-Norman influences, 56–9
Annaboy, Co. Antrim, 246
Anselm, St, 16
Antigua, 231
Antrim coastal fisheries, 242–4
Aran Islands, Co. Galway, 21, 26, 54, 112,
    234
Archaeology of fishing, 33–45
Arctic Circle, 67
Ardglass, Co. Down, 94, 161, 245, 290
Arklow, Co. Wicklow, 161, 94–5, 169–70,
    275–6, 278, 281
artistic representations, 9–12, 347–9
Assaroe Falls, Co. Donegal, 76, 103
Athlone, Co. Westmeath, 75–6
Aughinish, Co. Galway, 250
Aughris Head, Co. Sligo, 97
authority of skippers, 181, 183, 186
Avignon, France, 158

Balbriggan, Co. Dublin, 304, 309
Ballina, Co. Mayo, 248
Ballycotton, Co. Cork, 80
Ballyferriter, Co. Kerry, 37
Ballyteigue, Co. Galway, 274
Baltimore, Co. Cork, 95, 100–1, 198

Baltimore Fishery School, 334
Bann Estuary, 35
Bannow Bay, Co. Wexford, 36
Bantry, Co. Cork, 6, 203, 303
Barbary pirates, 151
Barry, J.H., 292
Barryscourt Castle, Co. Cork, 90
Bartlett, W.H., 21
Basking shark, 253–4
Basque fishermen, 156
Bayly, H.L., 170, 275–6
Beara Peninsula, Co. Cork, 190
Beattie, Seán, 185, 293
Beginish, Co. Kerry, 40
Bell, Sam Hanna, 7
Belmullet, Co. Mayo, 113
Bere Island, Co. Cork, 46
Black Death, 123
Black Sea, 156, 161
Blacksod Bay, Co. Mayo, 222
Blasket Islands, Co. Kerry, 185, 342
Bloody Foreland, Co. Donegal, 305
boat crews, 180
Boate, Gerard, 217–18
Bonny, Anne, 147
Book of Ballymote, 47
Bordeaux, France, 161
Bowles-Daly, James, 5, 290–2
Brabazon, Wallop, 4, 233, 248, 254, 282,
    284, 306, 309
Braudel, Fernand, 122, 160
Brendan the Navigator, 67, 156–7
Bridgewater, Devon, England, 199
Bristol, England, 121, 161, 199

Brittany, France, 36, 45
Broadhaven, Devon, England, 289
Brody, Hugh, 233–4, 236
Buncrana, Co. Donegal, 200
Bunratty, Co. Clare, 43, 93
Burren, Co. Clare, 223
Burton, F.W., 19–20
Burtonport, Co. Donegal, 21, 293

Cadiz, Spain, 161
Calvinist settlers, 95–6
Cape Clear, Co. Cork, 99, 101, 185,
    195–6, 225, 266, 269, 272, 309
Carlingford Lough, Co. Down, 51, 59,
    102, 107, 164, 169, 223, 245, 247, 299
Carlingford oyster boats, 223
Carlisle, Cumberland, England, 197
Carlyle, Thomas, 344
Carmarthen, Wales, 161
Carndonagh, Co. Donegal, 330
Carraroe, Co. Galway, 26
Carrickafoyle Castle, Co. Kerry, 85
Carrickfergus, Co. Antrim, 59, 63, 243
Carrowmore, Co. Galway, 41
Catalan fishermen, 174–5, 181
Catholic clergy, 4–6, 345
Causeway coast, Co. Antrim, 240
Cavan fishermen, 7
Céide, Co. Mayo, 42
Celtic Revival, 15
Census of boats, 228
Chambers, Anne, 150, 153
Chester, Cheshire, England, 161, 163
Christ Stopped at Eboli, 347
Cistercians, 53, 100
Claddagh, Co. Galway, 134, 145, 166,
    168, 174, 181, 195–6, 297, 301,
    314–18
Clare Island, Co. Mayo, 34
Clew Bay, Co. Mayo, 148–9

Clonmel, Co. Tipperary, 158
coastal famines, 190
coastal foraging, 2, 7, 33, 41
coastal towns, origins of, 32
Cobh, Co. Cork, 154
cod fishery, 113–14
coghill nets, 74
Cohen, Anthony, 185
Coleraine, Co. Derry, 35, 62, 148
Colfer, Billy, 57
colonial agents, 201
colonial art, 11
colonial conquest, 208, 213, 335, 349
colonial influences, 53–64
commercial fishing, 203–6, 310–12
Common Market, 1–2
community life, 185–7
Congested Districts, 23, 26, 235, 316, 320,
    329, 351
Connemara, Co. Galway, 19, 20, 21, 26,
    170, 294
conservation methods, 85–8
Copland Island, Co. Down, 244
Cork coastal fisheries, 262–71
Cork Harbour, 154
Cork, 33, 51, 55, 56, 69, 95 128, 161
Corkery, Daniel, 27, 342–3
Cornish fishermen, 290
Cornish fishing boats, 7, 302
Courtmacsherry, Co. Cork, 113
Cove fishing village, Co. Cork, 208
Cromwell, Oliver, 198
Cromwellian invasion, 215, 280
Crookhaven, Co. Cork, 207, 318
Culdaff, Co. Donegal, 200, 330
Cullen, Louis, 224, 226, 232
cultural nationalists, 29–30, 333
cultural outlook of fishermen, 177, 179,
    180–1, 186, 191
currachs, 298–303

customs collectors, 162
customs records, 63

Dalkey, Co. Dublin, 161–3
Dalriada, Scotland, 62
Danube, 161
David, Elizabeth, 203
de Courcy Ireland, John, 156, 161, 281, 289, 352
de Paor, Máire, 11
December Bride, 7
Degas, Edgar, 25
Denmark, 159
Dennis, Robert, 293, 303
Derricke, John, 7, 8
Derry coastal fisheries, 240–2
Derry, 161, 201–2, 204, 238, 241, 288
Devon Commission, 290
Devon, England, 283
Dieppe, France, 161
dietary change, 218–20
Dingle, Co. Kerry, 37, 94, 101, 105, 199, 267, 291–2, 322–3
Donaghadee, Co. Down, 244
Donegal fishing boats, 232
Donegal fishing grounds, 228–37
Dooey Island, Co. Donegal, 33
Doyle, J.P., 6
Drogheda, Co. Louth, 63, 80, 102, 105, 161, 169
Druidic remains, 11
Drumcliffe, Co. Sligo, 36
Drunkenness, 143–4, 265–6
Dublin Fishing Company, 284
Dublin port developments, 12–13
Dublin Society, 286, 288
Dublin, 12, 13, 43, 46, 55, 56, 60, 80, 94, 136–9, 161–2, 205–6
Dubourdieu, John, 242–4, 287, 311
Duiske Abbey, Co. Kilkenny, 48

Dunaff Bay, Co. Donegal, 35
Dunbrody Abbey, Co. Wexford, 79
Duncannon, Co. Wexford, 99, 131
Dundrum Bay, 66, 247, 311
Dungarvan, Co. Waterford, 6, 105, 118, 131, 135, 161, 270–2
Dunkirk, 152
Dunmore, Co. Down, 271
Dunshaughlin, Co. Meath, 44
Dursey, Co. Cork, 46, 56, 101, 326
Dutch fishermen, 96, 116–18, 152, 159, 207
Dutch sea power, 158

Early Christian Ireland, 49–53
early fishing craft, 45–8, 73–4
early shipbuilding techniques, 70–2
eel fisheries, 74–5, 163
Elias, Norbert, 122–3
Elizabethan policy, 194
emigration, 338–9, 345–6
English jurisdiction and Irish fisheries, 204–7
Enlightenment, 212, 341
equalitarianism, 185
Erris Head, Co. Mayo, 316
Estyn Evans, 6, 305–6
evolutionary theory, 295, 334

Faeroe Islands, 46
farmer-fishermen, 192
fast days, 77–80, 84
Ferriter's Cove, Co. Kerry, 37, 39, 48
Firth of Clyde, Scotland, 196
Fish
    companies, 202–4; consumption in medieval times, 65–77; curers, 185, 269; days, 86–7, 219; exports, 93–4, 105–7; factors, 199; famines, 236; levies, 206; management, 79–81;

Fish *(continued)*
    markets in medieval Ireland, 131–4,
    142–7; merchants, 132–4; middens,
    49–51; palaces, 109–10, 141–2; pies,
    71, 84–5; ponds, 86–7; presses, 214;
    processing, 215; racks, 37; shambles,
    121–3; spears, 220–1, 205, 220; tithes,
    72, 198, 207–8; traps, 164; weirs,
    72–7, 83; wives, 127, 130, 134, 144,
    169, 172
Fishamble Street, Dublin, 58, 126, 129,
    135
fishermen's dress, 182–3
fishing cotts, 63
fishing grounds, 229
fishing nets, 304–6
fishing rights, 65, 208
fishmongers, 126–8, 227
Flaherty, Robert, 13
Flanders, 161, 163
Fletcher, Nichola, 84
Flight of the earls, 202
food of fishermen, 173
forestallers, 127
Fox, E.W., 31–3
Fraser, Robert, 273–4
French fishermen, 117–19, 263
Furlong, Nicholas, 161

Gaeldom, bastions of, 344
Gaelic chieftains, 8, 105–8, 112–13, 116,
    119, 149–51
Gaelic culture, 12
Galicia, Spain, 36, 63
Galway coastal fisheries, 250–7
Galway fishermen, 164, 166
Galway, 4, 7, 20, 21, 63, 74, 76, 161
Gaskell, W.P., 331
Gauguin, Paul, 24
Gdansk, Poland, 161

gentrification processes, 121–9, 132–6.
Gilbard, Humphrey, 198
Giraldus Cambrensis, 62–3, 82, 158, 217
Glandore, Co. Cork, 66
Glasgow, Scotland, 161
Glengad, Co. Donegal, 239
Glengall, Earl of, 290
Gloucester, England, 199
Gola Island, Co. Donegal, 183, 233
Great Famine, 3, 5, 19, 238, 296, 319,
    313–20
Great Western Railway, 251
Greek Empire, 156
Green, W.S., 286–7, 325
Greencastle yawl, 308
Greencastle, Co. Donegal, 329
Greenland, 105, 197
Griffith, Arthur, 350
Griffith's Valuation, 315
Grotius, Hugo, 340–1
Gulf Stream, 295
Gunn, Neil, 184
Gweedore, Co. Donegal, 235
Gwynn, Stephen, 342–3

harbour facilities, 252, 274–5
Hack, James, 315
Hake fisheries, 98–100, 270
Hanseatic League, 310
Hanseatic merchants, 49
Hanseatic ports, 158
Hardiman, James, 167, 174, 182
Helvick, Co. Waterford, 54
Hempton Bank, 200
Henry, Paul, 7, 22
Herring busses, 159
Herring fisheries, 164, 231–4, 244–7
Herring gutters, 262
Herring seasons, 307, 310–11
Hickey, Patrick, 266–7, 318

Hill of Tara, Co. Meath, 62
Hill, George, 232, 252–3, 300, 307
Hobbes, Thomas, 212
Hoekers, 160
holding weirs, 121
Holdsworth, E.W.H., 256, 323–4
Hollanders, 158
Hood Head, Co. Wexford, 95
Horn Head, Co. Donegal, 286, 289
Howth, Co. Dublin, 102, 244
Hucksters, 129
Human types, 195
Hungary, 85

ice-houses, 203–4
Iceland, 46, 68
illegal fishing, 205–7
Illaunloughan, Co. Kerry, 47
Illustrated London News, 167, 181
immram, 157
Inch Island, Co. Donegal, 230
Inglis, Henry, 314
Inishowen, Co. Donegal, 35, 239
Inishtrahull, Co. Donegal, 237, 239
interlopers, 304
introduced species, 82
Irish commissioners of fishing, 288
Irish Fisheries Report, 228
Irish Sea, 158
'island-hopping', 238–40
Isle of Man, 232, 244
Italy, 159
Ivereagh Peninsula, Co. Kerry, 42, 215

Jerusalem, 158
Joyce, P.W., 74

Kattegat, 267
Keane, J.B., 347–8
Keating, Sean, 7, 22, 23

Kelly, Fergus, 39, 40
Kelly, Maria, 123–4
Kenmare, Co. Kerry, 198, 210, 261–2
Kerry coastal fisheries, 260–2, 341–5
Kiberd, Declan, 27, 346
Killala, Co. Mayo, 222
Killarney, Co. Kerry, 41
Killary Harbour, Co. Galway, 247–8, 288
Killorglin, Co. Kerry, 76
Killybegs, Co. Donegal, 161, 199, 200–1,
    289, 299, 319
Kilrush, Co. Clare, 104
King's Lynn, England, 162
Kinsale, Co. Cork, 63, 99, 105, 112, 154,
    155, 161, 164, 170, 263–6

La Rochelle, France, 95, 161
Labour aristocracy, 165–6
Laggan money, 236
Lagore crannog, Co. Meath, 74
lampreys, 63, 72, 129
Landing the Catch, 169
landlords, 296–7, 344–5
landscape artists, 9, 15, 21–3
Larne, Co. Antrim, 54
Larnian people, 37–8
law-tracts, 13, 43, 90–1
Lean, David, 13
lebensraum, 343
Lecale Peninsula, Co. Down, 60, 70, 192
Lecky, W.E.H., 6
lenten fasting, 71, 77–9, 87–8
Levi, Carlo, 347
Lewis, Samuel, 271
Limerick, 55, 63, 73, 121, 129
Lislaughtin, Co. Kerry, 78
Liverpool, England, 161, 204
lobster fishing season, 235
lobster pots, 306
lobstermen, 173–4, 182, 234

lobsters, 305
Locke, John, 340–1
long-line fishermen, 308–9
Lough Allua, Co. Cork, 224, 261
Lough Beg, Co. Antrim, 38
Lough Corrib, Co. Galway, 96
Lough Derravarragh, Co. Westmeath, 38
Lough Erne, Co. Fermanagh, 48
Lough Foyle, Co. Donegal, 45, 293
Lough Gur, Co. Limerick, 39
Lough Hyne, Co. Cork, 224, 261
Lough Neagh, 38, 202, 242
Lough Swilly, Co. Donegal, 35, 43, 199,
    210, 230, 261–2, 286, 289
Loughshinny, Co. Dublin, 352
Louisburg, Co. Mayo, 248
Lovett, Richard, 258, 314
Low Countries, 158
luggers, 301–2
lumpenproletariat, 166

MacEiteagain, Darren, 200
MacGill, Patrick, 18
MacGrail, Sean, 63
mackerel fishery, 325–7
MacNeill, Eoin, 53–4
MacParlan, James, 228, 247
Malahide, Co. Dublin, 102
Malin Head, Co. Donegal, 196, 237, 309,
    329
Man of Aran, 13
Manx fishermen, 290
mare clausum, 192, 316
mare liberum, 340
marginalisation of coastal Ireland, 28–30
marine biologists, 286–9
marine ecology, 290–5
maritime Ireland, 31–3, 192
maritime societies, characteristics, 31–3
Martello towers, 5

martyrdom, 66
Marvell, Andrew, 339
Maxwell, William, 249–50, 305
Mayo coastal fisheries, 247–51
McMahon, Brid, 86
Medieval cookbooks, 86
Mediterranean Sea, 160
Mellifont Abbey, Co. Louth, 78–9
mercantilism, 111
Mesolithic fisheries, 33–45
Mesolithic fish-traps, 44
Mesolithic farmer-fishers, 19–21
Milford, Co. Donegal, 161
Millet, Jean François, 24
Mitchell, Frank, 36–9
Mizen Head, Co. Cork, 267, 277, 321
Molloy, John, 351–2
Monastic fisheries, 51, 61, 62, 79, 80–1,
    87, 91
Monks and fishermen, 65–8
Montgomery, Alexander, 288
Moorish Spain, 83
Moriarty, Christopher, 33, 40
Mount Sandel, Co. Derry, 34–5
Moville, Co. Donegal, 329–30
Mull of Kintyre, Scotland, 62
Mullet, 249
Munster plantation, 189, 191, 193

Natural History Society of Dublin, 286
neglect of maritime tradition, 7–13
Nesbitt, William, 193
net-making, 164
New Guinea, 321
New Learning, 209–17
New Ross, Co. Wexford, 161, 273
New South Wales, Australia, 38
Newcastle, Co. Down, 243, 246
Newfoundland fisheries, 113–16, 159, 164,
    171, 196–7, 201, 252, 270, 275, 278–80

Newgrange, Co. Meath, 40
Newhaven, Surrey, England, 93
Newtonards, Co. Down, 53
Nicholls, Kenneth, 111
nomadism, 346–8
Norse place-names, 55–6
North Inishkea, Co. Mayo, 41
North Sea, 159, 267, 196
Northern Mists, 164
Norway, 159
Norwegian dealers, 204
Nymph Bank, 271

Oban, Scotland, 45
O'Brien, George, 6
O'Connell, Daniel, 336
Ó Criomhthain, Tomás, 177, 291, 297, 322–3
O'Donnell chieftains, 101–4
O'Donnell, Peadar, 16–8, 27, 185, 236–7
O'Flaherty, Donal, 149
O'Flaherty, Robert, 217
O'Grada, Cormac, 291
O'Kelly, Aloysius, 17, 19
O'Mahony, Colman, 262
O'Malley, Grace, 149–51, 153
O'Neill, Kevin, 11, 12
opposition to continental fishermen, 116–19
organic intelligentsia, 295
Ó Síocháin, Conchur, 327–8
Outer Hebrides, Scotland, 67
over-fishing, 283
oysters, 256–7
oyster consumption, 221
oyster fisheries, 259, 263, 283

paddle currachs, 299
Padstow, England, 102
Papa Stour, Scotland, 68

Passage West, Co. Cork, 131
Penzance, England, 102
perceptions of fishermen, 135–7
Petrie, George, 20
Petty, William, 179, 210–15, 217, 268
Phillip II of Spain, 198
Phoenicians, 156
phytoplankton, 285
pilchards, 207–8, 210, 216, 225, 289, 294
pilcher palaces, 210
pirates, 118, 146–9, 151
Plantations, 188–96, 192–6
Plunkett, David, 288
Plymouth, Devon, England, 278
poaching, 259–61
Pococke, Richard, 222
Political Anatomy of Ireland, 212–13
Political Arithmetic, 212
political demography, 232–4
Pollock, Vivienne, 244–6, 311
pollutants, 124–6, 139–42, 144–6
Poole, Dorset, England, 278
port life, 140–3
port officials, 162
Portmagee, Co. Kerry, 262
Portrush, Co. Derry, 201
post-Famine adjustments, 320–8
press gangs, 154–5
primacy of fishing, 184, 240
primitive rebels, 336
prisage, 198
public hygiene, 121–6, 131–7, 144
public pageants, 142–3

Quakers, 315, 318
Quinn, D.B., 8

Rathlin Island, Co. Antrim, 62
Rathmullan, Co. Donegal, 200
Ratzel, Friedrich, 28–9, 335–6

Read, Mary, 149
Red is the Harbour Light, 175
Rediker, Marcus, 151
rediscovery of coastal Ireland, 15–24
religious beliefs, 176–7
religious houses, 79–84
Ring Peninsula, Co. Wexford, 318
River Bann, 41, 72, 97, 202
River Boyne, 163
River Deel, 86
River Fergus, 53
River Lee, 40, 224
River Liffey, 90–1, 205–6
River Shannon, 40, 51, 63, 74, 77, 86, 162, 303
Robinson, Phillip, 193
Robinson, Tim, 313
Roman classics, 157
Roman Empire, 156
Roman historians, 45–6
Romania, 85
Rosses, Co. Donegal, 233
Rotterdam, Netherlands, 161
Rouen, France, 161
Royal Dublin Society, 286
Royal Navy, 168
rundale, 309
rural fundamentalism, 333–8
Rush, Co. Dublin, 102, 233, 311
Russia, 158
Ryan's Daughter, 13–15

Sacking of Baltimore, 151–3
St John's Point, Co. Donegal, 229
salmon consumption, 72
salmon fisheries, 241–2
salmon life cycle, 241
salt as preservative, 304–5
Saltee Islands, Co. Wexford, 56
Sampson, George, 240–1

Sandymount Strand, Co. Dublin, 223
Santiago de Compostela, Spain, 68
Sauer, Carl, 66, 68–9, 156
Scandinavian settlement, 60–3
Scania Peninsula, Sweden, 159
Scotch earnings, 236
Scotland, 158–9, 177, 224
Scottish Highlands, 344
sea charts, 321
sea fisheries, 1300–1600, 93–8
sea voyages, 65–6
seal fishery, 206, 286
sea-tales, 157
sedentary life, 340–1, 346, 378
seine netting, 268–9
Semeonis, Symon, 158
Seville, Spain, 161
Shannon Estuary, 292
Sheep Haven, Co. Donegal, 55
Sheephaven Bay, Co. Donegal, 305
Shetland Islands, Scotland, 102
shore food, 189
Skellig Michael, Co. Kerry, 66, 70
Skerries, Co. Dublin, 244, 304, 309
Skibbereen, Co. Cork, 261
Smerwick, Co. Kerry, 54
Smith, Adam, 341
Smith, Charles, 216–7, 224, 261
smugglers, 117, 158, 159
social borders, 185
Social Darwinism, 28–30, 334–6
social status, 185
Sommerville, Edith, 14–5
Southwell, Robert, 118
Spain, 159
Spanish fishermen, 101–02
speech patterns of fishermen, 171–2, 176
Spenser, Edmund, 97
spillards, 309

Strangford Lough, Co. Down, 52–53, 59, 162, 164, 169, 245, 247
street cries, 225
superstitions, 175–6, 180
Suskind, Patrick, 123
Sweden, 159
Swift, Jonathan, 225
Synge, J.M., 24–7

talamh na hEisc, 279
'tattie hokers', 350
taverns, 225–6
Templeton, John, 288
territorial state, 32, 111
The return of the fisherman, 17
The seaweed gatherers, 19
theories of underdevelopment, 1–7, 289–92, 333–9
Thompson, William, 288
Tír Conaill, 200, 206
tolls, 100
Tomelty, Joseph, 175
Torbay, England, 283, 287, 300
Tory Island, Co. Donegal, 185, 254, 329
Tranarossan, Co. Donegal, 41
transatlantic liners, 238–9
transhumance, 239
Traven, B., 347
trawlers, 322
trawl-nets, 282–5
Treaty of Antwerp, 96
Trevelyan, Charles, 318
tributary payments, 107–8, 116, 119, 155
Trondheim, Norway, 308

Ulster plantation, 188–9, 191, 193, 200–1, 203
uneven development, 311–12

United Provinces, 159
Ussher, James, 211

Valentia Island, Co. Kerry, 292
Valentia, Co. Kerry, 46
Van Gogh, Vincent, 24, 347–8
Venice, public hygiene policy, 121
Ventry, Co. Kerry, 262, 323
Viking boat building, 73
Viking settlement, 54–60

Wakeman, W.F., 52
water bailiffs, 131
Waterford, 73, 79, 115, 129, 130, 135, 161, 162, 170–1, 199
Went, A.E.J., 83, 98, 221
West Country fish merchants, 199
West Indies, 231, 290
Westport, Co. Mayo, 233, 255
Wexford, 115, 161
Weymouth, England, 162
Whale fishery, 196
Wherries, 256
Wilkins, Noel, 249
'winter kitchen', 222
women's role, 168, 170, 171, 184, 262
Woodham Smith, Cecil, 3, 289, 313
Woodman, Peter, 35–6, 39
work practices, 179–81, 183–5
Worthington, William, 282

Yarmouth, England, 108
yawls, 281, 321, 328
Yeats, Jack B., 17, 22, 23
Yeats, W.B., 311
Youghal, Co. Cork, 63, 95, 109, 112, 118, 170, 199, 203
Young, Arthur, 222, 230–1, 277, 288

Zealand, Denmark, 158